Oracle PL/SQL for DBAs

Other Oracle resources from O'Reilly

Related titles

Oracle PL/SQL Programming

Learning Oracle PL/SQL

Oracle PL/SQL Language
Pocket Reference

Oracle PL/SQL Programming:
A Developer's Workbook

Oracle Essentials: Oracle
Database 10g

Oracle in a Nutshell

Mastering Oracle SQL

Oracle SQL*Plus Pocket
Reference

Toad Pocket Reference
for Oracle

**Oracle Books
Resource Center**

oracle.oreilly.com is a complete catalog of O'Reilly's books on
Oracle and related technologies, including sample chapters and
code examples.

oreillynet.com is the essential portal for developers interested in
open and emerging technologies, including new platforms, programming languages, and operating systems.

Conferences

O'Reilly brings diverse innovators together to nurture the ideas
that spark revolutionary industries. We specialize in documenting the latest tools and systems, translating the innovator's
knowledge into useful skills for those in the trenches. Visit *con-
ferences.oreilly.com* for our upcoming events.

Safari Bookshelf (*safari.oreilly.com*) is the premier online reference library for programmers and IT professionals. Conduct
searches across more than 1,000 books. Subscribers can zero in
on answers to time-critical questions in a matter of seconds.
Read the books on your Bookshelf from cover to cover or simply flip to the page you need. Try it today with a free trial.

Oracle PL/SQL for DBAs

Arup Nanda and Steven Feuerstein

O'REILLY®

Beijing · Cambridge · Farnham · Köln · Paris · Sebastopol · Taipei · Tokyo

Oracle PL/SQL for DBAs
by Arup Nanda and Steven Feuerstein

Published by O'Reilly Media, Inc., 1005 Gravenstein Highway North, Sebastopol, CA 95472.

O'Reilly Media, Inc. books may be purchased for educational, business, or sales promotional use. On-line editions are also available for most titles (*safari.oreilly.com*). For more information, contact our corporate/institutional sales department: (800) 998-9938 or *corporate@oreilly.com*.

Editor:	Deborah Russell
Production Editor:	Darren Kelly
Cover Designer:	Karen Montgomery
Interior Designer:	David Futato

Printing History:

October 2005:	First Edition.

ISBN: 0-596-00587-3

[M]

Table of Contents

Preface

Millions of application developers and database administrators (DBAs) around the world use software provided by Oracle Corporation to build complex systems that manage vast quantities of data. At the heart of much of Oracle's software is PL/SQL— a programming language that provides procedural extensions to Oracle's version of Structured Query Language (SQL) and serves as the programming language within the Oracle Developer toolset.

PL/SQL figures prominently as an enabling technology in almost every new product released by Oracle Corporation. Software professionals use PL/SQL to perform many kinds of programming functions, including:

- Implementing crucial business rules in the Oracle Server with PL/SQL-based stored procedures and database triggers
- Generating and managing XML documents entirely within the database
- Linking web pages to an Oracle database
- Implementing and automating database administration tasks—from establishing row-level security to managing rollback segments within PL/SQL programs

PL/SQL was modeled after Ada,[*] a programming language designed for the United States Department of Defense. Ada is a high-level language that emphasizes data abstraction, information hiding, and other key elements of modern design strategies. As a result of this very smart design decision by Oracle, PL/SQL is a powerful language that incorporates many of the most advanced elements of procedural languages, including:

- A full range of datatypes from number to string, and including complex data structures such as records (which are similar to rows in a relational table), collections

---

[*] The language was named "Ada" in honor of Ada Lovelace, a mathematician who is regarded by many to have been the world's first computer programmer. For more information about Ada, visit *http://www.adahome. com*.

(which are Oracle's version of arrays), and XMLType (for managing XML documents in Oracle and through PL/SQL)

- An explicit and highly readable block structure that makes it easy to enhance and maintain PL/SQL applications
- Conditional, iterative, and sequential control statements, including a CASE statement and three different kinds of loops
- Exception handlers for use in event-based error handling
- Named, reusable code elements such as functions, procedures, triggers, object types (akin to object-oriented classes), and packages (collections of related programs and variables)

PL/SQL is integrated tightly into Oracle's SQL language: you can execute SQL statements directly from your procedural program without having to rely on any kind of intermediate Application Programming Interface (API) like Java DataBase Connectivity (JDBC) or Open DataBase Connectivity (ODBC). Conversely, you can also call your own PL/SQL functions from within a SQL statement.

While the majority of PL/SQL users are programmers, it is also a language used by many database administrators. A solid working knowledge of PL/SQL is, in fact, crucial for Oracle DBAs.

PL/SQL for DBAs

Why, specifically, is PL/SQL important to Oracle DBAs?

The most general answer to that question is simply that DBAs are generally responsible for anything that is in (and executes in) their databases, including the code. PL/SQL is a big part of that total picture. If you are ignorant of the PL/SQL language, you will not be able to evaluate programs for their security, maintainability, or performance. You will also not be able to take full advantage of the many advanced features that Oracle has built into its database and exposes *through* the PL/SQL language, usually through supplied, or built-in, packages.

Let's take a closer look at these different areas.

Securing the Database

Security has always been a key DBA responsibility, and knowing how to secure your database and applications has become all the more crucial in recent years. Many elements of security are handled directly via SQL statements and database configuration processes and parameters—for example, by establishing passwords and setting roles and privileges. Other, more complex aspects of security—including encryption, row-level security, fine-grained auditing, and the generation of random values—

require the use of PL/SQL. This book describes these more complex security topics in detail, focusing on the use of Oracle's built-in security packages.

Optimizing Performance

Wouldn't it be great if all developers (a) knew the ins and outs of optimizing SQL statements, (b) kept up with the latest developments in PL/SQL performance (like BULK COLLECT and FORALL), and (c) took the time to tune their code?

Many programmers do, in fact, pay close attention to how efficiently their code runs. Others are happy to get the program "working." The bottom line, however, is that this code is passed on to you, the DBA, to put into production. Therefore, depending on the policies of your specific organizations, it may become your responsibility to make sure this code will not create a problem in your production environment. At the least, sometimes you may have to be consulted on performance issues and suggest alternative approaches. You should be comfortable enough with PL/SQL and its latest upgrades to be able to review code, identify potential bottlenecks, and suggest ways that the development team can improve performance. The chapters of this book that describe ways of optimizing cursor and table function use will be particularly helpful in this area.

Fully Leveraging Oracle Utilities and Features

There was a time when DBAs got by with "straight" SQL and database configuration commands (either on the command line in SQL*Plus or through graphical interfaces like Oracle's Enterprise Manager). Today, DBAs must be able to write at least enough PL/SQL code to implement database and schema triggers, automate many administrative tasks through the use of native dynamic SQL (NDS) and other DDL execution mechanisms, and thoroughly utilize the many new features exposed through Oracle's built-in packages (from streams to queues to replication strategies to cost-based optimizer analysis). If PL/SQL is a stumbling block for you, in terms of your ability to provide optimal database administration for your organization, you will not be able to do your job as effectively as you should.

Mentoring New Developers and DBAs

Many of the developers and DBAs now entering the world of Oracle have relatively little experience in either database design or optimized programming. The more you know about PL/SQL—how it works and how to write good code—the more effective a resource you can be in moving your coworkers forward. The more professional they become, the easier your job will be, and the more widely you will be respected. The bottom line is that you should see PL/SQL as a means to a more senior DBA position within your organization and your industry.

About This Book

By reading and using the resources in this book, you will be better able to take advantage of the PL/SQL-based functionality in the Oracle database that is the most critical for DBAs.

We don't attempt to provide comprehensive coverage of the Oracle PL/SQL language in this book. We provide a solid overview of PL/SQL in Chapter 1, but otherwise assume a basic working knowledge of the language. If you are new to PL/SQL, we suggest that you get started by reading *Learning Oracle PL/SQL*. From there, *Oracle PL/SQL Programming*, Fourth Edition, will serve as a comprehensive reference and user guide. That 1,200-page volume is the classic book on both language fundamentals and advanced features.

Oracle PL/SQL for DBAs consists of eight chapters and one appendix, as follows:

Chapter 1, *Introduction to PL/SQL*, provides a whirlwind tour of the PL/SQL language, touching on all of the topics DBAs will need to become familiar with, from the basics of the PL/SQL block structure, identifier construction, and program data declarations, to the use of control and error-handling statements, to the construction of procedures, functions, packages, and triggers in PL/SQL.

Chapter 2, *Cursors*, describes PL/SQL cursors and how you can improve database performance by taking advantage of such features as cursor reuse, cursor soft-parsing and soft-closing, and various characteristics of implicit and explicit cursors. It also describes the use of REF CURSORs, bulk fetching, cursor parameters, and cursor expressions.

Chapter 3, *Table Functions*, explores the use of functions that can be used as data sources for queries and that are used frequently in Extraction, Transformation, and Loading (ETL) operations. Table functions are crucial when complex logic must be performed from within SELECT statements, usually to transform data. This chapter also explores how you can use pipelining, parallelizing, and nesting table functions to reap enormous performance benefits.

Chapter 4, *Data Encryption and Hashing*, explains how you can use Oracle's tools to build basic encryption and key management systems to protect sensitive data. Focusing on the use of the built-in DBMS_CRYPTO (for Oracle Database 10*g*) and DBMS_OBFUSCATION_TOOLKIT (for Oracle9*i* Database) packages, it describes encryption, decryption, cryptographic hashing, and Message Authentication Code (MAC) operations. It also describes the new Transparent Data Encryption (TDE) features introduced in Oracle Database 10*g* Release 2.

Chapter 5, *Row-Level Security*, explains how you can define policies on database tables so that you can restrict which rows particular users can see or change in those tables. Using the DBMS_RLS package, you can also effectively make tables and views read-only based on user credentials.

Chapter 6, *Fine-Grained Auditing*, shows how you can extend traditional Oracle auditing to capture both database changes and queries. Using the DBMS_FGA package, you can not only enforce security, but also analyze patterns of SQL usage and data access. This chapter also describes how FGA interacts with Oracle's flashback query and trigger features.

Chapter 7, *Generating Random Values*, discusses situations in which you may need to generate random values (e.g., creating temporary passwords or web site user IDs, generating statistically correct test data, or generating keys when building an encryption infrastructure). It focuses on the use of Oracle's built-in DBMS_RANDOM package.

Chapter 8, *Scheduling*, describes the use of the DBMS_SCHEDULER package (introduced in Oracle Database 10g and replacing the older DBMS_JOB package) in scheduling jobs to be performed at regular intervals (e.g., collecting statistics, gathering free space information, or notifying DBAs of problems).

Appendix A, *Quick Reference*, provides a summary of the built-in package specifications described in this book, as well as the data dictionary views related to these packages.

Conventions Used in This Book

The following conventions are used in this book:

Italic
> Used for file and directory names, for URLs, and for emphasis when introducing a new term.

`Constant width`
> Used for code examples.

`Constant width bold`
> Indicates user input in examples showing an interaction. Also, in some code examples, highlights the statements being discussed.

`Constant width italic`
> In some code examples, indicates an element (e.g., a filename) that you supply.

UPPERCASE
> In code examples, generally indicates PL/SQL keywords.

lowercase
> In code examples, generally indicates user-defined items such as variables, parameters, etc.

punctuation
> In code examples, enter exactly as shown.

indentation
> In code examples, helps to show structure but is not required.

\-\-
> In code examples, a double hyphen begins a single-line comment that extends to the end of a line.

/* and */
> In code examples, these characters delimit a multiline comment that can extend from one line to another.

.
> In code examples and related discussions, a dot qualifies a reference by separating an object name from a component name. For example, dot notation is used to select fields in a record and to specify declarations within a package.

[ ]
> In syntax descriptions, square brackets enclose optional items.

{ }
> In syntax descriptions, curly brackets enclose a set of items from which you must choose only one.

|
> In syntax descriptions, a vertical bar separates the items enclosed in curly brackets, as in {TRUE | FALSE}.

...
> In syntax descriptions, ellipses indicate repeating elements. An ellipsis also shows that statements or clauses irrelevant to the discussion were left out.

> Indicates a tip, suggestion, or general note. For example, we'll tell you if a certain setting is version-specific.

> Indicates a warning or caution. For example, we'll tell you if a certain setting has some kind of negative impact on the system.

About PL/SQL Versions

There are many versions of PL/SQL, and you may even find that you need to work with multiple versions in your database administration activities.

We assume for this book that Oracle Database 10g is the baseline PL/SQL version. However, where appropriate, we reference specific features introduced (or only available) in other, earlier versions. In cases where a feature is in any way version-dependent—for example, if you can use it only in Oracle Database 10g Release 2—we note that in the text.

Each version of the Oracle database comes with its own corresponding version of PL/SQL. As you use more up-to-date versions of PL/SQL, an increasing array of functionality will be available to you. One of our biggest challenges as users of PL/SQL is simply keeping up. We need to educate ourselves constantly about the new features in each version—figuring out how to use them and how to apply them to our applications, and determining which new techniques are so useful that we should modify existing applications to take advantage of them.

Table P-1 summarizes the major elements in each of the versions (past and present) of PL/SQL in the database. It offers a very high-level glimpse of the new features available in each version.

 The Oracle Developer product suite also comes with its own version of PL/SQL, and it generally lags behind the version available in the Oracle RDBMS itself. This chapter (and the book as a whole) concentrates on server-side PL/SQL.

Table P-1. Oracle database and corresponding PL/SQL versions

Oracle database release	PL/SQL version	Characteristics
6.0	1.0	This was the initial version of PL/SQL, used primarily as a scripting language in SQL*Plus (it was not yet possible to create named, reusable, and callable programs) and also as a programming language in SQL*Forms 3.
7.0	2.0	This was a major upgrade to PL/SQL 1.0. It added support for stored procedures, functions, packages, programmer-defined records, PL/SQL tables, and many package extensions.
7.1	2.1	This version supported programmer-defined subtypes, enabled the use of stored functions inside SQL statements, and offered dynamic SQL with the DBMS_SQL package. With PL/SQL 2.1, you could finally execute SQL DDL statements from within PL/SQL programs.
7.3	2.3	This version enhanced the functionality of PL/SQL tables, offered improved remote dependency management, added file I/O capabilities to PL/SQL with the UTL_FILE package, and completed the implementation of cursor variables.
8.0	8.0	The new version number reflected Oracle's effort to synchronize version numbers across related products. PL/SQL 8.0 was the version of PL/SQL that supported enhancements of Oracle8 Database, including large objects (LOBs), object-oriented design and development, collections (VARRAYs and nested tables), and Oracle/AQ (the Oracle/Advanced Queuing facility).
8.1	8.1	The first of Oracle's *i* series, the corresponding release of PL/SQL in Oracle8*i* Database offered a truly impressive set of added functionality, including a new version of dynamic SQL, support for Java in the database, the invoker rights model, the execution authority option, autonomous transactions, and high-performance "bulk" DML and queries.
9.1	9.1	Oracle9*i* Database Release 1 came fairly quickly on the heels of its predecessor. The first release of this version included support for inheritance in object types, table functions, and cursor expressions (allowing for parallelization of PL/SQL function execution), multi-level collections, and the CASE statement and CASE expression.

Table P-1. Oracle database and corresponding PL/SQL versions (continued)

Oracle database release	PL/SQL version	Characteristics
9.2	9.2	Oracle9*i* Database Release 2 put a major emphasis on Extensible Markup Language (XML), but also offered many other features, including associative arrays that can be indexed by VARCHAR2 strings in addition to integers, record-based DML (allowing you to perform an insert using a record, for example), and many improvements to UTL_FILE (which allows you to read/write files from within a PL/SQL program).
10.1	10.1	Oracle Database 10*g* Release 1 was unveiled in 2004 and focused on support for grid computing, with an emphasis on improved/automated database management. From the standpoint of PL/SQL, the most important new features were transparently available to developers: an optimized compiler and compile-time warnings.
10.2	10.2	Oracle Database 10*g* Release 2, first available in the fall of 2005, offered a small number of new features for PL/SQL developers, most notably support for preprocessor syntax that allows you to conditionally compile portions of your program, depending on Boolean expressions you define.

Resources for Developing PL/SQL Expertise

This book can do little more than introduce you to PL/SQL fundamentals before moving on to its main focus: DBA-specific features. There are, however, many other books and resources available to help you deepen your working knowledge of PL/SQL.

The following sections describe very briefly many of these resources. By taking full advantage of these resources, many of which are available either free or at a relatively low cost, you will greatly improve your experience (and resulting code) with the language.

The O'Reilly PL/SQL Series

Over the years, the Oracle PL/SQL series from O'Reilly has grown to include quite a long list of books. We've summarized below the books currently in print. Please check out the Oracle area of the O'Reilly web site (*http://oracle.oreilly.com*) for much more complete information.

Learning Oracle PL/SQL, by Bill Pribyl with Steven Feuerstein
> A comparatively gentle introduction to the language, ideal for new programmers and those who know a language other than PL/SQL. It also emphasizes PL/SQL development for Internet-based applications.

Oracle PL/SQL Programming, by Steven Feuerstein with Bill Pribyl
> The desk-side companion of a great many professional PL/SQL programmers and DBAs, this 1,200-page book is designed to cover every feature in the core PL/SQL language. The fourth edition covers PL/SQL up through Oracle Database 10*g* Release 2.

Oracle PL/SQL for DBAs, by Arup Nanda and Steven Feuerstein

> The book you are reading now provides a quick overview of the entire PL/SQL language and focuses on topics of special importance to DBAs: cursors, table functions, data encryption and hashing, row-level security, fine-grained auditing, generating random numbers, and scheduling. Current through Oracle Database 10g Release 2.

Oracle PL/SQL Best Practices, by Steven Feuerstein

> A concise book that describes more than 100 best practices that will help you produce high-quality PL/SQL code. Having this book is kind of like having a "lessons learned" document written by an in-house PL/SQL expert. Although written originally for Oracle8i Database, virtually all of the advice in this book is applicable to newer versions, as well.

Oracle PL/SQL Developer's Workbook, by Steven Feuerstein with Andrew Odewahn

> Contains a series of questions and answers intended to help PL/SQL programmers develop and test their understanding of the language. Current through Oracle8i Database.

Oracle Built-in Packages, by Steven Feuerstein, Charles Dye, and John Beresniewicz

> A reference guide to the prebuilt packages that Oracle supplies with the core database server. The use of these packages can sometimes simplify the difficult and tame the impossible. This book is current only through Oracle8 Database, but the discussion of the included packages should still be very helpful. For a more up-to-date summary of package specification syntax, check out *Oracle in a Nutshell*, by Rick Greenwald and David C. Kreines.

Oracle PL/SQL Language Pocket Reference, by Steven Feuerstein, Bill Pribyl, and Chip Dawes

> A small but very useful "quick reference" book that might actually fit in your coat pocket. Summarizes the syntax of the core PL/SQL language through Oracle Database 10g.

Oracle PL/SQL Built-ins Pocket Reference, by Steven Feuerstein, John Beresniewicz, and Chip Dawes

> Another helpful and concise guide summarizing built-in functions and packages through Oracle8 Database.

Oracle PL/SQL CD Bookshelf

> Contains an electronic version of most of the above books. Current through Oracle8i Database.

PL/SQL on the Internet

There are also some excellent web sites that will help you to develop additional PL/SQL expertise.

Oracle Technology Network

Join the Oracle Technology Network (OTN), which "provides services and resources that developers need to build, test, and deploy applications" based on Oracle technology. Boasting membership in the millions, OTN is a great place to download Oracle software, documentation, and lots of sample code. URL: *http://otn.oracle.com*

Quest Pipelines

Quest Software offers "a free Internet portal community...designed to inform, educate, and inspire IT professionals around the world." Originally the PL/SQL Pipeline, the Quest Pipelines now offer discussion forums, monthly tips, downloads, and, in essence, free consulting for developers and DBAs around the world on multiple database systems, including Oracle, DB2, SQL Server, and MySQL. URL: *http://www.quest-pipelines.com*

PLNet.org

PLNet.org is a repository of open source software, maintained by Bill Pribyl, that is written in PL/SQL or is otherwise for the benefit of PL/SQL developers. You can read more about the project's background or check out the Frequently Asked Questions (FAQ). You will also be directed to a number of utilities, such as utPLSQL, the unit-testing framework for PL/SQL developers. URL: *http://plnet.org*

Open Directory Project

Courtesy of the "dmoz" (Directory Mozilla) project, here you can find a choice set of links to PL/SQL sites. There is also a subcategory called "Tools" with a fairly comprehensive set of links to both commercial and noncommercial developer tools. URL: *http://dmoz.org/Computers/Programming/Languages/PL-SQL/*

Steven Feuerstein's Oracle PL/SQL Programming site

This web site offers trainings, downloads, and other resources for PL/SQL developers, mostly produced by Steven Feuerstein. You can download all of his seminar materials, plus supporting code. Examples from this book are also available there. URL: *http://www.oracleplsqlprogramming.com*

utPLSQL

utPLSQL is an open source unit-testing framework for PL/SQL developers. You can use it to standardize the way you unit-test programs and automate execution of those tests. URL: *http://utplsql.sourceforge.net*

Qnxo

Qnxo (Quality In, Excellence Out) is an active mentoring product designed by Steven Feuerstein that helps you generate, reuse, and test code more effectively. It contains a repository consisting of hundreds of PL/SQL templates and reusable programs. URL: *http://www.qnxo.com*

About the Code

We have provided all of the code included in this book on the book's web site. This is available from the O'Reilly site. Go to:

> *http://www.oreilly.com/catalog/oracleplsqldba*

and click on the Examples link to go to the book's web companion.

We also encourage you to visit Steven Feuerstein's "PL/SQL portal" at:

> *http://www.oracleplsqlprogramming.com*

where you will find training materials, code downloads, and more. All examples from the book are also available there.

To find a particular example on the book's web site, look for the filename cited in the text. For many examples, you will find filenames in the following form provided as a comment at the beginning of the example included in the book, as shown here:

```
/* File on web: fullname.pkg */
```

Using Code Examples

This book is here to help you get your job done. In general, you may use the code in this book in your programs and documentation. You do not need to contact O'Reilly for permission unless you're reproducing a significant portion of the code. For example, writing a program that uses several chunks of code from this book does not require permission. Selling or distributing a CD-ROM of examples from O'Reilly books *does* require permission. Answering a question by citing this book and quoting example code does not require permission. Incorporating a significant amount of example code from this book into your product's documentation *does* require permission.

We appreciate, but do not require, attribution. An attribution usually includes the title, author, publisher, and ISBN. For example: *Oracle PL/SQL for DBAs* by Arup Nanda and Steven Feuerstein. Copyright 2006 O'Reilly Media, Inc., 0-596-00587-3.

If you feel your use of code examples falls outside fair use or the permission given above, feel free to contact us at *permissions@oreilly.com*.

Comments and Questions

We have tested and verified the information in this book and in the source code to the best of our ability, but given the amount of text and the rapid evolution of technology, you may find that features have changed or that we have made mistakes. If so, please notify us by writing to:

O'Reilly Media, Inc.
1005 Gravenstein Highway North
Sebastopol, CA 95472
800-998-9938 (in the U.S. or Canada)
707-829-0515 (international or local)
707-829-0104 (FAX)

You can also send messages electronically. To be put on the mailing list or request a catalog, send email to:

info@oreilly.com

To ask technical questions or comment on the book, send email to:

bookquestions@oreilly.com

As mentioned in the earlier section, we have a web site for this book where you can find code, updated links, and errata (previously reported errors and corrections are available for public view). You can access this web site at:

http://www.oreilly.com/catalog/plsqldba

For more information about this book and others, see the O'Reilly web site:

http://www.oreilly.com

Safari® Enabled

 When you see a Safari® Enabled icon on the cover of your favorite technology book, it means the book is available online through the O'Reilly Network Safari Bookshelf.

Safari offers a solution that's better than e-books. It's a virtual library that lets you easily search thousands of top technology books, cut and paste code samples, download chapters, and find quick answers when you need the most accurate, current information. Try it for free at *http://safari.oreilly.com*.

Acknowledgments

First and foremost, we thank Darryl Hurley who wrote two chapters of this book: Chapter 2, *Cursors*, and Chapter 3, *Table Functions*. He stepped in at a critical moment in the development of the book, assumed significant responsibilities, and produced outstanding content. This text is far stronger for his involvement. Bryn Llewellyn, Oracle's PL/SQL Product Manager, provided crucial information on Oracle Database 10g's new features and answered many questions about various PL/SQL features.

We had a lot of help from our technical reviewers, especially because we asked them to test each code snippet and program in the book to keep to an absolute minimum the number of errors that made it into the printed version. We are deeply grateful to the following men and women of the Oracle PL/SQL world, who took time away from the rest of their lives to help make *Oracle PL/SQL for DBAs* the best book it could be. Jeffrey Hunter carefully reviewed all four security-related chapters under tight time pressure, and we are very grateful to him for his input. Daniel Wong provided key input on the security chapters as well. Many thanks to our chapter reviewers: John Beresniewicz, Dwayne King, Steve Jackson, Lorraine Pocklington, Mahraj Madala, Sean O'Keefe, and Yu-Ho Sikora.

Once we felt good about the technical content, it was time for the remarkable crew at O'Reilly Media, led by our good friend, Deborah Russell, to transform our many chapters and code examples into a book worthy of the O'Reilly imprint. Many thanks to Darren Kelly, production manager for the book; Rob Romano, who created the excellent figures; and the rest of the crew.

Finally, Arup thanks his wife, Anindita, and his son, Anish, who sacrificed precious family time to bring this book to fruition, especially Anish who was too young to verbalize his complaint but missed his father's playing with him terribly.

Steven thanks his wife, Veva Silva, and two sons, Chris Silva and Eli Silva Feuerstein, for their support and tolerance of the diversion of so much of his time and attention.

CHAPTER 1

Introduction to PL/SQL

PL/SQL stands for Procedural Language extensions to the Structured Query Language. SQL is the now-ubiquitous language for both querying *and* updating—never mind the name—of relational databases. Oracle Corporation introduced PL/SQL to overcome some limitations in SQL and to provide a more complete programming solution for those who sought to build mission-critical applications to run against the Oracle database. This chapter introduces PL/SQL and its origins, and it provides a quick overview of the basic elements of the language.

Our expectation is not to have you read this chapter and then immediately be able to write top-notch PL/SQL programs, but rather to make sure that you have sufficient grounding in the language to understand and work with the functionality and examples presented in the rest of this book. We'll try to give you an appreciation of the breadth of PL/SQL while focusing on the features that you are most likely to use as a DBA.

There is a lot more to PL/SQL than we have room to include in this chapter, long as it is. If you have not previously written PL/SQL programs and scripts, we encourage you to check out *Learning Oracle PL/SQL* and *Oracle PL/SQL Programming*, two other O'Reilly books on PL/SQL that will give you much more information and guidance.

What Is PL/SQL?

Oracle's PL/SQL language has several defining characteristics:

It is a highly structured, readable, and accessible language
> If you are new to programming, PL/SQL is a great place to start. You will find that it is an easy language to learn, and it is rich with keywords and structure that clearly express the intent of your code. If you are experienced in other programming languages, you will very easily adapt to the new syntax.

PL/SQL is a standard and portable language for Oracle development
> If you write a PL/SQL procedure or function to execute from within the Oracle database sitting on your laptop, you can move that same procedure to a database on your corporate network and execute it there without any changes (assuming compatibility of Oracle versions, of course). "Write once, run everywhere" was the mantra of PL/SQL long before Java appeared. For PL/SQL, though, "everywhere" means "everywhere there is an Oracle database."

PL/SQL is an embedded language
> PL/SQL was not designed to be used as a standalone language, but instead to be invoked from within a host environment. So, for example, you can run PL/SQL programs from within the database (through, say, the SQL*Plus interface). Alternatively, you can define and execute PL/SQL programs from within an Oracle Developer form or report (this approach is called *client-side PL/SQL*). You cannot, however, create a PL/SQL executable that runs all by itself.

PL/SQL is a high-performance, highly integrated database language
> These days, you have a number of choices when it comes to writing software to run against the Oracle database. You can use Java and JDBC; you can use Visual Basic and ODBC; you can go with Delphi, C++, and so on. You will find, however, that it is easier to write highly efficient code to access the Oracle database in PL/SQL than it is in any other language. In particular, Oracle offers certain PL/SQL-specific enhancements such as the FORALL statement that can improve database performance by an order of magnitude or more.

Basic PL/SQL Syntax Elements

This section introduces you to the fundamentals of PL/SQL program organization and syntax: its block structure; character set; and rules for identifiers, statement delimiters, and comments.

PL/SQL Block Structure

In PL/SQL, as in most other procedural languages, the smallest meaningful grouping of code is known as a *block*. A block is a unit of code that provides execution and scoping boundaries for variable declarations and exception handling. PL/SQL allows you to create *anonymous blocks* (blocks of code that have no name) and *named blocks*, which may be procedures, functions, or triggers.

In the sections below, we review the structure of a block and focus on the anonymous block. We'll explore the different kinds of named blocks later in this chapter.

Sections of the block

A PL/SQL block has up to four different sections, only one of which is mandatory. Figure 1-1 illustrates the block structure.

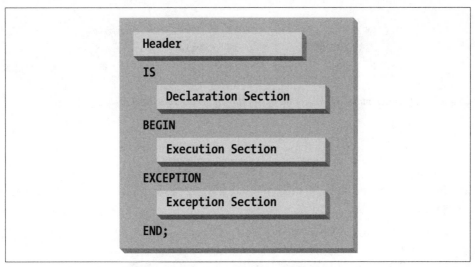

Figure 1-1. The PL/SQL block structure

Header
> Used only for named blocks. The header determines the way the named block or program must be called. Optional.

Declaration section
> Identifies variables, cursors, and sub-blocks that are referenced in the execution and exception sections. Optional.

Execution section
> Contains statements that the PL/SQL runtime engine will execute at runtime. Mandatory.

Exception section
> Handles exceptions to normal processing (warnings and error conditions). Optional.

Anonymous blocks

When someone wishes to remain anonymous, that person goes unnamed. The same is true of the anonymous block in PL/SQL, which is shown in Figure 1-2: it lacks a header section altogether, beginning instead with either DECLARE or BEGIN. That means that it cannot be called by any other block—it doesn't have a handle for reference. Instead, anonymous blocks serve as containers that execute PL/SQL statements, usually including calls to procedures and functions.

The general syntax of an anonymous PL/SQL block is as follows:

```
[ DECLARE
   ... declaration statements ... ]
BEGIN
   ... one or more executable statements ...
```

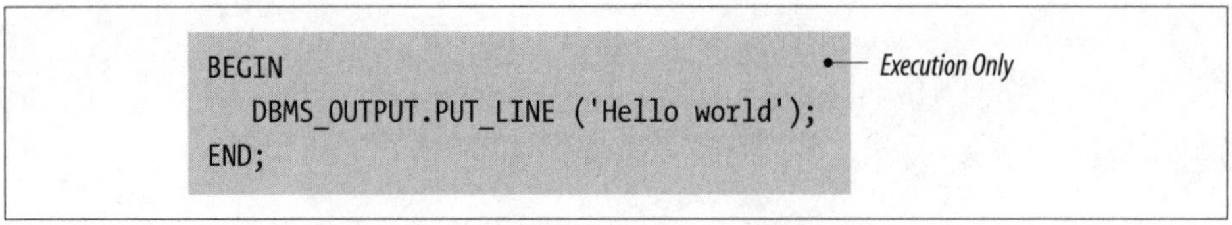

```
BEGIN                                              •—— Execution Only
    DBMS_OUTPUT.PUT_LINE ('Hello world');
END;
```

Figure 1-2. An anonymous block without declaration and exception sections

```
[ EXCEPTION
    ... exception handler statements ... ]
END;
```

The square brackets indicate an optional part of the syntax. You must have BEGIN and END statements, and you must have at least one executable statement. Here are a few examples:

- A bare minimum anonymous block:

```
BEGIN
    DBMS_OUTPUT.PUT_LINE(SYSDATE);
END;
```

- A functionally similar block, adding a declaration section:

```
DECLARE
    l_right_now VARCHAR2(9);
BEGIN
    l_right_now := SYSDATE;
    DBMS_OUTPUT.PUT_LINE (l_right_now);
END;
```

- The same block, but including an exception handler:

```
DECLARE
    l_right_now VARCHAR2(9);
BEGIN
    l_right_now := SYSDATE;
    DBMS_OUTPUT.PUT_LINE (l_right_now);
EXCEPTION
    WHEN VALUE_ERROR
    THEN
        DBMS_OUTPUT.PUT_LINE('I bet l_right_now is too small '
            || 'for the default date format!')
END;
```

The PL/SQL Character Set

A PL/SQL program consists of a sequence of statements, each made up of one or more lines of text. The precise characters available to you will depend on what database character set you're using. For example, Table 1-1 illustrates the available characters in the US7ASCII character set.

Table 1-1. Characters available to PL/SQL in the US7ASCII character set

Type	Characters
Letters	A–Z, a–z
Digits	0–9
Symbols	~ ! @ # $ % * ( ) _ - + = | : ; " ' < > , . ? / ^
Whitespace	Tab, space, newline, carriage return

Every keyword, operator, and token in PL/SQL is made from various combinations of characters in this character set. Now you just have to figure out how to put them all together!

Keep in mind that PL/SQL is a *case-insensitive language*. That is, it doesn't matter how you type keywords and identifiers; uppercase letters are treated the same way as lowercase letters unless surrounded by delimiters that make them a literal string. By convention, the authors of this book prefer uppercase for built-in language keywords and lowercase for programmer-defined identifiers.

A number of these characters—both singly and in combination with other characters—have a special significance in PL/SQL. Table 1-2 lists these special symbols.

Table 1-2. Simple and compound symbols in PL/SQL

Symbol	Description
;	Semicolon: terminates declarations and statements
%	Percent sign: attribute indicator (cursor attributes like %ISOPEN and indirect declaration attributes like %ROWTYPE); also used as multi-byte wildcard symbol with the LIKE condition
_	Single underscore: single-character wildcard symbol in LIKE condition
@	At-sign: remote location indicator
:	Colon: host variable indicator, such as :block.item in Oracle Forms
**	Double asterisk: exponentiation operator
< > or != or ^= or ~=	Ways to denote the "not equal" relational operator
||	Double vertical bar: concatenation operator
<< and >>	Label delimiters
<= and >=	Less than or equal to, greater than or equal to relational operators
:=	Assignment operator
=>	Association operator for positional notation
..	Double dot: range operator
--	Double dash: single-line comment indicator
/* and */	Beginning and ending multi-line comment block delimiters

Characters are grouped together into *lexical units*, also called *atomics* of the language because they are the smallest individual components. A lexical unit in PL/SQL is any of the following: identifier, literal, delimiter, or comment. These are described in the following sections.

Identifiers

An identifier is a name for a PL/SQL object, such as a variable, program name, or reserved word. The default properties of PL/SQL identifiers are summarized below:

- Up to 30 characters in length
- Must start with a letter
- Can include $ (dollar sign), _ (underscore), and # (pound sign)
- Cannot contain any "whitespace" characters

If the only difference between two identifiers is the case of one or more letters, PL/SQL treats those two identifiers as the same. For example, the following identifiers are all considered by PL/SQL to be the same:

```
lots_of_$MONEY$   LOTS_of_$MONEY$   Lots_of_$Money$
```

NULLs

The absence of a value is represented in Oracle by the keyword NULL. As shown in the previous section, variables of almost all PL/SQL datatypes can exist in a null state (the exception to this rule is any associative array type, instances of which are never null). Although it can be challenging for a programmer to handle NULL variables properly regardless of their datatype, strings that are null require special consideration.

In Oracle SQL and PL/SQL, a null string is *usually* indistinguishable from a literal of zero characters, represented literally as `''` (two consecutive single quotes with no characters between them). For example, the following expression will evaluate to TRUE in both SQL and PL/SQL:

```
'' IS NULL
```

While NULL tends to behave as if its default datatype is VARCHAR2, Oracle will try to implicitly cast NULL to whatever type is needed for the current operation. Occasionally, you may need to make the cast explicit, using syntax such as TO_NUMBER(NULL) or CAST(NULL AS NUMBER).

Literals

A literal is a value that is not represented by an identifier; it is simply a value.

String literals

A string literal is text surrounded by single quote characters, such as:

```
'What a great language!'
```

Unlike identifiers, string literals in PL/SQL are case-sensitive. As you should expect, the following two literals are different.

```
'Steven'
'steven'
```

So the following condition evaluates to FALSE:

```
IF 'Steven' = 'steven'
```

Numeric literals

Numeric literals can be integers or real numbers (a number that contains a fractional component). Note that PL/SQL considers the number 154.00 to be a real number of type NUMBER, even though the fractional component is zero and the number is actually an integer. Internally, integers and reals have a different representation, and there is some small overhead involved in converting between the two.

You can also use scientific notation to specify a numeric literal. Use the letter "E" (upper- or lowercase) to multiply a number by 10 to the nth power—for example, 3.05E19, 12e-5.

Beginning in Oracle Database 10g Release 1, a real can be either an Oracle NUMBER type or an IEEE 754 standard floating-point type. Floating-point literals are either binary (32-bit) (designated with a trailing F) or binary double (64-bit) (designated with a trailing D).

In certain expressions, you may use the named constants summarized in Table 1-3 as prescribed by the Institute of Electrical and Electronics Engineers (IEEE) standard.

Table 1-3. Named constants for BINARY_FLOAT and BINARY_DOUBLE

Description	BINARY_FLOAT (32-bit)	BINARY_DOUBLE (64-bit)
"Not a number" (NaN); result of divide by 0 or invalid operation	BINARY_FLOAT_NAN	BINARY_DOUBLE_NAN
Positive infinity	BINARY_FLOAT_INFINITY	BINARY_DOUBLE_INFINITY
Maximum finite number that is less than the overflow threshold	BINARY_FLOAT_MAX_NORMAL	BINARY_DOUBLE_MAX_NORMAL
Smallest normal number; underflow threshold	BINARY_FLOAT_MIN_NORMAL	BINARY_DOUBLE_MIN_NORMAL
Maximum positive number that is less than the underflow threshold	BINARY_FLOAT_MAX_SUBNORMAL	BINARY_DOUBLE_MAX_SUBNORMAL
Absolute minimum number that can be represented	BINARY_FLOAT_MIN_SUBNORMAL	BINARY_DOUBLE_MIN_SUBNORMAL

Boolean literals

PL/SQL provides two literals to represent Boolean values: TRUE and FALSE. These values are not strings; you should not put quotes around them. Use Boolean literals to assign values to Boolean variables, as in:

```
DECLARE
    enough_money BOOLEAN; -- Declare a Boolean variable
BEGIN
    enough_money := FALSE; -- Assign it a value
END;
```

On the other hand, you do not need to refer to the literal value when checking the value of a Boolean expression. Instead, just let that expression speak for itself, as shown in the conditional clause of the following IF statement:

```
DECLARE
    enough_money BOOLEAN;
BEGIN
    IF enough_money
    THEN
       ...
```

A Boolean expression, variable, or constant may also evaluate to NULL, which is neither TRUE nor FALSE.

The Semicolon Delimiter

A PL/SQL program is made up of a series of declarations and statements. These are defined logically, as opposed to physically. In other words, they are not terminated with the physical end of a line of code; instead, they are terminated with a semicolon (;). In fact, a single statement is often spread over several lines to make it more readable. The following IF statement takes up four lines and is indented to reinforce the logic behind the statement:

```
IF salary < min_salary (2003)
THEN
    salary := salary + salary * .25;
END IF;
```

There are two semicolons in this IF statement. The first semicolon indicates the end of the single executable statement within the IF-END IF construct. The second semicolon terminates the IF statement itself.

Comments

Inline documentation, otherwise known as *comments*, is an important element of a good program. While there are many ways to make your PL/SQL program self-documenting through good naming practices and modularization, such techniques are seldom enough by themselves to communicate a thorough understanding of a complex program.

PL/SQL offers two different styles for comments: single and multi-line block comments.

Single-line comment syntax

The single-line comment is initiated with two hyphens (--), which cannot be separated by a space or any other characters. All text after the double hyphen to the end of the physical line is considered commentary and is ignored by the compiler. If the double hyphen appears at the beginning of the line, the whole line is a comment.

In the following IF statement, I use a single-line comment to clarify the logic of the Boolean expression:

```
IF salary < min_salary (2003) -- Function returns min salary for year.
THEN
    salary := salary + salary*.25;
END IF;
```

Multi-line comment syntax

While single-line comments are useful for documenting brief bits of code or ignoring a line that you do not want executed at the moment, the multi-line comment is superior for including longer blocks of commentary.

Multiline comments start with a slash-asterisk (/*) and end with an asterisk-slash (*/). PL/SQL considers all characters found between these two sequences of symbols to be part of the comment, and they are ignored by the compiler.

The following example of multi-line comments shows a header section for a procedure. I use the vertical bars in the left margin so that, as the eye moves down the left edge of the program, it can easily pick out the chunks of comments:

```
PROCEDURE calc_revenue (company_id IN NUMBER)
/*
| Program: calc_revenue
| Author: Steven Feuerstein
*/
IS
```

Program Data

Almost every PL/SQL block you write will define and manipulate *program data*. Program data consists of data structures that exist only within your PL/SQL session (physically, within the Process Global Area, or PGA, for your session); they are not stored in the database. This section shows how to declare program data, covers the rules governing the format of the names you give them, and offers a quick reference to the different types of data supported in PL/SQL.

Before you can work with a variable or a constant, you must first declare it, and when you declare it, you give it a name and a datatype.

Here are two key recommendations for naming your variables, constants, and types:

Make sure each name accurately reflects its usage and is understandable at a glance
> You might even take a moment to write down—in noncomputer terms—what a variable represents. You can then easily extract an appropriate name from that statement. For example, if a variable represents the "total number of calls made about lukewarm coffee," a good name for that variable might be total_calls_on_cold_coffee, or tot_cold_calls, if you are allergic to five-word variable names. A bad name for that variable would be totcoffee, or t_#_calls_lwcoff, both too cryptic to get the point across.

Establish consistent, sensible naming conventions
> Such conventions usually involve the use of prefixes and/or suffixes to indicate type and usage. For example, all local variables should be prefixed with "l_" while global variables defined in packages have a "g_" prefix. All record types should have a suffix of "_rt" and so on. You can download a comprehensive set of naming conventions from O'Reilly's Oracle page at *http://oracle.oreilly.com*. Click on "Oracle PL/SQL Best Practices," then "Examples." The download contains a standards document for your use. (Currently, the direct URL is *http://examples.oreilly.com/orbestprac/*.)

Types of PL/SQL Datatypes

Whenever you declare a variable or a constant, you must assign it a datatype. (PL/SQL is, with very few exceptions, a *strongly typed* language.) PL/SQL offers a comprehensive set of predefined scalar and composite datatypes, and you can create your own user-defined types (also known as *abstract datatypes*).

Virtually all of these predefined datatypes are defined in the PL/SQL STANDARD package. Here, for example, are the statements that define the Boolean datatype and two of the numeric datatypes:

```
CREATE OR REPLACE PACKAGE STANDARD
IS
   type BOOLEAN is (FALSE, TRUE);
   type NUMBER is NUMBER_BASE;
   subtype INTEGER is NUMBER(38,);
```

When it comes to datatypes, PL/SQL supports the usual suspects and a whole lot more. This section provides only a quick overview of the various predefined datatypes.

Character data

PL/SQL supports both fixed- and variable-length strings as both traditional character and Unicode character data. CHAR and NCHAR are fixed-length datatypes; VARCHAR2 and NVARCHAR2 are variable-length datatypes. Here is a declaration of a variable-length string that can hold up to 2,000 characters:

```
DECLARE
   l_accident_description VARCHAR2(2000);
```

Oracle also supports very large character strings, known as LONGs and LOBs. These datatypes allow you to store and manipulate very large amounts of data—a LOB can hold up to 128 terabytes of information in Oracle Database 10g. (Use LONGs only for compatibility with existing code. The future lies with LOBs.) The character LOB datatypes are CLOB and NCLOB (multi-byte format). CLOB stands for *character large object*, and NCLOB for *National Language Support character large object.*

Numbers

PL/SQL supports an increasing variety of numeric datatypes. NUMBER has long been the workhorse of the numeric datatypes, and you can use it for decimal fixed- and floating-point values, and for integers. The following are examples of some possible NUMBER declarations:

```
DECLARE
    salary NUMBER(9,2); --fixed-point, seven to the left, two to the right
    raise_factor NUMBER; --decimal floating-point
    weeks_to_pay NUMBER(2); --integer
BEGIN
    salary := 1234567.89;
    raise_factor := 0.05;
    weeks_to_pay := 52;
END;
```

Because of its true decimal nature, NUMBER is particularly useful when working with monetary amounts. You won't incur any rounding error as a result of binary representation. For example, when you store 0.95, you won't come back later to find only 0.949999968.

Until Oracle Database 10g came along, NUMBER was the only one of PL/SQL's numeric datatypes to correspond directly to a database datatype. This is one reason you'll find NUMBER so widely used. Oracle Database 10g introduced two binary floating-point types: BINARY_FLOAT and BINARY_DOUBLE. As is the case with NUMBER, these new datatypes are also supported in both PL/SQL and the database. Given the right type of application, their use can lead to tremendous performance gains, as arithmetic involving the new types is performed in hardware (whenever the underlying platform allows).

PL/SQL supports several numeric types and subtypes that do not correspond to database datatypes but are, nevertheless, quite useful. Notable here is PLS_INTEGER, an integer type with its arithmetic implemented in hardware. FOR loop counters are implemented as PLS_INTEGERs.

Dates, timestamps, and intervals

Prior to Oracle9i Database, the Oracle world of dates was limited to the DATE datatype, which stores both dates and times (down to the nearest second). Oracle9i Database introduced two sets of new, related datatypes: INTERVALs and TIME-STAMPs. These datatypes greatly expand the capability of PL/SQL developers to write programs that manipulate and store dates and times with very high granularity, and also compute and store intervals of time.

Here is an example of a function that computes the age of a person:

```
CREATE OR REPLACE FUNCTION age (dob_in IN DATE)
    RETURN INTERVAL YEAR TO MONTH
IS
    retval INTERVAL YEAR TO MONTH;
BEGIN
    RETURN (SYSDATE - dob_in) YEAR TO MONTH;
END;
```

Booleans

PL/SQL supports a true Boolean datatype. A variable of this type can have one of only three values: TRUE, FALSE, and NULL.

Booleans help us write very readable code, especially involving complex logical expressions. Here's an example of a Boolean declaration, along with an assignment of a default value to that variable:

```
DECLARE
    l_eligible_for_discount BOOLEAN :=
        customer_in.balance > min_balance AND
        customer_in.pref_type = 'MOST FAVORED' AND
        customer_in.disc_eligibility;
```

Binary data

Oracle supports several forms of *binary data* (unstructured data that is not interpreted or processed by Oracle), including RAW, LONG RAW, BFILE, and BLOB. The BFILE datatype stores unstructured binary data in operating system files outside the database. RAW is a variable-length datatype like the VARCHAR2 character datatype, except that Oracle utilities do not perform character conversion when transmitting RAW data.

ROWIDs

Oracle provides two proprietary datatypes, ROWID and UROWID, used to represent the address of a row in a table. ROWID represents the unique address of a row in its table; UROWID represents the logical position of a row in an index-organized table (IOT). ROWID is also a SQL pseudonym that can be included in SQL statements.

REF CURSOR datatype

The REF CURSOR datatype allows you to declare cursor variables, which can be used with static and dynamic SQL statements to implement very flexible requirements. This datatype supports two forms: the strong REF CURSOR and the weak

REF CURSOR. The latter is one of the very few weakly typed datatypes you can declare.

Here is an example of a strong REF CURSOR declaration (I associate the cursor variable with a specific record structure with %ROWTYPE):

```
DECLARE
    TYPE  book_data_t IS REF CURSOR RETURN book%ROWTYPE;
    book_curs_var book_data_t;
```

And here are two weak REF CURSOR declarations in which I do not associate any particular structure with the resulting variable. The fourth line showcases SYS_REFCURSOR, a predefined weak REF CURSOR type.

```
DECLARE
    TYPE  book_data_t IS REF CURSOR;
    book_curs_var book_data_t;
    book_curs_var2 SYS_REFCURSOR
```

Internet datatypes

From Oracle9i Database onward, you'll find native support for several Internet-related technologies and types of data, specifically Extensible Markup Language (XML) and Universal Resource Identifiers (URIs). Oracle provides datatypes used to handle XML and URI data, as well as a class of URIs called DBUri-REFs used to access data stored within the database itself. Oracle also provides a new set of types to store and access both external and internal URIs from within the database.

The XMLType allows you to query and store XML data in the database using functions like SYS_XMLGEN and the DBMS_XMLGEN package. It also allows you to use native operators in the SQL language to perform searching with the XPath language.

The URI-related types, including URIType and HttpURIType, are all part of an object type inheritance hierarchy and can be used to store URLs to external web pages and files, as well as to refer to data within the database.

"Any" datatypes

Most of the time, our programming tasks are fairly straightforward and very specific to the requirements at hand. At other times, however, we write more generic kinds of code. For those situations, the "Any" datatypes might come in very handy.

The "Any" types were introduced in Oracle9i Database Release 1 and are very different from any other kind of datatype available in Oracle. They let you dynamically encapsulate and access type descriptions, data instances, and sets of data instances of any other SQL type. You can use these types (and the methods defined for them, as they are object types) to do things like determine the type of data stored in a particular nested table—without having access to the actual declaration of that table type!

The "Any" datatypes include AnyType, AnyData, and AnyDataSet.

Declaring Program Data

As I mentioned, before you can make a reference to a variable or a constant, you must declare it. (The only exception to this rule is for the index variables of FOR loops.) All declarations must be made in the declaration section of your anonymous block, procedure, function, trigger, object type body, or package body. You can declare many types of data and data structures in PL/SQL, including variables, constants, TYPEs (such as a type of collection or a type of record), and exceptions. This section focuses on the declarations of variables and constants.

Declaring a variable

When you declare a variable, PL/SQL allocates memory for the variable's value and names the storage location so that the value can be retrieved and changed. The declaration also specifies the datatype of the variable; this datatype is then used to validate values assigned to the variable.

The basic syntax for a declaration is:

```
name datatype [NOT NULL] [default_assignment];
```

where *name* is the name of the variable or constant to be declared, and *datatype* is the datatype or subtype that determines the type of data that can be assigned to the variable. You can include a NOT NULL clause, which means that if your code assigns a NULL to this variable, Oracle will raise an exception. The [*default_assignment*] clause allows you to initialize the variable with a value; this is optional for all declarations except those of constants.

The following examples illustrate declarations of variables of different datatypes:

```
DECLARE
    -- Simple declaration of numeric variable
    l_total_count NUMBER;

    -- Declaration of number that rounds to nearest hundredth (cent):
    l_dollar_amount NUMBER (10,2);

    -- A single date value, assigned a default value of "right now"
    -- and it can never be NULL
    l_right_now DATE NOT NULL  DEFAULT SYSDATE;

    -- Using the assignment operator for the default value specification
    l_favorite_flavor VARCHAR2(100) := 'Anything with chocolate, actually';

    -- Two-step declaration process for associative array.
    -- First, the type of table:
    TYPE list_of_books_t IS TABLE OF book%ROWTYPE INDEX BY BINARY_INTEGER;

    -- And now the specific list to be manipulated in this block:
    oreilly_oracle_books list_of_books_t;
```

The DEFAULT and assignment operator syntax for assigning a default value are equivalent and can be interchanged. So which should you use? I like to use the assignment operator (:=) to set default values for constants, and the DEFAULT syntax for variables. In the case of the constant, the assigned value is not really a default but an initial (and unchanging) value, so the DEFAULT syntax feels misleading to me.

Declaring constants

There are just two differences between declaring a variable and declaring a constant: for a constant, you include the CONSTANT keyword, and you must supply a default value (which isn't really a *default* at all, but rather is the *only* value). So the syntax for the declaration of a constant is:

```
name CONSTANT datatype [NOT NULL] := | DEFAULT default_value;
```

The value of a constant is set upon declaration and may not change thereafter.

Here are some examples of declarations of constants:

```
DECLARE
   -- The current year number; it's not going to change during my session.
   l_curr_year CONSTANT PLS_INTEGER :=
      TO_NUMBER (TO_CHAR (SYSDATE, 'YYYY'));

   -- Using the DEFAULT keyword
   l_author CONSTANT VARCHAR2(100) DEFAULT 'Bill Pribyl';

   -- Declare an object type as a constant
   -- this isn't just for scalars!
   l_steven CONSTANT  person_ot :=
     person_ot ('HUMAN', 'Steven Feuerstein', 175, '09-23-1958');
```

Unless otherwise stated, the information provided in the rest of this chapter for variables also applies to constants.

Anchored declarations

When you anchor a datatype, you tell PL/SQL to set the datatype of your variable based on the datatype of an already defined data structure—another PL/SQL variable, a predefined TYPE or SUBTYPE, a database table, or a specific column in a table. PL/SQL offers two kinds of anchoring:

Scalar anchoring
    Use the %TYPE attribute to define your variable based on a table's column or some other PL/SQL scalar variable.

Record anchoring
    Use the %ROWTYPE attribute to define your record structure based on a table or a predefined PL/SQL explicit cursor.

The syntax for an anchored datatype is:

```
variable_name_type attribute%TYPE [optional default value assignment];
variable_name table_name | cursor_name%ROWTYPE [optional default value assignment];
```

where *variable_name* is the name of the variable you are declaring, and *type_attribute* is either a previously declared PL/SQL variable name or a table column specification in the format *table.column*.

Here is an example of anchoring a variable to a database column:

```
l_company_id company.company_id%TYPE;
```

Here is an example of anchoring a record to a cursor:

```
DECLARE
    CURSOR book_cur IS
        SELECT author, title FROM book;
    l_book book_cur%ROWTYPE;
```

This anchoring reference is resolved at the time the code is compiled; there is no runtime overhead to anchoring. The anchor also establishes a dependency between the code and the anchored element (the table, cursor, or package containing the variable referenced). This means that if those elements are changed, the code in which the anchoring takes place is marked INVALID. When it is recompiled, the anchor will again be resolved, thereby keeping the code current with the anchored element.

Control Statements

There are two types of PL/SQL control statements: conditional control statements and sequential control statements. Almost every piece of code you write will require conditional control, which is the ability to direct the flow of execution through your program based on a condition. You do this with IF-THEN-ELSE and CASE statements (CASE statements are available in Oracle9*i* Database and Oracle Database 10*g*). There are also CASE expressions; while not the same as CASE statements, they can sometimes be used to eliminate the need for an IF or CASE statement altogether. Far less often, you will need to tell PL/SQL to transfer control unconditionally via the GOTO statement, or explicitly to do nothing via the NULL statement.

IF Statements

The IF statement allows you to design conditional logic into your programs, and comes in three flavors, as shown in Table 1-4.

Table 1-4. Types of IF statements

IF type	Characteristics
IF *condition* THEN END IF;	This is the simplest form of the IF statement. The condition between IF and THEN determines whether the set of statements between THEN and END IF should be executed. If the condition evaluates to FALSE, the code is not executed.

IF *condition* THEN
ELSE
END IF;
	This combination implements an either/or logic: based on the condition between the IF and THEN keywords, execute the code either between THEN and ELSE or between ELSE and END IF. One of these two sections of executable statements is performed.

Table 1-4. Types of IF statements (continued)

IF type	Characteristics

IF *condition1* THEN
ELSIF *condition2* THEN
ELSE
END IF;
	This last and most complex form of the IF statement selects an action from a series of mutually exclusive conditions and then executes the set of statements associated with that condition. If you're writing IF statements like this using any release from Oracle9*i* Database Release 1 onwards, you should consider using *searched CASE* statements instead.

CASE Statements and Expressions

The CASE statement allows you to select one sequence of statements to execute out of many possible sequences. CASE statements have been part of the SQL standard since 1992, although Oracle SQL didn't support CASE until the release of Oracle8*i* Database, and PL/SQL didn't support CASE until Oracle9*i* Database Release 1. From this release onward, the following types of CASE statements are supported:

Simple CASE statement
> Associates each of one or more sequences of PL/SQL statements with a value. Chooses which sequence of statements to execute based on an expression that returns one of those values.

Searched CASE statement
> Chooses which of one or more sequences of PL/SQL statements to execute by evaluating a list of Boolean conditions. The sequence of statements associated with the first condition that evaluates to TRUE is executed.

In addition to CASE statements, PL/SQL also supports CASE expressions. A CASE expression is very similar in form to a CASE statement and allows you to choose which of one or more expressions to evaluate. The result of a CASE expression is a single value, whereas the result of a CASE statement is the execution of a sequence of PL/SQL statements.

Simple CASE statement

A simple CASE statement allows you to choose which of several sequences of PL/SQL statements to execute based on the results of a single expression. Here is an example of a simple CASE statement that uses the employee type as a basis for selecting the proper bonus algorithm:

```
CASE employee_type
WHEN 'S' THEN
   award_salary_bonus(employee_id);
WHEN 'H' THEN
   award_hourly_bonus(employee_id);
WHEN 'C' THEN
   award_commissioned_bonus(employee_id);
ELSE
   RAISE invalid_employee_type;
END CASE;
```

This CASE statement has an explicit ELSE clause; however, the ELSE is optional. When you do not explicitly specify an ELSE clause of your own, PL/SQL implicitly uses the following:

```
ELSE
    RAISE CASE_NOT_FOUND;
```

Searched CASE statement

A searched CASE statement evaluates a list of Boolean expressions and, when it finds an expression that evaluates to TRUE, executes a sequence of statements associated with that expression. Essentially, a searched CASE statement is the equivalent of the CASE TRUE statement shown in the previous section. Here is an example of a searched CASE statement:

```
CASE
WHEN salary >= 10000 AND salary <=20000 THEN
    give_bonus(employee_id, 1500);
WHEN salary > 20000 AND salary <= 40000 THEN
    give_bonus(employee_id, 1000);
WHEN salary > 40000 THEN
    give_bonus(employee_id, 500);
ELSE
    give_bonus(employee_id, 0);
END CASE;
```

Loops in PL/SQL

PL/SQL offers three types of loops to provide you with the flexibility you need to write the most straightforward code to handle any particular situation. Most situations that require a loop could be written with any of the three loop constructs. If you do not pick the construct that is best suited for that particular requirement, however, you could end up having to write many additional lines of code. The resulting module would also be harder to understand and maintain.

To give you a feeling for the way the different loops solve their problems in different ways, consider the following three procedures. In each case, the procedure makes a call to display_total_sales for a particular year, for each year number between the start and end argument values.

In the following examples, the FOR loop clearly requires the smallest amount of code. Yet I can use it in this case only because I know that I will run the body of the loop a specific number of times. In many other situations, the number of times a loop must execute varies, so the FOR loop cannot be used.

Simple Loop

The simple loop is called simple for a reason: it starts simply with the LOOP keyword and ends with the END LOOP statement. The loop will terminate if you execute an EXIT, EXIT WHEN, or RETURN within the body of the loop (or if an exception is raised):

```
PROCEDURE display_multiple_years (
    start_year_in IN PLS_INTEGER
   ,end_year_in IN PLS_INTEGER
)
IS
   l_current_year PLS_INTEGER := start_year_in;
BEGIN
   LOOP
      EXIT WHEN l_current_year > end_year_in;
      display_total_sales (l_current_year);
      l_current_year :=  l_current_year + 1;
   END LOOP;
END display_multiple_years;
```

FOR Loop

Oracle offers both numeric and cursor FOR loops. With the numeric FOR loop, you specify the start and end integer values, and PL/SQL does the rest of the work for you, iterating through each intermediate value, and then terminating the loop:

```
PROCEDURE display_multiple_years (
    start_year_in IN PLS_INTEGER
   ,end_year_in IN PLS_INTEGER
)
IS
BEGIN
   FOR l_current_year IN start_year_in .. end_year_in
   LOOP
      display_total_sales (l_current_year);
   END LOOP;
END display_multiple_years;
```

The cursor FOR loop has the same basic structure, but, in this case, you supply an explicit cursor or SELECT statement in place of the low-high integer range:

```
PROCEDURE display_multiple_years (
    start_year_in IN PLS_INTEGER
   ,end_year_in IN PLS_INTEGER
)
IS
BEGIN
   FOR l_current_year IN (
      SELECT * FROM sales_data
       WHERE year BETWEEN start_year_in AND end_year_in)
   LOOP
      -- This procedure is now accepted a record implicitly declared
      -- to be of type sales_data%ROWTYPE...
      display_total_sales (l_current_year);
   END LOOP;
END display_multiple_years;
```

WHILE Loop

The WHILE loop is very similar to a simple loop, with a critical difference being that it checks the termination condition up front. It may not even execute its body a single time:

```
PROCEDURE display_multiple_years (
   start_year_in IN PLS_INTEGER
   ,end_year_in IN PLS_INTEGER
)
IS
   l_current_year PLS_INTEGER := start_year_in;
BEGIN
   WHILE (l_current_year <= end_year_in)
   LOOP
      display_total_sales (l_current_year);
      l_current_year :=  l_current_year + 1;
   END LOOP;
END display_multiple_years;
```

Exception Handling

In the PL/SQL language, errors of any kind are treated as *exceptions*—situations that should not occur—in your program. An exception can be one of the following:

- An error generated by the system (such as "out of memory" or "duplicate value in index")
- An error caused by a user action
- A warning issued by the application to the user

PL/SQL traps and responds to errors using an architecture of exception handlers. The exception handler mechanism allows you to cleanly separate your error processing code from your executable statements. It also provides an *event-driven* model, as opposed to a linear-code model, for processing errors. In other words, no matter how a particular exception is raised, it is handled by the same exception handler in the exception section.

When an error occurs in PL/SQL, whether it's a system error or an application error, an exception is raised. The processing in the current PL/SQL block's execution section halts, and control is transferred to the separate exception section of the current block, if one exists, to handle the exception. You cannot return to that block after you finish handling the exception. Instead, control is passed to the enclosing block, if any.

Defining Exceptions

Before an exception can be raised or handled, it must be defined. Oracle predefines thousands of exceptions, mostly by assigning numbers and messages to those exceptions. Oracle also assigns names to a relative few of these thousands—the most commonly encountered exceptions.

These names are assigned in the STANDARD package (one of two default packages in PL/SQL), as well as in other built-in packages such as UTL_FILE and DBMS_SQL. The code Oracle uses to define exceptions like NO_DATA_FOUND is the same code that you will write to define or declare your own exceptions. You can do this in two different ways, described in the following sections.

You can also declare your own exceptions by listing the name of the exception you want to raise in your program followed by the keyword EXCEPTION:

```
DECLARE
    exception_name EXCEPTION;
```

The names for exceptions are similar in format to (and "read" just like) Boolean variable names, but they can be referenced in only two ways:

- In a RAISE statement in the execution section of the program (to raise the exception), as in:

```
RAISE invalid_company_id;
```

- In the WHEN clauses of the exception section (to handle the raised exception), as in:

```
WHEN invalid_company_id THEN
```

Raising Exceptions

There are three ways that an exception may be raised in your application:

- Oracle might raise the exception when it detects an error.
- You might raise an exception with the RAISE statement.
- You might raise an exception with the RAISE_APPLICATION_ERROR built-in procedure.

We've already looked at how Oracle raises exceptions. Now let's examine the different mechanisms you can use to raise exceptions.

RAISE statement

Oracle offers the RAISE statement so that you can, at your discretion, raise a named exception. You can raise an exception of your own or a system exception. The RAISE statement can take one of three forms:

```
RAISE exception_name;
RAISE package_name.exception_name;
RAISE;
```

The first form (without a package name qualifier) can be used to raise an exception you have defined in the current block (or an outer block containing that block) or to raise a system exception defined in the STANDARD package.

The second form does require a package name qualifier. If an exception has been declared inside a package (other than STANDARD) and you are raising that exception outside that package, you must qualify your reference to that exception in your RAISE statement.

The third form of the RAISE statement does not require an exception name but can be used only within a WHEN clause of the exception section. Use this form when you want to re-raise (or propagate out) the same exception from within an exception handler.

Using RAISE_APPLICATION_ERROR

Oracle provides the RAISE_APPLICATION_ERROR procedure (defined in the default DBMS_STANDARD package) to raise application-specific errors in your application that need to be communicated back to the host environment.

The header for this procedure (defined in package DBMS_STANDARD) is shown here:

```
PROCEDURE RAISE_APPLICATION_ERROR (
    num binary_integer,
    msg varchar2,
    keeperrorstack boolean default FALSE);
```

where *num* is the error number and must be a value between -20,999 and -20,000 (just think: Oracle needs all the rest of those negative integers for its *own* exceptions!); *msg* is the error message and must be no more than 2K characters in length (any text beyond that limit will be ignored); and *keeperrorstack* indicates whether you want to add the error to any already on the stack (TRUE) or replace the existing errors (the default, FALSE).

Handling Exceptions

Once an exception is raised, the current PL/SQL block stops its regular execution and transfers control to the exception section. The exception is then either handled by an exception handler in the current PL/SQL block or passed to the enclosing block.

To handle or trap an exception once it is raised, you must write an exception handler for that exception. In your code, your exception handlers must appear after all the executable statements in your program but before the END statement of the block. The EXCEPTION keyword indicates the start of the exception section and the individual exception handlers. The syntax for an exception handler is as follows:

```
WHEN exception_name [ OR exception_name ... ]
THEN
    executable statements
```

or:

```
WHEN OTHERS
THEN
    executable statements
```

The WHEN OTHERS clause is optional; if it is not present, then any unhandled exception is immediately propagated back to the enclosing block, if any. The WHEN OTHERS clause must be the last exception handler in the exception section.

Built-in error functions

Oracle provides several built-in functions to help you identify, analyze, and respond to errors that occur in your PL/SQL application.

SQLCODE
> SQLCODE returns the error code of the most recently raised exception in your block. If there is no error, SQLCODE returns 0. SQLCODE also returns 0 when you call it outside of an exception handler.

SQLERRM
> SQLERRM is a function that returns the error message for a particular error code. If you do not pass an error code to SQLERRM, it returns the error message associated with the value returned by SQLCODE. The maximum length string that SQLERRM will return is 512 bytes (in some earlier versions of Oracle, only 255 bytes).

DBMS_UTILITY.FORMAT_ERROR_STACK
> This built-in function, like SQLERRM, returns the full message associated with the current error (i.e., the value returned by SQLCODE). As a rule, you should call this function inside your exception handler logic to obtain the full error message.

DBMS_UTILITY.FORMAT_ERROR_BACKTRACE
> Introduced in Oracle Database 10g Release 1, this function returns a formatted string that displays a stack of programs and line numbers leading back to the line on which the error was originally raised.

Unhandled exceptions

If an exception is raised in your program and it is not handled by an exception section in either the current or enclosing PL/SQL blocks, that exception is *unhandled*. PL/SQL returns the error that raised the unhandled exception all the way back to the application environment from which PL/SQL was run. That environment (a tool like SQL*Plus, Oracle Forms, or a Java program) then takes an action appropriate to the situation; in the case of SQL*Plus, a ROLLBACK of any DML changes from within that top-level block's logic is automatically performed.

Propagation of an unhandled exception

The scope rules for exceptions determine the block in which an exception can be raised. The rules for exception propagation address the way in which an exception is handled after it is raised.

When an exception is raised, PL/SQL looks for an exception handler in the current block (anonymous block, procedure, or function) of the exception. If it does not find a match, then PL/SQL propagates the exception to the enclosing block of that current block. PL/SQL then attempts to handle the exception by raising it once more in the enclosing block. It continues to do this in each successive enclosing block until there are no more blocks in which to raise the exception (see Figure 1-3).

```
PROCEDURE list_my_faults IS
BEGIN
   ...
   DECLARE                                                    Nested Block 1
      too_many_faults EXCEPTION;
   BEGIN
      ... executable statements before new block ...
      BEGIN                                                   Nested Block 2
         SELECT SUM (faults) INTO num_faults FROM profile ... ;
         IF num_faults > 100
         THEN
            RAISE too_many_faults;
         END IF;
      EXCEPTION
         WHEN NO_DATA_FOUND THEN ... ;
      END;
      ... executable statements after Nested Block 2 ...

   EXCEPTION
      WHEN too_many_faults THEN ... ;
   END;
   END list_my_faults;
```

Figure 1-3. Propagation of exception handling

When all blocks are exhausted, PL/SQL returns an unhandled exception to the application environment that executed the outermost PL/SQL block. An unhandled exception halts the execution of the host program.

Records

Each row in a table has one or more columns of various datatypes. Similarly, a record is composed of one or more fields. There are three different ways to define a record, but once defined, the same rules apply for referencing and changing fields in a record.

The block below demonstrates the declaration of a record that is based directly on an underlying database table. Suppose that I have defined a table to keep track of my favorite books:

```
CREATE TABLE books (
   book_id        INTEGER,
   isbn           VARCHAR2(13)
   title          VARCHAR2(200),
);
```

I can then easily create a record based on this table, populate it with a query from the database, and then access the individual columns through the record's fields:

```
DECLARE
   my_book    books%ROWTYPE;
BEGIN
   SELECT *
     INTO my_book
     FROM books
    WHERE title = 'Oracle PL/SQL Programming, 4th Edition';
END;
```

Declaring Records

You can declare a record in one of three ways:

Table-based record

Use the %ROWTYPE attribute with a table name to declare a record in which each field corresponds to—and has the same name as—a column in a table. In the following example, I declare a record named one_book with the same structure as the books table:

```
DECLARE
   one_book books%ROWTYPE;
```

Cursor-based record

Use the %ROWTYPE with an explicit cursor or cursor variable in which each field corresponds to a column or aliased expression in the cursor SELECT statement. In the following example, I declare a record with the same structure as an explicit cursor:

```
DECLARE
   CURSOR my_books_cur IS
      SELECT * FROM books
       WHERE author LIKE '%FEUERSTEIN%';

   one_SF_book my_books_cur%ROWTYPE;
```

Programmer-defined record

Use the TYPE RECORD statement to define a record in which each field is defined explicitly (with its name and datatype) in the TYPE statement for that record; a field in a programmer-defined record can even be another record. In the following example, I declare a record TYPE containing some information about my book-writing career and an "instance" of that TYPE, a record:

```
DECLARE
    TYPE book_info_rt IS RECORD (
        author books.author%TYPE,
        category VARCHAR2(100),
        total_page_count POSITIVE);

    steven_as_author book_info_rt;
```

Notice that when I declare a record based on a record TYPE, I do not use the %ROWTYPE attribute. The book_info_rt element already is a TYPE.

Working with Records

Regardless of how you define a record (based on a table, cursor, or explicit record TYPE statement), you work with the resulting record in the same ways. You can work with the data in a record at the record level, or you can work with individual fields of the record.

Record-level operations

When you work at the record level, you avoid any references to individual fields in the record. Here are the record-level operations currently supported by PL/SQL:

- You can copy the contents of one record to another (as long as they are compatible in structure—that is, have the same number of fields and the same or convertible datatypes).
- You can assign a value of NULL to a record with a simple assignment.
- You can define and pass the record as an argument in a parameter list.
- You can RETURN a record back through the interface of a function.

You can perform record-level operations on any records with compatible structures. In other words, the records must have the same number of fields and the same or convertible datatypes, but they don't have to be the same type. Suppose that I have created the following table:

```
CREATE TABLE cust_sales_roundup (
    customer_id NUMBER (5),
    customer_name VARCHAR2 (100),
    total_sales NUMBER (15,2)
    );
```

Then the three records defined as follows all have compatible structures, and I can mix and match the data in these records as shown:

```
DECLARE
    cust_sales_roundup_rec cust_sales_roundup%ROWTYPE;
```

```
    CURSOR cust_sales_cur IS SELECT * FROM cust_sales_roundup;
    cust_sales_rec cust_sales_cur%ROWTYPE;

    TYPE customer_sales_rectype IS RECORD
       (customer_id NUMBER(5),
        customer_name customer.name%TYPE,
        total_sales NUMBER(15,2)
        );
    prefererred_cust_rec customer_sales_rectype;
BEGIN
    -- Assign one record to another.
    cust_sales_roundup_rec := cust_sales_rec;
    prefererred_cust_rec := cust_sales_rec;
END;
```

Field-level operations

When you need to access a field within a record (to either read or change its value), you must use dot notation, just as you would when identifying a column from a specific database table. The syntax for such a reference is:

```
[schema_name.][package_name.]record_name.field_name
```

You need to provide a package name only if the record is defined in the specification of a package that is different from the one you are working on at that moment. You need to provide a schema name only if the package is owned by a schema different from that in which you are compiling your code.

Once you have used dot notation to identify a particular field, all the normal rules in PL/SQL apply as to how you can reference and change the value of that field. Let's take a look at some examples.

Collections

A *collection* is a data structure that acts like a list or a single-dimensional array. Collections are, in fact, the closest you can get to traditional arrays in the PL/SQL language. You can use collections to manage lists of information in your programs.

Types of Collections

Oracle supports three different types of collections. While these different types have much in common, they also each have their own particular characteristics.

Associative arrays
> These are single-dimensional, unbounded, sparse collections of homogeneous elements that are available only in PL/SQL. They were called *PL/SQL tables* in PL/SQL 2 and *index-by tables* in Oracle8 Database and Oracle8*i* Database (because, when you declare such a collection, you explicitly state that they are "indexed by" the row number). In Oracle9*i* Database, the name was changed to

associative arrays. The motivation for the name change was that starting with that release, the INDEX BY syntax could be used to "associate" or index contents by VARCHAR2 or PLS_INTEGER.

Nested tables

These are also single-dimensional, unbounded collections of homogeneous elements. They are initially dense but can become sparse through deletions. Nested tables can be defined in both PL/SQL and the database (for example, as a column in a table). Nested tables are *multisets*, which means that there is no inherent order to the elements in a nested table.

VARRAYs

Like the other two collection types, variable-sized arrays (VARRAYs) are also single-dimensional collections of homogeneous elements. However, they are always bounded and never sparse. When you define a type of VARRAY, you must also specify the maximum number of elements it can contain. Like nested tables, they can be used in PL/SQL and in the database. Unlike nested tables, when you store and retrieve a VARRAY, its element order is preserved.

Working with Collections

This section provides relatively simple examples of each of the different types of collections in this section, with explanations of the major characteristics.

Using an associative array

In the following example, I declare an associative array type and then a collection based on that type. I populate it with four rows of data and then iterate through the collection, displaying the strings in the collection. A more thorough explanation appears after the code.

```
 1  DECLARE
 2     TYPE list_of_names_t IS TABLE OF person.first_name%TYPE
 3        INDEX BY PLS_INTEGER;
 4     happyfamily    list_of_names_t;
 5     l_row PLS_INTEGER;
 6  BEGIN
 7     happyfamily (2020202020) := 'Eli';
 8     happyfamily (-15070) := 'Steven';
 9     happyfamily (-90900) := 'Chris';
10     happyfamily (88) := 'Veva';
11
12     l_row := happyfamily.FIRST;
13
14     WHILE (l_row IS NOT NULL)
15     LOOP
16        DBMS_OUTPUT.put_line (happyfamily (l_row));
17        l_row := happyfamily.NEXT (l_row);
18     END LOOP;
19* END;
```

```
SQL> /
Chris
Steven
Veva
Eli
```

Line(s)	Description
2–3	Declare the associative array TYPE, with its distinctive INDEX BY clause. A collection based on this type contains a list of strings, each of which can be as long as the first_name column in the person table.
4	Declare the happyfamily collection from the list_of_names_t type.
9–10	Populate the collection with four names. Notice that I can use virtually any integer value that I like. The row numbers don't have to be sequential in an associative array; they can even be negative!
12	Call the FIRST method (a function that is "attached" to the collection) to get the first or lowest defined row number in the collection.
14–18	Use a WHILE loop to iterate through the contents of the collection, displaying each row. Line 17 shows the use of the NEXT method to move from the current defined row to the next defined row "skipping over" any gaps.

Using a nested table

In the following example, I first declare a nested table type as a schema-level type. In my PL/SQL block, I declare three nested tables based on that type. I put the names of everyone in my family into the happyfamily nested table. I put the names of my children in the children nested table. I then use the Oracle Database 10g set operator, MULTISET EXCEPT, to extract just the parents from the happyfamily nested table; finally, I display the names of the parents. A more thorough explanation appears after the code.

```
REM Section A
SQL> CREATE TYPE list_of_names_t IS TABLE OF VARCHAR2 (100);
  2  /
Type created.

REM Section B
SQL>
  1  DECLARE
  2     happyfamily    list_of_names_t := list_of_names_t ();
  3     children       list_of_names_t := list_of_names_t ();
  4     parents        list_of_names_t := list_of_names_t ();
  5  BEGIN
  6     happyfamily.EXTEND (4);
  7     happyfamily (1) := 'Eli';
  8     happyfamily (2) := 'Steven';
  9     happyfamily (3) := 'Chris';
 10     happyfamily (4) := 'Veva';
 11
 12     children.EXTEND;
 13     children (1) := 'Chris';
 14     children.EXTEND;
 15     children (2) := 'Eli';
 16
```

```
    17      parents := happyfamily MULTISET EXCEPT children;
    18
    19      FOR l_row IN parents.FIRST .. parents.LAST
    20      LOOP
    21         DBMS_OUTPUT.put_line (parents (l_row));
    22      END LOOP;
    23* END;

SQL> /
Steven
Veva
```

Line(s)	Description
Section A	The CREATE TYPE statement creates a nested table type in the database itself. By taking this approach, I can declare nested tables in any PL/SQL block that has SELECT authority on the type. I can also declare columns in relational tables of this type.
2–4	Declare three different nested tables based on the schema-level type. Notice that in each case I also call a *constructor* function to initialize the nested table. This function always has the same name as the type and is created for us by Oracle. You must initialize a nested table before it can be used.
6	Call the EXTEND method to "make room" in my nested table for the members of my family. Here, in contrast to associative arrays, I must explicitly ask for a row in a nested table before I can place a value in that row.
7–10	Populate the happyfamily collection with our names.
12–15	Populate the children collection. In this case, I extend a single row at a time.
17	To obtain the parents in this family, I simply take the children out of the happyfamily. This is transparently easy to do in releases from Oracle Database 10*g* onward, where we have high-level set operators like MULTISET EXCEPT (very similar to the SQL MINUS).
19–22	Because I know that my parents collection is densely filled from the MULTISET EXCEPT operation, I can use the numeric FOR loop to iterate through the contents of the collection. This construct will raise a NO_DATA_FOUND exception if used with a sparse collection.

Using a VARRAY

In the following example, I demonstrate the use of VARRAYs as columns in a relational table. First, I declare two different schema-level VARRAY types. I then create a relational table, family, that has two VARRAY columns. Finally, in my PL/SQL code, I populate two local collections and then use them in an INSERT into the family table. A more thorough explanation appears after the code.

```
REM Section A
SQL> CREATE TYPE first_names_t IS VARRAY (2) OF VARCHAR2 (100);
  2 /
Type created.

SQL> CREATE TYPE child_names_t IS VARRAY (1) OF VARCHAR2 (100);
  2 /
Type created.

REM Section B
SQL> CREATE TABLE family (
  2      surname VARCHAR2(1000)
  3    , parent_names first_names_t
```

```
  4     , children_names child_names_t
  5   );

Table created.

REM Section C
SQL>
  1  DECLARE
  2     parents     first_names_t := first_names_t ();
  3     children    child_names_t := child_names_t ();
  4  BEGIN
  5     parents.EXTEND (2);
  6     parents (1) := 'Samuel';
  7     parents (2) := 'Charina';
  8     --
  9     children.EXTEND;
 10     children (1) := 'Feather';
 11
 12     --
 13     INSERT INTO family
 14                 (surname, parent_names, children_names
 15                 )
 16          VALUES ('Assurty', parents, children
 17                 );
 18  END;
SQL> /

PL/SQL procedure successfully completed.

SQL> SELECT * FROM family
  2  /

SURNAME
PARENT_NAMES
CHILDREN_NAMES
--------------------------------------------
Assurty
FIRST_NAMES_T('Samuel', 'Charina')
CHILD_NAMES_T('Feather')
```

Line(s)	Description
Section A	Use CREATE TYPE statements to declare two different VARRAY types. Notice that with a VARRAY, I must specify the maximum length of the collection. Thus, my declarations in essence dictate a form of social policy: you can have at most two parents and at most one child.
Section B	Create a relational table, with three columns: a VARCHAR2 column for the surname of the family and two VARRAY columns, one for the parents and another for the children.
Section C, lines 2–3	Declare two local VARRAYs based on the schema-level type. As with nested tables (and unlike with associative arrays), I must call the constructor function of the same name as the TYPE to initialize the structures.
5–0	Extend and populate the collections with the names of parents and then the single child. If I try to extend to a second row, Oracle will raise the *ORA-06532: Subscript outside of limit* error.
13–17	Insert a row into the family table, simply providing the VARRAYs in the list of values for the table. Oracle certainly makes it easy for us to insert collections into a relational table!

Collection Methods (Built-ins)

PL/SQL offers a number of built-in functions and procedures, known as *collection methods*, that let you obtain information about and modify the contents of collections. The following collection methods are available:

COUNT function
> Returns the current number of elements in a collection.

DELETE procedure
> Removes one or more elements from the collection. Reduces COUNT if the element is not already DELETEd. With VARRAYS, you can only delete the entire contents of the collection.

EXISTS function
> Returns TRUE or FALSE to indicate whether the specified element exists.

EXTEND procedure
> Increases the number of elements in a nested table or VARRAY. Increases COUNT.

FIRST, LAST functions
> Return the smallest (FIRST) and largest (LAST) subscripts in use.

LIMIT function
> Returns the maximum number of elements allowed in a VARRAY.

PRIOR, NEXT functions
> Return the subscript immediately before (PRIOR) or after (NEXT) a specified subscript. You should always use PRIOR and NEXT to traverse a collection, especially if you are working with sparse (or potentially sparse) collections.

TRIM procedure
> Removes collection elements from the end of the collection (highest defined subscript). Reduces COUNT if elements are not DELETEd.

These programs are referred to as *methods* because the syntax for using the collection built-ins is different from the normal syntax used to call procedures and functions. Collection methods employ a *member method* syntax that's common in object-oriented languages such as C++.

The general syntax for calling these associative array built-ins is either of the following:

- An operation that takes no arguments:

  ```
  table_name.operation
  ```

- An operation that takes a row index for an argument:

  ```
  table_name.operation(index_number [, index_number])
  ```

The following statement, for example, returns TRUE if the 15th row of the company_tab associative array is defined:

```
company_tab.EXISTS(15)
```

The collection methods are not available from within SQL; they can be used only in PL/SQL programs.

Procedures, Functions, and Packages

PL/SQL offers the following structures to modularize your code in different ways:

Procedure
> A program that performs one or more actions and is called as an executable PL/SQL statement. You can pass information into and out of a procedure through its parameter list.

Function
> A program that returns a single value and is used just like a PL/SQL expression. You can pass information into a function through its parameter list.

Package
> A named collection of procedures, functions, types, and variables. A package is not really a module (it's more of a meta-module), but it is so closely related that I mention it here.

Database trigger
> A set of commands that are triggered to execute (e.g., log in, modify a row in a table, execute a DDL statement) when an event occurs in the database.

Object type or instance of an object type.
> Oracle's version of (or attempt to emulate) an object-oriented class. Object types encapsulate state and behavior, combining data (like a relational table) with rules (procedures and functions that operate on that data).

In this section, we'll describe procedures, functions, and packages. Triggers are described in a later section. Object types are not covered in this chapter; few developers and even fewer database administrators use Oracle's version of object-oriented language features.

Procedures

A *procedure* is a module that performs one or more actions. Because a procedure call is a standalone executable statement in PL/SQL, a PL/SQL block could consist of nothing more than a single call to a procedure. Procedures are key building blocks of modular code, allowing you to both consolidate and reuse your program logic.

Structure of a procedure

The general format of a PL/SQL procedure is as follows:

```
PROCEDURE [schema.]name [( parameter [, parameter ...] ) ]
   [AUTHID DEFINER | CURRENT_USER]
IS
   [declaration statements]
```

```
BEGIN
    executable statements
[ EXCEPTION
    exception handler statements]
END [name];
```

where each element is used in the following ways:

schema
> Optional name of the schema that will own this procedure. The default is the current user. If different from the current user, that user will need privileges to create a procedure in another schema.

name
> Name of the procedure, which comes directly after the keyword PROCEDURE.

parameters
> Optional list of parameters that you define to both pass information into the procedure and send information out of the procedure back to the calling program.

AUTHID clause
> Determines whether the procedure will execute under the authority of the definer (owner) of the procedure or under the authority of the current user. The former is known as the *definer rights model*, the latter as the *invoker rights model*.

declaration statements
> Declarations of local identifiers for that procedure. If you do not have any declarations, there will be no statements between the IS and BEGIN statements.

executable statements
> Statements that the procedure executes when it is called. You must have at least one executable statement after the BEGIN and before the END or EXCEPTION keywords.

exception handler statements
> Optional exception handlers for the procedure. If you do not explicitly handle any exceptions, then you can leave out the EXCEPTION keyword and simply terminate the execution section with the END keyword.

Calling a procedure

A procedure is called as an executable PL/SQL statement. In other words, a call to a procedure must end with a semicolon (;) and be executed before and after other SQL or PL/SQL statements (if they exist) in the execution section of a PL/SQL block.

The following executable statement runs the apply_discount procedure:

```
BEGIN
    apply_discount( new_company_id, 0.15 );   -- 15% discount
END;
```

If the procedure does not have any parameters, then you call the procedure without any parentheses:

```
display_store_summary;
```

In Oracle8*i* Database and later, you can also include empty opening and closing parentheses, as in:

```
display_store_summary( );
```

Functions

A *function* is a module that returns a value. Unlike a procedure call, which is a standalone executable statement, a call to a function can exist only as part of an executable statement, such as an element in an expression or the value assigned as the default in a declaration of a variable.

Because a function returns a value, it is said to have a datatype. A function can be used in place of an expression in a PL/SQL statement having the same datatype as the function.

Functions are particularly important constructs for building modular code. For example, every business rule or formula in your application should be placed inside a function. Every single-row query should also be defined within a function, so that it can be easily and reliably reused.

 Some people prefer to rely less on functions and more on procedures that return status information through the parameter list. If this is your preference, make sure that your business rules, formulas, and single-row queries are tucked away into your procedures.

An application short on function definition and usage is likely to be difficult to maintain and enhance over time.

Structure of a function

The structure of a function is the same as that of a procedure, except that the function also has a RETURN clause. The general format of a function is as follows:

```
FUNCTION [schema.]name [( parameter [, parameter ...] ) ]
   RETURN return_datatype
   [AUTHID DEFINER | CURRENT_USER]
   [DETERMINISTIC]
   [PARALLEL ENABLE ...]
   [PIPELINED]
IS
   [declaration statements]

BEGIN
   executable statements
```

```
[EXCEPTION
    exception handler statements]

END [ name ];
```

where each element is used in the following ways:

schema

Optional name of the schema that will own this function. The default is the current user. If different from the current user, that user will need privileges to create a function in another schema.

name

Name of the procedure, which comes directly after the keyword FUNCTION.

parameters

Optional list of parameters that you define to both pass information into the procedure and send information out of the procedure back to the calling program.

return_datatype

Datatype of the value returned by the function. This is required in the function header.

AUTHID clause

Determines whether the procedure will execute under the authority of the definer (owner) of the procedure or under the authority of the current user. The former is known as the *definer rights model*, the latter as the *invoker rights model*.

DETERMINISTIC clause

Optimization hint that lets the system use a saved copy of the function's return result, if available. The query optimizer can choose whether to use the saved copy or re-call the function.

PARALLEL_ENABLE clause

Optimization hint that enables the function to be executed in parallel when called from within a SELECT statement.

PIPELINED clause

Specifies that the results of this table function should be returned iteratively via the PIPE ROW command.

declaration statements

Declarations of local identifiers for that function. If you do not have any declarations, there will be no statements between the IS and BEGIN statements.

executable statements

Statements the function executes when it is called. You must have at least one executable statement after the BEGIN and before the END or EXCEPTION keywords.

exception handler statements

Optional exception handlers for the function. If you do not explicitly handle any exceptions, then you can leave out the EXCEPTION keyword and simply terminate the execution section with the END keyword.

Calling a function

A function is called as part of an executable PL/SQL statement wherever an expression can be used. The following examples illustrate how various functions can be invoked.

- Assign the default value of a variable with a function call:

```
DECLARE
    v_nickname VARCHAR2(100) :=
        favorite_nickname ('Steven');
```

- Use a member function for the pet object type in a conditional expression:

```
DECLARE
    my_parrot pet_t :=
        pet_t (1001, 'Mercury', 'African Grey',
               TO_DATE ('09/23/1996', 'MM/DD/YYYY'));
BEGIN
    IF my_parrot.age < INTERVAL '50' YEAR -- 9i INTERVAL type
    THEN
        DBMS_OUTPUT.PUT_LINE ('Still a youngster!');
    END IF;
```

- Retrieve a single row of book information directly into a record:

```
DECLARE
    my_first_book books%ROWTYPE;
BEGIN
    my_first_book := book_info.onerow ('1-56592-335-9');
    ...
```

- Obtain a cursor variable to overdue book information for a specific user:

```
DECLARE
    my_overdue_info overdue_rct;
BEGIN
    my_overdue_info :=
        book_info.overdue_info ('STEVEN_FEUERSTEIN');
    ...
```

Parameters

Procedures and functions can both use *parameters* to pass information back and forth between the module and the calling PL/SQL block.

The parameters of a module are at least as important as the code that implements the module (the module's body). Sure, you have to make certain that your module fulfills its promise. But the whole point of creating a module is that it can be called, ideally by more than one other module. If the parameter list is confusing or badly designed, it will be very difficult for other programmers to make use of the module, and the result is that few will bother. And it doesn't matter how well you have implemented a program if no one uses it.

PL/SQL offers many different features to help you design parameters effectively. This section covers all elements of parameter definition.

Defining parameters

Formal parameters are defined in the parameter list of the program. A parameter definition parallels closely the syntax for declaring variables in the declaration section of a PL/SQL block. There are two important distinctions: first, a parameter has a passing mode while a variable declaration does not; and second, a parameter declaration must be unconstrained.

A *constrained declaration* is one that constrains or limits the kind of value that can be assigned to a variable declared with that datatype. An *unconstrained declaration* is one that does not limit values in this way. The following declaration of the variable company_name constrains the variable to 60 characters:

```
DECLARE
    company_name VARCHAR2(60);
```

When you declare a parameter, however, you must leave out the constraining part of the declaration:

```
PROCEDURE display_company (company_name IN VARCHAR2) IS ...
```

Actual and formal parameters

We need to distinguish between two different kinds of parameters: actual and formal parameters. The *formal parameters* are the names that are declared in the parameter list of the header of a module. The *actual parameters* are the values or expressions placed in the parameter list of the actual call to the module.

Let's examine the differences between actual and formal parameters using the example of tot_sales. Here, again, is the tot_sales header:

```
FUNCTION tot_sales
    (company_id_in IN company.company_id%TYPE,
     status_in IN order.status_code%TYPE := NULL)
    RETURN std_types.dollar_amount;
```

The formal parameters of tot_sales are:

company_id_in
    Primary key of the company

status_in
    Status of the orders to be included in the sales calculation

These formal parameters do not exist outside of the function. You can think of them as placeholders for real or actual parameter values that are passed into the function when it is used in a program.

How does PL/SQL know which actual parameter goes with which formal parameter when a program is executed? PL/SQL offers two ways to make the association:

Positional notation
 Associates the actual parameter implicitly (by position) with the formal parameter.

Named notation
 Associates the actual parameter explicitly (by name) with the formal parameter.

Parameter modes

When you define the parameter, you also specify the way in which it can be used. There are three different modes of parameters:

Mode	Description	Parameter usage
IN	Read-only	The value of the actual parameter can be referenced inside the module, but the parameter cannot be changed.
OUT	Write-only	The module can assign a value to the parameter, but the parameter's value cannot be referenced.
IN OUT	Read-write	The module can both reference (read) and modify (write) the parameter.

The mode determines how the program can use and manipulate the value assigned to the formal parameter. You specify the mode of the parameter immediately after the parameter name and before the parameter's datatype and optional default value. The following procedure header uses all three parameter modes:

```
PROCEDURE predict_activity
   (last_date_in IN DATE,
    task_desc_inout IN OUT VARCHAR2,
    next_date_out OUT DATE)
```

The predict_activity procedure takes in two pieces of information: the date of the last activity and a description of the activity. It then returns or sends out two pieces of information: a possibly modified task description and the date of the next activity. Because the task_desc_inout parameter is IN OUT, the program can both read the value of the argument and change the value of that argument.

Positional notation. In every example so far, I have employed positional notation to guide PL/SQL through the parameters. With positional notation, PL/SQL relies on the relative positions of the parameters to make the correspondence: it associates the Nth actual parameter in the call to a program with the Nth formal parameter in the program's header.

With the following tot_sales example, PL/SQL associates the first actual parameter, :order.company_id, with the first formal parameter, company_id_in. It then associates the second actual parameter, N, with the second formal parameter, status_in:

```
new_sales := tot_sales (:order.company_id, 'N');

FUNCTION tot_sales
   (company_id_in IN company.company_id%TYPE,
    status_in IN order.status_code%TYPE := NULL)
RETURN std_types.dollar_amount;
```

Now you know the name for the way compilers pass values through parameters to modules. Positional notation is certainly the most obvious and common method.

Named notation. With named notation, you explicitly associate the formal parameter (the name of the parameter) with the actual parameter (the value of the parameter) right in the call to the program, using the combination symbol =>.

The general syntax for named notation is:

```
formal_parameter_name => argument_value
```

Because you provide the name of the formal parameter explicitly, PL/SQL no longer needs to rely on the order of the parameters to make the association from actual to formal. So, if you use named notation, you do not need to list the parameters in your call to the program in the same order as the formal parameters in the header. You can call tot_sales for new orders in either of these two ways:

```
new_sales :=
   tot_sales (company_id_in => order_pkg.company_id, status_in =>'N');

new_sales :=
   tot_sales (status_in =>'N', company_id_in => order_pkg.company_id);
```

You can also mix named and positional notation in the same program call:

```
:order.new_sales := tot_sales (order_pkg.company_id, status_in =>'N');
```

If you do mix notation, however, you must list all of your positional parameters before any named notation parameters, as shown in the preceding example.

Packages

A *package* is a grouping or packaging together of PL/SQL code elements. Packages provide a structure (both logically and physically) in which you can organize your programs and other PL/SQL elements such as cursors, TYPEs, and variables. They also offer significant, unique functionality, including the ability to hide logic and data from view, and to define and manipulate global, or session-persistent, data.

Rules for building packages

The package is a deceptively simple construct. In a small amount of time, you can learn all the basic elements of package syntax and rules, but you can spend weeks (or more) uncovering all the nuances and implications of the package structure. In this section, we review the rules you need to know to build packages.

To construct a package, you must build a specification and, in almost every case, a package body. You must decide which elements go into the specification and which are hidden away in the body. You also can include a block of code that Oracle will use to initialize the package.

The package specification. The specification of a package lists all the elements in that package that are available for use in applications, and it provides all the information a developer needs to use elements defined in the package (often referred to as an API, or application programming interface). A developer should never have to look at the implementation code in a package body to figure out how to use an element in the specification.

Here are some rules to keep in mind for package specification construction:

- You can declare elements of almost any datatype, such as numbers, exceptions, types, and collections, at the package level (i.e., not within a particular procedure or function in the package). This is referred to as *package-level data*. Generally, you should avoid declaring variables in the package specification, although constants are always safe.

  You cannot declare cursor variables (variables defined from a REF CURSOR type) in a package specification (or body). Cursor variables are not allowed to *persist* at the session level (see the section "Package data" later in this chapter for more information about package data persistence).

- You can declare almost any type of data structure, such as a collection type, a record type, or a REF CURSOR type.

- You can declare procedures and functions in a package specification, but you can include only the header of the program (everything up to but not including the IS or AS keyword).

- You can include explicit cursors in the package specification. An explicit cursor can take one of two forms: it can include the SQL query as a part of the cursor declaration, or you can hide the query inside the package body and provide only a RETURN clause in the cursor declaration.

- If you declare any procedures or functions in the package specification or if you declare a CURSOR without its query, then you *must* provide a package body to implement those code elements.

- You can include an AUTHID clause in a package specification, which determines whether any references to data objects will be resolved according to the privileges of the owner of the package (AUTHID DEFINER) or of the invoker of the package (AUTHID CURRENT_USER).

- You can include an optional package name label after the END statement of the package, as in:

```
END my_package;
```

Here is a very simple package specification illustrating these rules:

```
1  CREATE OR REPLACE PACKAGE favorites_pkg
2     AUTHID CURRENT_USER
3  IS
4     -- Two constants; notice that I give understandable
5     -- names to otherwise obscure values.
6
7     c_chocolate CONSTANT PLS_INTEGER := 16;
8     c_strawberry CONSTANT PLS_INTEGER := 29;
9
10    -- A nested table TYPE declaration
11    TYPE codes_nt IS TABLE OF INTEGER;
12
13    -- A nested table declared from the generic type.
14    my_favorites codes_nt;
15
16    -- A REF CURSOR returning favorites information.
17    TYPE fav_info_rct IS REF CURSOR RETURN favorites%ROWTYPE;
18
19    -- A procedure that accepts a list of favorites
20    -- (using a type defined above) and displays the
21    -- favorite information from that list.
22    PROCEDURE show_favorites (list_in IN codes_nt);
23
24    -- A function that returns all the information in
25    -- the favorites table about the most popular item.
26    FUNCTION most_popular RETURN fav_info_rct;
27
28 END favorites_pkg; -- End label for package
```

As you can see, a package specification is, in structure, essentially the same as a declaration section of a PL/SQL block. One difference, however, is that a package specification may *not* contain any implementation code.

The package body. The package body contains all the code required to implement the package specification. A package body is not always needed, but it is required when any of the following conditions is true:

The package specification contains a cursor declaration with a RETURN clause
You will then need to specify the SELECT statement in the package body.

The package specification contains a procedure or function declaration
You will then need to complete the implementation of that module in the package body.

You wish to execute code in the initialization section of the package body
The package specification does not support an execution section (executable statements within a BEGIN...END); you can do this only in the body.

Structurally, a package body is very similar to a procedure definition. Here are some rules particular to package bodies:

- A package body can have declaration, execution, and exception sections. The declaration section contains the complete implementation of any cursors and programs defined in the specification, and also the definition of any private elements (not listed in the specification). The declaration section can be empty as long as there is an initialization section.

- The execution section of a package is known as the *initialization section*; this optional code is executed when the package is instantiated for a session.

- The exception section handles any exceptions raised in the initialization section. You can have an exception section at the bottom of a package body only if you have defined an initialization section.

- A package body may consist of the following combinations: just a declaration section; just an execution section; execution and exception sections; or declaration, execution, and exception sections.

- You may not include an AUTHID clause in the package body; it must go in the package specification. Anything declared in the specification may be referenced (used) within the package body.

- The same rules and restrictions for declaring package-level data structures apply to the body as well as to the specification—for example, you cannot declare a cursor variable.

- You can include an optional package name label after the END statement of the package, as in:

```
END my_package;
```

Here is an implementation of the favorites_pkg body:

```
CREATE OR REPLACE PACKAGE BODY favorites_pkg
IS
    -- A private variable
    g_most_popular   PLS_INTEGER := c_strawberry;

    -- Implementation of procedure
    PROCEDURE show_favorites (list_in IN codes_nt) IS
    BEGIN
        FOR indx IN list_in.FIRST .. list_in.LAST
        LOOP
            DBMS_OUTPUT.put_line (list_in (indx));
        END LOOP;
    END show_favorites;

    -- Implement the function
    FUNCTION most_popular RETURN fav_info_rct
    IS
        retval fav_info_rct;
        null_cv fav_info_rct;
```

```
   BEGIN
      OPEN retval FOR
      SELECT *
        FROM favorites
       WHERE code = g_most_popular;
      RETURN retval;
   EXCEPTION
      WHEN NO_DATA_FOUND THEN RETURN null_cv;
   END most_popular;

END favorites_pkg; -- End label for package
```

Rules for calling packaged elements

It doesn't really make any sense to talk about running or executing a package (after all, it is just a container for code elements). However, you will certainly want to run or reference those elements defined in a package.

A package owns its objects, just as a table owns its columns. To reference an element defined in the package specification *outside of* the package itself, you must use the same dot notation to fully specify the name of that element. Let's look at some examples.

The following package specification declares a constant, an exception, a cursor, and several modules:

```
CREATE OR REPLACE PACKAGE pets_inc
IS
   max_pets_in_facility CONSTANT INTEGER := 120;
   pet_is_sick EXCEPTION;

   CURSOR pet_cur (pet_id_in IN pet.id%TYPE) RETURN pet%ROWTYPE;

   FUNCTION next_pet_shots (pet_id_in IN pet.id%TYPE) RETURN DATE;
   PROCEDURE set_schedule (pet_id_in IN pet.id%TYPE);

END pets_inc;
```

To reference any of these objects, I preface the object name with the package name, as follows:

```
DECLARE
   -- Base this constant on the id column of the pet table.
   c_pet CONSTANT pet.id%TYPE:= 1099;
   v_next_apppointment DATE;
BEGIN
   IF pets_inc.max_pets_in_facility > 100
   THEN
      OPEN pets_inc.pet_cur (c_pet);
   ELSE
      v_next_appointment:= pets_inc.next_pet_shots (c_pet);
   END IF;
EXCEPTION
```

```
      WHEN pets_inc.pet_is_sick
      THEN
          pets_inc.set_schedule (c_pet);
   END;
```

To summarize, there are two rules to follow in order to reference and use elements in a package:

- When you reference elements defined in a package specification from outside of that package (an external program), you must use dot notation in the form *package_name.element_name*.

- When you reference package elements from within the package (specification or body), you do not need to include the name of the package. PL/SQL will automatically resolve your reference within the scope of the package.

Package data

Package data consists of variables and constants that are defined at the *package level*—that is, not within a particular function or procedure in the package. The scope of the package data is therefore not a single program, but rather the package as a whole. In the PL/SQL runtime architecture, package data structures *persist* (hold their values) for the duration of a session (rather than the duration of execution for a particular program).

If package data is declared inside the package body, then that data persists for the session but can be accessed only by elements defined in the package itself (private data).

If package data is declared inside the package specification, then that data persists for the session and is directly accessible (to both read and modify the value) by any program that has EXECUTE authority on that package (public data).

If a packaged procedure opens a cursor, that cursor remains open and is available throughout the session. It is not necessary to define the cursor in each program. One module can open a cursor while another performs the fetch. In addition, package variables can carry data across the boundaries of transactions because they are tied to the session rather than to a single transaction.

Querying Data

PL/SQL programs query information from the database with the SQL SELECT statement. Because PL/SQL is tightly integrated with the SQL language, you can execute this SELECT statement natively in your PL/SQL block, as shown below:

```
DECLARE
   l_employee employee%ROWTYPE;
BEGIN
   SELECT * INTO l_employee
     FROM employee
    WHERE employee_id = 7500;
END;
```

This SELECT INTO is an example of an *implicit cursor*, and is just one of several ways you can query data from within a PL/SQL block. You have these choices:

Implicit cursors

A simple and direct SELECT...INTO retrieves a single row of data into local program variables. It's the easiest (and often the most efficient) path to your data, but it can often lead to coding the same or similar SELECTs in multiple places in your code.

Explicit cursors

You can declare the query explicitly in your declaration section (local block or package). In this way, you can open and fetch from the cursor in one or more programs, with a granularity of control not available with implicit cursors.

Cursor variables

Offering an additional level of flexibility, cursor variables (declared from a REF CURSOR type) allow you to pass a *pointer* to a query's underlying result set from one program to another. Any program with access to that variable can open, fetch from, or close the cursor.

Cursor expressions

Introduced in Oracle9*i* Database, the CURSOR expression transforms a SELECT statement into a REF CURSOR result set and can be used in conjunction with table functions (described in Chapter 3) to improve the performance of applications.

Chapter 2 describes cursors in detail.

Typical Query Operations

Regardless of the type of query cursor, PL/SQL performs the same operations to execute a SQL statement from within your program. In some cases, PL/SQL takes these steps for you. In others, such as with explicit cursors, you will write the code for these steps yourself.

Parse

The first step in processing a SQL statement is to parse it to make sure it is valid and to determine the execution.

Bind

When you bind, you associate values from your program (host variables) with placeholders inside your SQL statement. With static SQL, the PL/SQL engine itself performs these binds. With dynamic SQL, you must explicitly request a binding of variable values if you wish to use bind variables.

Open

When you open a cursor, the bind variables are used to determine the result set for the SQL statement. The pointer to the active or current row is set to the first row. Sometimes you will not explicitly open a cursor; instead, the PL/SQL engine will perform this operation for you (as with implicit cursors or native dynamic SQL).

Execute

In the execute phase, the statement is run within the SQL engine.

Fetch

If you are performing a query, the FETCH command retrieves the next row from the cursor's result set. Each time you fetch, PL/SQL moves the pointer forward in the result set. When you are working with explicit cursors, remember that FETCH does nothing (does not raise an error) if there are no more rows to retrieve.

Close

This step closes the cursor and releases all memory used by the cursor. Once closed, the cursor no longer has a result set. Sometimes you will not explicitly close a cursor; instead, the PL/SQL engine will perform this operation for you (as with implicit cursors or native dynamic SQL).

Cursor Attributes

PL/SQL offers a set of *cursor attributes* that can be used to obtain information about the cursor's state. These attributes are shown in Table 1-5. Generally, if you try to reference one of these attributes for a cursor that has not yet been opened, Oracle will raise the INVALID_CURSOR exception.

Table 1-5. Cursor attributes

Name	Description
%FOUND	Returns TRUE if data was fetched, FALSE otherwise
%NOTFOUND	Returns TRUE if data was not fetched, FALSE otherwise
%ROWCOUNT	Returns number of rows fetched from cursor at that point in time
%ISOPEN	Returns TRUE if cursor is open, FALSE otherwise
%BULK_ROWCOUNT	Returns the number of rows modified by the FORALL statement for each collection element
%BULK_EXCEPTIONS	Returns exception information for rows modified by the FORALL statement for each collection element

To reference a cursor attribute, attach it to the name of the cursor or cursor variable about which you want information. Here are some examples:

- Is the explicit cursor still open?

```
DECLARE
   CURSOR happiness_cur IS SELECT simple_delights FROM ...;
BEGIN
   OPEN happiness_cur;
   ...
   IF happiness_cur%ISOPEN THEN ...
```

- How many rows did I retrieve with the implicit bulk query? (Notice that the "name" of my cursor in this case is the generic "SQL.")

```
DECLARE
   TYPE id_nt IS TABLE OF department.department_id;
   deptnums    id_nt;
BEGIN
   SELECT department_id
     BULK COLLECT INTO deptnums
     FROM department;

   DBMS_OUTPUT.PUT_LINE (SQL%BULK_ROWCOUNT);
END;
```

 You can reference cursor attributes in your PL/SQL code, as shown in the preceding example, but you cannot use those attributes inside a SQL statement. For example, if you try to use the %ROWCOUNT attribute in the WHERE clause of a SELECT:

```
SELECT caller_id, company_id
  FROM caller WHERE company_id = company_cur%ROWCOUNT;
```

you will get a compile error:

```
PLS-00229: Attribute expression within SQL expression
```

Implicit Cursors

PL/SQL declares and manages an implicit cursor every time you execute a SQL DML statement (INSERT, UPDATE, or DELETE) or a SELECT INTO that returns a single row from the database directly into a PL/SQL data structure. This kind of cursor is called *implicit* because Oracle implicitly or automatically handles many of the cursor-related operations for you, such as allocating a cursor, opening the cursor, fetching, and so on.

An implicit query is a SELECT statement that has the following special characteristics:

- The SELECT statement appears in the executable section of your block; it is not defined in the declaration section, as explicit cursors are.
- The query contains an INTO clause (or BULK COLLECT INTO for bulk processing). The INTO clause is a part of the PL/SQL (not the SQL) language and is the mechanism used to transfer data from the database into local PL/SQL data structures.
- You do not open, fetch, or close the SELECT statement; all of these operations are done for you.

The general structure of an implicit query is as follows:

```
SELECT column_list
  [BULK COLLECT] INTO PL/SQL variable list
  ...rest of SELECT statement...
```

If you use an implicit cursor, Oracle performs the open, fetches, and close for you automatically; these actions are outside your programmatic control. You can, however, obtain information about the most recently executed SQL statement by examining the values in the implicit SQL cursor attributes, as explained later in "Implicit SQL cursor attributes."

 In the following sections, the term *implicit cursor* means a SELECT INTO statement that retrieves (or attempts to retrieve) a single row of data. Later we'll discuss the SELECT BULK COLLECT INTO variation that allows you to retrieve multiple rows of data with a single implicit query.

Here is an example of an implicit query that retrieves an entire row of information into a record:

```
DECLARE
   l_book book%ROWTYPE;
BEGIN
   SELECT *
     INTO l_book
     FROM book
    WHERE isbn = '0-596-00121-5';
```

Error handling with implicit cursors

The implicit cursor version of the SELECT statement is a "black box." You pass the SQL statement to the SQL engine in the database, and it returns a single row of information. You can't get inside the separate operations of the cursor, such as the open, fetch, and close stages. You are also stuck with the fact that Oracle will automatically raise exceptions from within the implicit SELECT for two common outcomes:

- The query does not find any rows matching your criteria. In this case, Oracle raises the NO_DATA_FOUND exception.
- The SELECT statement returns more than one row. In this case, Oracle raises the TOO_MANY_ROWS exception.

Implicit SQL cursor attributes

Oracle allows you to access information about the most recently executed implicit cursor by referencing the special implicit cursor attributes shown in Table 1-6. The table describes the significance of the values returned by these attributes for an implicit SQL query (SELECT INTO). Because the cursors are implicit, they have no name and, therefore, the keyword "SQL" is used to denote the implicit cursor. These implicit cursors also apply to implicit DML statements: INSERT, UPDATE, and DELETE.

Table 1-6. Implicit query cursor attributes and their values

Name	Description
SQL%FOUND	Returns TRUE if one row (or more in the case of BULK COLLECT INTO) was fetched or modified, FALSE otherwise (in which case Oracle will also raise the NO_DATA_FOUND exception).
SQL%NOTFOUND	Returns TRUE if a row was not fetched or no rows were modified by a DML statement, FALSE otherwise.
SQL%ROWCOUNT	Returns the number of rows fetched from or modified by the specified cursor. For a SELECT INTO, this will be 1 if a row was found and 0 if Oracle raises the NO_DATA_FOUND exception.
SQL%ISOPEN	Always returns FALSE for implicit cursors, because Oracle opens and closes implicit cursors atomically.

All the implicit cursor attributes return NULL if no implicit cursors have yet been executed in the session. Otherwise, the values of the attributes always refer to the most recently executed SQL statement, regardless of the block or program from which the SQL statement was executed.

Explicit Cursors

An explicit cursor is a SELECT statement that is explicitly defined in the declaration section of your code and, in the process, assigned a name. There is no such thing as an explicit cursor for UPDATE, DELETE, and INSERT statements.

With explicit cursors, you have complete control over the different PL/SQL steps involved in retrieving information from the database. You decide when to OPEN the cursor, when to FETCH records from the cursor (and therefore from the table or tables in the SELECT statement of the cursor), how many records to fetch, and when to CLOSE the cursor. Information about the current state of your cursor is available through examination of cursor attributes. This granularity of control makes the explicit cursor an invaluable tool for your development effort.

Let's look at an example. The following function determines (and returns) the level of jealousy I should feel for my friends, based on their location.

```
 1  CREATE OR REPLACE FUNCTION jealousy_level (
 2     NAME_IN   IN   friends.NAME%TYPE) RETURN NUMBER
 3  AS
 4     CURSOR jealousy_cur
 5     IS
 6        SELECT location FROM friends
 7         WHERE NAME = UPPER (NAME_IN);
 8
 9     jealousy_rec   jealousy_cur%ROWTYPE;
10     retval         NUMBER;
11  BEGIN
12     OPEN jealousy_cur;
13
14     FETCH jealousy_cur INTO jealousy_rec;
15
16     IF jealousy_cur%FOUND
17     THEN
```

```
18        IF jealousy_rec.location = 'PUERTO RICO'
19           THEN retval := 10;
20        ELSIF jealousy_rec.location = 'CHICAGO'
21           THEN retval := 1;
22        END IF;
23     END IF;
24
25     CLOSE jealousy_cur;
26
27     RETURN retval;
28  END;
```

This PL/SQL block performs the following cursor actions:

Line(s)	Description
4–7	Declare the cursor
9	Declare a record based on that cursor
12	Open the cursor
14	Fetch a single row from the cursor
16	Check a cursor attribute to determine if a row was found
18–22	Examine the contents of the fetched row to calculate my level of jealousy
25	Close the cursor

To use an explicit cursor, you must first declare it in the declaration section of your PL/SQL block or in a package, as shown here:

```
CURSOR cursor_name [ ( [ parameter [, parameter ...] ) ]
    [ RETURN return_specification ]
    IS SELECT_statement
        [FOR UPDATE [OF [column list]]];
```

where *cursor_name* is the name of the cursor, *return_specification* is an optional RETURN clause for the cursor, and *SELECT_statement* is any valid SQL SELECT statement. You can also pass arguments into a cursor through the optional parameter list. Once you have declared a cursor, you can OPEN it and FETCH from it.

As with implicit cursors, Oracle provides attributes for explicit cursors. Table 1-7 shows you the attribute values you can expect to see both before and after the specified cursor operations.

Table 1-7. Explicit cursor "before and after" attribute values

	%FOUND	%NOTFOUND	%ISOPEN	%ROWCOUNT
Before OPEN	ORA-01001 raised	ORA-01001 raised	FALSE	ORA-01001 raised
After OPEN	NULL	NULL	TRUE	0
Before first FETCH	NULL	NULL	TRUE	0
After first FETCH	TRUE	FALSE	TRUE	1
Before subsequent FETCH(es)	TRUE	FALSE	TRUE	1

Table 1-7. Explicit cursor "before and after" attribute values (continued)

	%FOUND	%NOTFOUND	%ISOPEN	%ROWCOUNT
After subsequent FETCH(es)	TRUE	FALSE	TRUE	Data dependent
Before last FETCH	TRUE	FALSE	TRUE	Data dependent
After last FETCH	FALSE	TRUE	TRUE	Data dependent
Before CLOSE	FALSE	TRUE	TRUE	Data dependent
After CLOSE	Exception	Exception	FALSE	Exception

BULK COLLECT

Oracle8*i* Database introduced a very powerful new feature that improves the efficiency of queries in PL/SQL: the BULK COLLECT clause. With BULK COLLECT, you can retrieve multiple rows of data through either an implicit or an explicit query with a single roundtrip to and from the database. BULK COLLECT reduces the number of context switches between the PL/SQL and SQL engines and, thereby, reduces the overhead of retrieving data. The syntax for this clause is:

```
... BULK COLLECT INTO collection_name[, collection_name] ...
```

where *collection_name* identifies a collection. Here are some rules and restrictions to keep in mind when using BULK COLLECT:

- Prior to Oracle9*i* Database, you could use BULK COLLECT only with static SQL. With Oracle9*i* Database and Oracle Database 10*g*, you can use BULK COLLECT with both dynamic and static SQL.

- You can use BULK COLLECT keywords in any of the following clauses: SELECT INTO, FETCH INTO, and RETURNING INTO.

- The collections you reference can store only scalar values (strings, numbers, dates). In other words, you cannot fetch a row of data into a record structure that is a row in a collection.

- The SQL engine automatically initializes and extends the collections you reference in the BULK COLLECT clause. It starts filling the collections at index 1, inserts elements consecutively (densely), and overwrites the values of any elements that were previously defined.

- You cannot use the SELECT...BULK COLLECT statement in a FORALL statement.

- SELECT...BULK COLLECT will *not* raise NO_DATA_FOUND if no rows are found. Instead, you must check the contents of the collection to see if there is any data inside it.

- The BULK COLLECT operation empties the collection referenced in the INTO clause before executing the query. If the query returns no rows, this collection's COUNT method will return 0.

Limiting rows retrieved with BULK COLLECT

Oracle provides a LIMIT clause for BULK COLLECT that allows you to limit the number of rows fetched from the database. The syntax is:

```
FETCH cursor BULK COLLECT INTO ... [LIMIT rows];
```

where *rows* can be any literal, variable, or expression that evaluates to an integer (otherwise, Oracle will raise a VALUE_ERROR exception).

LIMIT is very useful with BULK COLLECT, because it helps you manage how much memory your program will use to process data. Suppose, for example, that you need to query and process 10,000 rows of data. You *could* use BULK COLLECT to retrieve all those rows and populate a rather large collection. However, this approach will consume lots of memory in the Process Global Area for that session. If this code is run by many separate Oracle schemas, your application performance may degrade because of PGA swapping.

The following block of code uses the LIMIT clause in a FETCH that is inside a simple loop. Notice that I check the %NOTFOUND attribute after the FETCH to see if any more rows were retrieved.

```
DECLARE
   CURSOR allrows_cur IS SELECT * FROM EMPLOYEE;

   TYPE employee_aat IS TABLE OF allrows_cur%ROWTYPE
      INDEX BY BINARY_INTEGER;

   l_employees employee_aat;
   l_row PLS_INTEGER;
BEGIN
   OPEN allrows_cur;
   LOOP
      FETCH allrows_cur BULK COLLECT INTO l_employees
         LIMIT 100;
      EXIT WHEN allrows_cur%NOTFOUND;

      -- Process the data by scanning through the collection.

      l_row := l_employees.FIRST;
      WHILE (l_row IS NOT NULL)
      LOOP
         upgrade_employee_status (l_employees(l_row).employee_id);
         l_row := l_employees.NEXT (l_row);
      END LOOP;
   END LOOP;

   CLOSE allrows_cur;
END;
```

Cursor Variables and REF Cursors

A *cursor variable* is a variable that points to or references an underlying cursor. Unlike an explicit cursor, which names the PL/SQL work area for the result set, a cursor variable is a reference to that work area. Explicit and implicit cursors are static in that they are tied to specific queries. The cursor variable can be opened for any query, even for different queries within a single program execution.

Declaring REF CURSOR types

You must perform two distinct declaration steps in order to work with a cursor variable:

1. Create a referenced cursor TYPE.
2. Declare the actual cursor variable based on that type.

The syntax for creating a referenced cursor type is as follows:

```
TYPE cursor_type_name IS REF CURSOR [ RETURN return_type ];
```

where *cursor_type_name* is the name of the type of cursor, and *return_type* is the RETURN data specification for the cursor type. The *return_type* can be any of the data structures valid for a normal cursor RETURN clause and is defined using the %ROWTYPE attribute or by referencing a previously defined record TYPE.

Notice that the RETURN clause is optional with the REF CURSOR type statement. Both of the following declarations are valid:

```
TYPE company_curtype IS REF CURSOR RETURN company%ROWTYPE;
TYPE generic_curtype IS REF CURSOR;
```

The first form of the REF CURSOR statement is called a *strong type* because it attaches a record type (or row type) to the cursor variable type at the moment of declaration. Any cursor variable declared using that type can be used only with SQL statement and FETCH INTO data structures that match the specified record type. The advantage of a strong REF TYPE is that the compiler can determine whether or not the developer has properly matched up the cursor variable's FETCH statements with its cursor object's query list.

The second form of the REF CURSOR statement, in which the RETURN clause is missing, is called a *weak type*. This cursor variable type is not associated with any record data structures. Cursor variables declared without the RETURN clause can be used in more flexible ways than the strong type. They can be used with any query, with any rowtype structure, and can vary even within the course of a single program.

Starting with Oracle9i Database, Oracle provides a predefined weak REF CURSOR type named SYS_REFCURSOR. You no longer need to define your own weak type; just use Oracle's:

```
DECLARE
    my_cursor SYS_REFCURSOR;
```

Declaring cursor variables

The syntax for declaring a cursor variable is:

```
cursor_name cursor_type_name;
```

where *cursor_name* is the name of the cursor, and *cursor_type_name* is the name of the type of cursor previously defined with a TYPE statement.

Here is an example of the creation of a cursor variable:

```
DECLARE
    /* Create a cursor type for sports cars. */
    TYPE sports_car_cur_type IS REF CURSOR RETURN car%ROWTYPE;

    /* Create a cursor variable for sports cars. */
    sports_car_cur sports_car_cur_type;
BEGIN
    ...
END;
```

Opening cursor variables

You assign a value (the cursor object) to a cursor when you OPEN the cursor. So the syntax for the traditional OPEN statement allows for cursor variables to accept a SELECT statement after the FOR clause, as shown below:

```
OPEN cursor_name FOR SELECT_statement;
```

where *cursor_name* is the name of a cursor or cursor variable and *SELECT_statement* is a SQL SELECT statement.

For strong REF CURSOR type cursor variables, the structure of the SELECT statement (the number and datatypes of the columns) must match or be compatible with the structure specified in the RETURN clause of the TYPE statement. If *cursor_name* is a cursor variable defined with a weak REF CURSOR type, you can OPEN it for any query, with any structure.

Fetching from cursor variables

As mentioned earlier, the syntax for a FETCH statement using a cursor variable is the same as that for static cursors:

```
FETCH cursor_variable_name INTO record_name;
FETCH cursor_variable_name INTO variable_name, variable_name ...;
```

When the cursor variable is declared with a strong REF CURSOR type, the PL/SQL compiler makes sure the data structures listed after the INTO keyword are compatible with the structure of the query associated with the cursor variable.

If the cursor variable is of the weak REF CURSOR type, the PL/SQL compiler cannot perform the same kind of check it performs for a strong REF CURSOR type. Such a cursor variable can FETCH into any data structures because the REF CURSOR type is not identified with a rowtype at the time of declaration. At compile time, there is no way to know which cursor object (and associated SQL statement) will be assigned to that variable.

Consequently, the check for compatibility must happen at runtime, when the FETCH is about to be executed. At this point, if the query and the INTO clause do not structurally match, then the PL/SQL runtime engine will raise the predefined ROWTYPE_MISMATCH exception. Note that PL/SQL will use implicit conversions if necessary and possible.

Changing Data

It is beyond the scope of this book to provide complete reference information about the features of DML statements in the Oracle SQL language. Instead, I provide a quick overview of the basic syntax, and then explore special features relating to DML inside PL/SQL, including:

- Examples of each DML statement
- Cursor attributes for DML statements
- Special PL/SQL features for DML statements, such as the RETURNING clause

For detailed information, I encourage you to peruse Oracle documentation or a SQL-specific text.

There are three DML statements available in the SQL language:

INSERT
    Inserts one or more new rows into a table

UPDATE
    Updates the values of one or more columns in an existing row in a table

DELETE
    Removes one or more rows from a table

The INSERT Statement

Here is the syntax of the two basic types of INSERT statements:

- Insert a single row with an explicit list of values.
  ```
  INSERT INTO table [(col1, col2, ..., coln)]
     VALUES (val1, val2, ..., valn);
  ```
- Insert one or more rows into a table as defined by a SELECT statement against one or more other tables.
  ```
  INSERT INTO table [(col1, col2, ..., coln)]
  AS
     SELECT ...;
  ```

Let's look at some examples of INSERT statements executed within a PL/SQL block. First, I insert a new row into the book table. Notice that I do not need to specify the names of the columns if I provide a value for each column.

```
BEGIN
    INSERT INTO book
        VALUES ('1-56592-335-9',
            'Oracle PL/SQL Programming',
            'Reference for PL/SQL developers,' ||
            'including examples and best practice ' ||
            'recommendations.',
            'Feuerstein,Steven, with Bill Pribyl',
            TO_DATE ('01-SEP-1997','DD-MON-YYYY'),
            987);
END;
```

I can also list the names of the columns and provide the values as variables, instead of literal values:

```
DECLARE
    l_isbn book.isbn%TYPE := '1-56592-335-9';
    ... other declarations of local variables
BEGIN
    INSERT INTO books (
        isbn, title, summary, author,
        date_published, page_count)
    VALUES (
        l_isbn, l_title, l_summary, l_author,
        l_date_published, l_page_count);
```

The UPDATE Statement

You can update one or more columns in one or more rows using the UPDATE statement. Here is the basic syntax:

```
UPDATE table
    SET col1 = val1
        [, col2 = val2, ... colN = valN]
[WHERE WHERE_clause];
```

The WHERE clause is optional; if you do not supply one, all rows in the table are updated. Here are some examples of UPDATEs:

- Uppercase all the titles of books in the book table.

```
UPDATE books SET title = UPPER (title);
```

- Run a utility procedure that removes the time component from the publication date of books written by specified authors (the argument in the procedure) and uppercases the titles of those books. As you can see, you can run an UPDATE statement standalone or within a PL/SQL block:

```
CREATE OR REPLACE PROCEDURE remove_time (
    author_in IN VARCHAR2)
```

```
   IS
   BEGIN
      UPDATE books
         SET title = UPPER (title),
             date_published =
                TRUNC (date_published)
      WHERE author LIKE author_in;
   END;
```

The DELETE Statement

You can use the DELETE statement to remove one, some, or all the rows in a table. Here is the basic syntax:

```
DELETE FROM table
   [WHERE WHERE_clause];
```

The WHERE clause is optional in a DELETE statement. If you do not supply one, all rows in the table are deleted. Here are some examples of DELETEs:

- Delete all the books from the books table:

```
DELETE FROM books;
```

- Delete all the books from the books table that were published prior to a certain date and return the number of rows deleted:

```
CREATE OR REPLACE PROCEDURE remove_books (
   date_in              IN        DATE,
   removal_count_out    OUT       PLS_INTEGER)
IS
BEGIN
   DELETE FROM books WHERE date_published < date_in;
   removal_count_out := SQL%ROWCOUNT;
END;
```

Of course, all of these DML statements can become qualitatively more complex as you deal with real-world entities. You can, for example, update multiple columns with the contents of a subquery. As of Oracle9*i* Database, you can replace a table name with a *table function* that returns a result set upon which the DML statement acts. See Chapter 3 for details.

Oracle provides several cursor attributes for the implicit cursors "behind" your DML statements, described in the next section.

Cursor Attributes for DML Operations

Oracle allows you to access information about the most recently executed native DML statement by referencing one of the implicit SQL cursor attributes (these are identical to those listed in Table 1-6). Table 1-8 describes the values returned by these attributes for DML statements.

Table 1-8. Implicit SQL cursor attributes for DML statements

Name	Description
SQL%FOUND	Returns TRUE if one or more rows were modified (created, changed, removed) successfully.
SQL%NOTFOUND	Returns TRUE if no rows were modified by the DML statement.
SQL%ROWCOUNT	Returns number of rows modified by the DML statement.

Now let's see how we can use cursor attributes with implicit cursors.

- Use SQL%FOUND to determine if your DML statement affected any rows. For example, from time to time an author will change his name and want a new name used for all of his books. So I create a small procedure to update the name and then report back via a Boolean variable whether any rows were modified:

```
CREATE OR REPLACE PROCEDURE change_author_name (
   old_name_in       IN       books.author%TYPE,
   new_name_in       IN       books.author%TYPE,
   changes_made_out  OUT      BOOLEAN)
IS
BEGIN
   UPDATE books
      SET author = new_name_in
    WHERE author = old_name_in;

   changes_made_out := SQL%FOUND;
END;
```

- Use SQL%ROWCOUNT when you need to know exactly how many rows were affected by your DML statement. Here is a reworking of the above name-change procedure that returns a bit more information:

```
CREATE OR REPLACE PROCEDURE change_author_name (
   old_name_in       IN       books.author%TYPE,
   new_name_in       IN       books.author%TYPE,
   rename_count_out  OUT      PLS_INTEGER)
IS
BEGIN
   UPDATE books
      SET author = new_name_in
    WHERE author = old_name_in;

   rename_count_out := SQL%ROWCOUNT;
END;
```

DML and Exception Handling

When an exception occurs in a PL/SQL block, Oracle does not roll back any of the changes made by DML statements in that block. It is up to you, the manager of the application's logical transaction, to decide what sort of behavior should occur. Here are some things to keep in mind in this regard:

- If your block is an autonomous transaction (described later in this chapter), then you must perform a rollback or commit (usually a rollback) when an exception is raised.

- You can use *savepoints* to control the scope of a rollback. In other words, you can roll back to a particular savepoint and thereby preserve a portion of the changes made in your session. Savepoints are also explored later in this chapter.

- If an exception propagates past the outermost block (i.e., it goes unhandled), then, in most host execution environments for PL/SQL, like SQL*Plus, an unqualified rollback is automatically executed, reversing any outstanding changes.

Bulk DML with the FORALL Statement

Oracle introduced a significant enhancement to PL/SQL's DML capabilities for Oracle8i Database and above with the FORALL statement. FORALL tells the PL/SQL runtime engine to bulk bind into the SQL statement all of the elements of one or more collections before sending anything to the SQL engine. Why would this be useful? We all know that PL/SQL is tightly integrated with the underlying SQL engine in the Oracle database. PL/SQL is the database programming language of choice for Oracle—even though you can now (at least theoretically) use Java inside the database, as well.

But this tight integration does not necessarily mean that no overhead is associated with running SQL from a PL/SQL program. When the PL/SQL runtime engine processes a block of code, it executes the procedural statements within its own engine but passes the SQL statements on to the SQL engine. The SQL layer executes the SQL statements and then returns information to the PL/SQL engine, if necessary.

This transfer of control between the PL/SQL and SQL engines is called a *context switch*. Each time a switch occurs, there is additional overhead. There are a number of scenarios in which many switches occur and performance degrades. Starting with Oracle8i Database, Oracle offers two enhancements to PL/SQL that allow you to bulk together multiple context switches into a single switch, thereby improving the performance of your applications. These enhancements are FORALL and BULK COLLECT (explained earlier).

When the statement is bulk bound and passed to SQL, the SQL engine executes the statement once for each index number in the range. In other words, the same SQL statements are executed, but they are all run in the same round trip to the SQL layer, minimizing the context switches. This is shown in Figure 1-4.

Syntax of the FORALL Statement

Although the FORALL statement contains an iteration scheme (i.e., it iterates through all the rows of a collection), it is not a FOR loop. Consequently, it has neither a LOOP nor an END LOOP statement. Its syntax is as follows:

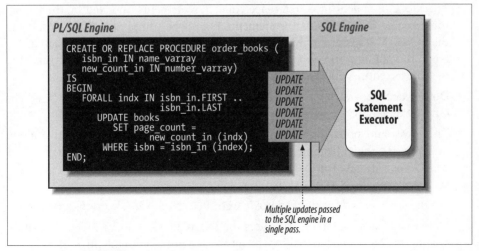

Figure 1-4. One context switch with FORALL

```
FORALL index_row IN
   [ lower_bound ... upper_bound |
     INDICES OF indexing_collection |
     VALUES OF indexing_collection
   ]
   [ SAVE EXCEPTIONS ]
   sql_statement;
```

where:

index_row

Specified collection that the FORALL will iterate through.

lower_bound

Starting index number (row or collection element) for the operation.

upper_bound

Ending index number (row or collection element) for the operation.

sql_statement

SQL statement to be performed on each collection element.

indexing_collection

PL/SQL collection used to select the indices in the bind array referenced in the *sql_statement*. The INDICES OF and VALUES_OF alternatives are available starting with Oracle Database 10g.

SAVE EXCEPTIONS

Optional clause that tells FORALL to process all rows, saving any exceptions that occur.

You must follow these rules when using FORALL:

- The body of the FORALL statement must be a single DML statement—an INSERT, UPDATE, or DELETE.

- The DML statement must reference collection elements, indexed by the *index_row* variable in the FORALL statement. The scope of the *index_row* variable is the FORALL statement only; you may not reference it outside of that statement. Note, though, that the upper and lower bounds of these collections do not have to span the entire contents of the collection(s).

- Do not declare a variable for *index_row*. It is declared implicitly as PLS_INTEGER by the PL/SQL engine.

- The lower and upper bounds must specify a valid range of consecutive index numbers for the collection(s) referenced in the SQL statement. Sparsely filled collections will raise the following error:

```
ORA-22160: element at index [3] does not exist
```

See the *diffcount.sql* file on the book's web site for an example of this scenario.

Note that Oracle Database 10g offers the INDICES OF and VALUES OF syntax to support sparse collections (in which rows are not filled sequentially).

- Fields within collections of records may not be referenced within the DML statement. Instead, you can only reference the row in the collection as a whole, whether the fields are collections of scalars or collections of more complex objects. For example, the code below:

```
DECLARE
    TYPE employee_aat IS TABLE OF employee%ROWTYPE
        INDEX BY PLS_INTEGER;
    l_employees    employee_aat;
BEGIN
    FORALL l_index IN l_employees.FIRST .. l_employees.LAST
        INSERT INTO employee (employee_id, last_name)
          VALUES (l_employees (l_index).employee_id
                , l_employees (l_index).last_name
          );
END;
```

will cause the following compilation error:

```
PLS-00436: implementation restriction: cannot reference fields of BULK In-BIND table
of records
```

- The collection subscript referenced in the DML statement cannot be an expression. For example, the following script:

```
DECLARE
    names name_varray := name_varray ();
BEGIN
    FORALL indx IN names.FIRST .. names.LAST
        DELETE FROM emp WHERE ename = names(indx+10);
END;
```

will cause the following error:

```
PLS-00430: FORALL iteration variable INDX is not allowed in this context
```

FORALL Examples

Here are some examples of the use of the FORALL statement:

- Let's rewrite the order_books procedure to use FORALL:

```
CREATE OR REPLACE PROCEDURE order_books (
   isbn_in IN name_varray,
   new_count_in IN number_varray)
IS
BEGIN
   FORALL indx IN isbn_in.FIRST .. isbn_in.LAST
      UPDATE books
         SET page_count = new_count_in (indx)
       WHERE isbn = isbn_in (indx);
END;
```

   Notice that the only changes in this example are to change FOR to FORALL, and to remove the LOOP and END LOOP keywords. This use of FORALL accesses and passes to SQL each of the rows defined in the two collections. Figure 1-4 shows the change in behavior that results.

- The next example shows how the DML statement can reference more than one collection. In this case, I have three collections: denial, patient_name, and illnesses. Only the first two are subscripted, and so individual elements of the collection are passed to each INSERT. The third column in health_coverage is a collection listing preconditions. Because the PL/SQL engine bulk binds only subscripted collections, the illnesses collection is placed in that column for each row inserted:

```
FORALL indx IN denial.FIRST .. denial.LAST
   INSERT INTO health_coverage
      VALUES (denial(indx), patient_name(indx), illnesses);
```

- Use the RETURNING clause in a FORALL statement to retrieve information about each separate DELETE statement. Notice that the RETURNING clause in FORALL must use BULK COLLECT INTO (the corresponding "bulk" operation for queries):

```
CREATE OR REPLACE FUNCTION remove_emps_by_dept (deptlist dlist_t)
   RETURN enolist_t
IS
   enolist enolist_t;
BEGIN
   FORALL aDept IN deptlist.FIRST..deptlist.LAST
      DELETE FROM emp WHERE deptno IN deptlist(aDept)
         RETURNING empno BULK COLLECT INTO enolist;
   RETURN enolist;
END;
```

- Use the indices defined in one collection to determine which rows in the binding array (the collection referenced inside the SQL statement) will be used in the dynamic INSERT.

```
FORALL indx IN INDICES OF l_top_employees
   EXECUTE IMMEDIATE
```

```
'INSERT INTO ' || l_table || ' VALUES (:emp_pky, :new_salary)
USING l_new_salaries(indx).employee_id,
      l_new_salaries(indx).salary;
```

Managing Transactions in PL/SQL

The Oracle RDBMS provides a very robust transaction model, as you might expect from a relational database. Your application code determines what constitutes a *transaction*, which is the logical unit of work that must be either saved with a COMMIT statement or rolled back with a ROLLBACK statement. A transaction begins implicitly with the first SQL statement issued since the last COMMIT or ROLLBACK (or with the start of a session), or continues after a ROLLBACK TO SAVEPOINT.

PL/SQL provides the following statements for transaction management:

COMMIT
> Saves all outstanding changes since the last COMMIT or ROLLBACK and releases all locks.

ROLLBACK
> Erases all outstanding changes since the last COMMIT or ROLLBACK and releases all locks.

ROLLBACK TO SAVEPOINT
> Erases all changes made since the specified savepoint was established, and releases locks that were established within that range of the code.

SAVEPOINT
> Establishes a savepoint, which then allows you to perform partial ROLLBACKs.

SET TRANSACTION
> Allows you to begin a read-only or read-write session, establish an isolation level, or assign the current transaction to a specified rollback segment.

LOCK TABLE
> Allows you to lock an entire database table in the specified mode. This overrides the default row-level locking usually applied to a table.

The following sections explore the COMMIT and ROLLBACK statements, as well as the *autonomous transaction* feature of PL/SQL.

The COMMIT Statement

When you COMMIT, you make permanent any changes made by your session to the database in the current transaction. Once you COMMIT, your changes will be visible to other Oracle sessions or users. The syntax for the COMMIT statement is:

```
COMMIT [WORK] [COMMENT text];
```

The WORK keyword is optional and can be used to improve readability.

The COMMENT keyword specifies a comment that is then associated with the current transaction. The text must be a quoted literal and can be no more than 50 characters in length. The COMMENT text is usually employed with distributed transactions and can be handy for examining and resolving in-doubt transactions within a two-phase commit framework. It is stored in the data dictionary along with the transaction ID.

Note that COMMIT releases any row and table locks issued in your session, such as with a SELECT FOR UPDATE statement. It also erases any savepoints issued since the last COMMIT or ROLLBACK.

Once you COMMIT your changes, you cannot roll them back with a ROLLBACK statement.

The following statements are all valid uses of COMMIT:

```
COMMIT;
COMMIT WORK;
COMMIT COMMENT 'maintaining account balance'.
```

The ROLLBACK Statement

When you perform a ROLLBACK, you undo some or all changes made by your session to the database in the current transaction. Why would you want to erase changes? From an ad hoc SQL standpoint, the ROLLBACK gives you a way to erase mistakes you might have made, as in:

```
DELETE FROM orders;
```

"No, no! I meant to delete only the orders before May 1995!" No problem—just issue ROLLBACK. From an application coding standpoint, ROLLBACK is important because it allows you to clean up or restart from a clean state when a problem occurs.

The syntax for the ROLLBACK statement is:

```
ROLLBACK [WORK] [TO [SAVEPOINT] savepoint_name];
```

There are two basic ways to use ROLLBACK: without parameters or with the TO clause to indicate a savepoint at which the ROLLBACK should stop. The parameterless ROLLBACK undoes all outstanding changes in your transaction.

The ROLLBACK TO version allows you to undo all changes and release all acquired locks that were issued since the savepoint identified by *savepoint_name* was marked. (See the next section on the SAVEPOINT statement for more information on how to mark a savepoint in your application.)

The *savepoint_name* is an undeclared Oracle identifier. It cannot be a literal (enclosed in quotes) or a variable name.

All of the following uses of ROLLBACK are valid:

```
ROLLBACK;
ROLLBACK WORK;
ROLLBACK TO begin_cleanup;
```

When you roll back to a specific savepoint, all savepoints issued after the specified *savepoint_name* are erased, but the savepoint to which you roll back is not. This means that you can restart your transaction from that point and, if necessary, roll back to that same savepoint if another error occurs.

Immediately before you execute an INSERT, UPDATE, or DELETE, PL/SQL implicitly generates a savepoint. If your DML statement then fails, a rollback is automatically performed to that implicit savepoint. In this way, only the last DML statement is undone.

Autonomous Transactions

When you define a PL/SQL block (anonymous block, procedure, function, packaged procedure, packaged function, database trigger) as an *autonomous transaction*, you isolate the DML in that block from the caller's transaction context. That block becomes an independent transaction that is started by another transaction, referred to as the *main transaction*.

Within the autonomous transaction block, the main transaction is suspended. You perform your SQL operations, commit or roll back those operations, and resume the main transaction. This flow of transaction control is illustrated in Figure 1-5.

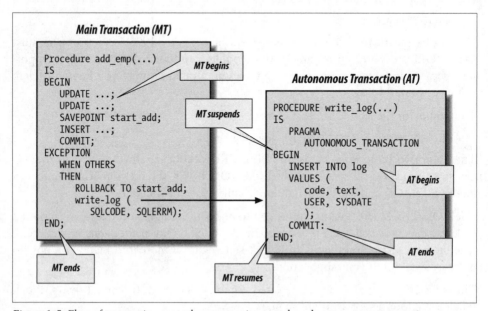

Figure 1-5. Flow of transaction control among main, nested, and autonomous transactions

There isn't much involved in defining a PL/SQL block as an autonomous transaction. You simply include the following statement in your declaration section:

```
PRAGMA AUTONOMOUS_TRANSACTION;
```

The pragma instructs the PL/SQL compiler to establish a PL/SQL block as autonomous or independent. For the purposes of the autonomous transaction, a PL/SQL block can be any of the following:

- Top-level (but not nested) anonymous PL/SQL blocks
- Functions and procedures, defined either in a package or as standalone programs
- Methods (functions and procedures) of an object type
- Database triggers

You can put the autonomous transaction pragma anywhere in the declaration section of your PL/SQL block. You would probably be best off, however, placing it before any data structure declarations. That way, anyone reading your code will immediately identify the program as an autonomous transaction.

This pragma is the only syntax change made to PL/SQL to support autonomous transactions. COMMIT, ROLLBACK, the DML statements—all the rest is as it was before. However, these statements have a different scope of impact and visibility when executed within an autonomous transaction, and you will need to include a COMMIT or ROLLBACK in your program.

Database Triggers

Database triggers are named program units that are executed in response to events that occur in the database. Five different types of events can have trigger code attached to them:

Data Manipulation Language (DML) statements
DML triggers are available to fire whenever a record is inserted into, updated in, or deleted from a table. These triggers can be used to perform validation, set default values, audit changes, and even disallow certain DML operations.

Data Definition Language (DDL) statements
DDL triggers fire whenever DDL is executed—for example, whenever a table is created. These triggers can perform auditing and prevent certain DDL statements from occurring.

Database events
Database event triggers fire whenever the database starts up or is shut down, whenever a user logs on or off, and whenever an Oracle error occurs. For Oracle8*i* Database and above, these triggers provide a means of tracking activity in the database.

INSTEAD OF

INSTEAD OF triggers are essentially alternatives to DML triggers. They fire when inserts, updates, and deletes are about to occur; your code specifies what to do in place of these DML operations. INSTEAD OF triggers control operations on views, not tables. They can be used to make non-updateable views updateable and to override the behavior of views that are updateable. These triggers are not covered further in this section, as they are a specialized topic that requires thorough coverage to be useful.

DML Triggers

Data Manipulation Language (DML) triggers fire when records are inserted into, updated within, or deleted from a particular table. These are the most common type of triggers, especially for developers; the other trigger types are used primarily by DBAs.

There are many options regarding DML triggers. They can fire after or before a DML statement or they can fire after or before each row is processed within a statement. They can fire for INSERT, UPDATE, or DELETE statements, or combinations of the three.

Transaction participation

By default, DML triggers participate in the transaction from which they were fired. This means that:

- If a trigger raises an exception, that part of the transaction will be rolled back.
- If the trigger performs any DML itself (such as inserting a row into a log table), then that DML becomes a part of the main transaction.
- You cannot issue a COMMIT or ROLLBACK from within a DML trigger.

 If you define your DML trigger to be an autonomous transaction, however, then any DML performed inside the trigger will be saved or rolled back—with your explicit COMMIT or ROLLBACK statement—without affecting the main transaction.

The following sections present the syntax for creating a DML trigger, provide reference information on various elements of the trigger definition, and explore an example that uses the many components and options for these triggers.

Creating a DML trigger

To create (or replace) a DML trigger, use the syntax shown here:

```
1  CREATE [OR REPLACE] TRIGGER trigger name
2  {BEFORE | AFTER}
```

```
 3  {INSERT | DELETE | UPDATE | UPDATE OF column list} ON table name
 4  [FOR EACH ROW]
 5  [WHEN (...)]
 6  [DECLARE ... ]
 7  BEGIN
 8   ... executable statements ...
 9  [EXCEPTION ... ]
10  END [trigger name];
```

The following table provides an explanation of these different elements:

Line(s)	Description
1	States that a trigger is to be created with the name supplied. Specifying OR REPLACE is optional. If the trigger exists and REPLACE is not specified, then your attempt to create the trigger anew will result in an ORA-4081 error. It is possible, by the way, for a table and a trigger (or procedure and trigger, for that matter) to have the same name. We recommend, however, that you adopt naming conventions to avoid the confusion that will result from this sharing of names.
2	Specifies if the trigger is to fire BEFORE or AFTER the statement or row is processed.
3	Specifies the type of DML to which the trigger applies: INSERT, UPDATE, or DELETE. Note that UPDATE can be specified for the whole record or just for a column list separated by commas. The columns can be combined (separated with an OR) and may be specified in any order. Line 3 also specifies the table to which the trigger is to apply. Remember that each DML trigger can apply to only one table.
4	If FOR EACH ROW is specified, then the trigger will activate for each row processed by a statement. If this clause is missing, the default behavior is to fire only once for the statement (a statement-level trigger).
5	An optional WHEN clause that allows you to specify logic to avoid unnecessary execution of the trigger.
6	Optional declaration section for the anonymous block that constitutes the trigger code. If you do not need to declare local variables, you do not need this keyword. Note that you should never try to declare the NEW and OLD pseudo-records. This is done automatically.
7–8	The execution section of the trigger. This is required and must contain at least one statement.
9	Optional exception section. This section will trap and handle (or attempt to handle) any exceptions raised in the execution section only.
10	Required END statement for the trigger. You can include the name of the trigger after the END keyword to explicitly document which trigger you are ending.

Here are a few examples of DML trigger usage:

- I want to make sure that whenever an employee is added or changed, all necessary validation is run. Notice that I pass the necessary fields of the NEW pseudo-record to individual check routines in this row-level trigger:

```
CREATE OR REPLACE TRIGGER validate_employee_changes
   AFTER INSERT OR UPDATE
   ON employee
   FOR EACH ROW
BEGIN
   check_age (:NEW.date_of_birth);
   check_resume (:NEW.resume);
END;
```

- The following BEFORE INSERT trigger captures audit information for the CEO compensation table. It also relies on the Oracle8*i* Database autonomous transaction feature to commit this new row without affecting the "outer" or main transaction:

```
CREATE OR REPLACE TRIGGER bef_ins_ceo_comp
   AFTER INSERT
   ON ceo_compensation
   FOR EACH ROW
DECLARE
   PRAGMA AUTONOMOUS_TRANSACTION;
BEGIN
   INSERT INTO ceo_comp_history
        VALUES (:NEW.name,
                :OLD.compensation, :NEW.compensation,
                'AFTER INSERT', SYSDATE);
   COMMIT;
END;
```

The WHEN clause

Use the WHEN clause to fine-tune the situations under which the body of the trigger code will actually execute. In the following example, I use the WHEN clause to make sure that the trigger code does not execute unless the new salary is changing to a *different* value:

```
CREATE OR REPLACE TRIGGER check_raise
   AFTER UPDATE OF salary
   ON employee
   FOR EACH ROW
WHEN (OLD.salary != NEW.salary) OR
     (OLD.salary IS NULL AND NEW.salary IS NOT NULL) OR
     (OLD.salary IS NOT NULL AND NEW.salary IS NULL)
BEGIN
   ...
```

In other words, if a user issues an UPDATE to a row and for some reason sets the salary to its current value, the trigger will and must fire, but the reality is that you really don't need any of the PL/SQL code in the body of the trigger to execute. By checking this condition in the WHEN clause, you avoid some of the overhead of starting up the PL/SQL block associated with the trigger.

> The *genwhen.sp* file on the book's web site offers a procedure that will generate a WHEN clause to ensure that the new value is actually different from the old.

In most cases, you will reference fields in the OLD and NEW pseudo-records in the WHEN clause, as in the example shown above. You may also, however, write code that invokes built-in functions, as in the following WHEN clause that uses SYSDATE to restrict the INSERT trigger to only fire between 9 A.M. and 5 P.M.:

```
CREATE OR REPLACE TRIGGER valid_when_clause
BEFORE INSERT ON frame
FOR EACH ROW
WHEN ( TO_CHAR(SYSDATE,'HH24') BETWEEN 9 AND 17 )
   ...
```

Working with NEW and OLD pseudo-records

Whenever a row-level trigger fires, the PL/SQL runtime engine creates and populates two data structures that function much like records. They are the NEW and OLD pseudo-records ("pseudo" because they don't share all the properties of real PL/SQL records). OLD stores the original values of the record being processed by the trigger; NEW contains the new values. These records have the same structure as a record declared using %ROWTYPE on the table to which the trigger is attached.

Here are some rules to keep in mind when working with NEW and OLD:

- With triggers on INSERT operations, the OLD structure does not contain any data; there *is* no "old" set of values.
- With triggers on UPDATE operations, both the OLD and NEW structures are populated. OLD contains the values prior to the update; NEW contains the values the row will contain after the update is performed.
- With triggers on DELETE operations, the NEW structure does not contain any data; the record is about to be erased.
- You cannot change the field values of the OLD structure; attempting to do so will raise the ORA-04085 error. You *can* modify the field values of the NEW structure.
- You cannot pass a NEW or OLD structure as a record parameter to a procedure or function called within the trigger. You can pass only individual fields of the pseudo-record. See the *gentrigrec.sp* script on the book's web site for a program that will generate code transferring NEW and OLD values to records that *can* be passed as parameters.
- When referencing the NEW and OLD structures within the anonymous block for the trigger, you must preface those keywords with a colon, as in:

  ```
  IF :NEW.salary > 10000 THEN...
  ```
- You cannot perform record-level operations with the NEW and OLD structures. For example, the following statement will cause the trigger compilation to fail:

  ```
  BEGIN :new := NULL; END;
  ```

Determining the DML action within a trigger

Oracle offers a set of functions (also known as *operational directives*) that allow you to determine which DML action caused the firing of the current trigger. Each of these functions returns TRUE or FALSE, as described below.

INSERTING

> Returns TRUE if the trigger was fired by an insert into the table to which the trigger is attached, and FALSE if not.

UPDATING

> Returns TRUE if the trigger was fired by an update of the table to which the trigger is attached, and FALSE if not.

DELETING

> Returns TRUE if the trigger was fired by a delete from the table to which the trigger is attached, and FALSE if not.

Using these directives, it is possible to create a single trigger that consolidates the actions required for each of the different types of operations.

DDL Triggers

Oracle allows you to define triggers that will fire when Data Definition Language (DDL) statements are executed. Simply put, DDL is any SQL statement used to create or modify a database object such as a table or an index. Here are some examples of DDL statements:

- CREATE TABLE
- ALTER INDEX
- DROP TRIGGER

Each of these statements results in the creation, alteration, or removal of a database object.

The syntax for creating these triggers is remarkably similar to that of DML triggers, except that the firing events differ and they are not applied to individual tables.

Creating a DDL Trigger

To create (or replace) a DDL trigger, use the syntax shown here:

```
1  CREATE [OR REPLACE] TRIGGER trigger name
2  {BEFORE | AFTER } {DDL event} ON {DATABASE | SCHEMA}
3  [WHEN (...)]
4  DECLARE
5  Variable declarations
6  BEGIN
7  ... some code...
8  END;
```

The following table summarizes what is happening in this code:

Line(s)	Description
1	Specifies that a trigger is to be created with the name supplied. Specifying OR REPLACE is optional. If the trigger exists and REPLACE is not specified, then good old Oracle error ORA-4081 will appear stating just that.

Line(s)	Description
2	This line has a lot to say. It defines whether the trigger will fire before, after, or instead of the particular DDL event, as well as whether it will fire for all operations within the database or just within the current schema. Note that the INSTEAD OF option is available only in Oracle9*i* Release 1 and higher.
3	An optional WHEN clause that allows you to specify logic to avoid unnecessary execution of the trigger.
4–7	These lines simply demonstrate the PL/SQL contents of the trigger.

Here's an example of a somewhat uninformed town crier trigger that announces the creation of all objects:

```
/* File on web: uninformed_town_crier.sql */
SQL> CREATE OR REPLACE TRIGGER town_crier
  2 AFTER CREATE ON SCHEMA
  3 BEGIN
  4   DBMS_OUTPUT.PUT_LINE('I believe you have created something!');
  5 END;
  6 /
Trigger created.
```

Database Event Triggers

Database event triggers fire whenever database-wide events occur. There are five database event triggers:

STARTUP
   Fires when the database is opened

SHUTDOWN
   Fires when the database is shut down normally

SERVERERROR
   Fires when an Oracle error is raised

LOGON
   Fires when an Oracle session begins

LOGOFF
   Fires when an Oracle session terminates normally

As any DBA will immediately see, these triggers offer stunning possibilities for automated administration and very granular control.

Creating a database event trigger

The syntax used to create these triggers is quite similar to that used for DDL triggers:

```
1 CREATE [OR REPLACE] TRIGGER trigger name
2 {BEFORE | AFTER} {database event} ON {DATABASE | SCHEMA}
3 DECLARE
4 Variable declarations
5 BEGIN
6 ... some code...
7 END;
```

There are restrictions regarding what events can be combined with what BEFORE and AFTER attributes. Some situations just don't make sense:

No BEFORE STARTUP triggers

Even if such triggers could be created, when would they fire? Attempts to create triggers of this type will be met by this straightforward error message:

```
ORA-30500: database open triggers and server error triggers cannot have BEFORE type
```

No AFTER SHUTDOWN triggers

Again, when would they fire? Attempts to create such triggers are deflected with this message:

```
ORA-30501: instance shutdown triggers cannot have AFTER type
```

No BEFORE LOGON triggers

It would require some amazingly perceptive code to implement these triggers: "Wait, I think someone is going to log on—do something!" Being strictly reality-based, Oracle stops these triggers with this message:

```
ORA-30508: client logon triggers cannot have BEFORE type
```

No AFTER LOGOFF triggers

"No wait, please come back! Don't sign off!" Attempts to create such triggers are stopped with this message:

```
ORA-30509: client logoff triggers cannot have AFTER type
```

No BEFORE SERVERERROR

These triggers would be every programmer's dream! Think of the possibilities...

```
CREATE OR REPLACE TRIGGER BEFORE_SERVERERROR
BEFORE SERVERERROR ON DATABASE
BEGIN
   diagnose_impending_error;
   fix_error_condition;
   continue_as_if_nothing_happened;
END;
```

Unfortunately, our dreams are shattered by this error message:

```
ORA-30500: database open triggers and server error triggers cannot have BEFORE type
```

Dynamic SQL and Dynamic PL/SQL

Dynamic SQL refers to SQL statements that are constructed and executed at runtime. Dynamic is the opposite of static. *Static SQL* refers to SQL statements that are fixed at the time a program is compiled. *Dynamic PL/SQL* refers to entire PL/SQL blocks of code that are constructed dynamically, then compiled and executed.

Ever since Oracle7 Release 1, we PL/SQL developers have been able to use the built-in DBMS_SQL package to execute dynamic SQL. In Oracle8i Database, we were given a second option for executing dynamically constructed SQL statements: *native dynamic SQL* (NDS). NDS is a *native* part of the PL/SQL language; it is much easier to use than DBMS_SQL, and, for many applications, it will execute more efficiently.

The EXECUTE IMMEDIATE Statement

Use EXECUTE IMMEDIATE to execute (immediately!) the specified SQL statement. Here is the syntax of this statement:

```
EXECUTE IMMEDIATE SQL_string
    [INTO {define_variable[, define_variable]... | record}]
    [USING [IN | OUT | IN OUT] bind_argument
        [, [IN | OUT | IN OUT] bind_argument]...];
```

where:

SQL_string

String expression containing the SQL statement or PL/SQL block.

define_variable

Variable that receives a column value returned by a query.

record

Record based on a user-defined TYPE or %ROWTYPE that receives an entire row returned by a query.

bind_argument

Expression whose value is passed to the SQL statement or PL/SQL block, or an identifier that serves as an input and/or output variable to the function or procedure that is called in the PL/SQL block.

INTO clause

Used for single-row queries; for each column value returned by the query, you must supply an individual variable or field in a record of a compatible type.

USING clause

Allows you to supply bind arguments for the SQL string. This clause is used for both dynamic SQL and PL/SQL, which is why you can specify a parameter mode. This usage is relevant only for PL/SQL; however, the default is IN, which is the only kind of bind argument you would have for SQL statements.

You can use EXECUTE IMMEDIATE for any SQL statement or PL/SQL block except for multiple-row queries. If *SQL_string* ends with a semicolon, it will be treated as a PL/SQL block; otherwise, it will be treated as a SELECT, DML (INSERT, UPDATE, or DELETE), or DDL (e.g., CREATE TABLE). The string may contain placeholders for bind arguments, but you cannot use bind values to pass in the names of schema objects, such as table names or column names.

 When you execute a DDL statement in your program, you will also perform a commit. If you don't want the DDL-driven commit to affect outstanding changes in the rest of your application, place the dynamic DDL statement within an autonomous transaction procedure. See *auton_ddl. sql* on the book's web site for a demonstration of this technique.

When the statement is executed, the runtime engine replaces each placeholder (an identifier with a colon in front of it, such as :salary_value) in the SQL string with its corresponding bind argument (by position). You can pass numeric, date, and string expressions. You cannot, however, pass a Boolean, because it is a PL/SQL datatype. Nor can you pass a NULL literal value. Instead, you must pass a variable of the correct type that has a value of NULL.

NDS supports all SQL datatypes. So, for example, define variables and bind arguments can be collections, large objects (LOBs), instances of an object type, and REFs. On the other hand, NDS does not support datatypes that are specific to PL/SQL, such as Booleans, associative arrays, and user-defined record types. The INTO clause may, however, contain a PL/SQL record.

Let's take a look at a few examples:

- Create an index:

```
EXECUTE IMMEDIATE 'CREATE INDEX emp_u_1 ON employee (last_name)';
```

  PL/SQL does not support native DDL statements; instead, you must use dynamic SQL.

- Obtain the count of rows in any table, in any schema, for the specified WHERE clause:

```
/* File on web: tabcount_nds.sf */
CREATE OR REPLACE FUNCTION tabcount (
    tab IN VARCHAR2, whr IN VARCHAR2 := NULL)
    RETURN PLS_INTEGER AUTHID CURRENT_USER
IS
    str     VARCHAR2 (32767) := 'SELECT COUNT(*) FROM ' || tab;
    retval  PLS_INTEGER;
BEGIN
    IF whr IS NOT NULL
    THEN
        str := str || ' WHERE ' || whr;
    END IF;

    EXECUTE IMMEDIATE str INTO retval;
    RETURN retval;
EXCEPTION
    WHEN OTHERS
    THEN
        DBMS_OUTPUT.put_line (
            'TABCOUNT ERROR: ' || DBMS_UTILITY.FORMAT_ERROR_STACK);
        DBMS_OUTPUT.put_line (str);
        RETURN NULL;
END;
/
```

  So now I never again have to write SELECT COUNT(*), whether in SQL*Plus or within a PL/SQL program. Instead, I can do the following:

```
BEGIN
    IF tabCount ('emp', 'deptno = ' || v_dept) > 100
```

```
      THEN
         DBMS_OUTPUT.PUT_LINE ('Growing fast!');
      END IF;
```

- Here's a function that lets you update the value of any numeric column in the employee table. It's a function because it returns the number of rows that have been updated.

```
/* File on web: updnval.sf */
CREATE OR REPLACE FUNCTION updNVal (
   col IN VARCHAR2,
   val IN NUMBER,
   start_in IN DATE,
   end_in IN DATE)
   RETURN PLS_INTEGER
IS
BEGIN
   EXECUTE IMMEDIATE
      'UPDATE employee SET ' || col || ' = :the_value
         WHERE hire_date BETWEEN :lo AND :hi'
      USING val, start_in, end_in;
   RETURN SQL%ROWCOUNT;
END;
```

That is a very small amount of code to achieve all that flexibility! This example introduces the bind argument: after the UPDATE statement is parsed, the PL/SQL engine replaces the :the_value, :lo, and :hi placeholders with the values in the USING clause. Notice also that I am able to rely on the SQL%ROWCOUNT cursor attribute that I have already been using for static DML statements.

As you can see, EXECUTE IMMEDIATE provides a very easy and accessible syntax!

The OPEN FOR Statement

The OPEN FOR statement was *not* introduced into PL/SQL for NDS; it was first offered in Oracle7 to support cursor variables. Now it is deployed in an especially elegant fashion to implement multiple-row dynamic queries. With DBMS_SQL, you go through a painful series of steps to implement multi-row queries: parse, bind, define each column individually, execute, fetch, extract each column value individually. That's a lot of code to write!

For native dynamic SQL, Oracle took an existing feature and syntax—that of cursor variables—and extended it in a very natural way to support dynamic SQL. Let's look at the syntax of the OPEN FOR statement:

```
OPEN {cursor_variable | :host_cursor_variable} FOR SQL_string
   [USING bind_argument[, bind_argument]...];
```

where:

cursor_variable
   Weakly typed cursor variable

:host_cursor_variable
> Cursor variable declared in a PL/SQL host environment such as an Oracle Call Interface (OCI) program

SQL_string
> Contains the SELECT statement to be executed dynamically

USING clause
> Follows the same rules as in the EXECUTE IMMEDIATE statement

 If you are using Oracle9*i* Database Release 2 or Oracle Database 10*g*, you can use EXECUTE IMMEDIATE with BULK COLLECT to retrieve multiple rows with a dynamic query. This approach requires much less code and can improve the performance of your query operation.

Following is an example that demonstrates the declaration of a weak REF CURSOR type, a cursor variable based on that type, and the opening of a dynamic query using the OPEN FOR statement:

```
CREATE OR REPLACE PROCEDURE show_parts_inventory (
    parts_table IN VARCHAR2,
    where_in IN VARCHAR2)
IS
    TYPE query_curtype IS REF CURSOR;
    dyncur query_curtype;
BEGIN
    OPEN dyncur FOR
        'SELECT * FROM ' || parts_table
        ' WHERE ' || where_in;
    ...
```

Once you have opened the query with the OPEN FOR statement, the syntax used to fetch rows, close the cursor variable, and check the attributes of the cursor are all the same as for static cursor variables and hardcoded explicit cursors.

Dynamic PL/SQL

Dynamic PL/SQL offers some of the most interesting and challenging coding opportunities. Think of it: while a user is running your application, you can take advantage of NDS to do any of the following:

- Create a program, including a package that contains globally accessible data structures
- Obtain (and modify) by name the value of global variables
- Call functions and procedures whose names are not known at compile time

There are some rules and tips you need to keep in mind when working with dynamic PL/SQL blocks and NDS:

- The dynamic string must be a valid PL/SQL block. It must start with the DECLARE or BEGIN keyword and end with an END statement and semicolon. The string will not be considered PL/SQL code unless it ends with a semicolon.

- In your dynamic block, you can access only PL/SQL code elements that have global scope (standalone functions and procedures, and elements defined in the specification of a package). Dynamic PL/SQL blocks execute outside the scope of the local enclosing block.

- Errors raised within a dynamic PL/SQL block can be trapped and handled by the local block in which the string was run with the EXECUTE IMMEDIATE statement.

Here is an example of using dynamic PLS/SQL. This is a true story, I kid you not. During a consulting stint at an insurance company in Chicago, I was asked to see what I could do about a particularly vexing program. It was very large and continually increased in size—soon it would be too large to even compile. Much to my amazement, this is what the program looked like:

```
CREATE OR REPLACE PROCEDURE process_line (line IN INTEGER)
IS
BEGIN
   IF    line = 1 THEN process_line1;
   ELSIF line = 2 THEN process_line2;
   ...
   ELSIF line = 514 THEN process_line514;
   ...
   ELSIF line = 2057 THEN process_line2057;
   END IF;
END;
```

For each line number, there was a "process_line" program that handled those details. And as the insurance company added more and more exceptions to the policy, the program got bigger and bigger. Not a very scalable approach to programming!

To avoid this kind of mess, a programmer should be on the lookout for repetition of code. If you can detect a pattern, you can either create a reusable program to encapsulate that pattern, or explore the possibility of expressing that pattern as a dynamic SQL construction.

I was able to replace those thousands of lines of code with nothing more than this:

```
CREATE OR REPLACE PROCEDURE process_line (line IN INTEGER)
IS
BEGIN
   EXECUTE IMMEDIATE
       'BEGIN process_line' || line || '; END;';
END;
```

From thousands of lines of code down to one executable statement! Of course, in most cases, identification of the pattern and conversion of that pattern into dynamic SQL will not be so straightforward. Still, the potential gains are enormous.

Conclusion: From Fundamentals to Applying PL/SQL

After reading this chapter, you should have a solid feeling for the fundamentals of the PL/SQL language. With that foundation (and, I hope, with some experience of actually writing PL/SQL programs), you can now proceed to the chapters that describe DBA-specific functionality that relies on PL/SQL to get its job done.

Cursors

A *cursor* is a vehicle for extracting data from an Oracle database. Cursors determine the columns and objects (tables, views, etc.) from which data will be extracted, and they provide criteria to determine exactly which records should be extracted. To start off our discussion, here are two very simple example cursors:

```
SELECT name
  FROM emp;

CURSOR curs_get_emp IS
SELECT name
  FROM emp;
```

Oracle DBAs are no doubt familiar with this basic cursor syntax but might describe the functionality (particularly of the first example) by using terms like "SELECT statement," "query," or "fetching data." On the surface, that is all cursors may appear to do—fetch data. Most DBAs know that cursors are a more integral part of database functionality, but they may not be aware of how understanding and manipulating cursors can dramatically improve the performance of their Oracle database applications.

Although traditionally used for querying data, cursors have become pervasive in PL/SQL. This chapter discusses how cursors and PL/SQL interact from a DBA perspective. It describes how reusing cursors can improve performance and discusses the differences between explicit and implicit cursors, and how each may affect your database. It also explores the performance benefits of Oracle's optimization of "soft-closed" cursors. The chapter also discusses REF (dynamic) cursors, cursor parameters, and cursor expressions (nested cursors).

There has been a great deal of spirited debate over the years about the proper use of cursors in the Oracle database. For example, DBAs and developers argue that one type of cursor is faster than another, or they question the effectiveness of Oracle's reuse model. Over the years, there have also been major advances in the cursor features provided in recent Oracle releases. This chapter does not try to persuade you to take one particular path in implementing and tuning cursors in your system. The proper use of cursors depends, to a large extent, on the characteristics of your organization and its data and applications. Here we simply try to explain the major features and provide some guidance to help you decide when to use them.

Reusing Cursors

Cursor reuse is basically a very simple concept—a cursor can be used and then used again. More specifically, the compiled version of the cursor can be reused to avoid a costly parse and recompilation.

Hard Parsing and Soft Parsing

The process of compiling a *new* cursor is referred to as *hard parsing* (and is worthy of a book all its own); within the context of this chapter it can be simplified to four steps:

Validation
> The SQL syntax of the cursor is validated for correctness, and the objects (tables and columns) to which it refers are verified.

Compilation
> The cursor is compiled into executable form and is loaded into the database's shared pool. Its location in the shared pool is referred to as its *address*.

Execution plan calculation
> Oracle's cost-based optimizer (CBO) determines the best execution plan for the cursor and attaches it to the cursor.

Hash calculation
> The ASCII value of each character in the cursor is totaled up and sent to a hash algorithm. The algorithm calculates a value to make the cursor easy to find for subsequent reuse. This value is referred to as the cursor's *hash value*. We'll look more at ASCII values later in this section.

A good deal of database latch activity takes place during these operations because Oracle cannot allow any underlying objects (tables and columns) to change while the cursor is being validated and compiled. The activity is almost entirely CPU-driven, so a portion of your database server's CPU will be consumed while compilation occurs. More importantly, the really important work of fetching records will be delayed. Subsequent executions of the same cursor (either by the same program or by another) can avoid incurring the costly hard-parse process and instead simply ensure that they have the required access to the objects (tables, views, etc.) involved and proceed directly to fetching records. This saves valuable time.

A running total of the hard parses a database has performed can be gleaned from the V$SYSSTAT table as follows:

```
SQL> SELECT name,
  2         value
```

```
  3    FROM v$sysstat
  4   WHERE name = 'parse count (hard)';

NAME                                VALUE
------------------------------- ----------
parse count (hard)                    676
```

If the number of hard parses in an application is steadily increasing, that is an indication that the application is not taking proper advantage of cursor reuse.

Even after a cursor has undergone a hard parse, it may require some amount of parsing during the course of reuse. However, that process will be a much less intrusive parse consisting of little more than a security check to ensure that the user attempting to reuse the cursor has the required access to its underlying objects. This somewhat limited work is referred to as a *soft parse*.

The running total of soft parses a database has performed may be calculated by taking total parses and subtracting hard parses.

```
SQL> SELECT ( SELECT value
  2               FROM v$sysstat
  3              WHERE name = 'parse count (total)' )
  4        - ( SELECT value
  5               FROM v$sysstat
  6              WHERE name = 'parse count (hard)' ) soft_parse
  7   FROM dual;

SOFT_PARSE
----------
      4439
```

The time a database has spent parsing (CPU and elapsed) is also available from the V$SYSSTAT table.

```
SQL> SELECT name,
  2          value
  3    FROM v$sysstat
  4   WHERE name LIKE 'parse time%';

NAME                                VALUE
------------------------------- ----------
parse time cpu                        381
parse time elapsed                   5933
```

Ideally, neither of these values should increase markedly while an application is running. They will, however, almost always increase somewhat because even the simplest soft parse requires *some* CPU.

Planning Cursor Use

It is good practice to limit the number of times a cursor has to be parsed—the optimal number of parses is one, of course. One option to achieve this ideal would be to preparse every possible cursor your application might ever execute. That way, every cursor would already be waiting in the shared pool when your application starts up. However, this approach would be extremely difficult to maintain in a large application or in one that allows ad hoc queries. Thus, it is better to take the hit the first time a cursor executes and then ensure that it is reused whenever possible later on.

 Except where explicitly stated otherwise in this chapter, the CURSOR_SHARING parameter for all examples is set to EXACT. See the later section "Matching Algorithms" for a discussion of exact matching versus similar matching.

The following subsections explain how Oracle decides whether to reuse a cursor. This is the most important information to have when devising a plan for cursor reuse. Many PL/SQL developers are, unfortunately, blissfully unaware of this whole concept, so it is doubly important for DBAs to understand the use and consequences of cursor reuse. First, we'll look at some details of Oracle's hash algorithm, and then we'll cover the nuances of cursor reuse. I encourage you to read this whole section before tackling any cursor reuse issues (real or perceived) in your applications.

How Oracle Decides To Share

Oracle uses a complex algorithm to decide whether a cursor that is about to be executed may reuse an already compiled version from the shared pool. Here is a simplified presentation of that algorithm:

1. Calculate the sum of the ASCII values of all characters in the cursor (excluding bind variables). For example, the total ASCII value of the following cursor is 2556:

   `SELECT order_date FROM orders`

   This is calculated as ASCII(S) + ASCII(E) + ASCII(L)...or 83 + 69 + 76 and so on.

2. Apply a hash algorithm to the ASCII total.

3. Peruse the shared pool for a cursor with the same hash value.

4. If one is found, it may be reused.

 Note that I say "may" be reused. Most of the time, a matching ASCII hash is enough to allow reuse, but not always, as I'll explain later in this section.

In item 1, I state that the ASCII value of *every* character is used. Thus, something as low level as mixing uppercase and lowercase has to be considered when planning for cursor reuse. Consider these two cursors run directly in SQL*Plus.

```
SQL> SELECT order_date
  2    FROM orders
  3    WHERE order_number = 11;
```

```
ORDER_DAT
---------
03-MAY-05

SQL> SELECT order_date
  2    FROM orders
  3   WHERE order_numbeR = 11;

ORDER_DAT
---------
03-MAY-05
```

The human eye can see that both of these examples do exactly the same thing—select the order date for order number 11. The only difference is that an uppercase R was used in the second one. That's just enough for Oracle to consider them different, though, so two cursors wind up in the shared pool.

```
SQL> SELECT sql_text,
  2          parse_calls,
  3          executions
  4    FROM v$sql
  5   WHERE INSTR(UPPER(sql_text),'ORDERS')  > 0
  6     AND INSTR(UPPER(sql_text),'SQL_TEXT') = 0
  7     AND command_type = 3;

SQL_TEXT                        PARSE_CALLS EXECUTIONS
------------------------------  ----------- ----------
SELECT order_date    FROM order          1          1
s  WHERE order_numbeR = 11

SELECT order_date    FROM order          1          1
s  WHERE order_number = 11
```

The EXECUTIONS column shows the number of times the particular cursor has been executed, and the PARSE_CALLS column shows the number of times the cursor has been parsed. Both cursors required a hard parse because the ASCII totals did not match up.

You may find the requirement for exact matching a little stern and unforgiving, but it has to be that way because the database can't afford to spend a lot of time preparsing or reformatting cursor text—it has better things to do, like running your application. Recent versions of Oracle have introduced some reformatting of literal values in cursors to aid in cursor reuse (see the "Matching Algorithms" section later in this chapter), but that reformatting introduces some overhead to each and every query containing a literal value.

One of the best ways to take advantage of automatically reformatting cursors to promote reuse is to put them into PL/SQL, as shown in this standalone block:

```
DECLARE
   CURSOR one IS
   SELECT order_date
     FROM orders
```

```
   WHERE order_number = 11;
 CURSOR two IS
 SELECT order_date
   FROM orders
  WHERE order_numbeR = 11;
 v_date DATE;
BEGIN
 -- open and close correct cursor
 OPEN one;
 FETCH one INTO v_date;
 CLOSE one;
 -- open and close misspelled cursor
 OPEN two;
 FETCH two INTO v_date;
 CLOSE two;
END;
```

The PL/SQL compiler reformats the mismatched cursors, thus producing a single cursor in the shared pool. On the surface, this may seem to be a very small improvement, but implemented across an application, it can produce big performance gains because the shared pool latches have fewer cursors to keep track of.

```
SQL_TEXT                        PARSE_CALLS EXECUTIONS
------------------------------- ----------- ----------
SELECT ORDER_DATE FROM ORDERS        2          2
WHERE ORDER_NUMBER = 11
```

This behavior is available in Oracle8i Database through Oracle Database 10g Release 2, with an unfortunate lapse in Oracle9i Database Release 2.

I like to think of the PL/SQL compiler as being a little more forgiving than the SQL one. Nevertheless, every execution of my standalone block necessitates that each cursor be validated and parsed. So, even though I'm down to a single cursor, my hard parse count is steadily increasing. Ten executions of my standalone block cause 20 hard parses:

```
SQL_TEXT                        PARSE_CALLS EXECUTIONS
------------------------------- ----------- ----------
SELECT ORDER_DATE FROM ORDERS        20         20
WHERE ORDER_NUMBER = 11
```

The good news is that PL/SQL can virtually eliminate all hard parses just by moving the cursors into a stored procedure, as follows:

```
CREATE OR REPLACE PROCEDURE simple_demo AS
  CURSOR one IS
  SELECT order_date
    FROM orders
   WHERE order_number = 11;
  CURSOR two IS
  SELECT order_date
     FROM orders
   WHERE order_numbeR = 11;
  v_date DATE;
```

```
BEGIN
  -- open and close correct cursor
  OPEN one;
  FETCH one INTO v_date;
  CLOSE one;
  -- open and close misspelled one allowing PL/SQL
  -- to reformat for me!
  OPEN two;
  FETCH two INTO v_date;
  CLOSE two;
END;
```

After executing the stored procedure 10 times in SQL*Plus like this:

```
SQL> BEGIN
  2    simple_demo;
  3  END;
```

the SGA shows these numbers:

```
SQL_TEXT                     PARSE_CALLS EXECUTIONS
---------------------------- ----------- ----------
SELECT ORDER_DATE FROM ORDERS           2         20
WHERE ORDER_NUMBER = 11
```

The two parses occurred when the procedure was first compiled. Once that happens, the procedure and all of its contents (including the cursors) are considered valid and do not require reparsing.

Simply by moving these two cursors into PL/SQL, you'll take advantage of two key features of PL/SQL that are particularly helpful for DBAs:

- The PL/SQL compiler promotes reuse by being more forgiving regarding the structure of cursors. The degree of forgiveness is discussed in the next section.

- Once a cursor is compiled into a PL/SQL procedure, package, or function, it is automatically considered valid and parsed as long as the procedure, package, or function remains valid.

PL/SQL Cursor Reformatting

As I mentioned, the PL/SQL compiler makes some extra effort to facilitate cursor reuse by checking for small differences like extra whitespace, uppercase versus lowercase, and line breaks. For example, only a single compiled cursor is created and reused in the shared pool for the following procedure:

```
CREATE OR REPLACE PROCEDURE forgiveness IS
  -- define two poorly structured cursors
  CURSOR curs_x IS
  SELECT order_date FROM orders;
  CURSOR curs_y IS
  SELECT order_date
    FROM    orders;
BEGIN
  -- let PL/SQL work its reformatting magic
```

```
    OPEN curs_x;
    CLOSE curs_x;
    OPEN curs_y;
    CLOSE curs_y;
END;
```

This preparsing is done to all cursors in PL/SQL to help with matching among all stored code. For example, the following cursor would reuse the compiled cursor from the forgiveness procedure.

```
CURSOR curs_x IS
SELECT order_date FROM ORDers;
```

Literal Values

Another factor to consider when planning for cursor reuse is the use of literal values. Consider the following simple code snippet that performs two straightforward queries. Pay close attention to the fact that the text of each query differs only in the specified literal order number.

```
CREATE OR REPLACE PROCEDURE two_queries
AS
   v_order_date DATE;
BEGIN
   -- get order 100
   SELECT order_date
     INTO v_order_date
     FROM orders
    WHERE order_number = 100;
   -- get order 200
   SELECT order_date
     INTO v_order_date
     FROM orders
    WHERE order_number = 200;
END;
```

After an initial execution, the shared pool contains two cursors.

```
SQL_TEXT                           PARSE_CALLS EXECUTIONS
---------------------------------- ----------- ----------
SELECT ORDER_DATE FROM ORDERS            1          1
WHERE ORDER_NUMBER = 100

SELECT ORDER_DATE FROM ORDERS            1          1
WHERE ORDER_NUMBER = 200
```

Each cursor was parsed and executed once because the ASCII totals did not match up. In addition, their only chance of further reuse will be when order 100 or 200 is explicitly queried. That's hardly optimal because, if there are tens of thousands of orders, there will be tens of thousands of hard parses to retrieve them.

Within PL/SQL, the easiest way to make these cursors available for reuse is to parameterize them as shown in this code:

```
CREATE OR REPLACE PROCEDURE two_queries AS
  -- define a parameterized cursor
  CURSOR get_date ( cp_order NUMBER ) IS
  SELECT order_date
    FROM orders
   WHERE order_number = cp_order;
  v_order_date DATE;
BEGIN
  -- get order 100
  OPEN get_date(100);
  FETCH get_date INTO v_order_date;
  CLOSE get_date;
  -- get order 200
  OPEN get_date(200);
  FETCH get_date INTO v_order_date;
  CLOSE get_date;
END;
```

After flushing the shared pool and executing the new function, here's what's in the shared pool.

```
SQL_TEXT                            PARSE_CALLS EXECUTIONS
---------------------------------- ----------- ----------
SELECT ORDER_DATE FROM ORDERS              1          2
WHERE ORDER_NUMBER = :B1
```

Only one cursor with an execution count of 2 exists in the shared pool, indicating that the cursor has already been reused.

At this point, any other code executing the same cursor to get the order date for an order can reuse the already compiled version. For example, the following procedure will reuse the compiled version of the cursor:

```
CREATE OR REPLACE PROCEDURE another_two_queries AS
  -- same cursor as above, just different parameter name
  CURSOR get_date ( cp_oid NUMBER ) IS
  SELECT order_date
    FROM orders
   WHERE order_number = cp_oid;
  v_order_date DATE;
BEGIN
  -- get order 300
  OPEN get_date(300);
  FETCH get_date INTO v_order_date;
  CLOSE get_date;
  -- get order 400
  OPEN get_date(400);
  FETCH get_date INTO v_order_date;
  CLOSE get_date;
END;
```

After running the new procedure, the shared pool holds this:

```
SQL_TEXT                        PARSE_CALLS EXECUTIONS
------------------------------- ----------- ----------
SELECT ORDER_DATE FROM ORDERS         2          4
WHERE ORDER_NUMBER = :B1
```

The compiled version of the cursor was reused by the second procedure. The parse required was only a soft one. It's clear from this example that it is good practice to keep from using literals in cursors whenever possible.

But what if the application is not adaptable because it's an off-the-shelf package or there just isn't enough time or money to change it? Oracle offers some help for such situations, as discussed in the next section.

Matching Algorithms

The default behavior for cursor reuse in the database is referred to as *exact matching*. Outside of PL/SQL this exactness is quite unforgiving—the ASCII values must match precisely. There is only black and white, no gray area at all. A cursor either matches or it does not. Within PL/SQL, the compiler does what it can by reformatting cursors to promote reuse, but it can only do so much. This limitation is especially maddening when cursors differ only in the text contained within literals. Consider these two cursors:

```
SELECT order_date FROM orders WHERE order_number = '1';
SELECT order_date FROM orders WHERE order_number = '4';
```

They both perform the same function of getting the order_date for a specific order, and their total ASCII values differ by a measly four digits. But under the exact matching algorithm, they both merit their own hard parse and space in the shared pool—even when embedded in PL/SQL.

```
SQL_TEXT                        PARSE_CALLS EXECUTIONS
------------------------------- ----------- ----------
SELECT order_date FROM orders         1          1
WHERE order_number = '4'

SELECT order_date FROM orders         1          1
WHERE order_number = '1'
```

Eventually, the shared pool may end up flooded with cursors like this that are so close to being reused—and yet so far. Some commercial off-the-shelf applications exhibit this behavior of using literals in cursors, and some older versions of ODBC rely on it, as well. To allow for this behavior, Oracle introduced a second algorithm for cursor sharing known as *similar matching*. "Similar" here means that cursors only need to match ASCII-wise outside of any literals.

The sharing algorithm applied is determined by the database initialization parameter CURSOR_SHARING:

```
SQL> SELECT name,
  2         value
  3    FROM v$parameter
  4   WHERE name = 'cursor_sharing';


NAME                 VALUE
-------------------- ---------------
cursor_sharing       EXACT
```

In addition to setting this parameter at the database level, you can set it for a single session using the ALTER SESSION command.

```
SQL> ALTER SESSION SET cursor_sharing = SIMILAR;

Session altered.
```

Here's what's in the shared pool after the cursors are executed with differing literals under the similar matching algorithm.

```
SQL> SELECT name,
  2         value
  3    FROM v$parameter
  4   WHERE name = 'cursor_sharing';

NAME                 VALUE
-------------------- ---------------
cursor_sharing       EXACT
```

In addition to setting this parameter at the database level, you can set it for a single session using the ALTER SESSION command.

```
SQL> ALTER SESSION SET cursor_sharing = SIMILAR;

Session altered.
```

Here's what's in the shared pool after the cursors are executed with differing literals under the similar matching algorithm.

```
SQL_TEXT             PARSE_CALLS EXECUTIONS
-------------------- ----------- ----------
SELECT order_date FRO          2          2
M orders WHERE order_
number = :"SYS_B_0"
```

The literal value was translated into a bind variable, which means that it is now far more likely to be reused.

The SIMILAR setting does not mean that Oracle will blindly substitute bind variables for every single literal it encounters. For example, it won't do so if the execution plan chosen by the cost-based optimizer would change drastically, as shown in this example with some very skewed orders by region.

```
SQL> SELECT region_id,
  2         count(*)
  3    FROM orders
  4  GROUP BY region_id;

REGION_ID   COUNT(*)
---------- ----------
        1       9999
        2          1
```

If the optimizer statistics are up to date, Oracle will be aware of this skew and will utilize different execution plans for getting records from each region. For region 1, it will choose a full table scan because it has to touch all but one record anyway. For region 2, it will hone in on a single row using an index on the REGION_ID field. I'll execute the queries with AUTOTRACE to show this behavior.

```
SQL> SELECT COUNT(*)
  2    FROM ( SELECT *
  3             FROM orders
  4            WHERE region_id = 1 );

COUNT(*)
----------
      9999


Execution Plan
----------------------------------------------------------
   0      SELECT STATEMENT Optimizer=ALL_ROWS (Cost=3 Card=1 Bytes=2)
   1    0   SORT (AGGREGATE)
   2    1     TABLE ACCESS (FULL) OF 'ORDERS' (TABLE) (Cost=3 Card=21 Bytes=42)

SQL> SELECT COUNT(*)
  2    FROM ( SELECT *
  3             FROM orders
  4            WHERE region_id = 2 );

COUNT(*)
----------
         1


Execution Plan
----------------------------------------------------------
   0      SELECT STATEMENT Optimizer=ALL_ROWS (Cost=1 Card=1 Bytes=2)
   1    0   SORT (AGGREGATE)
   2    1     INDEX (RANGE SCAN) OF 'ORDER_REGION' (INDEX) (Cost=1 Card=1 Bytes=2)
```

The really interesting thing is the resulting cursors in the shared pool.

```
SQL_TEXT              PARSE_CALLS EXECUTIONS
---------------------  ----------- ----------
SELECT COUNT(*)    FRO       1          1
M ( SELECT *
   FROM orders
    WHERE region_id =
 :"SYS_B_0" )

SELECT COUNT(*)    FRO       1          1
M ( SELECT *
   FROM orders
    WHERE region_id =
 :"SYS_B_0" )
```

Even though the text of the cursors is exactly the same after making the substitution, another cursor was created because Oracle recognized that the execution plan would change too drastically. This behavior ensures that performance is not adversely affected when you choose the SIMILAR setting for cursor sharing.

A third setting is available for the CURSOR_SHARING parameter: FORCE. And it does just that—force cursors to be shared strictly on the basis of the text they contain after translating literals into bind variables. This method blindly performs literal substitution and forces the CBO to create an execution plan based on it. This is not always optimal, because the CBO might make a better decision if it knew the explicit value, as shown in the preceding REGION_ID.

After executing the count of region 1 and 2 records using the FORCE setting, the shared pool contains a single cursor.

```
SQL_TEXT              PARSE_CALLS EXECUTIONS
---------------------  ----------- ----------
SELECT COUNT(*)    FRO       2          2
M ( SELECT *
   FROM orders
    WHERE region_id =
 :"SYS_B_0" )
```

The FORCE setting was introduced in Oracle8*i* Database (8.1.6) before the SIMILAR setting was made available in Oracle9*i* Database. SIMILAR was introduced because many DBAs and developers viewed the FORCE setting as being an overly brute-force method with regard to query performance (as shown in the examples above). If you decide to implement either of these settings, I strongly encourage you to perform a substantial amount of performance testing to make sure that the benefit of cursor sharing is not being outweighed by query performance degradation.

Remember: although the SIMILAR and FORCE settings may come in handy, there remains no substitute for well-thought-out, consistent use of cursors in your code.

Text Matching Might Not Be Enough

Beyond matching the text of a cursor, there are several other factors influencing cursor reuse—for example, optimizer statistics and Globalization Support (previously

National Language Support, or NLS) setting mismatches. In such cases, it's not enough to simply match ASCII values.

Let's look at the example of setting the optimizer mode in this example.

```
SQL> ALTER SESSION SET optimizer_mode = FIRST_ROWS;

Session altered.

SQL> SELECT COUNT(*)
  2    FROM orders;

  COUNT(*)
----------
     10000

SQL> ALTER SESSION SET optimizer_mode = ALL_ROWS;

Session altered.

SQL> SELECT COUNT(*)
  2    FROM orders;

  COUNT(*)
----------
     10000
```

Astute DBAs know that two cursors will be created in this case: even though the text matched, the optimizer mode used was different, so Oracle built a different execution plan for each cursor. Here's what's in the shared pool.

```
SQL> SELECT sql_id,
  2         sql_text,
  3         parse_calls,
  4         executions
  5    FROM v$sql
  6   WHERE INSTR(UPPER(sql_text),'ORDERS') > 0
  7     AND INSTR(UPPER(sql_text),'SQL_TEXT') = 0
  8     AND command_type = 3;

SQL_ID        SQL_TEXT              PARSE_CALLS EXECUTIONS
------------- --------------------- ----------- ----------
d8ksp6aaxa26d SELECT COUNT(*) FRO             1          1
              M orders

d8ksp6aaxa26d SELECT COUNT(*) FRO             1          1
              M orders
```

 Starting with Oracle Database 10g Release 1, the column SQL_ID is used to uniquely identify a cursor in views such as V$SQL and V$OPEN_CURSOR. Earlier releases use a combination of the HASH_VALUE and ADDRESS columns for this purpose.

Oracle obviously recognized that the cursors were exactly the same because it assigned them the same ID but made the second one a child of the first.

We know in this case that two cursors were required because the optimizer mode changed, but what if we didn't have that information? How could we figure out why a child cursor was required? Enter the V$SQL_SHARED_CURSOR view.

```
SQL> SELECT sql_id,
  2         child_number,
  3         optimizer_mismatch
  4    FROM v$sql_shared_cursor
  5   WHERE sql_id = 'd8ksp6aaxa26d';

SQL_ID        CHILD_NUMBER O
------------- ------------ -
d8ksp6aaxa26d            0 N
d8ksp6aaxa26d            1 Y
```

The "Y" in the second column means that Yes, the optimizer mismatch necessitated a child cursor. I carefully limited the query to confirm the reason that the cursor was not shared by including only the OPTIMIZER_MISMATCH column. However, the V$SQL_SHARED_CURSOR view contains a lot of fields (39 in Oracle Database 10g Release 1, for example), one for each possible reason a cursor might not have been shared.

I've always wondered why this view isn't named V$SQL_UNSHARED_SQL_CURSOR because that's what it actually shows. Either way, it's a very handy view for diagnosing cursor-sharing issues, so I encourage you to check it out.

Using Explicit Cursors Versus Implicit Cursors

A topic that has inspired much debate over the years is the choice between explicit and implicit cursors—or put another way, the "OPEN, FETCH, CLOSE" versus the "SELECT INTO" debate. In this section, I will completely set aside the debate about performance because Oracle has done a lot of work in recent releases to render the point moot. Instead, I'll focus on the effects on the database and discuss the differing PL/SQL usage of both cursor types including the fact they don't always match up in the database's shared pool.

What's the Difference?

In PL/SQL, an *implicit cursor* is one that is defined as it is being executed. Here's an example:

```
DECLARE
  v_date DATE;
BEGIN
  SELECT order_date
    INTO v_date
```

```
     FROM orders
   WHERE order_number = 100;
END;
```

As the code was executing, it created a cursor to select the order_date for order 100. Thus, the cursor was implicitly defined when the code executed.

An *explicit cursor* is one that is defined before it actually gets executed. Here's a simple example:

```
DECLARE
  CURSOR curs_get_od IS
  SELECT order_date
    FROM orders
   WHERE order_number = 100;
  v_date DATE;
BEGIN
  OPEN curs_get_od;
  FETCH curs_get_od INTO v_date;
  CLOSE curs_get_od;
END;
```

The implicit version was much easier to write and required a lot less typing, so the initial reaction may be to go with that choice. However, explicit cursors have other benefits that make the extra typing worthwhile within PL/SQL code, as described in the next two sections.

Cursor Attributes

A key benefit of explicit cursors is the attributes they provide to facilitate logical programming. Consider the following example. Here, we want to look for an order and do something if it is found. The first procedure using implicit cursors has to rely on exception handling to determine whether a record was found or not.

```
CREATE OR REPLACE PROCEDURE demo AS
  v_date       DATE;
  v_its_there BOOLEAN := TRUE;
BEGIN
  BEGIN
    SELECT order_date
      INTO v_date
      FROM orders
     WHERE order_number = 1;
  EXCEPTION
    WHEN no_data_found THEN
      v_its_there := FALSE;
    WHEN OTHERS THEN
      RAISE;
  END;
  IF NOT v_its_there THEN
    do_something;
  END IF;
END;
```

The following code, now using explicit cursors, is easier to follow because the availability of the cursor's %NOTFOUND attribute makes it obvious what is being checked. There is also no need to embed extra PL/SQL blocks (BEGIN–END) just to handle logic.

```
CREATE OR REPLACE PROCEDURE demo AS
  CURSOR curs_get_date IS
  SELECT order_date
    FROM orders
   WHERE order_number = 1;
  v_date DATE;
BEGIN
  OPEN curs_get_date;
  FETCH curs_get_date INTO v_date;
  IF curs_get_date%NOTFOUND THEN
    do_something;
  END IF;
  CLOSE curs_get_date;
END;
```

Oracle supports the following cursor attributes:

Attribute	Description
%BULK_ROWCOUNT	Number of records returned by a bulk fetch (BULK COLLECT INTO) operation.
%FOUND	TRUE if the last FETCH was successful, FALSE if not.
%NOTFOUND	TRUE if the last FETCH was not successful, FALSE if it was.
%ISOPEN	TRUE if the cursor is open, FALSE if not.
%ROWCOUNT	Number of the record currently fetched from the cursor.

You probably are aware that some of these attributes are available for implicit cursors, as well. However, they lend themselves better to programming logic with explicit cursors, especially when you are using multiple cursors as shown in this brief example:

```
IF curs_get_order%ROWCOUNT = 1 THEN
  IF curs_get_details%FOUND THEN
    process_order_detail;
```

Cursor Parameters

As I mentioned earlier in this chapter, you can further promote cursor reuse in PL/SQL by parameterizing your cursors. Here's my simple order_date procedure with a parameterized cursor:

```
DECLARE
  CURSOR curs_get_od ( cp_on NUMBER ) IS
  SELECT order_date
    FROM orders
   WHERE order_number = cp_on;
  v_date DATE;
```

```
BEGIN
  OPEN curs_get_od(100);
  FETCH curs_get_od INTO v_date;
  CLOSE curs_get_od;
END;
```

If later on in the program I wanted to get order 200, 300, and 500, I could simply reopen the cursor. Doing so promotes cursor reuse within the PL/SQL program itself as well as in the shared pool.

Mixing but not Matching

Explicit and implicit cursors do not match up in the shared pool. What do I mean by that? I'll explain with an example.

```
DECLARE
  CURSOR get_region IS
  SELECT region_id FROM orders WHERE region_id = 2;
  v_region NUMBER;
BEGIN
  OPEN get_region;
  FETCH get_region INTO v_region;
  CLOSE get_region;
  SELECT region_id INTO v_region FROM orders WHERE region_id = 2;
END;
```

How many shared pool cursors does this produce? The answer is two.

SQL_TEXT	PARSE_CALLS	EXECUTIONS
SELECT REGION_ID FROM ORDERS W HERE REGION_ID = 2	1	1
SELECT REGION_ID FROM ORDERS W HERE REGION_ID = 2	1	1

Even though these cursors look identical and share the same address in the shared pool, they differ just enough (perhaps the INTO clause?) for Oracle to store two separate ones. The moral is that you can't assume that explicit and implicit cursors will match up in the shared pool. It's best to stick with one way or the other.

Soft-Closing Cursors

When I am building applications, I am a firm believer in extending assumptions in order to squeeze out every little bit of extra performance or throughput. I'm forever asking questions—for example, if the same Oracle session executes my PL/SQL function repeatedly, why don't I cache some of the setup information instead of querying it each time? Or, if I know that underlying data changes only hourly, why can't I cache the result sets and avoid requerying the database until 60 minutes pass?

One assumption that Oracle itself extends is that once a session uses a cursor, it will eventually reuse it—even if it is explicitly closed. The trickery used to accomplish this feat is known as *soft closing,* or what I refer to as "the close that's not a close."

Consider this simple example of an implicit cursor.

```
SQL> SELECT NULL
  2    FROM DUAL;

N
-


1 row selected
```

The implicit cursor was created, opened, fetched, and closed—all in the SELECT statement. So now it should be disassociated with the session that executed it, right? Not so fast. In order to take better advantage of potential reuse, the cursor is soft-closed only within the session to make subsequent reuse by that session faster.

The cursors associated with a particular session are shown in the V$OPEN_CURSOR view. That view includes any cursors currently open as well as those that have been soft-closed. Here's what the view shows for the session querying the DUAL table.

```
SQL> SELECT sql_text
  2    FROM v$open_cursor
  3   WHERE sid = 43;

SQL_TEXT
-------------------------
SELECT NULL   FROM DUAL
```

This soft-closing occurs whenever cursors are closed explicitly via the CLOSE statement or implicitly when they go out of scope.

To avoid keeping every single cursor in this soft-closed state forever, you can specify a per-session limit in the OPEN_CURSORS database initialization parameter. The list stays current by flushing the least-recently-used entries whenever space is needed for new entries. However, if a session attempts to actually open more than this limit at one time, it will encounter the *ORA-01000: maximum open cursors exceeded* error.

Explicit and Implicit Open Cursors

The list of open cursors is another area where explicit and implicit cursors are treated differently, as shown in the following example with OPEN_CURSORS set to 20. First, I'll execute several implicit cursors:

```
DECLARE
  v_dummy varchar2(10);
BEGIN
  SELECT 'A' INTO v_dummy  FROM orders;
  SELECT 'B' INTO v_dummy  FROM orders;
```

```
...and so on through lower and upper case alphabets...
   SELECT 'x' INTO v_dummy  FROM orders;
   SELECT 'y' INTO v_dummy  FROM orders;
   SELECT 'z' INTO v_dummy  FROM orders;
END;
```

The session's list of associated cursors now looks like this:

```
SQL> SELECT oc.sql_text
  2    FROM v$open_cursor oc,
  3         v$sql          sq
  4   WHERE user_name = 'DRH'
  5     AND oc.sql_id = sq.sql_id
  6     AND command_type = 3;

SQL_TEXT
--------------------------------
SELECT 'n' FROM ORDERS
SELECT 'z' FROM ORDERS
SELECT 'o' FROM ORDERS
SELECT 'q' FROM ORDERS
SELECT 'x' FROM ORDERS
SELECT 'l' FROM ORDERS
SELECT 'v' FROM ORDERS
SELECT 's' FROM ORDERS
SELECT 'p' FROM ORDERS
SELECT 'w' FROM ORDERS
SELECT 'm' FROM ORDERS
SELECT 'u' FROM ORDERS
SELECT 'k' FROM ORDERS
SELECT 'j' FROM ORDERS
SELECT 'i' FROM ORDERS
SELECT 'y' FROM ORDERS
SELECT 'r' FROM ORDERS
SELECT 't' FROM ORDERS
SELECT 'h' FROM ORDERS

19 rows selected.
```

Only the last cursors remained behind as soft-closed. The others were flushed out to make room for newer ones.

Now, I'll execute several explicit cursors by opening and closing each one.

```
DECLARE
   CURSOR curs_65 IS SELECT 'A' FROM orders;
   CURSOR curs_66 IS SELECT 'B' FROM orders;
...and so on through the lowercase and uppercase alphabets
...ASCII 65 through 122
   CURSOR curs_122 IS SELECT 'z' FROM orders;
BEGIN
   OPEN curs_65;
   CLOSE curs_65;
...and so on...
   OPEN curs_122;
```

```
    CLOSE curs_122;
  END;
```

I'll wind up with a list of associated cursors that is very similar to the list I had for the implicit run. But imagine what would happen if I were lazy and decided not to close the explicit cursors, as in this code.

```
DECLARE
  CURSOR curs_65 IS SELECT 'A' FROM orders;
  CURSOR curs_66 IS SELECT 'B' FROM orders;
...and so on through the lowercase and uppercase case alphabets
...ASCII 65 through 122
  CURSOR curs_122 IS SELECT 'z' FROM orders;
BEGIN
  OPEN curs_65;
  OPEN curs_66;
...and so on...
  OPEN curs_122;
END;
```

At or near the 20th cursor, I get this error because the session tried to go beyond its limit of 20 open cursors.

```
ERROR at line 1:
ORA-01000: maximum open cursors exceeded
ORA-06512: at line 21
ORA-06512: at line 80
```

This is one of the reasons why it's important to always close explicit cursors.

So, what's a good setting for the OPEN_CURSORS parameter? That's easy: set it to whatever you need plus one. That may not seem to be a very helpful answer, but there is no tried-and-true method for setting this parameter. If the value is too low, the code won't run because of the ORA-1000 error. If the value is too high, then cursors (explicit and implicit) may remain soft-closed forever. The good news is that the space is not pre-allocated, so setting this value high does not have to factor into your overall memory sizing.

This query provides a good value to use by determining the maximum number of cursors (open or soft-closed) associated with a current session. I run this at regular intervals early in the application's life cycle.

```
SYS> SELECT *
  2   FROM ( SELECT sid,
  3                 COUNT(*)
  4            FROM v$open_cursor
  5           GROUP BY sid
  6           ORDER BY COUNT(*) DESC)
  7  WHERE ROWNUM = 1;

       SID   COUNT(*)
---------- ----------
        46         20
```

I then set OPEN_CURSORS to the highest maximum plus a safety buffer of 10 or 20.

Native Dynamic SQL

Native Dynamic SQL (NDS) is also generally able to take advantage of soft-closed cursors and cursor reuse, but it does best when bind variables are used. Consider the following two procedures; they do the same thing except that one uses bind variables while the other uses concatenation.

```
CREATE OR REPLACE PROCEDURE bind ( p_on NUMBER ) AS
  v_od DATE;
BEGIN
  EXECUTE IMMEDIATE 'SELECT order_date ' ||
                    ' FROM orders '      ||
                    ' WHERE order_number = :v_on'
         INTO v_od
         USING p_on;
END;

CREATE OR REPLACE PROCEDURE concatenate ( p_on NUMBER ) AS
  v_od DATE;
BEGIN
  EXECUTE IMMEDIATE 'SELECT order_date ' ||
                    ' FROM orders '      ||
                    ' WHERE order_number = ' || p_on
         INTO v_od;
END;
```

First, I'll execute the bind version three times:

```
SQL> BEGIN
  2    FOR counter IN 1..3 LOOP
  3      bind(counter);
  4    END LOOP;
  5  END;
  6  /

PL/SQL procedure successfully completed.
```

The open cursors list shows one very familiar cursor:

```
SELECT order_date  FROM orders
  WHERE order_number = :v_on
```

The parse and execution counts are, as expected, 1 and 3:

```
SQL_TEXT                       PARSE_CALLS EXECUTIONS
------------------------------ ----------- ----------
SELECT order_date  FROM orders      1           3
  WHERE order_number = :v_on
```

Now I'll run the concatenation version three times.

```
SQL> BEGIN
  2    FOR counter IN 1..3 LOOP
  3      concatenate(counter);
  4    END LOOP;
```

```
5  END;
6  /
```

```
PL/SQL procedure successfully completed.
```

The open cursor list looks like this because only the very last one is kept around, hoping for re-execution.

```
SQL_TEXT
-------------------------------
SELECT order_date  FROM orders
  WHERE order_number = 3
```

The parse calls and execution counts are interesting. Three separate cursors all parsed once and executed once. That's just plain wasteful.

```
SQL_TEXT                          PARSE_CALLS EXECUTIONS
-------------------------------   ----------- ----------
SELECT order_date  FROM orders         1           1
  WHERE order_number = 3
SELECT order_date  FROM orders         1           1
  WHERE order_number = 1

SELECT order_date  FROM orders         1           1
  WHERE order_number = 2
```

Dynamic SQL is a powerful and handy tool. With just a little forethought, you can ensure that it takes advantage of all of the cursor reuse features of normal PL/SQL.

Using Cursors for More Than Queries

As the Oracle database has evolved over time, so has the humble cursor. In addition to providing the performance improvements described in earlier sections, cursor functionality now extends beyond queries, and it is integral to the design and building of applications. This section describes a variety of additional cursor capabilities not explored in previous sections.

Bulk fetching, REF cursors, cursor parameters, and cursor expressions are especially handy tools for DBAs who need ways to investigate and improve the performance of applications. The features discussed here are particularly helpful if you are working with very busy databases where keeping the number of records touched to an absolute minimum is very important. For example, REF cursors can be used to control data access from client applications that may not even be aware of the way that tables are structured. Cursor parameters allow data access to be spread out. (Chapter 3 discusses additional tools for accomplishing this goal.) And cursor expressions (nested cursors) go a long way toward ensuring that only the work that needs to be done actually is done.

Bulking Up

If you fetch records, one by one, via a PL/SQL loop, you will incur the overhead of context switching between SQL and PL/SQL once per record. This will dramatically increase the elapsed time if you are processing a large number of records. You can reduce the number of context switches by using a bulk fetch (BULK COLLECT INTO) to query records in sets or all at once.

First, here is an example of what I mean by fetching one record at a time:

```
CREATE OR REPLACE PROCEDURE one_at_a_time AS
  CURSOR curs_get_ord IS
  SELECT order_number,
         order_date
    FROM orders
  ORDER BY order_number;
  v_order_number NUMBER;
  v_order_date   DATE;
BEGIN
  FOR v_order_rec IN curs_get_ord LOOP
    do_something;
  END LOOP;
END;
```

If the ORDERS table contains 100 records, then 100 context switches would occur. Here is the bulk fetch version of the code.

```
CREATE OR REPLACE PROCEDURE all_at_once AS
  CURSOR curs_get_ord IS
  SELECT order_number,
         order_date
    FROM orders
  ORDER BY order_number;

  -- local collections to hold bulk fetched values
  TYPE v_number_t IS TABLE OF NUMBER;
  TYPE v_date_t   IS TABLE OF DATE;
  v_order_number v_number_t;
  v_order_date   v_date_t;

BEGIN
  -- get all orders at once
  OPEN curs_get_ord;
  FETCH curs_get_ord BULK COLLECT INTO v_order_number, v_order_date;
  CLOSE curs_get_ord;
  -- if any orders were found then loop through the local
  -- collections to process them
  IF NVL(v_order_number.COUNT,0) > 0 THEN
    FOR counter IN v_order_number.FIRST..v_order_number.LAST LOOP
      do_something;
    END LOOP;
  END IF;
END;
```

For large record sets, the performance gain can be huge, so I highly recommend that you use this option whenever you can.

There is also another, less obvious advantage to performing bulk fetches: the database does not have to maintain a read-consistent view of the data while the records it retrieves are processed. Let's look again at the previous example. If the mythical DO_SOMETHING procedure took five seconds to process each of the 100 records retrieved from the ORDERS table, Oracle would have to maintain a read-consistent copy of the records in the result set for more than eight minutes. If the ORDERS table is busy with many other DML operations, then the database's rollback segments will be busy keeping a view of the data in synch for the long operation.

 In this case, there is a potential snag resulting from switching to a bulk fetch method: the DO_SOMETHING procedure will have to handle situations where the orders it wants to process no longer exist because they were deleted after the bulk fetch occurred.

The alternative is to query all records into memory right away with a bulk fetch and then process them. This operation also drastically reduces the chances of getting the troublesome *ORA-01555 – Snapshot Too Old (Rollback Segment Too Small)* error.

Because the bulk fetch feature brings records into session memory, a balance must be struck with session memory limits. If session memory is a concern for your application, then you can use the LIMIT clause to restrict the number of entries queried at one time. For example:

```
OPEN curs_get_ord;
LOOP
  -- get next 1,000 orders
  FETCH curs_get_ord BULK COLLECT INTO v_order_number, v_order_date LIMIT 1000;
  -- if any more orders found then loop through them
  IF NVL(v_order_number.COUNT,0) > 0 THEN
    FOR counter IN v_order_number.FIRST..v_order_number.LAST LOOP
      do_something;
    END LOOP;
  ELSE
    EXIT;
  END IF;
END LOOP;
CLOSE curs_get_ord;
```

I make frequent use of the bulk fetch feature when querying Oracle's performance (V$) tables because the last thing I want is for the database to do extra work just so I can see, for example, how many reads and writes each session did. Here is the algorithm I follow:

```
BEGIN
  bulk fetch current sessions from V$SESSION
  for each session
    query session stats for reads and writes
```

```
    end if
  END;
```

I recommend using this feature frequently when querying from the busier Oracle performance views.

REF Cursors

REF cursors provide placeholders for eventual *real* cursors. Using REF cursors, a program may utilize Oracle's cursor features without being terribly explicit about what data is to be accessed until runtime. Here is a really simple example:

```
CREATE OR REPLACE PROCEDURE ref_curs AS
  v_curs SYS_REFCURSOR;
BEGIN
  OPEN v_curs FOR 'SELECT order_number ' ||
                  ' FROM orders';
  CLOSE v_curs;
END;
```

At compile time, Oracle has no idea what the query text will be—all it sees is a string variable. But the REF cursor tells it to be ready to provide cursor functionality in some manner.

The most useful application of REF cursors is to provide "black box" data access to other applications with functions building and returning REF cursors as shown here:

```
CREATE OR REPLACE FUNCTION all_orders ( p_id NUMBER )
                  RETURN SYS_REFCURSOR  IS
  v_curs SYS_REFCURSOR;
BEGIN
  OPEN v_curs FOR 'SELECT * ' ||
                  ' FROM orders ' ||
                  ' WHERE order_number = ' || p_id;
  RETURN v_curs;
END;
```

The calling program simply passes an order_number value to the function and is returned access to the underlying data without having to know anything about it beforehand. External applications, such as Microsoft's .NET, can interrogate the returned REF cursor to determine attributes such as column names and datatypes to decide how to display them.

Here is how the all_orders function might be issued from PL/SQL:

```
DECLARE
  v_curs     SYS_REFCURSOR;
  v_order_rec ORDERS%ROWTYPE;
BEGIN
  v_curs := all_orders(1);
  FETCH v_curs INTO v_order_rec;
  IF v_curs%FOUND THEN
    DBMS_OUTPUT.PUT_LINE('Found It');
```

```
    END IF;
    CLOSE v_curs;
END;
```

Strong vs. weak REF cursors

There are two types of REF cursors, strongly typed and weakly typed. The difference
is that weakly typed REF cursors have no idea up front what data set they will be
returning, while strongly typed ones are told explicitly what their return set will look
like.

 The SYS_REFCURSOR datatype shown in the two previous examples
became available in Oracle9i Database, allowing for the quick definition of weakly typed REF cursors. In previous versions, they were
declared like this:

```
DECLARE
    TYPE v_curs_t IS REF_CURSOR;
    v_curs v_curs_t;
```

Weakly typed REF cursors can be reused by almost any query because they are not
tied to an explicit return structure.

```
DECLARE
    v_curs SYS_REFCURSOR;
BEGIN
    OPEN v_curs FOR 'SELECT order_number ' ||
                    ' FROM orders';
    CLOSE v_curs;
    OPEN v_curs FOR 'SELECT * ' ||
                    ' FROM orders';
    CLOSE v_curs;
END;
```

The actual query provided for the REF cursor winds up being validated, parsed, and
held in the System Global Area just like any other cursor.

SQL_TEXT	PARSE_CALLS	EXECUTIONS
SELECT * FROM orders	1	1
SELECT order_number FROM orde rs	1	1

Note, however, that REF cursors are not soft-closed, so they cannot take advantage
of being opened extra-super-duper quickly later on. Thus, REF cursors will not work
as fast as normal cursors.

Weakly typed REF cursors will also incur overhead when Oracle figures out the
structure of the return set on the fly. So, for the best performance, strongly typed
REF cursors should be used whenever possible. Here are some examples of strongly
typed REF cursors:

```
DECLARE
  -- type for order records
  TYPE v_order_curs IS REF CURSOR RETURN orders%ROWTYPE;
  v_oc v_order_curs;
  -- type for order numbers only
  TYPE v_order_number_t IS RECORD ( order_number orders.order_number%TYPE );
  TYPE v_order_number_curs IS REF CURSOR RETURN v_order_number_t;
  v_ocn v_order_number_curs;
```

Attempts to use a REF cursor with a non-matching return data set will be met with
the rather generic ORA-06550 message.

```
OPEN v_ocn FOR SELECT * FROM ORDERS;
                     *
ERROR at line 10:
ORA-06550: line 10, column 18:
PLS-00382: expression is of wrong type
```

REF cursor attributes

REF cursors have the same full suite of attributes as explicit cursors, as shown in this
example:

```
DECLARE
  v_curs SYS_REFCURSOR;
  v_on   NUMBER;
BEGIN
  OPEN v_curs FOR 'SELECT order_number ' ||
                  ' FROM orders';
  FETCH v_curs INTO v_on;
  LOOP
    EXIT when v_curs%NOTFOUND;
    IF v_curs%ROWCOUNT = 1 THEN
      NULL;
    END IF;
    FETCH v_curs INTO v_on;
  END LOOP;
  CLOSE v_curs;
END;
```

Dynamic data access

REF cursors are very handy in situations in which query text is not known beforehand, but logical processing is. For example, the following procedure will be passed
the text of a query, and it will open a REF cursor for it. It will then send the REF cursor off to another procedure to fetch from (and eventually close).

```
CREATE OR REPLACE PROCEDURE order_cancel ( p_sql  VARCHAR2 ) IS
  v_curs SYS_REFCURSOR;
BEGIN
  IF v_curs%ISOPEN THEN
    CLOSE v_curs;
  END IF;
  BEGIN
```

```
      OPEN v_curs FOR p_sql;
    EXCEPTION
      WHEN OTHERS THEN
        RAISE_APPLICATION_ERROR(-20000,'Unable to open cursor');
    END;
    order_cancel_details(v_curs);
    CLOSE v_curs;
  END;
```

The order_cancel function could then be executed like this:

```
BEGIN
  order_cancel('SELECT order_number FROM orders
               WHERE due_date <= TRUNC(SYSDATE)');
END;
```

Cursor Parameters

As the examples in the previous section suggest, it is possible to pass cursors as parameters using straight SQL. This can also be done in a SELECT statement using the CURSOR keyword.

```
SELECT count_valid(CURSOR(SELECT order_number
                           FROM orders
                           WHERE processed IS NULL))
    FROM dual;
```

The count_valid function might look something like this:

```
CREATE OR REPLACE FUNCTION count_valid( p_curs SYS_REFCURSOR )
                RETURN NUMBER IS
  v_on NUMBER;
  v_ret_val NUMBER := 0;
BEGIN
  FETCH p_curs INTO v_on;
  LOOP
    EXIT WHEN p_curs%NOTFOUND;
    IF extensive_validation(v_on) THEN
      v_ret_val := v_ret_val + 1;
    END IF;
    FETCH p_curs INTO v_on;
  END LOOP;
  RETURN(v_ret_val);
END;
```

The SELECT statement is passed right into the function that then loops through the records it returns, validating them and then returning a count of those deemed valid. This results in two cursors in the shared pool and the soft-closed list for the user.

```
SQL_TEXT
-------------------------------------------
SELECT "A2"."ORDER_NUMBER" "ORDER_NUMBER
" FROM "ORDERS" "A2" WHERE "A2"."PROCESS
ED" IS NULL
```

```
SELECT count_valid(CURSOR(SELECT order_n
umber                              FROM o
rders                             WHERE p
rocessed IS NULL))    FROM dual
```

Cursor Expressions

Cursor expressions are essentially nested cursors. When I refer to a "cursor expression," I am not talking about nested subqueries that determine a result set; instead, I am talking about nested queries that return nested result sets. Let me explain with an example.

```
SELECT order_number,
       CURSOR ( SELECT order_line_amt
                  FROM order_lines ol
                 WHERE ol.order_number = orders.order_number )
   FROM orders;
```

This query returns a list of orders plus a cursor to find the lines of that order later. Here's how it might be used in a PL/SQL procedure:

```
/* File on web: nested_cursor.sql */
CREATE OR REPLACE PROCEDURE nested AS

   -- cursor to get orders plus a nested cursor
   -- to its line amounts
   CURSOR curs_orders IS
   SELECT order_number,
          CURSOR ( SELECT order_line_amt
                     FROM order_lines ol
                    WHERE ol.order_number = orders.order_number )
      FROM orders;
   lines_curs SYS_REFCURSOR;  -- for order lines
   v_order_id NUMBER;

   -- local variables for bulk fetch of lines
   TYPE v_number_t IS TABLE OF NUMBER;
   v_line_amt  v_number_t;

BEGIN

   OPEN curs_orders;
   FETCH curs_orders INTO v_order_id, lines_curs;

   -- for every order...
   LOOP
     EXIT WHEN curs_orders%NOTFOUND;

     -- only process even numbered orders
     IF MOD(v_order_id,2) = 0 THEN

        -- get all lines for the order at once
        FETCH lines_curs BULK COLLECT INTO v_line_amt;
```

```
      -- loop through the order lines
    IF NVL(v_line_amt.COUNT,0) > 0 THEN
      FOR counter IN v_line_amt.FIRST..v_line_amt.LAST LOOP
        process_lines;
      END LOOP;
    END IF;

  END IF;  -- only even numbered orders

  FETCH curs_orders INTO v_order_id, lines_curs;
  END LOOP;  -- every order

  CLOSE curs_orders;

END;
```

Cursor expressions have slightly esoteric syntax, but they offer some advantages. The main advantage is they provide a direct link between logical and physical processing for both the Oracle optimizer and the code itself. The optimizer benefits from being explicitly informed of the physical link between the two tables (ORDERS and ORDER_LINES), so it can make better decisions when it is eventually asked to get order lines. The code itself limits physical work by logically deciding whether or not to even get certain order lines. This avoids querying records only to ignore them later.

What's even more interesting is what is loaded into the SGA after executing the nested procedure against 1,000 orders.

SQL_TEXT	PARSE_CALLS	EXECUTIONS
SELECT ORDER_NUMBER, CURSOR (SELECT ORDER_LINE_AMT FROM ORDER_LINES WHERE ORDER_NUMBER = ORDERS.ORDER_NUMBER) FROM ORDERS	1	1
SELECT "A2"."ORDER_LINE_AMT" "ORDER_LINE_AMT" FROM "ORDER_LINES" "A2" WHERE "A2"."ORDER_NUMBER"=:CV1$	500	500

Notice that the right side of the nested query's WHERE clause was changed to a cursor bind variable. That's how it is linked back to the main cursor. Also notice that the parse and execution counts are at 500 for the second cursor—that's because it executed only the absolutely required 500 times. More importantly, the underlying data was accessed only 500 times.

After the procedure has been run, the only cursor left open for the session is the main one. However, there are actually many more open during execution. You can expose this fact by adding a sleep of 10 seconds to the code and checking V$OPEN_CURSORS while the sleep occurs.

```
SQL_TEXT
------------------------------
SELECT ORDER_NUMBER, CURSOR (
SELECT ORDER_LINE_AMT FROM ORD
ER_LINES WHERE ORDER_NUMBER =
ORDERS.ORDER_NUMBER ) FROM ORD
ERS

SELECT "A2"."ORDER_LINE_AMT" "
ORDER_LINE_AMT" FROM "ORDER_LI
NES" "A2" WHERE "A2"."ORDER_NU
MBER"=:CV1$
```

It turns out that 500 of the second cursor will actually be listed as being open before the procedure finishes and closes them (because they have gone out of scope). All 500 of the nested cursors will make use of the already compiled version in the SGA, as you can see by the cursors' ever-increasing parse and execution counts after six runs of the nested procedure.

```
SQL_TEXT                            PARSE_CALLS EXECUTIONS
------------------------------      ----------- ----------
SELECT "A2"."ORDER_LINE_AMT" "         3000        3000
ORDER_LINE_AMT" FROM "ORDER_LI
NES" "A2" WHERE :CV1$=:CV1$
```

As written, however, all 500 will not take advantage of soft-closed cursors. As a matter of fact, they bring me unnecessarily close to my session's maximum OPEN_CURSORS limit. Thus, it's best in such cases to explicitly close the nested cursor when you are finished with it. (This may not be obvious because the nested cursor does not have an explicit open to associate with.) Here is the changed section of code:

```
-- process only even numbered orders
IF MOD(v_order_id,2) = 0 THEN

  -- implcitly opened
  FETCH lines_curs BULK COLLECT INTO v_line_amt;

    IF NVL(v_line_amt.COUNT,0) > 0 THEN
      FOR counter IN v_line_amt.FIRST..v_line_amt.LAST LOOP
        Process_lines;
    END LOOP;

END IF;  -- only even numbered orders

-- close the nested cursor
CLOSE lines_curs;

END IF;
```

At this point, I'm sure you are wondering if the example I'm using would not be better written as a single cursor—perhaps something like this:

```
SELECT o.order_number,
       order_line_amt
```

```
        FROM orders      o,
              order_lines ol
      WHERE ol.order_number = o.order_number;
```

Then I could check to see whether the order number is evenly divisible by two in the PL/SQL code. The difference between these two approaches is the number of rows processed during the query. The nested cursor approach shows these values:

```
SQL_TEXT                            ROWS_PROCESSED
------------------------------- --------------
SELECT ORDER_NUMBER, CURSOR (            1000
SELECT ORDER_LINE_AMT FROM ORD
ER_LINES OL WHERE OL.ORDER_NUM
BER = ORDERS.ORDER_NUMBER ) FR
OM ORDERS

SELECT "A2"."ORDER_LINE_AMT" "            5000
ORDER_LINE_AMT" FROM "ORDER_LI
NES" "A2" WHERE "A2"."ORDER_NU
MBER"=:CV1$
```

On the other hand, the single cursor approach shows these numbers:

```
SQL_TEXT                            ROWS_PROCESSED
------------------------------- --------------
SELECT O.ORDER_NUMBER, ORDER_L           10000
INE_AMT FROM ORDERS O, ORDER_L
INES OL WHERE OL.ORDER_NUMBER
= O.ORDER_NUMBER
```

Four thousand fewer rows had to be processed by Oracle to build the results set(s). That may seem like a small number, but in a busy system, that is 4,000 fewer records for which Oracle has to keep a read-consistent copy for the duration of the query.

Another option would be to add "MOD(order_number,2) = 0" directly to the query, and that is perfectly viable syntactically. However, the Oracle optimizer may choose a query plan geared to returning all of the order lines and then weed out the odd ones in memory. Of course, you could use a function-based index to work around that, but there is overhead there, as well.

Changing it to a single query negates the further benefit of bulk fetching the order lines, as well.

 Oracle does not maintain read-committed result sets across nested cursors. Result sets are maintained only between the implicit open and the subsequent close of the nested cursor. The main cursor, however, still experiences full read-committed consistency.

Another equally viable alternative would be two cursors, one to get the orders and one to get the lines. However the optimizer is then forced to treat them as two separate cursors because it has not been told of the link.

Conclusion

This chapter has covered the interaction of cursors and PL/SQL from two different angles. The first is integral to the daily work of database administration: mechanics like cursor reuse, cursor parsing, and the often-overlooked cursor soft-parsing are required knowledge for all DBAs because they underlie virtually every Oracle application. The second is more oriented to application development; while not necessarily everyday usage for DBAs, topics like bulk fetching and REF cursors are also important for you to understand. Your job entails not only monitoring and diagnosing database problems, but also recommending development alternatives that may get your database performance back on track.

CHAPTER 3

Table Functions

A *table function* is a function that can be used as a data source for a query. For example, you can include a table function in the FROM clause of a SELECT statement in a PL/SQL program. Even more exciting is the fact that a table function can return records. (In fact, it returns a collection of objects.) These two behaviors alone make table functions very useful in situations where complex processing needs to be hidden behind a single SELECT statement, such as in reports and API components. Add to these features the ability to pipeline and parallelize table functions and you have a very powerful tool for transformative processes like Data Warehouse Extraction, Transformation, Loading (ETL).

It's clear that table functions provide benefits to report developers and Data Warehouse techies, but you may be wondering why DBAs should care about them. The short answer is that you need to know about them because others in your organization might not. Many developers aren't even aware that table functions exist, let alone how they can help in building better and faster applications—and that's where DBAs come in. Consider a developer whose report query has become increasingly complex as requirements have changed, until performance is now unacceptable. He may have tried every combination of subquery and outer join, all to no avail. The processing is obviously much too complex to expect a single SELECT statement to handle it, but the report interface dictates that it needs it to remain a single statement. In such situations, DBAs are often right there in the trenches, trying to help developers by running explain plans and partitioning and repartitioning tables in the hope of making things faster. You may have reached your collective wits' end and wish there were some way of mimicking Oracle's own query mechanisms so that you could assemble result sets yourself. With table functions, you can!

This chapter describes how table functions work and how you can take advantage of them in your environment. It also describes how table functions interact with cursors and how you can pipeline, nest, and parallelize these functions for even greater performance. Finally, the chapter discusses the use of table functions in a variety of real applications.

Why Table Functions?

Let's start with a simple example of what table functions look like and what they can do for you.

A Simple Example

Earlier, I mentioned the idea of querying a table function with a SELECT statement. Here is an example.

```
SELECT *
  FROM TABLE(company_balance_sheet);
```

At first glance, this might look like just another query, but note that company_balance_sheet is a function. Let's suppose here that it is a function that can peruse millions of lengthy accounting records from potential acquisitions to see how they would affect a parent company's bottom line. The large amount of data and stringent accounting rules may seem best suited to a program all their own, but what if the results must be available via a simple query from a web page? Table functions to the rescue...

Here is an example of a table function embedded in PL/SQL. Notice that here it is used just like any other cursor. However, this function might be scanning mountains of detailed sales transactions to summarize them in real time by region to enable managers to make decisions toward make-or-break sales quotas.

```
DECLARE
  CURSOR curs_get_western_sales IS
  SELECT *
    FROM TABLE(total_sales_by_region)
   WHERE region = 'Western';
  v_western_sales NUMBER;
BEGIN
  OPEN curs_get_western_sales;
  FETCH curs_western_sales INTO v_western_sales;
  CLOSE curs_get_western_sales;
END;
```

This example shows how a table function can accept parameters that may be used to control business processing. In the next example, the function examines reams of intricate test samples looking for anomalies before presenting results that must be accurate for real-time grant requests aimed at funding important cancer research:

```
SELECT *
  FROM TABLE(cancer_research_results( sdate => SYSDATE, edate => SYSDATE + 1 );
```

On a much less grand scale (but just as important to your own business), you might use a table function in a query that needs to apply complex logic to find all unscheduled work orders within three seconds so the calling application won't time out. Or you might use a table function to prevent a simple .NET query screen—one that needs to display all available backup equipment—from being seen as unreliable because it takes too long to work through a formula to find replacement parts for a broken water main.

In the world of data transformation processing, table functions allow results from nested transformations to be sent downstream for further work, one by one. There are many situations in which a long transformation is essentially waiting on itself, because the full result set from an initial transformation must be assembled before further transformations can even start—even though they could logically begin as soon as the first record is available. You can use table functions in a mode known as *pipelining* to handle this situation, and you can use *parallelized table functions* to throw even more power at a transformation.

You're still not sure that table functions make the DBA's life easier? Well, consider the fact that table functions allow you to embed actual business logic into a query to ensure that it does only what it absolutely has to. For example, instead of worrying about rollback segment space for frequent long-running queries, you could cache the results in memory, knowing that the underlying data set changes only hourly. You can also implement performance features like bulk fetching and use of associative arrays (formerly known as index-by tables) within table functions to reduce overall stress on a database.

We'll look at these and other examples in this chapter. First, we'll cover some basics.

Calling a Table Function

Most DBAs know that Oracle allows functions to be called in queries like the following:

```
SELECT SYSDATE
  FROM DUAL;
```

Oracle permits this type of query because the structure of its return set is defined: it will return a single column of type DATE in a single record.

Most DBAs also know that for any object (e.g., a table, a view, or another type of object) to be part of a SELECT statement, it must have a defined result set structure. Otherwise, the database will have no idea in what format the results will be returned. But you may be wondering how functions that have historically returned single scalar values can possibly return a multi-column, multi-record result set like this:

```
SQL> SELECT order_number,
  2         creation_date,
  3         assigned_date,
  4         closed_date
  5    FROM TABLE(order_history_function(region_id => 22))
  6   WHERE region = 11;
```

```
ORDER_NUMBER CREATION_DATE ASSIGNED_DATE CLOSED_DATE
------------ ------------- ------------- -----------
       10987    10-JAN-05     11-JAN-05   22-JAN-05
       10989    12-JAN-05     15-JAN-05   20-JAN-05
       10993    20-JAN-05     21-JAN-05   28-JAN-05
```

Defining the Result Set Structure

PL/SQL is pretty smart about resolving the result set of a table or a view. The language makes it easy for us not to worry about datatypes by substituting %TYPE and %ROWTYPE variables as follows.

```
DECLARE
  v_order_row orders%ROWTYPE;
BEGIN
  SELECT order_id,
         region_id
    INTO v_order_row
    FROM orders;
END;
```

However, PL/SQL will be at a loss to decipher the structure returned by a table function because it has no basis from which to work. You must provide that basis explicitly via Oracle objects and collections. This is illustrated in this example of declaring an object and then a collection of that object.

```
CREATE TYPE rowset_o AS OBJECT ( col1 NUMBER,
                                 col2 VARCHAR2(30));
/
CREATE TYPE rowset_t AS TABLE OF rowset_o;
/
```

The "multi-recordness" of the collection is what allows it to be used as the result set of a function.

```
CREATE OR REPLACE FUNCTION simple RETURN rowset_t AS
  v_rowset rowset_t := rowset_t();
BEGIN
  v_rowset.EXTEND(3);
  v_rowset(1) := rowset_o(1,'Value 1');
  v_rowset(2) := rowset_o(2,'Value 2');
  v_rowset(3) := rowset_o(3,'Value 3');
  RETURN(v_rowset);
END;
```

All the function does is assemble three objects into a collection and return them. Now the function can be called from a SELECT statement using the TABLE keyword to tell Oracle to treat the returned collection as if it were a set of records.

```
SQL> SELECT *
  2    FROM TABLE(simple);

      COL1 COL2
---------- ----------------
         1 Value 1
```

```
     2 Value 2
     3 Value 3

 3 rows selected.
```

The full power of Oracle SQL can be applied to the result set returned by a PL/SQL table function, just as if a table or a view had been queried.

```
SQL> SELECT *
  2    FROM TABLE(simple)
  3   WHERE col1 = 2;

      COL1 COL2
---------- --------------
         2 Value 2

SQL> SELECT col2
  2    FROM TABLE(SIMPLE)
  3   GROUP BY col2;

COL2
------------------------
Value 1
Value 2
Value 3
```

A table function can perform any work that could be performed in a standard function, including queries and conditional logic.

The topic of table functions is a very large one, so, in this chapter, I won't be able to explore in detail every possible application of table functions. All of the applications I've mentioned, however, share a common requirement: they take advantage of the temporary and fast storage of data (in a collection). For example, consider the cancer research application we mentioned earlier. Each research experiment record needs to be evaluated for completeness before being considered for inclusion in the final result set, and every individual experiment has to be evaluated for completeness before any subsequent processing can occur. If 1,000 experiments have to be looked at, and each takes 2 seconds to evaluate for completeness, it will be more than half an hour (2,000 seconds) before any upstream processing can occur. This application would be far more efficient if each experiment could be passed upstream for subsequent processing as soon as it passed evaluation. Table functions make this possible, as I describe in the next section.

Cursors, Pipelining, and Nesting

So far, table functions may strike you as a performance booster that might help you out occasionally when you're in a tight spot. The features described in this section, however—the use of cursors, pipelining, and nesting with table functions—are powerful enough that they might persuade you to actually tailor your code to make use of them.

Cursors

The omnipresent cursor makes an appearance in table functions as both a parameter datatype and a SQL function to allow SELECT statements to be passed right into a table function to be processed.

Pipelining

This feature allows a table function to send its results back one by one, rather than having to assemble a full result set. The effect is to allow downstream processing to begin much faster. Going back to the cancer research example I mentioned earlier, what if the function had to parse 100 results that each took three seconds? That means that any downstream processing would have to wait five minutes before it could begin. With pipelined functions, the downstream work would begin after only three seconds.

Nesting

Table functions can be nested to perform multiple tasks on data. This is especially powerful for Data Warehouse ETL work.

I think the best way to demonstrate all of these capabilities is with an example from a Data Warehouse ETL process that extracts information about work orders. The specific function I'll show extracts components of the creation, assignment, and close date of the orders. These components are then passed on for further processing in the ETL.

Cursors

We looked carefully at cursors in Chapter 2, and here they are again! How do cursors and table functions interact? Let's start by looking at a non-pipelined version of a table function.

```
/* File on web: date_parser.sql */
CREATE OR REPLACE FUNCTION date_parse ( p_curs SYS_REFCURSOR )
                RETURN order_date_t AS

  v_order_rec orders%ROWTYPE;
  v_ret_val   order_date_t := order_date_t( );

BEGIN

  -- for every order in the cursor...
  LOOP
    FETCH p_curs INTO v_order_rec;
    EXIT WHEN p_curs%NOTFOUND;

    -- extend the array by 3 and populate with cmoponents of the
    -- orders creation, assignment and close date
    v_ret_val.EXTEND(3);
    v_ret_val(v_ret_val.LAST - 2) := order_date_o(v_order_rec.order_number,
                                       '0',
                              TO_CHAR(v_order_rec.create_date,'YYYY'),
                              TO_CHAR(v_order_rec.create_date,'Q'),
```

```
                                TO_CHAR(v_order_rec.create_date,'MM'));
        v_ret_val(v_ret_val.LAST - 1) := order_date_o(v_order_rec.order_number,
                                          'A',
                                TO_CHAR(v_order_rec.assign_date,'YYYY'),
                                TO_CHAR(v_order_rec.assign_date,'Q'),
                                TO_CHAR(v_order_rec.assign_date,'MM'));
        v_ret_val(v_ret_val.LAST) := order_date_o(v_order_rec.order_number,
                                        'C',
                                TO_CHAR(v_order_rec.close_date,'YYYY'),
                                TO_CHAR(v_order_rec.close_date,'Q'),
                                TO_CHAR(v_order_rec.close_date,'MM'));
        END LOOP;  -- every order in ths cursor

        RETURN(v_ret_val);

    END;
```

And here are the results when three orders are queried.

ORDER_NUMBER	D	YEAR	QUARTER	MONTH
1	0	2005	3	8
1	A	2005	3	8
1	C	2005	3	8
2	0	2005	4	10
2	A	2005	4	10
2	C	2005	4	10
3	0	2005	4	12
3	A	2005	4	12
3	C	2005	4	12

You'll notice that I said three orders were queried, but I was careful not to say where they were queried from. The answer is that they are queried from the cursor passed to the function as shown here.

```
SELECT *
  FROM TABLE(date_parse(CURSOR(SELECT *
                                 FROM orders)));
```

The TABLE keyword indicates the call to the date_parse function. The CURSOR keyword indicates that the text that follows (in parentheses) is to be used as the cursor in the table function. It is implicitly opened, and the function fetches records from it. It is implicitly closed when the table function goes out of scope. The ability to pass cursor text to the function is extremely powerful because all it requires is valid SQL. It can be called (and hence reused) in many places. For example, if I want to process only today's orders, I would call it like this:

```
SELECT *
  FROM TABLE(date_parse(CURSOR(SELECT *
                                 FROM orders
                                WHERE create > TRUNC(SYSDATE)))));
```

If I want to further restrict it to orders from a specific region, I would add that restriction to the SELECT statement as follows:

```
SELECT *
  FROM TABLE(date_parse(CURSOR(SELECT *
                                 FROM orders
                                WHERE create > TRUNC(SYSDATE)
                                  AND region_id = 33)));
```

The only restriction on the SELECT statement here is it has to select every column from the ORDERS table because within the table function, the record variable it selects into is declared as such (orders%ROWTYPE). You don't always have to be this restrictive, however, and there are plenty of options for matching up SELECT statements, cursor parameter types, and local variables. I'll discuss those options later in this chapter.

Pipelined Table Functions

A pipelined table function is one that returns a result set as a collection, but it does so iteratively. In other words, Oracle does not wait for the function to run to completion, storing all the rows it computes in the PL/SQL collection before returning it. Instead, as each row is ready to be assigned to the collection, it is "piped out" of the function. Let's see a pipelined table function in action.

```
/* File on web: date_parser_pipelined.sql */
CREATE OR REPLACE FUNCTION date_parse ( p_curs SYS_REFCURSOR )
                 RETURN order_date_t
                 PIPELINED AS

  v_order_rec orders%ROWTYPE;

BEGIN

  -- for every order in the cursor...
  LOOP
    FETCH p_curs INTO v_order_rec;
    EXIT WHEN p_curs%NOTFOUND;

    -- pipe out the components of the orders open data
    PIPE ROW(order_date_o(v_order_rec.order_number,
                          'O',
                          TO_CHAR(v_order_rec.create_date,'YYYY'),
                          TO_CHAR(v_order_rec.create_date,'Q'),
                          TO_CHAR(v_order_rec.create_date,'MM')));

    -- pipe out the components of the orders assign date
    PIPE ROW(order_date_o(v_order_rec.order_number,
                          'A',
                          TO_CHAR(v_order_rec.assign_date,'YYYY'),
                          TO_CHAR(v_order_rec.assign_date,'Q'),
                          TO_CHAR(v_order_rec.assign_date,'MM')));
```

```
        -- pipe out the components of the orders close date
     PIPE ROW(order_date_o(v_order_rec.order_number,
                           'C',
                           TO_CHAR(v_order_rec.close_date,'YYYY'),
                           TO_CHAR(v_order_rec.close_date,'Q'),
                           TO_CHAR(v_order_rec.close_date,'MM')));

   END LOOP;  -- every order in the cursor

   RETURN;

 END;
```

There are four main syntax changes between the non-pipelined version and the pipelined version:

- The PIPELINED keyword is added to the function's header to tell Oracle to pipe results back as requested, rather than assembling a full result set and returning it.
- The PIPE ROW command indicates the point at which the function sends back a single result.
- The poor lonely RETURN keyword is left with nothing to do but...return. All of the results will already have been piped back via the PIPE ROW command.
- The datatype returned (order_date_o) differs from the return datatype declared for the function (order_date_t). Though syntactically different, they must be related, as discussed in the next paragraph.

Oracle won't allow just any old datatype to be piped back from any old table function. The collection specified as the return type of the function must be *of* the object type. The two datatypes declared for my example were declared like this:

```
CREATE OR REPLACE TYPE order_date_o AS OBJECT ( order_number NUMBER,
                                                date_type    VARCHAR2(1),
                                                year         NUMBER,
                                                quarter      NUMBER,
                                                month        NUMBER );
/
CREATE TYPE order_date_t AS TABLE OF order_date_o;
/
```

To demonstrate how much pipelining helps in this situation, I'll beef up the number of orders to 10,000 and run the following query against both the non-pipelined and the pipelined versions of the function.

```
SELECT *
  FROM TABLE(date_parse(CURSOR(SELECT *
                                 FROM orders)))
 WHERE ROWNUM <= 10;
```

This query is perfect for this situation because it will show exactly how long the function took to send back its 10th result. And the winner is...

- In second place with a respectable time of 2.73 seconds is the non-pipelined version.
- In first place with an astounding duration of 0.07 seconds is the pipelined version.

The pipelined version runs 2.66 seconds or almost 93% faster. More fulfilling from a DBA point of view is that behind the scenes the database had to spend 93% less time maintaining a read-consistent copy of the ORDERS table to satisfy the query, and there is 93% less chance of requiring excess physical reads because the query ran so long. I could go on and on.

Even more pleasing from a DBA point of view is the reduction in the amount of Oracle session memory required to execute the pipelined version. For the sake of simplicity here, I'll restrict the concept of session memory to the User Global Area (UGA) and the Process Global Area (PGA). Table 3-1 shows a comparison between the UGA and the PGA required to execute both versions of the function. These stats were gathered after signing onto the database and executing the pipelined and non-pipelined functions once each.

Table 3-1. Pipelined versus non-pipelined Oracle session memory

	Non-pipelined	Pipelined	Difference
UGA maximum	7,105,168	90,284	7,014,884
PGA maximum	12,815,736	242,708	12,573,028

That's a 98% reduction in both session UGA and session PGA—the database has less to keep track of, so it can spend more time being fast.

Nested Table Functions

The *nesting* of table functions refers to the execution of several table functions in a nested manner: the results of one are sent to the next for further processing, and those results are sent on to the next, and so on. This process is sometimes known as *daisy-chaining*. Combined with pipelining, the nesting of table functions provides a particularly powerful technique for ETL processing.

I'll demonstrate by coding a function that accepts the results of my date_parse table function via a cursor and performs an operation on them. To avoid the clutter of explaining a complex ETL transformation, we'll stick to a simple one by adding up the order_number, year, quarter, and month values queried. Here's the function.

```
/* File on web: next_in_line.sql */
CREATE OR REPLACE FUNCTION next_in_line ( p_curs SYS_REFCURSOR )
             RETURN next_t
             PIPELINED IS

  v_ret_val next_t := next_t();

  -- local variables for cursor results
```

```
            v_on NUMBER;
            v_dt VARCHAR2(1);
            v_yr NUMBER;
            v_qt NUMBER;
            v_mt NUMBER;

        BEGIN

            -- for all date components from the cursor...
            LOOP

                FETCH p_curs INTO v_on, v_dt, v_yr, v_qt, v_mt;
                EXIT WHEN p_curs%NOTFOUND;
                -- pipe out the sum of the components
                PIPE ROW(next_o(v_on + v_yr + v_qt + v_mt));

            END LOOP;  -- every date component

            RETURN;

        END;
```

We've already covered most of the syntax in this example. Only the syntax used to nest the two functions together in a query is new:

```
SELECT *
  FROM TABLE(next_in_line
              (CURSOR
                (SELECT *
                  FROM TABLE(date_parse
                              (CURSOR
                                (SELECT *
                                  FROM orders))))));
```

With my nifty indentation, it even looks nested with the embedded TABLE and CURSOR keywords. Simply put, what this example does is start the date_parse function, which pipes results to the next_in_line function, which pipes them to the world.

Parallelizing Table Functions

Moving functions into the paradigm of SELECT statements allows them to take advantage of another powerful facet of Oracle—parallel query processing.

Oracle has long provided parallelism as a way to conquer large queries by splitting processing among multiple Parallel Query (PQ) servers, using each to calculate a portion of the results, then assembling a final result set at the end. Behind the scenes, Oracle decides how to distribute the work across the available PQ servers to get the best results. The DBA can influence Oracle's decision somewhat by setting degrees of parallelism for tables or implementing specific partitioning schemes, but, in the end, the database decides how best to execute the query.

Taking Advantage of Parallel Query

Parallelization helps all types of queries, whether or not they use table functions. Queries that do not use table functions take advantage of the extra throughput of PQ to assemble their final result set faster. Queries that do use table functions also benefit from the added throughput of PQ servers, but they take things a step further by assembling results sets along the way.

Let's illustrate using the following table, which holds one record for every single transaction at a large bank:

```
SQL> DESC acct_transactions
 Name                                    Null?    Type
 --------------------------------------- -------- ------------
 AREA                                             VARCHAR2(10)
 TRX_DATE                                         DATE
 TRX_AMT                                          NUMBER
```

Suppose that I want to build a function to summarize the transactions by area. The first thing I considered implementing here was a query grouped by area. But that is negated by the need for a series of complex validation processes; for the sake of demonstration, I've hidden those in the function named super_complex_validation in the following examples.

Here are the results I'm looking for based on a demonstration data set, assuming that all transactions pass the complex validation.

```
SQL> SELECT area,
  2         SUM(trx_amt)
  3    FROM acct_transactions
  4   GROUP BY area;

AREA       SUM(TRX_AMT)
---------- ------------
1                   460
10                  550
2                   470
3                   480
4                   490
5                   500
6                   510
7                   520
8                   530
9                   540
```

To achieve this result faster with a large number of records, I decide to use parallel processing. With table functions, this means that Oracle will run multiple instances of the table function in parallel and distribute results from the passed-in REF cursor among them, as shown in Figure 3-1.

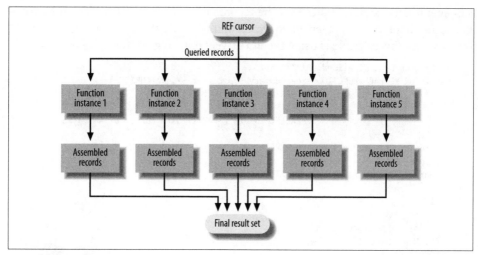

Figure 3-1. Parallel table function

Distributing Records

One really cool thing about parallel table functions is that you can tell Oracle how to distribute records among the parallel function instances. Two different aspects of distribution can be specified. The first is *partitioning*—how Oracle should decide which records to send to which function instance. The second is *streaming*—how each function instance should order the records partitioned to it. The options for each are shown below.

Partitioning
> Records can be partitioned based on ranges of one or more columns, hash values based on one or more columns, or simply as Oracle sees fit. The PARTITION BY clause specifies the specific partitioning option for the table function, as shown in the following examples.

Streaming
> Records can be ordered or clustered by specific columns. The ORDER or CLUSTER keyword specifies the specific streaming option for the table function, as shown in the following examples.

I'll explain each of these components and how they interact while working through development of my account transaction summary function.

Random partitioning (PARTITION BY ANY)

First, I'll set up the function and tell Oracle to run it in parallel, but simply partition the records as it sees fit. The PARALLEL_ENABLE clause in the function header tells Oracle that this function has been coded with parallelism in mind and that it would really like to take advantage of this feature. The PARTITION BY ANY parameter supplied in this example states that the records returned by the REF cursor be partitioned randomly, in whatever order Oracle wants across the available PQ servers. In other words, this example is using the PQ servers only to gain throughput.

```
/* File on web: pipelined.sql */
CREATE OR REPLACE FUNCTION area_summary ( p_cursor SYS_REFCURSOR )
                          RETURN area_summary_t
                          PIPELINED
                          PARALLEL_ENABLE ( PARTITION p_cursor BY ANY ) AS

  v_row    acct_transactions%ROWTYPE;
  v_total NUMBER := NULL;
  v_area  acct_transactions.area%TYPE;

BEGIN

  -- for every transaction
  FETCH p_cursor INTO v_row;
  LOOP
    EXIT WHEN p_cursor%NOTFOUND;

    -- if we pass the extensive validation check
    IF super_complex_validation(v_row.trx_date,v_row.trx_amt) THEN

       -- set initial total or add to current area total
       -- or return an area total as required
       IF v_total IS NULL THEN
         v_total := v_row.trx_amt;
         v_area := v_row.area;
       ELSIF v_row.area = v_area THEN
            v_total := v_total + v_row.trx_amt;
       ELSE
         PIPE ROW(area_summary_o(v_area,v_total));
         v_total := v_row.trx_amt;
         v_area := v_row.area;
       END IF;

    END IF;  -- extensive validation

    FETCH p_cursor INTO v_row;

  END LOOP; -- every transaction

  PIPE ROW(area_summary_o(v_area,v_total));

END;
```

The function is executed using a SELECT statement with a SELECT statement as a parameter. I still get a kick out of saying that!

```
SELECT *
  FROM TABLE(area_summary(CURSOR(SELECT *
                                  FROM acct_transactions)));
```

The results will be random and unpredictable because the function relies on receiving records ordered by area, but Oracle has been left on its own to decide how to actually disperse the records. Thus, specifying PARTITION BY ANY will not help my function. (I do, however, get the incorrect results really fast!)

Range partitioning (PARTITION BY RANGE)

To take best advantage of parallel processing, I need to tell Oracle that all records for any particular area must be sent to the same function instance. For example, if three parallel function instances are run, then all records for area 7 must go to instance 1, 2, or 3. This method is specified using the RANGE clause, as shown in the new function header here:

```
CREATE OR REPLACE FUNCTION area_summary ( p_cursor ref_cursors.acct_trx_curs )
                    RETURN area_summary_t
                    PIPELINED
                    PARALLEL_ENABLE ( PARTITION p_cursor BY RANGE(area) ) AS
```

Notice that the passed REF cursor has been changed to a strongly typed version. That is, if Oracle is to correctly partition records, it has to know what their structure is beforehand. My ref_cursors package contains a single line of code:

```
PACKAGE ref_cursors IS
   TYPE acct_trx_curs IS REF CURSOR RETURN acct_transactions%ROWTYPE;
END;
```

Now, the results should be better.

```
SQL> SELECT *
  2    FROM TABLE(area_summary(CURSOR(SELECT *
  3                                     FROM acct_transactions)));
```

AREA	AMT
6	96
7	97
8	98
9	99
6	414
7	423
8	432
9	441
1	369
10	450
2	378
3	387
4	396
5	405
1	91
2	92
3	93
4	94
5	95

```
    10                100

20 rows selected.
```

Order streaming (ORDER)

That's still not quite what I'm looking for. The problem is that even though records are being partitioned across function instances by area, they aren't being ordered within each function instance. For example, the records for area 6 all went to the same function instance, but another area was mingled in, which caused redundant, incomplete summaries for area 6. I need to advise Oracle that entries must be ordered by area within each function instance, as well. That's done using the ORDER clause shown below.

```
CREATE OR REPLACE FUNCTION area_summary ( p_cursor ref_cursors.acct_trx_curs )
                    RETURN area_summary_t
                    PIPELINED
                    PARALLEL_ENABLE ( PARTITION p_cursor BY RANGE(area) )
                    ORDER p_cursor BY (area) AS
```

Now let's see what I get.

```
SQL> SELECT *
  2    FROM TABLE(area_summary(CURSOR(SELECT *
  3                                     FROM acct_transactions)));

AREA             AMT
---------- ----------
1                460
10               550
2                470
3                480
4                490
5                500
6                510
7                520
8                530
9                540

10 rows selected.
```

Success! The totals are now correct because the records returned by the cursor were partitioned across multiple parallel function instances by area *and* ordered by area within them, as shown in Figure 3-2.

Hash partitioning (PARTITION BY HASH)

The preceding examples demonstrated random (ANY) partitioning and range partitioning. If you select the third partitioning option, known as *hash partitioning*, a hash value is calculated based on specified columns, and that value determines the function instance to which a record should be sent. Duplicate values will produce the same hash, so it's safe to assume that record distribution will work for my account

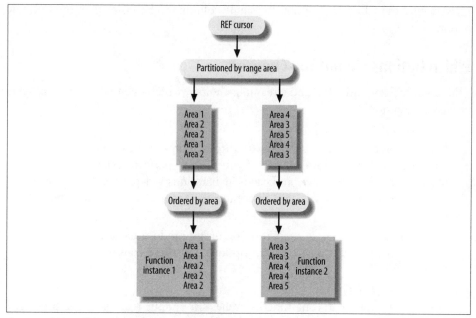

Figure 3-2. Parallel table function partitioned and ordered by area

transaction summary function. As a matter of fact, the PARTITION BY HASH option is usually a little bit faster than the PARTITION BY RANGE option.

Here's the syntax:

```
CREATE OR REPLACE FUNCTION area_summary ( p_cursor ref_cursors.acct_trx_curs )
                          RETURN area_summary_t
                          PIPELINED
                          PARALLEL_ENABLE ( PARTITION p_cursor BY HASH(area) )
                          ORDER p_cursor BY (area) AS
```

Cluster streaming (CLUSTER)

In an earlier version of my summary function, I specified the ORDER clause because that function relies on records being ordered by area within each function instance. Another option, CLUSTER, guarantees that records with the same values for the specified columns will be clustered within the function instance. Note, however, that this option does not order the values.

Because my function cares only about a single column, I can easily switch to clustering. Here's the syntax for that.

```
CREATE OR REPLACE FUNCTION area_summary ( p_cursor ref_cursors.acct_trx_curs )
                          RETURN area_summary_t
                          PIPELINED
                          PARALLEL_ENABLE ( PARTITION p_cursor BY HASH(area) )
                          CLUSTER p_cursor BY (area) AS
```

I have found the CLUSTER option for single columns to be faster than the ORDER option.

Which Options Should You Choose?

With all of these partitioning and streaming choices, which one makes sense for your particular situation?

PARTITION BY ANY (random)
> Use this option if you just want extra throughput *and* the ordering of records is not important at all. For example, if you need to perform calculations on every record from the REF cursor and each calculation is independent, then this is the way to go because Oracle will distribute the records without worrying about their order.
>
> I have yet to come across a situation requiring random partitioning in conjunction with the ORDER or CLUSTER options, but these combinations are syntactically allowed.

PARTITION BY RANGE
> Specify this option if your function relies on certain records being processed together *and* the records are spread evenly among the values. This will ensure that each parallel function instance gets a similar amount of work to do.
>
> Combining this partitioning option with either ORDER BY or CLUSTER BY is valid. Note that the clustering approach will be slightly faster.

PARTITION BY HASH
> Specify this option if your function relies on certain records being processed together *and* the spread is somewhat skewed. The hash algorithm provides a better chance of each parallel function instance's getting a similar amount of work to do.
>
> Combining this partitioning option with either ORDER BY or CLUSTER BY is valid. Note that the clustering approach will be slightly faster.

What Does Oracle Do?

At this point, you might be wondering how the database partitions the query results. Does Oracle execute one query per parallel function instance or does it execute a single query and partition its results? Let's find out by looking in the shared pool.

```
SQL> SELECT sql_text,
  2         parse_calls,
  3         executions
  4    FROM v$sql
  5   WHERE INSTR(UPPER(sql_text),'ACCT_TRANSACTIONS')  > 0
  6     AND INSTR(UPPER(sql_text),'SQL_TEXT') = 0
  7     AND command_type = 3;
```

```
SQL_TEXT                    PARSE_CALLS EXECUTIONS
-------------------------   ----------- ----------
SELECT *   FROM TABLE(are        1          1
a_summary(CURSOR(SELECT *
FROM acct_transactions)))

SELECT "A3"."AREA" "AREA"        1          1
,"A3"."TRX_DATE" "TRX_DAT
E","A3"."TRX_AMT" "TRX_AM
T" FROM "ACCT_TRANSACTION
S" "A3" ORDER BY "A3"."AR
EA"
```

There are only two cursors here: the one I executed and the one executed within the table function, each with a parse and execute count of 1. That means that a single cursor is used and that Oracle partitions the returned rows as requested.

Number of PQ Servers to Use

For most parallel query operations, it is possible to limit (or at least influence) the number of parallel query servers that may be used for a particular operation. For example, the degree of parallelism can be specified for a table, and Oracle will do its best to provide the specified number of PQ servers for queries of that table. It's also possible to specify the degree of parallelism (and hence the number of PQ servers used) for any particular query by specifying the appropriate optimizer hints.

Unfortunately, no such option exists for parallelized table functions.

I wish something like the following syntax were available:

```
CREATE OR REPLACE FUNCTION area_summary ( p_cursor ref_cursors.acct_trx_curs )
                RETURN area_summary_t
                PIPELINED
                PARALLEL_ENABLE ( PARTITION p_cursor BY HASH(area) )
                DEGREE 3 - invalid - DRH dream syntax
                ORDER p_cursor BY (area) AS...
```

That way, I could define the maximum number of PQ servers allocated to a single execution of the table function. Despite this minor quibble, I do have to admit that Oracle does a pretty good job of determining the number of PQ servers to utilize.

Using Table Functions

In this section, I'll show the use of table functions in a real-world example based on a large cable company's attempt to track repeat orders. Simply put, a repeat order occurs when a technician is dispatched to a location more than once within a 30-day period to perform the same type of work or to repair the original work. A repeat visit doesn't always have a negative connotation—it could result from an installation occurring within 30 days of a pre-sales call.

Locations are identified by preassigned ID values. These can map to anything from a specific neighborhood cable outlet to a house or a large shopping mall. The type of work is identified using order type IDs. For example, type 1 might be "Cable Installation," and type 2 might be "Cable Upgrade."

The company is divided into several regions, each with its own set of location codes, order types, and repeat-order criteria. These criteria define sets of two order types that must occur at the same location within 30 days of each other to be considered a repeat order. The two order types may or may not be the same; for example, a "Cable Installation" followed by a subsequent "Cable Repair" might be deemed a repeat order in the same way that two "Cable Installations" would.

The criteria are held in this table:

```
SQL> DESC repeat_order_criteria
 Name                                        Null?    Type
 ------------------------------------------- -------- ------
 REGION_ID                                            NUMBER
 START_DATE                                           DATE
 FIRST_TYPE_ID                                        NUMBER
 REPEAT_TYPE_ID                                       NUMBER
```

The table holds each region's repeat-order definitions, including the date they are in effect. Here's an example record.

```
SQL> SELECT *
  2    FROM repeat_order_criteria;

REGION_ID START_DAT FIRST_TYPE_ID REPEAT_TYPE_ID
---------- --------- ------------- --------------
        1 19-APR-05            44            102
```

This record states that any order of type 44 followed by an order of type 102 at the same location in region 1 within 30 days constitutes a repeat order.

The ORDERS table contains the fields necessary to determine an order's "repeatedness."

```
SQL> DESC orders
 Name                                        Null?    Type
 ------------------------------------------- -------- ------
 ORDER_NUMBER                                NOT NULL NUMBER
 ORDER_DATE                                  NOT NULL DATE
 REGION_ID                                   NOT NULL NUMBER
 TYPE_ID                                     NOT NULL NUMBER
 LOCATION_ID                                 NOT NULL NUMBER
```

The requirement is made a little more complex by the fact that this company processes tens of thousands of orders every day, and the repeat-order criteria can change at any time, so a new result set has to be available quickly. The large number of records combined with the serialized processing of one record at a time to create the result set makes this application a perfect candidate for table functions.

The Function Header

I'll start things off by explaining the header for the function I'll write.

```
1 CREATE FUNCTION repeat_order_finder ( p_curs cursors.repeat_orders_curs )
2                 RETURN repeat_region_location_t
3                 PIPELINED
4                 PARALLEL_ENABLE ( PARTITION p_curs BY RANGE(region_id) )
5                 ORDER p_curs BY (location_id, order_date) IS
```

As far as function headers go, this one has a lot to say, so let's look at it line by line.

Line 1

States the function name and its parameter—a strongly typed REF cursor declared in another package like this:

```
CREATE OR REPLACE PACKAGE cursors AS
  TYPE repeat_orders_rec IS RECORD (order_number NUMBER,
                                    order_date   DATE,
                                    region_id    NUMBER,
                                    type_id      NUMBER,
                                    location_id  NUMBER );

  TYPE repeat_orders_curs IS REF CURSOR RETURN repeat_orders_rec;
END;
```

When the function is executed, I'll be passing it a SELECT statement getting all orders from the past 30 days.

Line 2

Explains the structure of the rows this function will return. It was created using the following SQL defining an object and a collection:

```
CREATE TYPE repeat_region_location_o AS OBJECT ( region_id      NUMBER,
                                                 location_id    NUMBER,
                                                 first_type_id  NUMBER,
                                                 repeat_type_id NUMBER );
/
CREATE TYPE repeat_region_location_t AS TABLE OF repeat_region_location_o;
/
```

Line 3

Explains that this function will pipe rows back upstream as soon as they are calculated.

Line 4

Defines the way that records from the passed-in REF cursor will be partitioned across the multiple parallel instances of this function. They are to be partitioned by values in the REGION_ID column. This means that all values for a particular region will be processed by the same function instance. It does *not* mean there will be one instance per region. Oracle will allocate available PQ servers as it sees fit to run instances of the function. This means that a single instance may process more than one region.

Line 5

States that, within each function instance, the records are to be further ordered by their LOCATION_ID and ORDER_DATE values.

Just working through the header has exposed most of the power behind the table function. This function allows me to throw the power of parallel processing at what would have been serial processing of tens of thousands of records. It even allows me to define what records go to each parallel function instance so I can make some assumptions in my code. Topping that off with not having to wait for all records to be processed before sending results upstream makes me think I've achieved nirvana!

Enough time on the pulpit! Let's get back to the function.

The Basic Loop

The main algorithm of the function is a loop that fetches records from the REF cursor as shown in this pseudo-code.

```
BEGIN

  -- for every order...
  LOOP

    FETCH p_curs INTO v_order;
    EXIT WHEN p_curs%NOTFOUND;

    IF it's a repeat order then
      PIPE ROW( );
    END IF;

  END LOOP;  -- every order

  RETURN;

END;
```

It's very straightforward. Just fetch records from the passed-in cursor and evaluate them against repeat-order criteria. If a match is found, then pipe a record upstream. Now I'll add in the loading of the regions' repeat-order criteria.

Bulk Fetching the Criteria

Because my table function guarantees that records will be grouped by region, I can safely assume that any time the region ID value of a fetched record changes, I will have moved on to the next region. And the first thing I want to do for each region is load its repeat-order criteria into a PL/SQL associative array. I'll accomplish this using a cursor as shown here.

```
CURSOR curs_get_criteria ( cp_region NUMBER ) IS
  SELECT *
```

```
          FROM repeat_order_criteria
       WHERE region_id = cp_region;
```

Then, within the function, I implement a simple "last region id" check to see when the value changes, and, if it does, I bulk load the criteria:

```
-- if it's a new region...
IF NVL(v_last_region,0) <> v_order.region_id THEN

   -- set the local region ID and bulk load
   -- its criteria
   v_last_region := v_order.region_id;
   OPEN curs_get_criteria(v_order.region_id);
   FETCH curs_get_criteria BULK COLLECT INTO v_criteria;
   CLOSE curs_get_criteria;

END IF;  -- new region
```

This exposes another benefit of table functions—the ability to implement focused data access within the function itself. This means that the database can focus on getting the orders with one query and the repeat criteria with another.

Getting back to the function, the pseudo-code looks like this now that I've added the query to get the criteria:

```
BEGIN

   -- for every order...
   LOOP

      FETCH p_curs INTO v_order;
      EXIT WHEN p_curs%NOTFOUND;

      IF first record or new region THEN
         Load region criteria
      END IF;

      IF it's a repeat order then
         PIPE ROW();
      END IF;

   END LOOP;  -- every order

   RETURN;

END;
```

Identifying Potential Repeats

Now for the slightly difficult part—finding repeat orders. I've decided to do this in two distinct operations. The first operation determines if the order is a potential outage by matching its order type and date with the first order type in a criterion. The second operation decides if the order is a genuine repeat by matching its location and order type with the repeat-order type of a potential outage.

I'll explain further with some example data. Consider the following order criterion record:

```
START_DAT FIRST_TYPE_ID REPEAT_TYPE_ID
--------- ------------- --------------
19-APR-05           801             87
```

This record states that an order on or after April 19, 2005, with an order type of 334 that is followed within 30 days by an order of type 87 at the same location is considered a repeat order.

Now consider the following three orders.

```
ORDER_NUMBER ORDER_DAT  TYPE_ID LOCATION_ID
------------ --------- ---------- ----------
        1016 19-APR-05        801        343
        1863 20-APR-05         87        343
        2228 21-APR-05         87        343
```

When processed by my function order, 1016 would become a potential repeat order for order type 801 and location 343. Any subsequent order of type 87 within 30 days at location 343 would be considered a genuine repeat order. Thus, orders 1863 and 2228 would be counted as genuine repeats by my function.

To find genuine repeat orders, I need to discover potential repeats first. For the sake of clean code, I'll implement the "potential repeats" logic as a sub-function named load_potential_repeat. First I'll show you the code, and then I'll explain it.

```
/*------------------------------------------------------------------*/
PROCEDURE load_potential_repeat ( p_location_id NUMBER,
                                  p_type_id     NUMBER,
                                  p_date        DATE ) IS
/*------------------------------------------------------------------*/
  v_hash NUMBER;
BEGIN

  -- for every criteria...
  FOR counter IN 1..v_criteria.LAST LOOP

    -- if the order type of the order matches that of the criteria
    IF v_criteria(counter).first_type_id = p_type_id THEN

      -- if date range is valid
      IF v_criteria(counter).start_date <= p_date THEN

        -- create a hash based on the location and two repeat criteria
        v_hash := DBMS_UTILITY.GET_HASH_VALUE(p_location_id || ':' ||
                      v_criteria(counter).first_type_id || ':' ||
                      v_criteria(counter).repeat_type_id,
                      -32767,65533);

        -- if the criteria is not already in the potential list then
        -- put it there
        IF NOT v_potential_repeat.EXISTS(v_hash) THEN
```

```
          v_potential_repeat(v_hash).location_id := p_location_id;
          v_potential_repeat(v_hash).first_type_id :=
                            v_criteria(counter).first_type_id;
          v_potential_repeat(v_hash).repeat_type_id :=
                            v_criteria(counter).repeat_type_id;
      END IF;

    END IF;  -- date range is valid

  END IF;  -- order type matches

 END LOOP;  -- every criteria

 END load_potential_repeat;
```

It may look a little daunting, but it's actually a rather simple algorithm. For every criterion for the region, ask:

- Does the first order type of the criterion match that of the order being processed? If yes, then carry on.
- Is the criterion date less than or equal to the order date? If yes, then carry on.
- Manufacture a hash value based on the location of the order, the first order type of the criterion, and the repeat-order type from the criterion.
- Has an entry already been created in the associative array at the index point indicated by the manufactured hash? If no, then carry on.
- Add the location, first order type, and repeat-order type to the associative array at the index point indicated by the manufactured hash.

For example, if three separate potential repeats were found, the associative array would look something like this:

```
INDEX LOCATION_ID FIRST_TYPE_ID REPEAT_TYPE_ID
----- ----------- ------------- --------------
-3421         874          1876            202
  -99        1098             2             18
88862          18           100             88
```

Thus, any subsequent orders of type 202 and location 874 would be considered repeats, as would any orders of type 18 at location 1098 or type 88 at location 18.

Now, let's move on to find the genuine repeats.

Finding Genuine Repeats

Finding genuine repeats is straightforward. If the order type matches the repeat type of a criteria record, and if a corresponding match is found in the associative array containing potential repeats, then we have found a genuine repeat. I've put this code into a sub-function, as well.

```
  /*------------------------------------------------------------------*/
  FUNCTION order_is_a_repeat ( p_location_id NUMBER,
                               p_type_id     NUMBER,
                               p_date        DATE )
           RETURN NUMBER IS
  /*------------------------------------------------------------------*/
    v_hash NUMBER;
  BEGIN

    -- for every criteria...
    FOR counter IN 1..v_criteria.LAST LOOP

      -- if order type matches the repeat order type of a criteria
      IF v_criteria(counter).repeat_type_id = p_type_id THEN

        -- calculate a hash of the location, first and repeat order types
        v_hash := DBMS_UTILITY.GET_HASH_VALUE(p_location_id || ':' ||
                           v_criteria(counter).first_type_id || ':' ||
                           v_criteria(counter).repeat_type_id,
                           -32767,65533);

        -- if logged as a potential repeat then its safe to assume
        -- we are repeating now
        IF v_potential_repeat.EXISTS(v_hash) THEN
          RETURN(v_hash);
        END IF;

      END IF;  -- order type match

    END LOOP;  -- every criteria

    RETURN(NULL);

  END order_is_a_repeat;
```

The algorithm is as follows. For every criterion for the region:

- Does the order type of the order being processed match the repeat-order type of the criterion? If yes, then carry on.

- Manufacture a hash value based on the location of the order, the first order type of the criterion, and the repeat-order type of the criterion.

- If an entry exists in the associative array of potential repeat orders at the index point denoted by the hash value, then we've found a genuine repeat order.

- Return the manufactured hash so the correct row can be found and piped upstream immediately.

The Final Function

Now that all facets of the function are in place, it's time to take one last look at the function's pseudo-code.

```
BEGIN

  -- for every order...
  LOOP

    FETCH p_curs INTO v_order;
    EXIT WHEN p_curs%NOTFOUND;

    IF first revord or new region THEN
      Load region criteria
    END IF;

    IF it's a potential repeat then add to associative array.
    IF it's a repeat order then
      PIPE ROW( );
    END IF;

  END LOOP;  -- every order

  RETURN;
END;
```

The complete function code is available in the *repeat_orders.sql* file on the book's web site.

Running the Function

The function is executed using a SQL SELECT statement that is passed another SQL SELECT statement. I know that may still take some getting used to, but believe me—it's worth checking out. Here's the SQL used to run the function:

```
/* File on web: repeat_orders.sql */
SQL> SELECT *
  2    FROM TABLE(repeat_order_finder(CURSOR(
  3                   SELECT order_number,
  4                          order_date,
  5                          region_id,
  6                          type_id,
  7                          location_id
  8                     FROM orders
  9                    WHERE order_date >= SYSDATE - 30
 10                )))
 11  /

REGION_ID LOCATION_ID FIRST_TYPE_ID REPEAT_TYPE_ID
---------- ----------- ------------- --------------
         1           1             1              2
         2           2             2              3
         3           3             3              4
         4           4             4              5
         4           4             4              5
         5           5             5              6
         6           6             6              7
```

7	7	7	8
8	8	8	9
9	9	9	10
10	10	10	11

```
11 rows selected.
```

The result set is treated just as if it came from an Oracle table or view. Criteria could be applied to limit the result set—for example, "WHERE first_type_id = 3". Even more exciting is the fact that the results of a somewhat convoluted business process are available as a simple SQL query upon which reports can easily be built. All of the business logic to assemble the result set is done in the database.

Pipelining the function serves records up to be processed right away, saving even more valuable time.

The Totaling Function

Next, I'll build another table function to total the repeat orders by region, and then I'll nest it right into the SQL shown in the previous section. The new function looks like this.

```
/* File on web: repeat_orders_summary.sql */
CREATE OR REPLACE FUNCTION summarize_repeat_orders ( p_curs cursors.repeat_summary_curs )
             RETURN repeat_summary_t
             PIPELINED
             PARALLEL_ENABLE ( PARTITION p_curs BY RANGE(region_id) ) AS

  v_summary_rec cursors.repeat_summary_rec;
  v_last_region NUMBER;
  v_count       NUMBER := 0;

BEGIN

  -- for every repeat order
  LOOP

    -- fetch the repeat order
    FETCH p_curs INTO v_summary_rec;
    EXIT WHEN p_curs%NOTFOUND;

    -- if this is the first record then set the local
    -- region ID
    IF p_curs%ROWCOUNT = 1 THEN
      v_last_region := v_summary_rec.region_id;
    END IF;

    -- if this is a new region then pipe the region count
    -- out and reset the local variables
    IF v_summary_rec.region_id <> v_last_region THEN
      PIPE ROW(repeat_summary_o(v_last_region,v_count));
      v_last_region := v_summary_rec.region_id;
```

```
      v_count := 0;
    END IF;

    v_count := v_count + 1;

  END LOOP;  -- every repeat order

  -- don't forget the last record
  IF v_count > 0 THEN
    PIPE ROW(repeat_summary_o(v_last_region,v_count));
  END IF;

  RETURN;

END;
```

The algorithm is a straightforward loop through the fetched repeat orders, summarizing them by region. Whenever the region ID value changes in the repeat order, a result must be piped out.

The summary function is activated using the SQL SELECT statement shown here.

```
SQL> SELECT *
  2    FROM TABLE(summarize_repeat_orders(CURSOR(
  3       SELECT *
  4        FROM TABLE(repeat_order_finder(CURSOR(
  5           SELECT order_number,
  6                  order_date,
  7                  region_id,
  8                  type_id,
  9                  location_id
 10            FROM orders
 11           WHERE order_date >= SYSDATE - 30
 12                )))
 13             )));

REGION_ID REPEAT_COUNT
---------- ------------
        1            1
        2            1
        3            1
        4            2
        5            1
        6            1
        7            1
        8            1
        9            1
       10            1

10 rows selected.
```

The method shown here (using multiple table functions) illustrates the nesting (or daisy-chaining) of table functions that we introduced earlier. The work is split out among several functions, passing result sets upstream, record by record, until the final result set is assembled. Factor in the parallelization of each function along the way, and it's easy to see the enormous benefits of table functions.

Table Function Examples

This section contains a number of additional examples that demonstrate some handy applications of using table functions to handle such tasks as performing extra tracing, establishing time limits, and using timed data refreshes. Each example takes advantage of the fact that table functions allow code to be written with a SELECT statement.

Tracing

Most PL/SQL tracing tools (SQL Trace, DBMS_TRACE, etc.) require you to run an operation and then look elsewhere for the trace output. Even Oracle's DBMS_OUTPUT package (the simplest debug tool of all) requires separate output when using a development tool like Toad or PL/SQL Developer.

Table functions allow debug information to be included within query results. When combined with autonomous transactions, they can even provide tracing for DML operations. Consider the following function.

```
/* File on web: tracer.sql */
CREATE OR REPLACE FUNCTION tracer
                RETURN debug_t AS
  PRAGMA AUTONOMOUS_TRANSACTION;
  v_debug debug_t := debug_t();
BEGIN
  v_trace.EXTEND;
  v_trace(v_debug.LAST) := 'Started Insert At ' ||
                        TO_CHAR(SYSDATE,'HH24:MI:SS');
  INSERT INTO a_table VALUES(1);
  COMMIT;
  v_trace.EXTEND;
  v_trace(v_debug.LAST) := 'Completed Insert At ' ||
                        TO_CHAR(SYSDATE,'HH24:MI:SS');
  RETURN(v_trace);
END;
```

Without the AUTONOMOUS TRANSACTION clause, I would get the error *ORA-14551: cannot perform a DML operation inside a query* when executing the query. With this clause in place, I can run the function using a SELECT statement.

```
SQL> SELECT *
  2    FROM a_table;

no rows selected

SQL> SELECT *
```

```
  2    FROM TABLE(debug);
```

```
COLUMN_VALUE
---------------------------
Started Insert At 22:04:28
Completed Insert At 22:04:28
```

```
SQL> SELECT *
  2    FROM a_table;

      COL1
----------
         1
```

Establishing Time Limits

One very useful application of table functions is to use them to establish time limits for returning records from queries. This is great if you want to test an application using a subset of queried records without having to wait for the whole list. The following function pipes records back from a query for the number of seconds passed in. Once the number of seconds is reached, a value of negative 1 is piped out and the function is exited.

```
/* File on web: time_limit.sql */
CREATE OR REPLACE FUNCTION get_a_table
        ( p_limit NUMBER )
        RETURN rowset_t
        PIPELINED AS
  CURSOR curs_get_a IS
  SELECT *
    FROM a_table;
  v_start DATE;
BEGIN
  v_start := SYSDATE;
  FOR v_a_rec IN curs_get_a LOOP
    PIPE ROW(rowset_o(v_a_rec.col1));
    IF SYSDATE - v_start >= ( p_limit * 0.000011574 ) THEN
      PIPE ROW(rowset_o(-1));
      EXIT;
    END IF;
  END LOOP;
END;
```

Here's an example of selecting from a table with 1,000 records in it.

```
SQL> SELECT *
  2    FROM TABLE(get_a_table(1));

      COL1
----------
       661
       662
       663
```

```
              664
               -1

    5 rows selected.
```

If the query takes more than p_limit seconds to return, the function will exceed its time limit.

Enabling Nested Cursors

Table functions can also be used to help queries perform better by adding application knowledge to a query. The classic example is the multiple "OR EXISTS" type of query shown in this example.

```
SELECT *
  FROM main_table mt
 WHERE col1 = 1
   AND ( EXISTS ( SELECT 1
                    FROM or_table_one
                   WHERE col11 = mt.col1 )
      OR EXISTS ( SELECT 1
                    FROM or_table_two
                   WHERE col21 = mt.col1 )
      OR EXISTS ( SELECT 1
                    FROM or_table_three
                   WHERE col31 = mt.col1 ) );
```

It will return a record if a corresponding record is found in any of three other tables. The AUTOTRACE output for the query shows that the Oracle optimizer looked at each table involved in order to get the single resultant record.

```
Execution Plan
----------------------------------------------------------
       0      SELECT STATEMENT Optimizer=ALL_ROWS (Cost=1 Card=1 Bytes=4)
     1    0   FILTER
     2    1    TABLE ACCESS (BY INDEX ROWID) OF 'MAIN_TABLE' (TABLE) (Cost=1 Card=1
                  Bytes=4)
     3    2     INDEX (UNIQUE SCAN) OF 'SYS_C003477' (INDEX (UNIQUE)) (Cost=0
                  Card=1)
     4    1    INDEX (UNIQUE SCAN) OF 'SYS_C003479' (INDEX (UNIQUE)) (Cost=0 Card=1
                  Bytes=2)
     5    1    INDEX (UNIQUE SCAN) OF 'SYS_C003481' (INDEX (UNIQUE)) (Cost=1 Card=1
                  Bytes=3)
     6    1    INDEX (UNIQUE SCAN) OF 'SYS_C003483' (INDEX (UNIQUE)) (Cost=1 Card=1
                  Bytes=3)


Statistics
----------------------------------------------------------
         0  recursive calls
         0  db block gets
        13  consistent gets
         0  physical reads
         0  redo size
```

```
446  bytes sent via SQL*Net to client
511  bytes received via SQL*Net from client
  2  SQL*Net roundtrips to/from client
  0  sorts (memory)
  0  sorts (disk)
  1  rows processed
```

The Statistics section shows the amount of work Oracle had to do to provide the result set, including 13 consistent gets.

But what if I know that there is a 90% chance of a match in the OR_TABLE_ONE table and only a 10% chance of a match in the other tables? I'd want to look in OR_TABLE_ONE and only go to the others if I didn't find a record there. One solution is to use nested cursors within a table function so the whole operation can still be done as a query.

```
CREATE OR REPLACE FUNCTION nested
                  RETURN number_t AS

  -- get a main table record
  CURSOR curs_get_mt IS
  SELECT mt.col1,
         CURSOR ( SELECT 1
                    FROM or_table_one
                   WHERE col11 = mt.col1 ),
         CURSOR ( SELECT 1
                    FROM or_table_two
                   WHERE col21 = mt.col1 ),
         CURSOR ( SELECT 1
                    FROM or_table_three
                   WHERE col31 = mt.col1 )
    FROM main_table mt
   WHERE col1 = 1;

  v_col1        NUMBER;
  cursor_one    SYS_REFCURSOR;
  cursor_two    SYS_REFCURSOR;
  cursor_three  SYS_REFCURSOR;
  v_dummy       NUMBER;

  v_ret_val number_t := number_t();

BEGIN

  OPEN curs_get_mt;
  FETCH curs_get_mt INTO v_col1,
                         cursor_one,
                         cursor_two,
                         cursor_three;

  IF curs_get_mt%FOUND THEN
    -- look in the first OR table
    FETCH cursor_one INTO v_dummy;
```

```
        IF cursor_one%FOUND THEN
          v_ret_val.EXTEND;
          v_ret_val(v_ret_val.LAST) := v_col1;
        ELSE
          -- look in the seconds OR table
          FETCH cursor_two INTO v_dummy;
          IF cursor_two%FOUND THEN
            v_ret_val.EXTEND;
            v_ret_val(v_ret_val.LAST) := v_col1;
          ELSE
            - look in the third OR table
            FETCH cursor_three INTO v_dummy;
            IF cursor_two%FOUND THEN
              v_ret_val.EXTEND;
              v_ret_val(v_ret_val.LAST) := v_col1;
            END IF;
          END IF;
        END IF;
      END IF;
      IF cursor_one%ISOPEN THEN
        CLOSE cursor_one;
      END IF;
      IF cursor_two%ISOPEN THEN
        CLOSE cursor_two;
      END IF;
      IF cursor_three%ISOPEN THEN
        CLOSE cursor_three;
      END IF;
      CLOSE curs_get_mt;
      RETURN(v_ret_val);
    END;
```

The AUTOTRACE output for the function looks like this.

```
SQL> SELECT *
  2    FROM TABLE(nested);

COLUMN_VALUE
------------
           1

Execution Plan
----------------------------------------------------------
   0      SELECT STATEMENT Optimizer=ALL_ROWS (Cost=25 Card=8168 Bytes=16336)
   1    0   COLLECTION ITERATOR (PICKLER FETCH) OF 'NESTED'

Statistics
----------------------------------------------------------
          13  recursive calls
           0  db block gets
           3  consistent gets
           0  physical reads
           0  redo size
         397  bytes sent via SQL*Net to client
```

```
511  bytes received via SQL*Net from client
  2  SQL*Net roundtrips to/from client
  0  sorts (memory)
  0  sorts (disk)
  1  rows processed
```

The optimizer cost of the function evaluated much higher than the query, 25 to 1. But the database had to do a little less work, 3 consistent gets versus 13.

 A word of caution: switch to this implementation only when you have identified a bottleneck and only after thorough testing. The performance gains may not be worth the extra lines of code you have to write, debug, and then maintain.

Tips for Working with Table Functions

I'll wrap up this chapter with a few tips to help you take full advantage of table functions.

The Case Against SYS_REFCURSOR

Oracle's SYS_REFCURSOR function provides a way to quickly declare a weakly typed REF cursor that can process almost any cursor. The fact that SYS_REFCURSOR can be specified as the datatype means that any old SELECT statement can be passed in, as long as the cursor isn't actually manipulated in the function. For example, this function is wide open to any SELECT.

```
CREATE OR REPLACE FUNCTION wide_open ( p_curs SYS_REFCURSOR )
                RETURN number_t IS
  v_ret_val number_t := number_t( );
BEGIN
  v_ret_val.EXTEND;
  v_ret_val(v_ret_val.LAST) := 99;
  RETURN v_ret_val;
END;
```

Any valid SELECT will work.

```
SQL> SELECT *
  2    FROM TABLE(wide_open(CURSOR(SELECT NULL
  3                                  FROM DUAL)));

COLUMN_VALUE
------------
          99

SQL> SELECT *
  2    FROM TABLE(wide_open(CURSOR(SELECT *
  3                                  FROM orders)));
```

```
COLUMN_VALUE
------------
         99
```

But things have to become more isolated because, presumably, records will be fetched within the function. Thus, local variables are required to fetch into.

```
CREATE OR REPLACE FUNCTION wide_open ( p_curs SYS_REFCURSOR )
                    RETURN number_t IS
  v_ret_val    number_t := number_t( );
  v_order_rec orders%ROWTYPE;
BEGIN
  FETCH p_curs INTO v_order_rec;
  v_ret_val.EXTEND;
  v_ret_val(v_ret_val.LAST) := 99;
  RETURN v_ret_val;
END;
```

Only SELECT statements getting all columns from the ORDERS table can now be passed to this function. Others will raise the ORA-01007 error.

```
SQL> SELECT *
  2    FROM TABLE(wide_open(CURSOR(SELECT NULL
  3                                  FROM DUAL)));
  FROM TABLE(wide_open(CURSOR(SELECT NULL
                  *
ERROR at line 2:
ORA-01007: variable not in select list
ORA-06512: at "SCOTT.WIDE_OPEN", line 6

SQL> SELECT *
  2    FROM TABLE(wide_open(CURSOR(SELECT *
  3                                  FROM orders)));

COLUMN_VALUE
------------
         99
```

At this point, the function can accept absolutely any SELECT statement, but it will fail if it doesn't query the ORDERS table. The flexibility of SYS_REFCURSOR and weakly typed REF cursors, in general, is rendered moot.

Because of this behavior, I prefer to completely remove the illusion of flexibility by using strongly typed REF cursors declared in a central package as follows:

```
CREATE OR REPLACE PACKAGE cursors AS
  TYPE order_curs IS REF CURSOR RETURN orders%ROWTYPE;
END;
```

and then use them in a table function.

```
CREATE OR REPLACE FUNCTION wide_open ( p_curs cursors.order_curs )
                    RETURN number_t IS
  v_ret_val    number_t := number_t( );
  v_order_rec p_curs%ROWTYPE;
BEGIN
```

```
    FETCH p_curs INTO v_order_rec;
    v_ret_val.EXTEND;
    v_ret_val(v_ret_val.LAST) := 99;
    RETURN v_ret_val;
  END;
```

This has the added benefit of linking the datatype of the local variable I select into directly to the strongly typed cursor. This saves time during execution because Oracle will not have to waste time figuring out what the returned structure will be. It also allows me to coordinate the SELECT statements and cursor parameters via a single central package, should I ever want to change them. There is no need to change every function to stay in synch.

REF Cursors and Nesting

Because table functions return collections, there is no easy way to declare strongly typed REF cursors to handle them when nesting. Thus, I have to declare records with the same structure as the collection and then tie a REF cursor to them like this.

```
CREATE OR REPLACE PACKAGE cursors
  TYPE v_number_rec IS RECORD ( number_col NUMBER );
  TYPE number_curs IS REF CURSOR RETURN v_number_rec;
END;
```

Now the strongly typed REF cursor can be used in table functions ready for nesting.

```
CREATE OR REPLACE FUNCTION nested_number ( p_curs cursors.number_curs )...
```

Applying Criteria

When applying criteria to a function, be cognizant of performance, especially when deciding whether to pass parameter values into the function for use when assembling the result set or applying them to the returned result set. Here are two examples of what I mean. The first applies the criterion (col1 = 'A') to returned records after they are assembled by the function.

```
SELECT *
  FROM TABLE(a_function)
  WHERE col1 = 'A';
```

This next example passes the criterion directly into the function so it can be used when assembling records.

```
SELECT *
  FROM TABLE(a_function('A'));
```

Examine the complexity of the algorithm and the size of the data set to determine which approach will work best for you.

Standardizing Object and Collection Names

After implementing table functions in several applications, I was alarmed to see the number of duplicate object and collection types I had implemented. For example, I had created these two objects:

```
SQL> DESC experiment_results_o
 Name                                      Null?    Type
 ---------------------------------------- -------- ------
 SAMPLE_AMT                                         NUMBER


SQL> DESC research_tallies_o
 Name                                      Null?    Type
 ---------------------------------------- -------- ------
 TALLY_TOTAL                                        NUMBER
```

And then rolled them up into collections with similar names—replacing the "_o" (underscore o) suffix with "_t". This is just the simplest example of the clutter I created because I hadn't focused on the database as a whole. I've since gone back and replaced the two objects with a single one like this:

```
SQL> DESC number_o
 Name                                      Null?    Type
 ---------------------------------------- -------- ------
 COL1                                               NUMBER
```

I also have similar generic objects for other datatypes including several standard lengths of VARCHAR2 fields.

Another standard I follow is that my object names have "_o" appended while my collections (or tables) have "_t" appended. This allows me to discern quickly what type they are.

Beware of Unhandled Exceptions

Moving functions into the realm of SELECT statements makes handling exceptions a whole new ball game. It's no longer as simple as causing the function to fail and raising the error to the calling application. For example, how should we handle the situation when the following function raises the NO DATA FOUND exception?

```
CREATE OR REPLACE FUNCTION unhandled
                  RETURN number_t AS
  v_ret_val number_t := number_t();
  v_dummy    NUMBER;
BEGIN
  SELECT 1
    INTO v_dummy
    FROM DUAL
   WHERE 1 = 2;
  v_ret_val.EXTEND;
  v_ret_val(v_ret_val.LAST) := 1;
  RETURN(v_ret_val);
END;
```

Should the exception be returned from a SELECT statement like this?

```
SQL> SELECT *
  2    FROM TABLE(unhandled);

COLUMN_VALUE
------------------------
ORA-01403: no data found
```

That would require Oracle to keep track of two possible result set structures—one for successful execution and one with a single VARCHAR2 column to hold a potential error message. That might be possible but would wreak havoc with nested table functions, because they too would have to handle two different return structures. That would get far too complicated far too fast.

Perhaps the SELECT should just fail outright?

```
SQL> SELECT *
  2    FROM TABLE(unhandled);

ORA-01403: no data found
```

That's better than returning an error message but could be a little confusing.

The answer is that Oracle takes the relatively easy way out by stating that the failing function simply returned no rows.

```
SQL> SELECT *
  2    FROM TABLE(unhandled);

no rows selected
```

You need to be very careful to handle all possible exceptions or your table functions may silently fail.

Passing Objects Instead Of Cursors

It's a little-known fact that table functions can accept collections as well as cursors as parameters. Here's a simple example.

```
CREATE OR REPLACE FUNCTION give_me_a_collection ( p_col number_t )
               RETURN number_t IS
  v_ret_val number_t := number_t();
BEGIN
  v_ret_val.EXTEND(p_col.COUNT);
  FOR counter IN v_ret_val.FIRST..v_ret_val.LAST LOOP
    v_ret_val(counter) := p_col(counter);
  END LOOP;
  RETURN(v_ret_val);
END;
```

And here's one way to execute it in a SELECT.

```
SQL> SELECT *
  2    FROM TABLE(give_me_a_collection(number_t(1,2,3)));
```

```
COLUMN_VALUE
------------
           1
           2
           3
```

Not Read Committed

Even though table functions execute within the domain of a SELECT statement, they cannot take advantage of Oracle's read-committed architecture for their duration. Any queries performed within the table function can do so, but the table function itself works just like any other function in this regard. Consider this example table function.

```
CREATE OR REPLACE FUNCTION not_committed
                  RETURN number_t IS
  v_ret_val NUMBER_T := NUMBER_T();
  v_count   NUMBER;
BEGIN
  SELECT COUNT(*)
    INTO v_count
    FROM orders;
  v_ret_val.EXTEND;
  v_ret_val(v_ret_val.LAST) := v_count;
  DBMS_LOCK.SLEEP(10);
  SELECT COUNT(*)
    INTO v_count
    FROM orders;
  v_ret_val.EXTEND;
  v_ret_val(v_ret_val.LAST) := v_count;
  RETURN(v_ret_val);
END;
```

It queries the number of records in the ORDERS table, waits 10 seconds, and then does it again, returning the two counts as a result set. If you execute the table function in one session and then delete (and commit) 5 orders in another session (presumably during the 10-second pause), you'll see the following results.

```
SQL> SELECT *
  2    FROM TABLE(not_committed);

COLUMN_VALUE
------------
       10000
        9995
```

Be sure to factor this into your decision-making when considering the use of table functions versus queries. If you determine that read-committed access is pivotal through the operation, then table functions may not be the way to go.

Conclusion

When you use a table function, the table is the program. What do I mean by that? In effect, a program (your table function) becomes a queryable source of results—just like a table. Table functions are perfect for situations where complex logic must be performed by a SELECT statement, as is often the case when you must interface Oracle with third-party applications. Combine that functionality with the extra power provided by parallelizing table functions, and you end up with an extremely handy tool for DBAs.

CHAPTER 4
Data Encryption and Hashing

In the simplest terms, *encryption* means disguising data, or altering the contents in such a way that only the creator of the original data knows the secret of how to put the data back together again. This chapter describes Oracle's support for encryption, focusing on the concepts and features of most use to DBAs. The emphasis here is on the use of Oracle's built-in packages, DBMS_CRYPTO (available in releases from Oracle Database 10g Release 1 onward) and DBMS_OBFUSCATION_TOOL-KIT (used primarily with earlier releases). I'll also focus on the protection of data on disk, as opposed to the protection of data being transmitted between the client and the database or the protection of data during authentication, both of which require the use of Oracle's extra-cost Advanced Security Option (ASO). The only exception to the rule is transmission of passwords, which are always encrypted, regardless of the use of ASO.

In this chapter, you will learn how to build a basic encryption system that will protect sensitive data from access by unauthorized users. You will learn how to build a key management system that effectively protects your encryption keys while seamlessly providing the application users unrestrained access to the data. You'll also learn about cryptographic hashing and the use of Message Authentication Code (MAC). I'll also describe Transparent Data Encryption (TDE), a new feature introduced in Oracle Database 10g Release 2 that can be used to encrypt sensitive data in a way that allows you to comply with many regulations with the least amount of effort.

Oracle recommends that if you are now running Oracle Database 10g, you start using the DBMS_CRYPTO package as opposed to the older DBMS_OBFUSCATION_TOOLKIT package. However, because so many sites are still running Oracle9i Database, we'll look first at the facilities provided by that package, and then move on to the Oracle Database 10g implementation. Even if you are running the new release, you might want to read this section of the chapter first to make sure you are properly grounded in encryption concepts.

DBMS_CRYPTO offers a number of advantages over DBMS_OBFUSCATION_TOOLKIT:

- More choices for encryption algorithms, particularly support for the newest standard, the Advanced Encryption Standard (AES)
- The ability to do stream ciphering, which allows a stream of data to be encrypted
- Support for the Secure Hash Algorithm 1 (SHA-1)
- The ability to create MAC
- Encryption of large objects (LOBs) in their *native* format

I'll explore all of these features in this chapter. In Appendix A, you will find a quick reference to the procedures and functions provided in the DBMS_CRYPTO and DBMS_OBFUSCATION_TOOLKIT packages.

This book does not discuss the details of cryptographic algorithms or the art and science of computer encryption, a field that demands much more detailed coverage than we can possibly accomplish in a book of this kind. Our objective is to get readers started on building an encryption system, using Oracle's built-in tools, not to reinvent the wheel by writing actual algorithms. For additional information on cryptoanalysis, mathematical encryption, and related topics, you can refer to the many very good, publicly available books.

Introduction to Encryption

Let's suppose that you carry your laptop home from work every day, bring it back to the office the following morning, and then tether it to your desktop with a locking cable protected by a combination lock. You know how important it is to remember the lock combination, don't you? If you ever forget it, your laptop will end up married to your desk until you pry it free by cutting the cable. Maybe you remember numbers easily, but I don't. It's hard enough for me to even remember my own telephone number, let alone the plethora of secret numbers in my life—my Social Security number, bank account PIN, voice mail password, and anniversary (oops!). To make things easier, I have devised an ingenious method for remembering that lock combination—I have written down the code on a label and put that label *on* the lock itself!

And now you must be wondering if you would ever be able to trust me with something secure!

Like the rest of humanity, I have a brain that is part hard drive (disk) and part random-access memory (RAM), and numbers seem to go into RAM more often than not. After a period of usage, the numbers are conveniently aged out to make room for more (not unlike the System Global Area of an Oracle instance) and are forgotten. In computers, this process is expected and is built into the design. Database systems are designed to store information and make it accessible to users when asked.

Historically, the assumption has been that users who demand access will already have been authenticated to establish that they are who they claim to be. The mere storage of sensitive information, therefore, has not been considered a potential security breach.

That may have been true at one time, but not today, with intruders seemingly everywhere—they may be curiosity seekers; they may be planning to sell account data to your competitors; or they may be seeking to disrupt your system for revenge. The attack might come from outside, via the Internet, or inside your organization. (Indeed, research shows that most hacking does come from within.) As countless security breaches have shown, sensitive data clearly needs to be protected from anyone not authorized to see that data. What options does Oracle provide for that protection?

Pan back to my lock combination—it's 3451. Not being a complete idiot, I don't write that number on my lock. Instead, I have a secret number that I *always* remember—6754, and using this number I modify the lock combination by adding the corresponding digits:

```
3 + 6 = 9
4 + 7 = 11
5 + 5 = 10
1 + 4 = 5
```

The resulting numbers are 9, 11, 10, and 5. In my scheme, I use only single-digit numbers, so I wrap the double-digit numbers around the number 10; hence, 10 becomes 0, 11 becomes 1, and so on. Using my secret key 6754, I have transformed the number 3451 into 9105. It's the *latter* number that I write on the combination lock, not the actual code. If I forget the combination, I will be able to read that number and use my magic number 6754 to reverse the logic I applied earlier so I can use the number 3451 to unlock the key. The number 9105 is for the whole world to see, but the thief still won't be able to unlock the combination unless he also knows the key, 6754.

In this way, I have *encrypted* the number represented by my lock combination. The number 6754 is the *key* to the encryption process. This type of encryption I've performed here is known as *symmetric encryption* because the same key is used to encrypt and decrypt. (In contrast, with asymmetric encryption, described later in this chapter, there are two distinct keys: a public key and a private key.) The logic I described to encrypt the code is a very simplistic implementation of an *encryption algorithm*.

Encryption Components

Let's summarize what we have learned so far. An encryption system has several basic components, as shown in Figure 4-1.

- The algorithm
- The key
- The type of encryption (symmetric, in this case, because the same key is used both to encrypt and to decrypt)

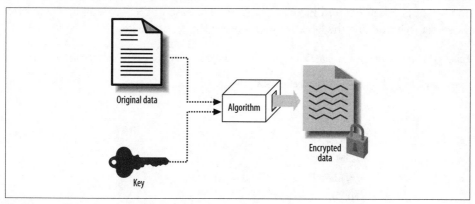

Figure 4-1. Symmetric encryption components

Let's assume that a thief intent on stealing my laptop is trying to open the lock. What does she need in order to succeed? First, she has to know the algorithm; let's assume here that that she knows it, perhaps because I boasted about my cleverness at work, or she read this book, or this algorithm is public knowledge. Second, she needs to learn the key. That is something I can protect. Even if the thief knows about the algorithm, I can still hide the key effectively. But as there are only 4 digits in the key, it takes only up to 10^4, or 10,000, attempts by the thief to guess the key. And because each attempt has an equal probability of getting it right or wrong, in theory, the thief has a 1 in 5,000 chance to guess the right key. Can she do it? In this case, the thief will have to *manually* turn the wheels of the combination lock 5,000 times. That's daunting, but theoretically possible. Suddenly, I don't feel so secure anymore.

What are the ways that I can protect my lock combination?

- I can hide the algorithm.
- I can make the key difficult to guess.
- I can take both of these steps together.

The first option is impossible if I am using a publicly known algorithm. I could develop my own, but the time and effort may not be worth it. It might later be found out anyway, and changing an algorithm is a very difficult task. That rules out the third option, too, leaving the second option as the only viable one.

The Effects of Key Length

My lock combination is the digital equivalent of sensitive data. If an intruder wants to crack the encrypted key, 10,000 iterations to guess the code is trivial—he'll be able to crack it in under a second. What if I use an alphanumeric key instead of an all-numeric one? That gives 36 possible values for each character of the key, so the intruder will have to guess up to 36^4, or 1,679,616, combinations—more difficult than 10,000, but still not beyond reach. The key must be strengthened, or "hardened," by making it longer than 4 characters. Table 4-1 shows how the maximum number of guesses required increases with the increase in the key length. Therefore, the secret to hardening the key is to increase the length of the key.

Table 4-1. Alphanumeric key length and maximum number of guesses required to crack the key

Key length	Maximum number of guesses required
4	1,679,616
5	60,466,176
6	2,176,782,336
7	78,364,164,096
8	2,821,109,907,456
9	101,559,956,668,416
10	3,656,158,440,062,976

Remember that computers think in terms of bits and bytes (i.e., binary numbers), not alphanumeric characters. The possible values of a key position are 0 and 1, so the 10-digit key needs only 2^{10}, or 1024, combinations, an extremely easy number to handle. Practically speaking, a key must be much longer. The length of a key is described in bits, so a key of 64 numbers is said to be of 64-bit. Table 4-2 shows the relationship between key length and number of guesses required for a binary type key.

Table 4-2. Binary key length and maximum number of guesses required to crack the key

Key length	Maximum number of guesses required
56	72,057,594,037,927,936
57	144,115,188,075,855,872
58	288,230,376,151,711,744
59	576,460,752,303,423,488
60	1,152,921,504,606,846,976
61	2,305,843,009,213,693,952
62	4,611,686,018,427,387,904
63	9,223,372,036,854,775,808
64	18,446,744,073,709,551,616
65	36,893,488,147,419,103,232

The longer the key, the more difficult it is to crack the encryption. But longer keys also extend the elapsed time needed to do encryption and decryption, as the CPU has to do more work. In designing an encryption infrastructure, you may need to make a compromise between key size and reduced security.

Symmetric Encryption Versus Asymmetric Encryption

In the earlier example, the same key is used to encrypt and decrypt. As I mentioned, this type of encryption is known as *symmetric encryption*. There is an inherent problem with this type of encryption: because the same key must be used to decrypt the data, the key must be made known to the recipient. The key, which is generally referred to as the *secret key*, has to be either known by the recipient before she receives the encrypted data (i.e., there needs to be a "knowledge-sharing agreement") or the key has to be sent as a part of the data transmission. For data at rest (on disk), the key will have to be stored as a part of the database in order for an application to decrypt it. There are obvious risks in this situation. A key that is being transmitted may be intercepted by an intruder, and a key that is stored in the database may be stolen.

To address this problem, another type of encryption is often used, one in which the key used to encrypt is different from the one used to decrypt. Because the keys differ, this is known as *asymmetric encryption*. Because two keys are generated—a public key and a private key—it is also known as *public-key encryption*. The *public key*, which is required for the encryption, is made known to the sender and, in fact, can be freely shared. The other key, the *private key*, is used only to decrypt the data encrypted by the public key and must be kept secret.

Let's see how public-key encryption might work in real life. As shown in Figure 4-2, John (on the left) is expecting a message from Jane (on the right). Here are the steps in the encryption process:

1. John generates two keys—a public key and a private key.
2. He sends the public key to Jane.
3. Jane has an original message (known as the *cleartext*) that she encrypts using the public key, and she sends the encrypted message to John.
4. John decrypts it using the private key he generated earlier.

Note carefully here that there is no exchange of decryption keys between the parties. The public key is sent to the sender, but because that is not what is needed to decrypt the value, it does not pose a threat from a potential key theft.

However, you should be aware of the effect of spoofing or phishing here, which can render this process of data encryption insecure. Here is a scenario:

1. John generates a public-private key pair and hands the public key over to Jane.

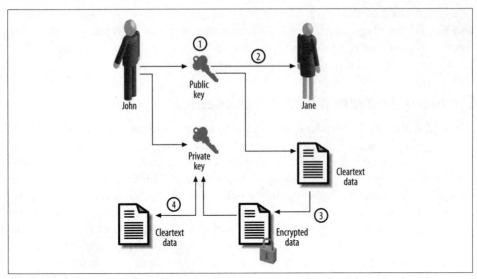

Figure 4-2. Basic asymmetric encryption

2. An intruder is sniffing the communication line and obtains John's public key. Sometimes that's not even necessary, as John may have made his public key available to the public intentionally.

3. The intruder creates *another* public-private key pair with his software (using John's name so the public key looks like it was from him).

4. The intruder sends "his" new public key that he generated with his software, not the original one created by John. Jane does not know the difference; she thinks it is John's real public key.

5. Jane encrypts the message using this public key and sends the encrypted message to John.

6. However, the intruder is still sniffing the line and intercepts this message. He has the private key for the public key, so he can decrypt the message. In an instant, the intended security advantage is lost.

7. There is a slight problem, though. When John eventually gets the encrypted message and tries to decrypt it, he will be unsuccessful, because the private key that needs to be used is not the correct one. He will get suspicious. To prevent this, the intruder will just have to re-encrypt the message using John's real public key and pass on the encrypted message to him. John is unlikely to know that something like this has happened.

Scary? Of course. So, what's the solution? The solution is to somehow verify the authenticity of the public key and ascertain its source as the correct sender. This can be done using a *fingerprint match*. The topic is beyond the scope of this book, but essentially, when Jane encrypts with the public key, she checks the fingerprint of the key to make sure the key does indeed belong to John. (This discussion also high-lights how the communication lines between the source and the destination must be highly secure.)

The key used to encrypt is not the key used to decrypt, so how does the decryption process know the key used during the encryption process? Recall that both keys are generated at the same time by the receiver, which ensures that there is a mathematical relationship between them. One is simply the inverse of the other: whatever one does, the other simply undoes it. The decryption process can therefore decipher the value without knowing the encryption key.

Because public and private keys are mathematically related, it is theoretically possible to guess the private key from the public key, although it is a rather laborious process that requires factoring an extremely large number. So, to reduce the risk of brute-force guessing, very high key lengths are used, typically 1,024-bit keys, instead of the 56-, 64-, 128-, or 256-bit keys used in symmetric encryption. Note that a 1,024-bit key is typical, not the norm. Keys of shorter lengths are also used.

Oracle provides asymmetric encryption at two points:

- During transmission of data between the client and the database
- During authentication of users

Both of these functions require use of Oracle's Advanced Security Option (ASO), an extra-cost option that is not provided by default. That tool simply enables asymmetric key encryption on those functions; it does not provide a simple ready-to-use interface that you can use to build a data-at-rest encryption solution.

The only developer-oriented encryption tools freely available in Oracle provide for symmetric encryption. For this reason, I focus on symmetric encryption, not asymmetric encryption, in this chapter.

 Because asymmetric encryption systems use different keys to encrypt and decrypt, the source and destination need not know the key that will be used to decrypt. In contrast, symmetric encryption systems do use the same key, so safeguarding the keys when using such systems is very important.

Encryption Algorithms

There are many widely used and commercially available encryption algorithms, but we'll focus here on the symmetric key algorithms supported by Oracle for use in PL/SQL applications. The DES and Triple DES algorithms are supported by both of Oracle's built-in encryption packages: DBMS_CRYPTO and DBMS_OBFUSCATION_TOOLKIT; only DBMS_CRYPTO, introduced in Oracle Database 10g Release 1, supports AES, however.

Data Encryption Standard (DES)

Historically, DES has been the predominant standard used for encryption. It was developed more than 20 years ago for the National Bureau of Standards (which later became the National Institute of Standards and Technology, or NIST), and subsequently DES became a standard of the American National Standards Institute (ANSI). There is a great deal to say about DES and its history, but my purpose here is not to describe the algorithm but simply to summarize its adaptation and use inside the Oracle database. This algorithm requires a 64-bit key, but discards 8 of them, using only 56 bits. An intruder would have to use up to 72,057,594,037,927,936 combinations to guess the key.

DES was an adequate algorithm for quite a while, but the decades-old algorithm shows signs of age. Today's powerful computers might find it easy to crack open even the large number of combinations needed to expose the key.

Triple DES (DES3)

NIST went on to solicit development of another scheme based on the original DES that encrypts data twice or thrice, depending upon the mode used. An intruder trying to guess a key would face 2,112 and 2,168 combinations, in two-pass and three-pass encryption routines, respectively. DES3 uses a 128-bit or 192-bit key, depending on whether it is using a two-pass or three-pass scheme.

Triple DES is now also showing signs of age and, like DES, has become susceptible to determined attacks.

Advanced Encryption Standard (AES)

In November 2001, the Federal Information Processing Standards (FIPS) Publication 197 announced the approval of a new standard, the Advanced Encryption Standard, which became effective in May 2002. The full text of the standard can be obtained from NIST at *http://csrc.nist.gov/CryptoToolkit/aes/round2/r2report.pdf* (or visit the book's web site for the link).

Later in this chapter, I'll show how you can use these algorithms by specifying options or selecting constants in Oracle's built-in packages.

Padding and Chaining

When a piece of data is encrypted, it is not encrypted as a whole by the algorithm. It's usually broken into chunks of eight bytes each, and then each chunk is operated on independently. Of course, the length of the data may not be an exact multiple of eight; in such a case, the algorithm adds some characters to the last chunk to make it exactly eight bytes long. This process is known as *padding*. This padding also has to be done right so an attacker won't be able to figure out what was padded and then guess the key from there. To securely pad the values, you can use a pre-developed padding method, which is available in Oracle, known as *Public Key Cryptography System #5* (PKCS#5). There are several other padding options that allow for padding with zeros and for no padding at all. Later in this chapter, I'll show how you can use padding by specifying options or selecting constants in Oracle's built-in packages.

When data is divided into chunks, there needs to be a way to connect back together those chunks, a process known as *chaining*. The overall security of an encryption system depends upon how chunks are connected and encrypted—independently or in conjunction with the adjacent chunks. Oracle supports the following chaining methods:

CBC
Cipher Block Chaining, the most common chaining method.

ECB
Electronic Code Book

CFB
Cipher Feedback

OFB
Output Feedback

Later in this chapter, I'll show how you can use these methods by specifying options or selecting constants in Oracle's built-in packages.

Encryption in Oracle9*i* Database

Let's start our detailed discussion of encryption of Oracle data by looking at the DBMS_OBFUSCATION_TOOLKIT package. Although Oracle now recommends that you use the newer DBMS_CRYPTO package, most organizations have not yet converted their applications to use the new capabilities, so it makes sense to begin with the older package.

 If you are running Oracle Database 10g and starting a new project, you will want to use the features described in the "Encryption in Oracle Database 10g" section. However, to make sure you are properly grounded in encryption concepts, you might still want to read this section first.

Encrypting Data

It's time to see encryption in action in the Oracle database. I'll show a simple example and then explain the details. Let's assume here that you are trying to get the encrypted value of the string "SHHH..TOP SECRET". The following snippet of code does the trick, invoking the DES3ENCRYPT program in the DBMS_OBSFUSCATION_ TOOLKIT package:

```
1  DECLARE
2     l_enc_val   VARCHAR2 (200);
3  BEGIN
```

```
    4        DBMS_OBFUSCATION_TOOLKIT.des3encrypt
    5                         (input_string        => 'SHHH..TOP SECRET',
    6                          key_string          => 'ABCDEFGHIJKLMNOP',
    7                          encrypted_string     => l_enc_val
    8                         );
    9                         DBMS_OUTPUT.put_line ('Encrypted Value = ' || l_enc_val);
   10    END;
```

The output is:

```
Encrypted Value = ¿jVªå¬F.(e) ?«?0
```

Line 6 specifies the key string used to encrypt the value, a key that is 16 characters long. The encrypted value is a VARCHAR2 value but is full of control characters. This type of output may not be useful in real-life applications, especially if you want to store it, print it, or tell someone what it is; we may have to make it more manageable by changing it into readable characters. Note, however, that sometimes you don't want to convert the values from or to the RAW datatype; see the sidebar "When Should You Use Raw Encryption?" later in this chapter. Our first task is to convert the value to the RAW datatype using the built-in package UTL_RAW.

```
    l_enc_val := utl_raw.cast_to_raw(l_enc_val);
```

Next, I convert this to hexadecimal using the function RAWTOHEX to make it easier to manipulate:

```
    l_enc_val := rawtohex(utl_raw.cast_to_raw(l_enc_val));
```

This will change my PL/SQL block to:

```
DECLARE
    l_enc_val    VARCHAR2 (200);
BEGIN
    DBMS_OBFUSCATION_TOOLKIT.des3encrypt (input_string      => 'SHHH..TOP SECRET',
                                          key_string        => 'ABCDEFGHIJKLMNOP',
                                          encrypted_string => l_enc_val
                                         );
    l_enc_val := RAWTOHEX (UTL_RAW.cast_to_raw (l_enc_val));
    DBMS_OUTPUT.put_line ('Encrypted Value = ' || l_enc_val);
END;
```

The output is:

```
Encrypted Value = A86A56A6EE92462E28652903ECAEC730
```

The output is now a hexadecimal string, easily stored and manipulated in VARCHAR2 fields of tables. You could also convert the output to a number for even easier numeric manipulation, but you are generally better off using only hexadecimal values as characters, as they convey meaning as encrypted data while numbers do not.

```
    l_enc_val := to_number('A86A56A6EE92462E28652903ECAEC730',
    'XXXXXXXXXXXXXXXXXXXXXXXXXXXXXXXX')

    223862444271805716712258987042708309808
```

Using the encryption programs in the DBMS_OBFUSCATION_TOOLKIT package as a base, I'll build some wrapper functions around them to make things easier and more flexible to use.

 This example uses the DES3ENCRYPT function to invoke Triple DES encryption. There are a number of other functions and procedures in the ENCRYPT family; see Appendix A for a full list of specifications.

```
/* File on web: get_enc_val_1.sql */

CREATE OR REPLACE FUNCTION get_enc_val (p_in_val IN VARCHAR2, p_key IN VARCHAR2)
   RETURN VARCHAR2
IS
   l_enc_val   VARCHAR2 (200);
BEGIN
   l_enc_val :=
      DBMS_OBFUSCATION_TOOLKIT.des3encrypt (input_string    => p_in_val,
                                            key_string      => p_key
                                           );
   l_enc_val := RAWTOHEX (UTL_RAW.cast_to_raw (l_enc_val));
   RETURN l_enc_val;
END;
```

Using this function from the earlier example, I get the desired results.

```
SQL> SET SERVEROUTPUT ON

SQL> DECLARE
  2>    v_enc   VARCHAR2 (200);
  3> BEGIN
  4>    v_enc := get_enc_val ('SHHH..TOP SECRET', 'ABCDEFGHIJKLMNOP');
  5>    DBMS_OUTPUT.put_line ('Encrypted value = ' || v_enc);
  6> END;
  7> /

Encrypted value = A86A56A6EE92462E28652903ECAEC730

PL/SQL procedure successfully completed.
```

Note that the actual value produced on your system could be different, as a result of character set differences; this is a very important concept that I'll explain later in this chapter. You can use this encryption function in a variety of ways—inserting data into encrypted columns, passing encrypted data to other functions or procedures, and much more.

Before going further, let's test this function by passing it different input. In the earlier example, we used a specific string to encrypt—"SHHH..TOP SECRET". Here we will use a different value to encrypt:

```
DECLARE
   v_enc   VARCHAR2 (200);
BEGIN
```

```
   v_enc := get_enc_val ('A DIFFERENT VALUE', 'ABCDEFGHIJKLMNOP');
   DBMS_OUTPUT.put_line ('Encrypted value = ' || v_enc);
END;
/
```

Uh-oh. This time it throws an error immediately.

```
DECLARE
*
ERROR at line 1:
ORA-28232: invalid input length for obfuscation toolkit
ORA-06512: at "SYS.DBMS_OBFUSCATION_TOOLKIT_FFI", line 0
ORA-06512: at "SYS.DBMS_OBFUSCATION_TOOLKIT", line 216
ORA-06512: at "SCOTT.GET_ENC_VAL", line 10
ORA-06512: at line 4
```

What went wrong here? The only thing that changed was the input string: the first
one I passed was 16 characters long, but the second one was 17 characters. It turns
out that the input to the function DES3ENCRYPT must be an exact multiple of eight
characters; if it is not, the exception will trigger an ORA-28232 error. In this type of
encryption, known as *block ciphering*, the encryption routines work on a block of
characters at a time (where a block is eight characters long). If the length of the input
value is not a multiple of eight, the string has to be padded to make it so, as discussed earlier in the "Padding and Chaining" section. I can easily modify the input
string to make it such inside the function, as follows:

```
/* File on web: get_enc_val_2.sql */

CREATE OR REPLACE FUNCTION get_enc_val (p_in_val IN VARCHAR2, p_key IN VARCHAR2)
   RETURN VARCHAR2
IS
   l_enc_val   VARCHAR2 (200);
   l_in_val    VARCHAR2 (200);
BEGIN
   l_in_val := RPAD (p_in_val, (8 * ROUND (LENGTH (p_in_val) / 8, 0) + 8));
   l_enc_val :=
      DBMS_OBFUSCATION_TOOLKIT.des3encrypt (input_string    => l_in_val,
                                            key_string      => p_key
                                           );
   l_enc_val := RAWTOHEX (UTL_RAW.cast_to_raw (l_enc_val));
   RETURN l_enc_val;
END;
/
```

The only difference here is that I have modified the input string to right-pad it with
blank spaces to make it a multiple of eight bytes. If you use this modified function,
you can pass strings of any length to be encrypted.

 If you are using the DBMS_CRYPTO package in Oracle Database 10g,
you need not pad the input explicitly; padding is done by the package
itself. As mentioned earlier, that package also offers additional choices
of encryption algorithms and padding and chaining methods.

Specifying an Initialization Vector

The encryption described in the previous section works very well for most situations. However some intruders are still one step ahead of us. One of the code-cracking tools (also known as *cryptoanalysis*) they employ is to check the header information of the encrypted data to identify a pattern. To prevent this, you can add a non-data-related random value to the beginning of your actual data. This is a bit like creating some very simple encrypted data of your own. For example, if your actual data is 12345678, you could affix a random value, say 6675, before it to make it 667512345678, which can then be encrypted. The header information then contains some value related to 6675, not the actual data. When decrypting, you need to make sure to remove these random characters.

The random characters prefixed to the data are known as the *initialization vector* (IV). In the DBMS_OBFUSCATION_TOOLKIT, you specify this initialization vector in the DES3ENCRYPT function as an additional parameter called iv_string. Because the IV is prefixed to the actual data, the length of the combined string, not just the data, must be a multiple of eight. Let's modify our encryption function to accept this parameter and make the length a multiple of eight.

```
/* File on web get_enc_val_3.sql */

CREATE OR REPLACE FUNCTION get_enc_val (
    p_in_val    IN   VARCHAR2,
    p_key       IN   VARCHAR2,
    p_iv        IN   VARCHAR2 := NULL
)
    RETURN VARCHAR2
IS
    l_enc_val   VARCHAR2 (200);
    l_in_val    VARCHAR2 (200);
    l_iv        VARCHAR2 (200);
BEGIN
    l_in_val := RPAD (p_in_val, (8 * ROUND (LENGTH (p_in_val) / 8, 0) + 8));
    l_iv := RPAD (p_iv, (8 * ROUND (LENGTH (p_iv) / 8, 0) + 8));
    l_enc_val :=
        DBMS_OBFUSCATION_TOOLKIT.des3encrypt (input_string    => l_in_val,
                                              key_string      => p_key,
                                              iv_string       => l_iv
                                             );
    l_enc_val := RAWTOHEX (UTL_RAW.cast_to_raw (l_enc_val));
    RETURN l_enc_val;
END;
```

Decrypting Data

So far, I have focused on encrypting the data; let's see how to decrypt it to get back the original value with the DES3DECRYPT function. In the following PL/SQL block, I will create an encrypted value from *cleartext* and then decrypt it.

```
DECLARE
    l_enc_val    VARCHAR2 (2000);
    l_dec_val    VARCHAR2 (2000) := 'Clear Text Data';
    l_key        VARCHAR2 (2000) := 'ABCDEFGHIJKLMNOP';
BEGIN
    l_enc_val := get_enc_val (l_dec_val, l_key, '12345678');
    l_dec_val :=
        DBMS_OBFUSCATION_TOOLKIT.des3decrypt
                (input_string        => UTL_RAW.cast_to_varchar2
                                                    (HEXTORAW (l_enc_val)
                                                    ),
                key_string          => l_key
                );
    DBMS_OUTPUT.put_line ('Decrypted Value = ' || l_dec_val);
END;
/
```

The output is:

```
Decrypted Value = s}?2+  ¬xt Data

PL/SQL procedure successfully completed.
```

Wait! The decrypted value is *different* from the input given. What went wrong?

Note the parameters to the DES3DECRYPT function. Have you supplied the IV to it? Because an IV was specified during the encryption process, it must be specified during decryption, as well. Let's rewrite the block with the IV value of 12345678:

```
DECLARE
    l_enc_val    VARCHAR2 (2000);
    l_dec_val    VARCHAR2 (2000) := 'Clear Text Data';
    l_key        VARCHAR2 (2000) := 'ABCDEFGHIJKLMNOP';
BEGIN
    l_enc_val := get_enc_val (l_dec_val, l_key, '12345678');
    l_dec_val :=
        DBMS_OBFUSCATION_TOOLKIT.des3decrypt
                (input_string        => UTL_RAW.cast_to_varchar2
                                                    (HEXTORAW (l_enc_val)
                                                    ),
                key_string          => l_key,
                iv_string           => '12345678'
                );
    DBMS_OUTPUT.put_line ('Decrypted Value = ' || l_dec_val);
END;
/
```

The output is as expected:

```
Decrypted Value = Clear Text Data

PL/SQL procedure successfully completed.
```

If you use an IV when encrypting data, you must use the *same* IV when decrypting it.

In a way, IV acts as a key or a part of the key, but it can't be relied on as a key as such. Why? Consider the following code.

```
DECLARE
    l_enc_val    VARCHAR2 (2000);
    l_dec_val    VARCHAR2 (2000) := 'Clear Text Data';
    l_key        VARCHAR2 (2000) := 'ABCDEFGHIJKLMNOP';
BEGIN
    l_enc_val := get_enc_val (l_dec_val, l_key, '12345678');
    l_dec_val :=
        DBMS_OBFUSCATION_TOOLKIT.des3decrypt
                (input_string      => UTL_RAW.cast_to_varchar2
                                                    (HEXTORAW (l_enc_val)
                                                    ),
                key_string        => l_key,
                iv_string         => '1234567X'
                );
    DBMS_OUTPUT.put_line ('Decrypted Value = ' || l_dec_val);
END;
/
```

The output is:

```
Decrypted Value = Clear T?xt Data

PL/SQL procedure successfully completed.
```

The IV parameter is 12345678 during encryption but 1234567X during decryption; only the eighth character has changed. That's because the decrypted value is not exactly the same as the input value; the eighth character is a nonprintable one instead of the letter *e*. Although the returned data is not exactly the same, it might be easier to guess by supplying random values for the initialization vector, a procedure known as a *brute-force attack*. Because IVs are typically shorter than keys, that guess may take less time, so you should not rely on the IV as a key.

The initialization vector simply modifies the input cleartext value to prevent repetition; it is not a substitute for the encryption key.

Encrypting RAW Data

We've talked a bit about the use of RAW data. Here we'll explore how you can encrypt data whose datatype is RAW by taking advantage of the fact that within the DBMS_OBFUSCATION_TOOLKIT package, the DES3ENCRYPT and DES3DECRYPT programs are overloaded. That means that they have several variants. Each has a procedure format in which exactly the same parameters are passed as input parameters and the return value is passed back to the user using an OUT parameter named either encrypted_string or decrypted_string (depending on whether you are encrypting or decrypting). The functions and procedures are also overloaded to accommodate the RAW datatype for the parameters. You will use these variants if you need to manipulate raw data such as large objects (LOBs).

It is certainly possible to convert RAW values as shown here when doing encryption and decryption:

```
/* File on web: enc_raw.sql */

CREATE OR REPLACE FUNCTION enc_raw (
    p_in_val   IN    VARCHAR2,
    p_key      IN    VARCHAR2,
    p_iv       IN    VARCHAR2
)
    RETURN VARCHAR2
IS
    l_enc_val    RAW (200);
    l_in_val     RAW (200);
    l_iv         RAW (200);
BEGIN
    l_in_val :=
        UTL_RAW.cast_to_raw (RPAD (p_in_val,
                                  (8 * ROUND (LENGTH (p_in_val) / 8, 0) + 8
                                  )
                                  )
                            );
    l_iv :=
        UTL_RAW.cast_to_raw (RPAD (p_iv, (8 * ROUND (LENGTH (p_iv) / 8, 0) + 8)));
    l_enc_val :=
        DBMS_OBFUSCATION_TOOLKIT.des3encrypt (input       => l_in_val,
                                              KEY         => p_key,
                                              iv          => l_iv
                                             );
    RETURN RAWTOHEX (UTL_RAW.cast_to_raw (l_enc_val));
END;
/
```

However, the additional processing required for conversion between the RAW and VARCHAR2 datatypes might actually *hurt* performance, rather than help it. In my tests, this version for VARCHAR2 and NUMBER datatypes underperformed the plain string version by about 50%. Because encryption is a CPU-intensive process, this measurement may vary widely based on the host system. However, the general rule of thumb is to avoid this raw manipulation if possible if your data is primarily character-based and you use only one type of character set.

Performing Multi-Pass Encryption

Earlier in this chapter, in the "Encryption Algorithms" section, I mentioned that the DES standard had been enhanced so that content could pass through the process *two*

When Should You Use Raw Encryption?

One situation in which you should use raw encryption is when are you are using the BLOB datatype, as explained earlier.

Another situation is when non-English characters are used in the database. If you are using *Oracle Globalization Support* (previously known as *National Language Support,* or NLS), RAW encryption and decryption can handle such characters very well without necessitating any additional manipulations, especially while exporting and importing data. The encrypted data can be moved across databases without fear of corruption.

or three times, leading to the name *Triple DES*, or DES3. Oracle's implementation of DES3 through the function DES3ENCRYPT uses the two-pass scheme by default. However, you can instruct the function to use three passes via a new parameter called *which*. The default value, 0, indicates only two passes, and 1 indicates three. Performing three passes, of course, provides stronger encryption.

To use the three-pass scheme, you must use a key of at least 24 bytes, instead of the 16-byte one we've been using up until now. I can change the original function as follows to allow the user to specify the two-pass or three-pass process.

```
/* File on web: get_enc_val_4.sql */

CREATE OR REPLACE FUNCTION get_enc_val (
   p_in_val    IN    VARCHAR2,
   p_key       IN    VARCHAR2,
   p_iv        IN    VARCHAR2,
   p_which     IN    NUMBER := 0
)
   RETURN VARCHAR2
IS
   l_enc_val    VARCHAR2 (200);
   l_in_val     VARCHAR2 (200);
   l_iv         VARCHAR2 (200);
BEGIN
   l_in_val := RPAD (p_in_val, (8 * ROUND (LENGTH (p_in_val) / 8, 0) + 8));
   l_iv := RPAD (p_iv, (8 * ROUND (LENGTH (p_iv) / 8, 0) + 8));
   l_enc_val :=
      DBMS_OBFUSCATION_TOOLKIT.des3encrypt (input_string    => l_in_val,
                                            key_string      => p_key,
                                            iv_string       => l_iv,
                                            which           => p_which
                                           );
   l_enc_val := RAWTOHEX (UTL_RAW.cast_to_raw (l_enc_val));
   RETURN l_enc_val;
END;
/
```

Changing the number of passes during encryption also means that, during decryption three passes, instead of two, must be used. During the decryption process, I must explicitly set the *which* parameter to 1.

```
DECLARE
   l_enc_val   VARCHAR2 (2000);
   l_dec_val   VARCHAR2 (2000) := 'Clear Text Data';
   l_key       VARCHAR2 (2000) := 'ABCDEFGHIJKLMNOPQRSTUVWXY';
BEGIN
   l_enc_val := get_enc_val (l_dec_val, l_key, '12345678', 1);
   l_dec_val :=
      DBMS_OBFUSCATION_TOOLKIT.des3decrypt
            (input_string      => UTL_RAW.cast_to_varchar2
                                                (HEXTORAW (l_enc_val)
                                                ),

             key_string        => l_key,
             iv_string         => '12345678',
             which             => 1
            );
   DBMS_OUTPUT.put_line ('Decrypted Value = ' || l_dec_val);
END;
/
```

The length of the key is now 24 bytes, the minimum required for the three-pass encryption process.

Putting It Together

Now that you've learned about the components of the encryption process, let's put it all together to build our own unified tool. I'll modify our old faithful get_enc_val function as follows.

```
/* File on web: get_enc_val_5.sql */

CREATE OR REPLACE FUNCTION get_enc_val (
   p_in_val   IN   VARCHAR2,
   p_key      IN   VARCHAR2,
   p_iv       IN   VARCHAR2 := NULL,
   p_which    IN   NUMBER := 0
)
   RETURN VARCHAR2
IS
   l_enc_val   VARCHAR2 (200);
   l_in_val    VARCHAR2 (200);
   l_iv        VARCHAR2 (200);
BEGIN
   IF p_which = 0
   THEN
      IF LENGTH (p_key) < 16
      THEN
         raise_application_error
                        (-20001,
                         'Key length less than 16 for two-pass scheme'
                        );
```

```
         END IF;
      ELSIF p_which = 1
      THEN
         IF LENGTH (p_key) < 24
         THEN
            raise_application_error
                         (-20002,
                          'Key length less than 24 for three-pass scheme'
                         );
         END IF;
      ELSE
         raise_application_error (-20003,
                              'Incorrect value of which '
                          || p_which
                          || '; must be 0 or 1'
                         );
      END IF;

      l_in_val := RPAD (p_in_val, (8 * ROUND (LENGTH (p_in_val) / 8, 0) + 8));
      l_iv := RPAD (p_iv, (8 * ROUND (LENGTH (p_iv) / 8, 0) + 8));
      l_enc_val :=
         DBMS_OBFUSCATION_TOOLKIT.des3encrypt (input_string    => l_in_val,
                                               key_string      => p_key,
                                               iv_string       => l_iv,
                                               which           => p_which
                                              );
      l_enc_val := RAWTOHEX (UTL_RAW.cast_to_raw (l_enc_val));
      RETURN l_enc_val;
   END;
   /
```

I'll also build a similar function for decryption, named get_dec_val, as follows.

```
/* File on web: get_dec_val_1.sql */

CREATE OR REPLACE FUNCTION get_dec_val (
   p_in_val    VARCHAR2,
   p_key       VARCHAR2,
   p_iv        VARCHAR2 := NULL,
   p_which     NUMBER := 0
)
   RETURN VARCHAR2
IS
   l_dec_val   VARCHAR2 (2000);
   l_iv        VARCHAR2 (2000);
BEGIN
   IF p_which = 0
   THEN
      IF LENGTH (p_key) < 16
      THEN
         raise_application_error
                      (-20001,
                       'Key length less than 16 for two-pass scheme'
                      );
```

```
                END IF;
        ELSIF p_which = 1
        THEN
            IF LENGTH (p_key) < 24
            THEN
                raise_application_error
                            (-20002,
                             'Key length less than 24 for three-pass scheme'
                            );
            END IF;
        ELSE
            raise_application_error (-20003,
                                     'Incorrect value of which '
                            || p_which
                            || '; must be 0 or 1'
                            );
        END IF;

        l_iv := RPAD (p_iv, (8 * ROUND (LENGTH (p_iv) / 8, 0) + 8));
        l_dec_val :=
            DBMS_OBFUSCATION_TOOLKIT.des3decrypt
                    (input_string      => UTL_RAW.cast_to_varchar2
                                                    (HEXTORAW (p_in_val)
                                                    ),
                    key_string        => p_key,
                    iv_string         => l_iv,
                    which             => p_which
                    );
        RETURN RTRIM (l_dec_val);
    END;
    /
```

Note that I have padded the IV parameter to make its length a multiple of eight. Remember that during encryption I padded the input value to make its length a multiple of eight; after decryption, I have to remove those added blank spaces, as we did in the return string of the above function.

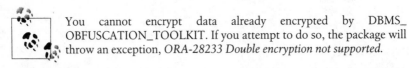 You cannot encrypt data already encrypted by DBMS_OBFUSCATION_TOOLKIT. If you attempt to do so, the package will throw an exception, *ORA-28233 Double encryption not supported.*

Generating Keys

It should be apparent from the discussion so far that the weakest link in the chain is the encryption key. To successfully decrypt the encrypted data, the key is literally that—*the key*, and to protect the encryption, you must make that key very difficult to guess. In the examples we have presented so far, we have used a 16-byte key for DES3 two-pass encryption and a 24-byte key for DES3 three-pass encryption.

There are two important points to remember about using a proper encryption key:

- The longer the key is, the more difficult it is to guess. The two-pass method accepts a key of 128 bits, and the three-pass method accepts a key of 192 bits. To have an acceptable level of encryption, you should use as large a key as possible.

- In addition to being long, the key should be one that does not follow a pattern or format prone to guessing. In the earlier examples, I used the value 1234567890123456 as the key, a sequence of numbers in a predictable order. This is not acceptable. A value of a2H8s7X40Ys8346yp2 is better.

Using DES3GETKEY

The DBMS_OBFUSCATION_TOOLKIT provides a function, DES3GETKEY (and as usual, a procedure, and both formats are overloaded with multiple datatypes) that allows you to generate a cryptographically acceptable key. The function needs a seed value as a starting point to generate a random value that can be used as a key.

The DBMS_CRYPTO package available in Oracle Database 10*g* has a function named GETRANDOMBYTES that can be used to produce cryptographically random keys.

You can call the function as follows:

```
l_ret := DBMS_OBFUSCATION_TOOLKIT.des3getkey (
   seed_string => l_seed
);
```

The value of l_seed must be a random string of 80 characters; a longer value is accepted, but only 80 characters will be used. The value returned is a VARCHAR2, stored in the variable l_ret. Because the seed length must be 80 characters, let's use a simple scheme to generate the value. Note that this is not the actual key; it is just the seed. (For a detailed discussion of seeds, see Chapter 7.)

```
l_seed varchar2(2000) :=
    '1234567890'||
    '1234567890'||
    '1234567890'||
    '1234567890'||
    '1234567890'||
    '1234567890'||
    '1234567890'||
    '1234567890'
```

This function DES3GETKEY returns a value in binary format, which probably should be converted to a usable type such as VARCHAR2, so I can modify the returned key as follows:

```
l_ret := rawtohex(utl_raw.cast_to_raw(l_ret));
```

This converts the key to RAW and then to a hexadecimal value. One more parameter—*which*—is used to specify either the two-pass or three-pass method.

Putting everything together, my function to generate the key looks like this.

```
/* File on web: get_key_1.sql */

 1  CREATE OR REPLACE FUNCTION get_key (
 2     p_seed    VARCHAR2 :=   '1234567890'
 3                          || '1234567890'
 4                          || '1234567890'
 5                          || '1234567890'
 6                          || '1234567890'
 7                          || '1234567890'
 8                          || '1234567890'
 9                          || '1234567890',
10     p_which   NUMBER := 0
11  )
12     RETURN VARCHAR2
13  IS
14     l_seed   VARCHAR2 (80);
15     l_ret    VARCHAR2 (2000);
16  BEGIN
17     l_seed := RPAD (p_seed, 80);
18     l_ret :=
19        DBMS_OBFUSCATION_TOOLKIT.des3getkey (seed_string    => l_seed,
20                                             which          => p_which
21                                            );
22     l_ret := RAWTOHEX (UTL_RAW.cast_to_raw (l_ret));
23     RETURN l_ret;
24* END;
```

The following table explains the significant elements of this code.

Lines	Description
2–9	One very important parameter is the seed value, which defaults to a string, 1234567890, repeated 8 times to create an 80-byte string. Obviously, this is not secure, so use any 80-byte string constant here. Longer strings will not give any better randomness, as only the first 80 bytes will be used.
10	I assume the default 2-pass DES3 key generation, so the "which" parameter is 0. The three-pass method would require this parameter to be 1.
17	The seed must be 80 bytes long. If the user supplies a smaller string, the function will accept it and pad it to 80 bytes rather than throw an error.
18	The function DES3GETKEY returns a VARCHAR2.
22	The value returned is VARCHAR2 but is full of control characters. We first convert it to a RAW datatype and then to a hexadecimal value.

This function will return a cryptographically random value each time it is called. Let's see how it works.

```
BEGIN
    DBMS_OUTPUT.put_line ('Key=' || get_key);
    DBMS_OUTPUT.put_line ('Key=' || get_key);
    DBMS_OUTPUT.put_line ('Key=' || get_key);
    DBMS_OUTPUT.put_line ('Key=' || get_key);
    DBMS_OUTPUT.put_line ('Key=' || get_key);
END;
```

The output is:

```
Key=4992D7CCC6B9428F11D7EC612E728C02
Key=4DB67B0610E3EB2EB6B7B6B39DC4DB13
Key=4DC1F80A3FE4FC266A667CE2A11E25C9
Key=111768ECC7E6F0C5DFAD6B9B0C146C9A
Key=75FE17395B8209FC578C41B26E22CBC7
```

Note how the key generated is different in each case, even though the seed is the same. The actual output may be different when you run this; this is supposed to be random.

Using the key in encryption

Using the functions developed above, I can satisfactorily encrypt sensitive data. Let's see a very simple example.

```
DECLARE
    l_key    VARCHAR2 (80);
    l_enc    VARCHAR2 (2000);
BEGIN
    l_key := get_key;
    l_enc := get_enc_val ('Input Value', l_key);
    DBMS_OUTPUT.put_line ('Key = ' || l_key || ' Encrypted Value = ' || l_enc);
END;
/
```

The output is:

```
Key = 3DA5335923D784F21B0C27B61496D1AD Encrypted Value =
076A5703A745D03934B56F7500C1DCB4
```

Generating Keys in Older Oracle Releases

Unfortunately, the DES3GETKEY function is not available in Oracle8i Database. You must create your own random string generator to generate an appropriate key. Here is where our knowledge of random string generation (see Chapter 7) comes in handy. In earlier releases, you can write your own get_key function, as follows.

```
1  CREATE OR REPLACE FUNCTION get_key
2     RETURN VARCHAR2
3  IS
4     l_ret    VARCHAR2 (200);
5  BEGIN
6     l_ret := DBMS_RANDOM.STRING ('x', 24);
7     l_ret := RAWTOHEX (UTL_RAW.cast_to_raw (l_ret));
8     RETURN l_ret;
9* END;
```

In line 6, I generate a printable random string of 24 bytes. In line 7, I cast the line to a RAW datatype and then convert it to hexadecimal as I did in my Oracle9i Database example. Finally, I return the string as the key.

This process works, but the generated string is not sufficiently random to be crypto-graphically strong. However, because earlier Oracle releases do not provide a facility to generate keys, the only alternative is to supply keys manually, a process that may not be possible in real-world implementations. This approach is pretty much the only option, but use it with caution.

Let's decrypt the encrypted value using the same key.

```
DECLARE
   l_key   VARCHAR2 (80)    := '3DA5335923D784F21B0C27B61496D1AD';
   l_enc   VARCHAR2 (2000) := '076A5703A745D03934B56F7500C1DCB4';
   l_dec   VARCHAR2 (2000);
BEGIN
   l_dec := get_dec_val (l_enc, l_key);
   DBMS_OUTPUT.put_line ('Decrypted Value = ' || l_dec);
END;
/
```

The output is:

```
Decrypted Value = Input Value
```

Using the functions get_key, get_enc_val, and get_dec_val we can build a complete encryption system, as you'll see in the next section.

A Practical Encryption Example

How can we use our newfound knowledge of encryption in a system that we might encounter in the real world? Let's examine a table named ACCOUNTS. The table looks like this.

```
SQL> DESC accounts
 Name                                      Null?    Type
 ----------------------------------------- -------- -------------------
 ACCOUNT_NO                                NOT NULL NUMBER
 BALANCE                                            NUMBER
 ACCOUNT_NAME                                       VARCHAR2(200)
```

I want to protect the data by encrypting the columns BALANCE and ACCOUNT_NAME. As I've said many times, the most important element is the key, and it must be an appropriate one. I can generate a key, use it to encrypt the column value, and then store the key and the encrypted value somewhere to be retrieved later. How exactly can I do this? I have a few choices:

- I could define a view on the table as follows:

  1. Add the columns ENC_BALANCE and ENC_ACCOUNT_NAME to the table to store the encrypted values of the corresponding columns.

  2. Add another column named ENC_KEY to store the key used for encryption.

  3. Create a view called VW_ACCOUNTS defined as follows:

     ```
     CREATE OR REPLACE VIEW vw_accounts
     AS
        SELECT account_no.enc_balance AS balance
             , enc_account_name AS account_name
          FROM accounts
     /
     ```

  4. Create INSTEAD OF triggers to handle updates and inserts to the view, if needed.

  5. Create a public synonym ACCOUNTS for the view VW_ACCOUNTS.

  6. Grant all privileges on VW_ACCOUNTS and revoke all privileges on ACCOUNTS.

  This arrangement ensures that the schema owner, as well as any users who have been given direct privileges on the ACCOUNTS table, will see the cleartext values. All others will see only the encrypted values.

- I could encrypt the columns themselves, and use the view to show the decrypted data, as follows:

  1. Add the column ENC_KEY to store the key for that row.

  2. Store the encrypted values of BALANCE and ACCOUNT_NAME in those columns.

  3. Create a view named VW_ACCOUNTS as follows:

     ```
     CREATE OR REPLACE VIEW vw_accounts
     AS
        SELECT account_no.get_dec_val (balance, enc_key) AS balance,
               get_dec_val (enc_account_name, enc_key) AS account_name
          FROM accounts
     /
     ```

4. Now, the table will show the encrypted value, but the view will show the cleartext values; privileges on those values can be granted to users.

5. Create triggers on the table to convert the values to encrypted values before inserting or updating the columns.

The advantage of this approach is that the table itself need not be changed.

- I could store the keys separate from the table. Both of the approaches described above have a serious flaw—the key is stored in the table. If someone has the access required to select from the table, he will be able to see the key and decrypt the values. A better approach is to store the keys separate from the source table, as follows:

    1. Create a table called ACCOUNT_KEYS with only two columns:

        ACCOUNT_NO: corresponds to the ACCOUNT_NO of the record in the ACCOUNTS table.

        ENC_KEY: the key used to encrypt the value.

    2. Make the actual table ACCOUNTS contain the encrypted values, not the cleartext values.

    3. Create triggers on the ACCOUNTS table. The AFTER INSERT trigger generates a key, uses it to encrypt the actual value given by the user, changes the value to the encrypted value before storing, and finally stores the key in the ACCOUNT_KEYS table.

    4. Create a view to display decrypted data by joining both of the tables.

Storing the Keys

Storing the keys is the most crucial part of the encryption exercise. If you don't do this properly, the whole point of safeguarding data by encrypting it becomes moot. There are a variety of storage options:

In database tables
This approach, illustrated in the example above, is the most convenient way to handle keys. It suffers from a serious drawback, however: it offers no protection from the DBA who is able to access all tables.

In an operating system file
The file can be created at runtime by the client process via either the built-in package UTL_FILE or external tables, and it can then be used for decryption. After the read, the file can be destroyed. This approach offers protection from all other users, including the DBA.

Issued by the user
At runtime, the user can provide the key to the function for decryption. This is the most secure, but the most impractical, approach of the three. The disadvantage is that the user may forget the key, which means that it will be impossible to ever decrypt the encrypted data.

Encryption in Oracle Database 10*g*

Starting with Oracle Database 10*g* Release 1, Oracle provides the DBMS_CRYPTO package for encryption. In this section, I'll show how to generate keys and encrypt data using this new package. First, though, let's look at the differences between the DBMS_CRYPTO and the DBMS_OBFUSCATION_TOOLKIT packages.

The DBMS_OBFUSCATION_TOOLKIT package remains available in Oracle Database 10*g*, although Oracle recommends that you start using the new package as the capabilities of the old package are limited compared with those of DBMS_CRYPTO.

Differences Between DBMS_CRYPTO and DBMS_OBFUSCATION_TOOLKIT

There are a number of key differences between the DBMS_CRYPTO and DBMS_OBFUSCATION_TOOLKIT packages, summarized below:

Advanced Encryption Standard
> The DES and DES3 algorithms have been showing signs of age, and many organizations are now using a more secure symmetric encryption algorithm, the Advanced Encryption Standard (AES). The DBMS_OBFUSCATION_TOOLKIT package does not support encryption using this newer standard, but DBMS_CRYPTO does.

Stream ciphering
> Encryption can be performed on a block of data at a time via a process known as *block ciphering*. This method is the most common and the easiest to implement. However, some systems may not have the luxury of getting data in uniform chunks—for example, encrypted content relayed through the public media or other outlets. In such cases, the content must be encrypted, as it comes in, via a process known as *stream ciphering*. The DBMS_OBFUSCATION_TOOLKIT package does not support stream ciphering, but DBMS_CRYPTO does.

Secure Hash Algorithm
> The DBMS_OBFUSCATION_TOOLKIT package supports only the Message Digest (MD5) function for cryptographic hashing, not more modern and secure algorithms such as the Secure Hash Algorithm 1 (SHA-1) provided by DBMS_CRYPTO.

Message Authentication Code
> The use of a Message Authentication Code (MAC) allows the creation of a hashed value of the message to be transmitted; that value may then be compared with the value calculated on the message at the other end to ensure the integrity of that message. This process is similar to hashing except that a key must be supplied (as with encryption) to create the hash value. The DBMS_

OBFUSCATION_TOOLKIT package does not support the creation of a MAC, but DBMS_CRYPTO does.

Large objects

The DBMS_OBFUSCATION_TOOLKIT package does not support large objects (LOBs) in their *native* format, but DBMS_CRYPTO does. Encryption of LOBs with the older package requires that they be converted first to RAW format using the built-in UTL_RAW package. This could create some difficulty in writing applications.

 In certain circumstances, you may still want to use the DBMS_OBFUSCATION_TOOLKIT package even if you are running Oracle Database 10*g*. For example, if you are deploying an application in both Oracle9*i* Database and Oracle Database 10*g*, you will have to use the older package because both Oracle versions support it. Similarly, if you are encrypting data in Oracle Database 10*g* that may be decrypted in Oracle9*i* Database, you will again have to use DBMS_OBFUSCATION_TOOLKIT.

Generating Keys

As mentioned earlier, the DBMS_OBFUSCATION_TOOLKIT function used to generate an encryption key, DES3GETKEY, is not available in the DBMS_CRYPTO package. A new function, RANDOMBYTES, takes its place. If you want to use my get_key function in Oracle Database 10*g*, you will need to change this function to use RANDOMBYTES instead.

You need to be aware of the following differences when switching key generation methods:

- In the DBMS_OBFUSCATION_TOOLKIT, the DES3GETKEY function could generate a key with a datatype of either VARCHAR2 or RAW. In DBMS_CRYPTO, all encryptions involving VARCHAR2 are done through RAW, so a VARCHAR2 key is not useful, and the RANDOMBYTES function returns only a RAW key.

- In DBMS_CRYPTO, you do not need to specify the seed as you do in the DBMS_OBFUSCATION_TOOLKIT. The function gets the seed from the parameter SQLNET.CRYPTO_SEED inside the file *SQLNET.ORA*. This parameter, therefore, must have a valid value of any combination of characters between 10 and 70 bytes long. Here is an example setting of the parameter:

```
SQLNET.CRYPTO_SEED =
weipcfwe0cu0we98c0wedcpoweqdufd2d2df2dk2d2d23fv43098fpiwef02uc2ecw1x982jd23d908d
```

Let's see how I need to change my get_key function to accommodate these changes.

```
/* File on web: get_key_2.sql */

CREATE OR REPLACE FUNCTION get_key (p_length IN PLS_INTEGER)
```

```
      RETURN RAW
   IS
      l_ret    RAW (4000);
   BEGIN
      l_ret := dbms_crypto.randombytes (p_length);
      RETURN l_ret;
   END;
   /
```

Note that there is no *which* parameter, either. In addition, I have specified the length of the key to be generated, which is important during encryption.

 The package DBMS_CRYPTO may not have been granted to PUBLIC by default, or there may not be a public synonym for it. If you want all developers to be able to use DBMS_CRYPTO, make sure you have a public synonym and proper grants in place. You can execute the following statements as SYS to accomplish this.

```
GRANT EXECUTE ON dbms_crypto TO PUBLIC;

CREATE PUBLIC SYNONYM dbms_crypto FOR sys.dbms_crypto;
```

Note that if the public synonym already exists, the statement will fail, but that will not cause any problems in your database.

The RANDOMBYTES function is a very simple one, and you may decide that you do not need a wrapper function to simplify it further. However, you may still want to wrap the function inside get_key for the following reasons.

- If your existing code uses the get_key function, you would have to create a function to ensure backward compatibility anyway.

- It takes fewer characters to type "get_key", which can enhance code readability.

- Uniformity usually helps in developing quality code, so wrapping may be beneficial for that reason alone.

In addition to generating keys in RAW via the RANDOMBYTES function, DBMS_CRYPTO can be used to produce numbers and binary integers. The RANDOMINTEGER function generates a binary integer key, as shown in this code segment:

```
l_ret := DBMS_CRYPTO.randominteger;
```

The RANDOMNUMBER function generates a key of the integer datatype with a length of 2^{128} as follows:

```
l_ret := DBMS_CRYPTO.randomnumber;
```

You may be wondering why we need an integer and a binary integer when the encryption relies on the RAW datatype only. They are not needed, strictly speaking, for encryption, but may be useful in generating pseudo-random numbers for other processing.

Encrypting Data

After the key is generated, I have to encrypt my data. I do that with the ENCRYPT program in the DBMS_CRYPTO package. As with its DBMS_OBFUSCATION_ TOOLKIT encryption cousin, ENCRYPT is overloaded; it provides both function and procedure variants. But in contrast to DBMS_OBFUSCATION_TOOLKIT, this overloading has a purpose in DBMS_CRYPTO. The function variant accepts only a RAW datatype as an input value, while the procedure variant accepts only CLOB and BLOB as input values.

Let's look at the simplest case of RAW encryption in the ENCRYPT function. Here is the declaration of the function:

```
DBMS_CRYPTO.encrypt(
    src IN RAW,
    typ IN PLS_INTEGER,
    key IN RAW,
    iv  IN RAW          DEFAULT NULL)
  RETURN RAW;
```

You should already be familiar with three of these parameters:

src
: The input value to be encrypted

key
: The encryption key

iv
: The initialization vector.

The second parameter, *typ*, however, is new and requires a more detailed explanation.

Specifying the encryption type

The DBMS_OBFUSCATION_TOOLKIT and DBMS_CRYPTO packages differ in how they allow you to select the type of encryption. DBMS_OBFUSCATION_ TOOLKIT provides specific functions (and corresponding procedures) for each algorithm—for example, DESENCRYPT for DES and DES3ENCRYPT for Triple DES. DBMS_CRYPTO, on the other hand, provides only a single function, and the encryption type is specified via a parameter. Table 4-3 shows the algorithms available in the encryption process and their corresponding constants. You specify the desired constant in the form *PackageName.Constant.Name*; to select Triple DES, for example, you would use the constant DBMS_CRYPTO. ENCRYPT_3DES. Note that the AES variants and RC4 are not supported by the older package.

Table 4-3. Types of encryption in DBMS_CRYPTO

Constant	Description	Effective key length
ENCRYPT_DES	Data Encryption Standard (DES)	56
ENCRYPT_3DES_2KEY	Modified Triple Data Encryption Standard (3DES); operates on a block 3 times with 2 keys	112
ENCRYPT_3DES	Triple Data Encryption Standard (3DES); operates on a block 3 times	156
ENCRYPT_AES128	Advanced Encryption Standard	128
ENCRYPT_AES192	Advanced Encryption Standard	192
ENCRYPT_AES256	Advanced Encryption Standard	256
ENCRYPT_RC4	Streaming cipher (the only one)	

You specify the desired type of encryption by selecting the correct value for the typ parameter; however, this value is only a *part* of the value of the parameter, which encodes other information as well, as the next section describes.

Specifying chaining

While encrypting data, each block to be encrypted can be either independently encrypted or chained with previous blocks to produce a more cryptographically secure system. The latter produces a more secure encrypted value. You choose the desired chaining method by selecting the appropriate constant from Table 4-4 and providing it as part of the typ parameter—for example, DBMS_CRYPTO.CHAIN_OFB.

Table 4-4. Types of chaining in DBMS_CRYPTO

Constant	Description
CHAIN_CBC	Cipher Block Chaining format
CHAIN_ECB	Electronic Code Book format
CHAIN_CFB	Cipher Feedback format
CHAIN_OFB	Output Feedback format

Specifying padding

Remember that in block ciphering the data must be in units of blocks. What if the data is not an exact multiple? With DBMS_OBFUSCATION_TOOLKIT, you have to pad the data explicitly to make its length a multiple. However, this practice is not considered cryptographically secure. DBMS_CRYPTO allows you to specify the type of padding; most organizations use the PKCS#5 method.

You choose the desired padding method by selecting the appropriate constant from Table 4-5 and providing it as part of the typ parameter—for example, DBMS_CRYPTO.PAD_PKCS5.

Table 4-5. *Types of padding in DBMS_CRYPTO*

Constant	Description
PAD_PKCS5	Padding with Public Key Cryptography System #5
PAD_ZERO	Padding with zeros
PAD_NONE	No padding is done; the data must be an exact multiple of the block size to be encrypted (a multiple of eight)

Combining options in the typ parameter

Now let's see how to put these various options together. Suppose that you want to select these encryption options:

Padding method
    Pad with zeros (PAD_ZERO)

Encryption algorithm
    128-bit key Advanced Encryption Standard (ENCRYPT_AES128)

Chaining method
    Block chaining via Cipher Feedback (CHAIN_CFB)

You can set the typ parameter as follows to express this combination of different settings—a rather lengthy string of values:

```
typ => DBMS_CRYPTO.pad_zero + DBMS_CRYPTO.encrypt_aes128 + DBMS_CRYPTO.chain_cfb
```

Using the same principle, you can specify any combination of options to the ENCRYPT function. Here is a typical complete call to the function:

```
DECLARE
    l_enc   RAW(2000);
    l_in    RAW(2000);
    l_key   RAW(2000);
BEGIN
    l_enc :=
        DBMS_CRYPTO.encrypt (src    => l_in,
                             KEY    => l_key,
                             typ    =>   DBMS_CRYPTO.pad_zero
                                       + DBMS_CRYPTO.encrypt_aes128
                                       + DBMS_CRYPTO.chain_cfb

                            );
END;
```

To make things more convenient, the package provides two constants with a predefined combination of values for these three parameters. Table 4-6 shows these constants and the set of encryption, padding, and chaining options they represent.

Table 4-6. *DBMS_CRYPTO constants with predefined sets for the typ parameter*

Constant	Encryption	Padding	Block chaining
DES_CBC_PKCS5	ENCRYPT_DES	PAD_PKCS5	CHAIN_CBC
DES3_CBC_PKCS5	ENCRYPT_3DES	PAD_PKCS5	CHAIN_CBC

Assuming that I still want to specify the DES algorithm, PKCS#5 padding, and cipher block chaining (CBC), I would use the combination constant as follows.

```
DECLARE
    l_enc   RAW(2000);
    l_in    RAW(2000);
    l_key   RAW(2000);
BEGIN
    l_enc :=
        DBMS_CRYPTO.encrypt (src      => l_in,
                             KEY      => l_key,
                             typ      => DBMS_CRYPTO.des_cbc_pkcs5
                             );
END;
/
```

Now let's rewrite the original function to encrypt a value as follows.

```
CREATE OR REPLACE FUNCTION get_enc_val (
    p_in_val    IN    RAW,
    p_key       IN    RAW,
    p_iv        IN    RAW := NULL
)
    RETURN RAW
IS
    l_enc_val    RAW (4000);
BEGIN
    l_enc_val :=
        DBMS_CRYPTO.encrypt (src      => p_in_val,
                             KEY      => p_key,
                             iv       => p_iv,
                             typ      =>   DBMS_CRYPTO.encrypt_aes128
                                         + DBMS_CRYPTO.chain_cbc
                                         + DBMS_CRYPTO.pad_pkcs5

                             );
    RETURN l_enc_val;
END;
/
```

Handling and converting RAW data

This function accepts the input values in RAW and assumes that you want to use the 128-bit AES encryption algorithm, PKCS#5 padding, and Cipher Block Chaining. In real-world applications, these assumptions may be too constraining. For instance, the input values are usually in VARCHAR2 or some numeric datatype, not RAW. Let's make the function more generic by having it accept VARCHAR2 instead of RAW. Because the ENCRYPT function requires RAW input, that means I will have to convert my original input to RAW. I can do this as follows:

```
l_in := UTL_I18N.string_to_raw (p_in_val, 'AL32UTF8');
```

You may recall that earlier in the chapter I used the built-in UTL_RAW package to convert from VARCHAR to RAW. But here I am using the function UTL_I18N.

STRING_TO_RAW, rather than UTL_RAW.CAST_TO_RAW, to do that conversion. Why?

The ENCRYPT function requires the input to be RAW, but it also requires a specific character set—AL32UTF8, which may not be the character set of the database. So I actually have to perform two conversions:

- From the current database character set to the character set AL32UTF8
- From VARCHAR2 to RAW

The CAST_TO_RAW function can't perform the character set conversion, but the STRING_TO_RAW function in the built-in package UTL_i18n can handle both.

 The UTL_i18n package is provided as part of Oracle's Globalization Support and is used to perform *globalization* (or *internationalization*, which is often shortened to "i18n"; the name is made up of the starting letter "i," the ending letter "n," and the 18 letters in between). You can find out more about PL/SQL and internationalization in Chapter 24 of *Oracle PL/SQL Programming*, 4th edition.

ENCRYPT also returns a RAW datatype, which may not be convenient to store in the database or easy to manipulate. I can convert the value from RAW to VARCHAR2 as follows:

```
l_enc_val := rawtohex(l_enc_val);
```

Specifying the encryption algorithm

Recall from the earlier discussion that the choice of algorithm depends on several factors—for example, upgrading from Oracle9i Database to Oracle Database 10g. If the source or destination of the encrypted data is in Oracle9i Database, you will not have access to the DBMS_CRYPTO package. Instead, you have to use DBMS_OBFUSCATION_TOOLKIT, which does not offer the AES algorithms. So even though AES algorithms are more secure and efficient, you will have no choice but to use something else, such as DES. For additional security, you might want to use 3DES (but be aware that it is slower than DES). In many cases you may need to choose different algorithms to satisfy different conditions, while the other two modifiers—padding and chaining—will remain the same. Unfortunately, the ENCRYPT function does not allow you to define the type of encryption algorithm directly; it must be passed as a parameter along with other modifiers (e.g., padding and chaining).

You can accomplish this yourself, however, by using a new parameter (p_algorithm) included in my user-defined generic encryption package. That parameter will accept only the following values, indicating the types of algorithms supported by DBMS_CRYPTO:

DES
3DES_2KEY

3DES
AES128
AES192
AES256
RC4

The passed value is then appended to the term "ENCRYPT_" and passed to the ENCRYPT function. The following code does just that:

```
l_enc_algo :=
    CASE p_algorithm
        WHEN 'DES'
            THEN DBMS_CRYPTO.encrypt_des
        WHEN '3DES_2KEY'
            THEN DBMS_CRYPTO.encrypt_3des_2key
        WHEN '3DES'
            THEN DBMS_CRYPTO.encrypt_3des
        WHEN 'AES128'
            THEN DBMS_CRYPTO.encrypt_aes128
        WHEN 'AES192'
            THEN DBMS_CRYPTO.encrypt_aes192
        WHEN 'AES256'
            THEN DBMS_CRYPTO.encrypt_aes256
        WHEN 'RC4'
            THEN DBMS_CRYPTO.encrypt_rc4
    END;
```

Putting it together

Putting everything together, the get_enc_val function now looks like this:

```
/* File on web: get_enc_val_6.sql */

CREATE OR REPLACE FUNCTION get_enc_val (
    p_in_val      IN    VARCHAR2,
    p_key         IN    VARCHAR2,
    p_algorithm   IN    VARCHAR2 := 'AES128',
    p_iv          IN    VARCHAR2 := NULL
)
    RETURN VARCHAR2
IS
    l_enc_val     RAW (4000);
    l_enc_algo    PLS_INTEGER;
    l_in          RAW (4000);
    l_iv          RAW (4000);
    l_key         RAW (4000);
    l_ret         VARCHAR2 (4000);
BEGIN
    l_enc_algo :=
        CASE p_algorithm
            WHEN 'DES'
                THEN DBMS_CRYPTO.encrypt_des
            WHEN '3DES_2KEY'
```

```
            THEN DBMS_CRYPTO.encrypt_3des_2key
        WHEN '3DES'
            THEN DBMS_CRYPTO.encrypt_3des
        WHEN 'AES128'
            THEN DBMS_CRYPTO.encrypt_aes128
        WHEN 'AES192'
            THEN DBMS_CRYPTO.encrypt_aes192
        WHEN 'AES256'
            THEN dbms_crypto.encrypt_aes256
        WHEN 'RC4'
            THEN DBMS_CRYPTO.encrypt_rc4
      END;
   l_in  := utl_i18n.string_to_raw (p_in_val, 'AL32UTF8');
   l_iv  := utl_i18n.string_to_raw (p_iv, 'AL32UTF8');
   l_key := utl_i18n.string_to_raw (p_key, 'AL32UTF8');
   l_enc_val :=
      DBMS_CRYPTO.encrypt (src      => l_in,
                           KEY      => l_key,
                           iv       => l_iv,
                           typ      =>  l_enc_algo
                                      + DBMS_CRYPTO.chain_cbc
                                      + DBMS_CRYPTO.pad_pkcs5
                          );
   l_ret := RAWTOHEX (l_enc_val);
   RETURN l_ret;
END;
```

After this function is created, let's test it.

```
SQL> SELECT get_enc_val ('Test','1234567890123456')
  2>    FROM dual
  3> /

GET_ENC_VAL('TEST','1234567890123456')
---------------------------------------
2137F30B29BE026DFE7D61A194BC34DD
```

That's it; we have just built a generic encryption function that can optionally take the encryption algorithm and an initialization vector (IV). It assumes PKCS#5 padding and ECB chaining, which are common practice. If these encryption characteristics meet your requirements, this program could become your wrapper function to perform everyday encryption.

Decrypting Data

On the other side of the coin is the decryption process, which decodes the encrypted string using the same key used originally for encryption. Let's write a new function for decryption, called get_dec_val, using the DBMS_CRYPTO package, as follows.

```
/* File on web: get_dec_val_2.sql */

CREATE OR REPLACE FUNCTION get_dec_val (
   p_in_val      IN   VARCHAR2,
```

```
      p_key           IN    VARCHAR2,
      p_algorithm     IN    VARCHAR2 := 'AES128',
      p_iv            IN    VARCHAR2 := NULL
   )
      RETURN VARCHAR2
IS
   l_dec_val    RAW (4000);
   l_enc_algo   PLS_INTEGER;
   l_in         RAW (4000);
   l_iv         RAW (4000);
   l_key        RAW (4000);
   l_ret        VARCHAR2 (4000);
BEGIN
   l_enc_algo :=
      CASE p_algorithm
         WHEN 'DES'
            THEN DBMS_CRYPTO.encrypt_des
         WHEN '3DES_2KEY'
            THEN DBMS_CRYPTO.encrypt_3des_2key
         WHEN '3DES'
            THEN DBMS_CRYPTO.encrypt_3des
         WHEN 'AES128'
            THEN DBMS_CRYPTO.encrypt_aes128
         WHEN 'AES192'
            THEN DBMS_CRYPTO.encrypt_aes192
         WHEN 'AES256'
            THEN DBMS_CRYPTO.encrypt_aes256
         WHEN 'RC4'
            THEN DBMS_CRYPTO.encrypt_rc4
      END;
   l_in := hextoraw(p_in_val);
   l_iv := utl_i18n.string_to_raw (p_iv, 'AL32UTF8');
   l_key := utl_i18n.string_to_raw (p_key, 'AL32UTF8');
   l_dec_val :=
      DBMS_CRYPTO.decrypt (src     => l_in,
                           KEY     => l_key,
                           iv      => l_iv,
                           typ     =>   l_enc_algo
                                      + DBMS_CRYPTO.chain_cbc
                                      + DBMS_CRYPTO.pad_pkcs5
                          );
   l_ret := utl_i18n.raw_to_char (l_dec_val, 'AL32UTF8');
   RETURN l_ret;
END;
```

Let's test this function. To decrypt the value encrypted earlier, I can use:

```
SQL> SELECT get_dec_val ('2137F30B29BE026DFE7D61A194BC34DD', '1234567890123456')
  2> FROM DUAL
  3> /

GET_DEC_VAL('2137F30B29BE026DFE7D61A194BC34DD','1234567890123456')
--------------------------------------------------------------------------
Test
```

There it is; I just got back my original value. Note that I am using the same key employed to encrypt earlier. When you are decrypting an encrypted value, you must use exactly the same key, algorithm, padding method, and chaining method used during encryption.

You might consider using get_dec_val as a generic program to decrypt encrypted values. For simplicity, ease of management, and security, I suggest that you place this set of encryption and decryption functions inside a package of your own construction.

Before closing this section, let me mention an important concept. In the previous two examples, I used VARCHAR2 input and output values. Recall, however, that encryption and decryption is done inside the database as RAW, so we had to convert the data and key from RAW to VARCHAR2 and then back to RAW again. Although doing this simplified our presentation, it may not be acceptable in some cases. See the sidebar "When Should You Use Raw Encryption?" earlier in the chapter.

Key Management in Oracle Database 10*g*

You've learned the basics of how to use encryption and decryption, as well as how to generate keys. But that's the easy part; for the most part, we've simply used Oracle's supplied programs and built wrappers around them to get the job done. Now comes the more challenging aspect of the encryption infrastructure—managing the key. Our applications will need to have access to the key to decrypt the encrypted values, and this access mechanism should be as simple as possible. On the other hand, the key should not be so simple as to be accessible to hackers. A proper key management system balances the simplicity of key access against prevention of unauthorized access to the keys.

There are essentially three different types of key management:

- A single key for the entire database
- A different key for each row of tables with encrypted data
- A combination approach

The following sections describe these different approaches to key management.

The discussions in this chapter use features of Oracle Database 10*g*, but the concepts apply equally well to Oracle9*i* Database, so if you are still using that version, you will still find this section helpful.

Using a Single Key

With this approach, a single key is used to access any data in the database. As shown in Figure 4-3, the encryption routine reads only one key from the key location and encrypts all the data that needs to be protected. This key could be stored in a variety of locations:

In the database

This is the simplest strategy of all. The key is stored in a relational table, perhaps in a schema used specifically for this purpose. Because the key is inside the database, it is automatically backed up as a part of the database; older values can be obtained by flashback queries or the database, and the key is not vulnerable to theft from the operating system. The simplicity of this approach is also its weakness: because the key is just data in a table, anyone with the authority to modify that table (such as any DBA) could alter the key and disrupt the encryption infrastructure.

In the filesystem

The key is stored in a file, which may then be read by the encryption procedure, using the UTL_FILE built-in package. By setting the appropriate privileges on that file, you can ensure that it cannot be changed from within the database.

On some removable media controlled by the end user

This approach is the safest one; no one except the end user can decrypt the values or alter the key, not even the DBA or system administrator. Examples of removable media include a USB stick, a DVD, and a removable hard drive. A major disadvantage of removable media is the possibility of key loss or key theft. The responsibility of safekeeping the key lies with the end user. If the key is ever lost, the encrypted data is also lost—permanently.

The biggest advantage of using a single key is that the encryption/decryption routines will not need to select keys from tables or store them every time a record is manipulated in the base table. The result is that performance is generally better because of reduced CPU cycles and I/O operations. The biggest disadvantage of this approach is its dependence on a single point of failure. If an intruder breaks into the database and determines the key, the entire database becomes immediately vulnerable. In addition, if you want to change the key, you will need to change all of the rows in all of the tables, which may be quite an extensive task in a large database (see Figure 4-3).

Because of these disadvantages, particularly the consequences of key theft, this approach is used only infrequently. There are a few cases where it may be useful. One example is a data publication system where a key is generally used only once during transmission of data; after transmission, the key is destroyed and a new key is used for the next transmission. Such a system might be used by financial-data publication houses sending analytical data to customers or in a situation where one division of a company is sending confidential corporate data to the other divisions or to company headquarters.

Using a Key for Each Row

With the second approach, a different key is used for each row of a table, as shown in Figure 4-4. This approach is far more secure than the one discussed in the previous

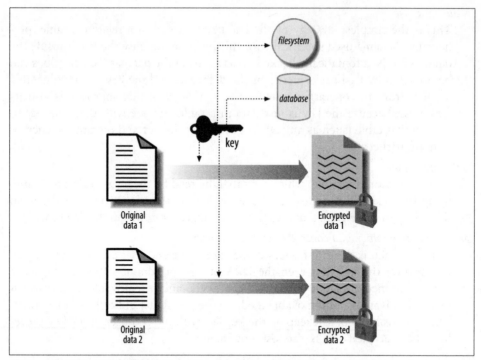

Figure 4-3. Single database-key approach

section. Even if a thief succeeds in stealing a key, only one row will be compromised, not the entire table or the database. There are some disadvantages of this approach: the proliferation of keys makes it extremely difficult to manage them. Also, because encryption and decryption operations need to generate or retrieve a different key for each row, performance will suffer. Nevertheless, the added security provided by this approach makes it preferable in most encryption systems.

Using a Combined Approach

In some cases, neither of the approaches I've described so far may be suitable. Let's examine the pros and cons of the two options.

- With the one-key approach:

    a. The key management is extremely simple. There is only one key to manage—create, access, and back up.

    b. The key can be placed in many places convenient for the applications to access.

    c. On the other hand, if the key is ever stolen, the entire database becomes vulnerable.

- With the one-key-per-row approach:

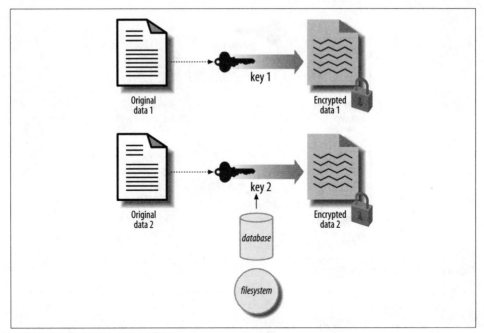

Figure 4-4. Single-key-per-row approach

> a. The number of keys equates to the number of rows, increasing the complexity of key management—more data to back up, more storage, and so on.
>
> b. On the other hand, if a single key is stolen, only that corresponding row is compromised, not the entire database. This adds to the overall security of the system.

Clearly, neither approach is perfect, and you will have to find a middle ground—that is, choose an approach somewhere between the two approaches we've discussed. Perhaps you will use a single key per column, where the same key applies to all the rows; or a key per table regardless of the number of columns; or a key per schema; and so on. The number of keys to be managed would decrease dramatically with any of these approaches, but of course the vulnerability of the data would increase.

Let's take a look at a third approach—I will adopt a combination of keys, as shown in Figure 4-5:

- One key for each row, plus
- A master key for the entire database

This is not the same as encrypting the encrypted value (in fact, that isn't even possible). Although I have defined one key per row, the actual key used during encryption is *not* the key stored for the row; it is, instead, the bitwise exclusive OR (XOR) of *two* values—the stored key and a *master* key. The master key can be stored in a location different from the location of the other keys, as shown in Figure 4-6. An intruder must find both keys if she is to successfully decrypt an encrypted value.

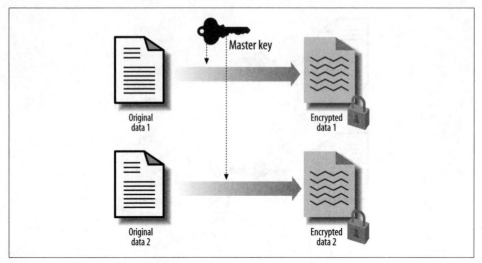

Figure 4-5. The master-key approach

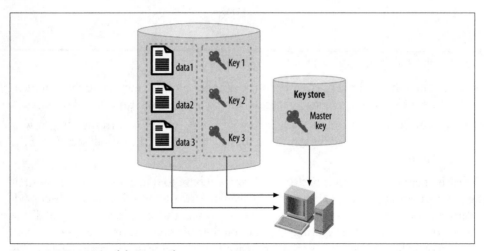

Figure 4-6. Location of the master key

The built-in UTL_RAW package provides the BIT_XOR function, which I can use to perform a bitwise XOR operation. Here I'll perform a bitwise XOR for two values—12345678 and 87654321.

```
/* File on web: bit_xor.sql */

1  DECLARE
2     l_bitxor_val    RAW (2000);
3     l_val_1         VARCHAR2 (2000) := '12345678';
4     l_val_2         VARCHAR2 (2000) := '87654321';
5  BEGIN
6     l_bitxor_val :=
7        UTL_RAW.bit_xor (utl_i18n.string_to_raw (l_val_1, 'AL32UTF8'),
```

```
 8                         utl_i18n.string_to_raw (l_val_2, 'AL32UTF8')
 9                      );
10      DBMS_OUTPUT.put_line (    'Raw Val_1:       '
11                         || RAWTOHEX (utl_i18n.string_to_raw (l_val_1,
12                                                         'AL32UTF8'
13                                                         )
14                                    )
15                      );
16      DBMS_OUTPUT.put_line (    'Raw Val_2:       '
17                         || RAWTOHEX (utl_i18n.string_to_raw (l_val_2,
18                                                         'AL32UTF8'
19                                                         )
20                                    )
21                      );
22      DBMS_OUTPUT.put_line ('After bit XOR: ' || RAWTOHEX (l_bitxor_val));
23   END;
```

To perform a bitwise operation, I first need to convert the values to the RAW datatype, as shown in line 8, where the call to the UTL_I18N.STRING_TO_RAW function converts the value to RAW. In line 7, I call the bitwise XOR function, and at the end, I display the two input values converted to RAW, along with the XOR'ed value.

After executing the above block, I get this output:

```
Raw Val_1:      3132333435363738
Raw Val_2:      3837363534333231
After bit XOR: 0905050101050509
```

Note how the bitwise XOR'ed value is very different from both of the input values. Using this technique, if I pull one value as the stored key for the row and the other as a master key, I can generate a different key that will be used in actual encryption. You will need *both* of the values, not just one, to arrive at the XOR'ed value. Thus, even someone who knows one of the values will not be able to decipher the XOR'ed value and thus get the actual encryption value.

 This approach is not the same as re-encrypting the encrypted value with a different key. The DBMS_CRYPTO package does not allow you to re-encrypt an encrypted value. If you attempt to do so, you will encounter the *ORA-28233 source data was previously encrypted* error.

I can change my original encryption/decryption program to use this master key, as shown below. I add a new variable called l_master_key in line 6, which accepts a value from the user (the substitution variable &master_key). In lines 15 through 17, I have XOR'ed the key and the master key, which was used instead of the l_key variable as the encryption key in line 22.

```
/* File on web: enc_dec_master.sql */

1   REM
2   REM Define a variable to hold the encrypted value
```

```
 3  VARIABLE enc_val varchar2(2000);
 4  DECLARE
 5     l_key           VARCHAR2 (2000) := '1234567890123456';
 6     l_master_key    VARCHAR2 (2000) := '&master_key';
 7     l_in_val        VARCHAR2 (2000) := 'Confidential Data';
 8     l_mod           NUMBER
 9        :=    DBMS_CRYPTO.encrypt_aes128
10            + DBMS_CRYPTO.chain_cbc
11            + DBMS_CRYPTO.pad_pkcs5;
12     l_enc           RAW (2000);
13     l_enc_key       RAW (2000);
14  BEGIN
15     l_enc_key :=
16        UTL_RAW.bit_xor (utl_i18n.string_to_raw (l_key, 'AL32UTF8'),
17                         utl_i18n.string_to_raw (l_master_key, 'AL32UTF8')
18                        );
19     l_enc :=
20        DBMS_CRYPTO.encrypt (utl_i18n.string_to_raw (l_in_val, 'AL32UTF8'),
21                             l_mod,
22                             l_enc_key
23                            );
24     DBMS_OUTPUT.put_line ('Encrypted=' || l_enc);
25     :enc_val := RAWTOHEX (l_enc);
26  END;
27  /
28  DECLARE
29     l_key           VARCHAR2 (2000) := '1234567890123456';
30     l_master_key    VARCHAR2 (2000) := '&master_key';
31     l_in_val        RAW (2000)      := HEXTORAW (:enc_val);
32     l_mod           NUMBER
33        :=    DBMS_CRYPTO.encrypt_aes128
34            + DBMS_CRYPTO.chain_cbc
35            + DBMS_CRYPTO.pad_pkcs5;
36     l_dec           RAW (2000);
37     l_enc_key       RAW (2000);
38  BEGIN
39     l_enc_key :=
40        UTL_RAW.bit_xor (utl_i18n.string_to_raw (l_key, 'AL32UTF8'),
41                         utl_i18n.string_to_raw (l_master_key, 'AL32UTF8')
42                        );
43     l_dec := DBMS_CRYPTO.decrypt (l_in_val, l_mod, l_enc_key);
44     DBMS_OUTPUT.put_line ('Decrypted=' || utl_i18n.raw_to_char (l_dec));
45  END;
```

When I execute this block, this is what the output looks like. Note that first I supply the master key to encrypt the value, and then I provide the same master key while decrypting.

```
Enter value for master_key: MasterKey0123456
old   3:    l_master_key varchar2(2000) := '&master_key';
new   3:    l_master_key varchar2(2000) := 'MasterKey0123456';
Encrypted=C2CABD4FD4952BC3ABB23BD50849D0C937D3EE6659D58A32AC69EFFD4E83F79D
```

```
PL/SQL procedure successfully completed.

Enter value for master_key: MasterKey0123456
old    3:    l_master_key varchar2(2000) := '&master_key';
new    3:    l_master_key varchar2(2000) := 'MasterKey0123456';
Decrypted=ConfidentialData

PL/SQL procedure successfully completed.
```

My program asked for the master key, which I supplied correctly, and the correct value came up. But what if I supply a wrong master key?

```
Enter value for master_key: MasterKey0123456
old    3:    l_master_key varchar2(2000) := '&master_key';
new    3:    l_master_key varchar2(2000) := 'MasterKey';
Encrypted=C2CABD4FD4952BC3ABB23BD50849D0C937D3EE6659D58A32AC69EFFD4E83F79D

PL/SQL procedure successfully completed.

Enter value for master_key: MasterKey0123455
old    3:    l_master_key varchar2(2000) := '&master_key';
new    3:    l_master_key varchar2(2000) := 'WrongMasterKey';
declare
*
ERROR at line 1:
ORA-28817: PL/SQL function returned an error.
ORA-06512: at "SYS.DBMS_CRYPTO_FFI", line 67
ORA-06512: at "SYS.DBMS_CRYPTO", line 41
ORA-06512: at line 15
```

Note the error here: the use of a wrong master key did not expose the encrypted data. This enhanced security mechanism relies on two different keys, and both keys must be present to successfully decrypt it. If you hide the master key, it will be enough to prevent unauthorized decryption.

Because the master key is stored with the client, and it is sent over the network, a potential attacker could use a tool to "sniff" the value as it passes by. To prevent this from occurring, you can use a variety of approaches:

- You could create a virtual local area network (VLAN) between the application server and the database server. The VLAN protects the network traffic between the servers to a great extent.

- You could modify the master key in some predetermined way, such as by reversing the characters so that an attacker could potentially get the master key that passed over the network, but not the master key actually used.

- Finally, for a really secure solution, you could use Oracle Advanced Security (an extra-cost option) to secure the network traffic between the client and the server.

There is no perfect key-management solution. The approach you choose will be determined by the nature of your application and your best attempts to balance security against ease of access. The three approaches described in the previous sections represent three major types of key-management techniques and are intended to give you a jump start on figuring out your own key management approach. You might very well come up with a better idea that could be more appropriate to your specific situation. For example, you might consider a hybrid approach, such as using different keys for critical tables.

Protection from the DBA?

Do you need to protect the encrypted data from your own DBA? It's a question that is bound to come up while designing the system, so you will have to address it one way or the other.

A key is stored either in the database or the filesystem. If the key store is the database, then—because the DBA is authorized to select from *any* table (including the table where the keys are stored)—he can therefore decrypt any encrypted data. If the key store is the filesystem, it has to be available to the Oracle software owner so that it may be read using UTL_FILE, which the DBA may have access to. Thus, either way, protecting encrypted data from the DBA is probably a fruitless exercise. Is that an acceptable risk in your organization? The answer depends upon your organization's security policies and guidelines. In many cases, the risk is managed by placing trust in the DBA, so this may be a moot point. But in other cases, the encrypted data must be protected even from the DBA.

The only solution in that case is to store the keys on a location that the DBA will not be able to access—such as on the application server. But doing so makes key management difficult. You will have to ensure that the keys are backed up and protected from theft.

You can use a more complex system for key management using the master key approach described above. The master key may be placed in a digital *wallet*, and the application server can request the key every time it needs to encrypt and decrypt the data. Although this makes the key inaccessible to the DBA, it also makes the system complex and increases processing time.

If your objective is to prevent the DBA from altering the key, yet you want her to still be able to see it, you can use the same master-key approach. The master key can be placed in a filesystem that is read-only but accessible to the Oracle software owner to read it. This enables the database (and the DBA) to use it in encryption, but the DBA will not be able to alter it.

To keep your system manageable, especially if you want to make sure that your applications are minimally affected, then you will have to make the keys available to the Oracle software owner, either in a filesystem or inside the database in a table. In that case, it will be impossible to hide them from a DBA.

Transparent Data Encryption in Oracle Database 10g Release 2

When you store both the encryption key and the encrypted data in the database, another potential security hole opens up—if the disks containing the entire database are stolen, the data becomes immediately vulnerable. One way around this problem is to encrypt all the data elements and store the keys separately on a different location away from the disk drives where the data resides.

If your database is completely isolated, you may not feel that you need to encrypt its data. However, you may still want to protect the data in case of a disk theft. One solution would be to create a view to show the decrypted value. In this case, if the key is stored elsewhere, a physical disk theft will not make the data vulnerable. This approach works, but it requires an extensive and elaborate setup.

To address these types of situations, Oracle has introduced a new feature known as Transparent Data Encryption (TDE), available starting with Oracle Database 10g Release 2. TDE uses a combination of two keys—one master key stored outside the database in a *wallet* and one key for each table. The same key is used for all rows in a table, and a unique key is generated for each table (as illustrated in Figure 4-7).

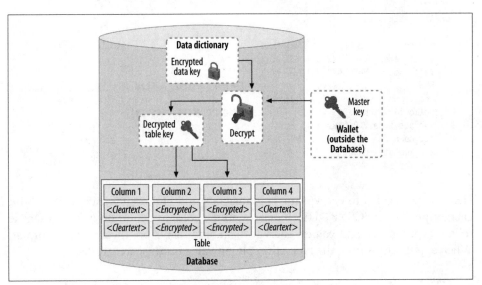

Figure 4-7. The Transparent Data Encryption model

With TDE, you may define a subset of columns as encrypted. For example, if a table has four columns, as shown in the figure, and columns 2 and 3 are encrypted, Oracle will generate a key and use it to encrypt those columns. On the disk, columns 1 and 4 will be stored as cleartext, and the other two as encrypted text.

When a user selects encrypted columns, Oracle transparently retrieves the key from the wallet, decrypts the columns, and shows them to the user. If the data on the disk is stolen, it cannot be retrieved without the keys, which reside in the wallet encrypted by the master key, which is not stored as cleartext itself. The result is that the thief can't decrypt the data, even if he steals the disks or copies the files.

The goal of Transparent Data Encryption (TDE) is to satisfy the need to protect data stored on media such as disks and tapes, a requirement for compliance with many national and international regulatory frameworks and rules such as Sarbanes-Oxley, HIPAA, Visa Cardholder Information Security Program, etc.

TDE is not a full-scale encryption solution and should not be used as such. Note, for example, that it decrypts the encrypted columns regardless of who actually selects them, a scenario that is not likely to satisfy your security needs. For more comprehensive solutions, you will need to build your own tool using the techniques described in this chapter.

To take advantage of TDE, add an ENCRYPT clause (available in Oracle Database 10*g* Release 2 only) to your table creation statement for each column to be encrypted:

```
/* File on web: cr_accounts.sql */

CREATE TABLE accounts
(
    acc_no        NUMBER       NOT NULL,
    first_name    VARCHAR2(30) NOT NULL,
    last_name     VARCHAR2(30) NOT NULL,
    SSN           VARCHAR2(9)              ENCRYPT USING 'AES128',
    acc_type      VARCHAR2(1)  NOT NULL,
    folio_id      NUMBER                   ENCRYPT USING 'AES128',
    sub_acc_type  VARCHAR2(30),
    acc_open_dt   DATE         NOT NULL,
    acc_mod_dt    DATE,
    acc_mgr_id    NUMBER
);
```

Here I have decided to encrypt the columns SSN and FOLIO_ID using AES 128-bit encryption. The ENCRYPT USING clause in the column definition instructs Oracle to intercept the cleartext values, encrypt them, and then store the encrypted format. When a user selects from the table, the column value is transparently decrypted.

You cannot enable Transparent Data Encryption on tables owned by SYS.

Setting Up TDE

Before you start using TDE, you have to set up the wallet where the master key is stored and secure it. Here is a step-by-step approach to wallet management.

1. Set the wallet location.

   When you enable TDE for the first time, you need to create the wallet where the master key is stored. By default, the wallet is created in the directory *$ORACLE_BASE/admin/$ORACLE_SID/wallet*. You can also choose a different directory by specifying it in the file *SQLNET.ORA*. For instance, if you want the wallet to be in the */oracle_wallet* directory, place the lines in the *SQLNET.ORA* file as shown here. In this example, I assume that the default location is chosen.

   ```
   ENCRYPTION_WALLET_LOCATION =
     (SOURCE=
         (METHOD=file)
         (METHOD_DATA=
             (DIRECTORY=/oracle_wallet)))
   ```

   Make sure to include the wallet as a part of your regular backup process.

2. Set the wallet password.

   Now you have to create the wallet and set the password to access it. This is done in one step by issuing:

   ```
   ALTER SYSTEM SET ENCRYPTION KEY IDENTIFIED BY "pooh";
   ```

   This command does three things:

   a. It creates the wallet in the location specified in Step 1.

   b. It sets the password of the wallet as "pooh".

   c. It opens the wallet for TDE to store and retrieve keys.

   The password is case-sensitive, and you must enclose it in double quotes.

3. Open the wallet.

   The previous step opens the wallet for operation. However, after the wallet is created once, you do not need to re-create it. After the database comes up, you just have to open it using the same password via the command:

   ```
   ALTER SYSTEM SET ENCRYPTION WALLET OPEN IDENTIFIED BY "pooh";
   ```

   You can close the wallet by issuing the command:

   ```
   ALTER SYSTEM SET ENCRYPTION WALLET CLOSE;
   ```

   The wallet needs to be open for TDE to work. If the wallet is not open, all non-encrypted columns are accessible, but the encrypted columns are not.

Adding TDE to Existing Tables

In the example in the previous section, you saw how to use TDE while creating a new table. You can encrypt a column of an existing table, as well. To encrypt the column SSN of the table ACCOUNTS, specify:

```
ALTER TABLE accounts MODIFY (ssn ENCRYPT);
```

This operation does two things:

- It creates a key for the column SSN.
- It converts all values in the column to encrypted format.

The encryption is then performed inside the database. By default, the AES (with 192-bit key) algorithm is used for the encryption. You can choose a different algorithm by specifying it in the command. For instance, to choose 128-bit AES encryption, you would specify:

```
ALTER TABLE accounts MODIFY (ssn ENCRYPT USING 'AES128');
```

You can choose AES128, AES256, or 3DES168 (168-bit Triple DES algorithm) as parameters. After encrypting a column, let's look at the table:

```
SQL> DESC accounts
 Name        Null? Type
 --------- ----- ------------
 ACC_NO            NUMBER
 ACC_NAME          VARCHAR2(30)
 SSN               VARCHAR2(9) ENCRYPT
```

Note the clause ENCRYPT after the datatype. To find the encrypted columns in the database, search the new data dictionary view DBA_ENCRYPTED_COLUMNS.

What about the performance impact of TDE? There is no overhead when working with non-encrypted columns. You can expect to see a small amount of overhead when accessing encrypted columns. If encryption is no longer required, you can turn it off for that column by specifying:

```
ALTER TABLE account MODIFY (ssn DECRYPT);
```

Performing TDE Key and Password Management

What if someone discovers your TDE keys somehow? You can simply re-create the encrypted values by issuing a simple command. While you are at it, you may also want to choose a different encryption algorithm such as AES256. You can do both by issuing:

```
ALTER TABLE accounts REKEY USING 'aes256';
```

If someone discovers the wallet password, you can change it using a graphical tool called Oracle Wallet Manager. From the command line, type owm, which brings up the tool as shown in Figure 4-8. From the top menu, choose Wallet → Open and choose the wallet location you have specified. You will have to supply the password of the wallet. After that, choose Wallet → Change Password to change the password. Note that changing the password does not change the keys.

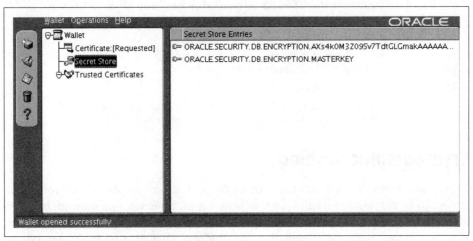

Figure 4-8. Oracle Wallet Manager

Adding Salt

Encryption is all about hiding data, and sometimes encrypted data is easier to guess if there is repetition in the cleartext. For example, a table that contains salary information is quite likely to contain repeated values, and, in that case, the encrypted values will also be the same. Even if an intruder can't decrypt the actual values, she will be able to tell which entries have the same salary, and this information may be valuable. To prevent such a thing from happening, *salt* is added to the data, which makes the encrypted value different even if the input data is the same. TDE, by default, applies *salt*.

In some cases, patterns of data may improve your database performance, and adding salt may degrade it. With certain indexes, for example, a pattern may establish the b-tree structure and make the searching of LIKE predicates faster, as in the following query:

```
SELECT ... FROM accounts WHERE ssn LIKE '123%';
```

In this case, b-tree indexes will have to travel along only one branch to get the data, because all account numbers start with the digits 123. If salt is added, the actual values will be stored all over the b-tree structure, making index scans more expensive, and the optimizer will most likely choose a full table scan. In such cases, you will have to remove the salt from the indexed columns. You can do so by specifying:

```
ALTER TABLE accounts MODIFY (ssn ENCRYPT NO SALT);
```

Removing the salt does not significantly affect the security, so the risk of vulnerability probably does not outweigh the performance benefits of indexing.

 You cannot use TDE on columns that have any of the following characteristics:

- Those with datatypes BLOB or CLOB
- Those used in indexes other than regular b-tree indexes, such as bitmap indexes, function-based indexes, etc.
- Those used as partitioning keys

Lack of support for TDE in these cases is also another reason why TDE is not a candidate for all types of encryption.

Cryptographic Hashing

Encryption provides a way to ensure that only authorized people can see your data. It does so by disguising sensitive data. In some cases, however, you may not be interested in disguising data, but simply in protecting it from manipulation. Suppose that you have stored payment information for vendors. That data by itself may not be sensitive enough to require encryption, but you may want a way to ensure that someone does not alter the numbers to increase a payment amount. How can you do that? The answer lies in a process known as *cryptographic hashing*. Let's start by looking at a real-world example.

The Case of the Suspicious Sandwich

Let's suppose that you leave your sandwich open on your desk when you go over to the fax machine to pick up an important fax. When you come back, you feel somehow that the sandwich has shifted a little to the left. Has someone tampered with your sandwich, perhaps placing some barbiturate in it to knock you out so that he can steal your cool new wireless mouse? Or perhaps he's after the PL/SQL book hidden in your drawer? Maybe it's not drugs, but sand, in your sandwich? The possibilities spin madly through your mind, and you lose your appetite.

To calm your fears, you decide to challenge the integrity of the sandwich. Being the careful fellow you are, you had previously weighed the sandwich and recorded its weight out to the 10th digit after the decimal point. Confronted with the possibility of an altered sandwich, you weigh it again and compare the results. They are exactly the same, down to that 10th digit of precision.What a relief! If someone had actually changed the sandwich in any way—for example, by adding barbiturates or sand—the weights would have been different, thus revealing the adulteration.

Pay close attention to the concepts presented here. You did not "hide" the sandwich (i.e., *encrypt* it); you simply created your own method of calculating a value that represents the sandwich. You could then compare the before and after values. The value you arrived at could have been based on any algorithm—in this case, it was the weight of the sandwich.

If you were examining data, rather than sliced bread and meat, an algorithm could be used to generate the value. This process is known as *hashing*. It's different from encryption in that it is one-way only—you can decrypt encrypted data, but you can't de-hash hashed values. Hashing the same piece of data more than once produces the same value regardless of the number of times it is done. If data has been modified in any way, the generated hash value will not be the same, thus revealing the contamination.

There is always a theoretical risk that two different pieces of data will hash to the same value, but you can minimize the probability of this happening by using a sufficiently sophisticated hashing algorithm. One such algorithm is known as a *Message Digest* (MD). One MD variant known as MD5 was once a standard, but it did not prove secure enough to maintain its standardization; a newer standard called *Secure Hash Algorithm Version 1* (SHA-1) is more often used today and is available in Oracle Database 10g.

MD5 Hashing in Oracle9*i* Database

Let's see how we can use hashing in real-life database administration. When a sensitive piece of information is sent to a different location, you might calculate the hash value beforehand and send it in another shipment or transmission. The recipient can then calculate the hash value of the received data and compare it against the hash value that you sent out.

In Oracle9*i* Database, the DBMS_OBFUSCATION_TOOLKIT package provides a hashing function for MD5, an implementation of the Message Digest protocol. To hash a string, I might specify:

```
DECLARE
    l_hash      VARCHAR2 (2000);
    l_in_val    VARCHAR2 (2000);
BEGIN
    l_in_val := 'Account Balance is 12345.67';
    l_hash := DBMS_OBFUSCATION_TOOLKIT.md5 (input_string => l_in_val);
    l_hash := RAWTOHEX (UTL_RAW.cast_to_raw (l_hash));
    DBMS_OUTPUT.put_line ('Hashed Value = ' || l_hash);
END;
/
```

Here I provided a simple string "Account Balance is 12345.67", and got its hash value. The MD5 function returns a VARCHAR2 value, but as in the encryption process observed earlier, it contains control characters. Hence, I must convert it to RAW and then to hexadecimal for easy storage. The above code segment returns:

```
Hashed Value = A09308E539C35C97CD612E918BA58B4C
```

In this example, you will note two important differences between hashing and encryption:

- In hashing, the input string does not have to be padded to make it a certain length, whereas it does in encryption.
- In hashing, there is no key. Because there is no key involved, there is no need to store or supply the key at any point of the send-receive process, which makes a hashing system extremely simple.

Because I may want to obtain this value and transmit it to the recipient, I can create a stored function that does that for us. Let's use the same code example and create the function, as follows.

```
/* File on web: get_hash_val_9i.sql */

CREATE OR REPLACE FUNCTION get_hash_val (p_in VARCHAR2)
    RETURN VARCHAR2
IS
    l_hash    VARCHAR2 (2000);
BEGIN
    l_hash :=
        RAWTOHEX
            (UTL_RAW.cast_to_raw
                (DBMS_OBFUSCATION_TOOLKIT.md5 (input_string    => p_in)
                )
            );
    RETURN l_hash;
END;
```

Let's generate some representative outputs from this function.

```
BEGIN
    DBMS_OUTPUT.put_line (    'Hashed = '
                        || get_hash_val ('Account Balance is 12345.67')
                    );
    DBMS_OUTPUT.put_line (    'Hashed = '
                        || get_hash_val ('Account Balance is 12345.67')
                    );
END;
```

The output is:

```
Hashed = A09308E539C35C97CD612E918BA58B4C
Hashed = A09308E539C35C97CD612E918BA58B4C
```

As you can see, the function returns an *identical* value each time for the same input string, a fact that can be used in validating the integrity of that particular piece of data. Note that here I am referring to the integrity of the *data*, not the database; the latter is assured by the Oracle database in enforcing constraints and in transactions. When a legitimate user updates a value that does not violate defined constraints, the data (but not the database) becomes corrupt. For example, if someone updates an account balance via ad hoc SQL from $12,345.67 to $21,345.67, that fact may not be detected at all unless the organization provides tracking capabilities.

If the hash value for a column like Social Security number was calculated beforehand and stored somewhere, and then after retrieval the recalculated hash value is compared against the stored one, it will signal a possibly malicious data manipulation because the hash values will not be the same. Let's see how this works.

```
DECLARE
    l_data    VARCHAR2 (200);
BEGIN
    l_data := 'Social Security Number = 123-45-6789';
    DBMS_OUTPUT.put_line ('Hashed = ' || get_hash_val (l_data));
    --
    -- someone manipulated the data and changed it
    --
    l_data := 'Social Security Number = 023-45-6789';
    DBMS_OUTPUT.put_line ('Hashed = ' || get_hash_val (l_data));
END;
```

The output is:

```
Hashed = 098D833A81B279E54992BFB1ECA6E428
Hashed = 6682A974924B5611FA9D809357ADE508
```

Note how the hash values differ. The resulting hash value will be different if the data was modified in any way, even if the value itself is unchanged. If a space, punctuation, or anything else is modified, the hash value will not be the same.

> It is theoretically possible that two different input values will produce the same hash value. However, by relying on widely used algorithms such as MD5 and SHA-1, you are ensured that the probability of a *hash conflict* is usually a statistically remote 1 in 10^{38} (depending on the algorithm chosen). If you cannot afford to take even that chance, you will need to write conflict-resolution logic around your use of the hash function.

SHA-1 Hashing in Oracle Database 10g

As mentioned earlier, the MD5 protocol is not considered sufficiently secure for modern data protection, and SHA-1 is often used instead. SHA-1 is not available in the DBMS_OBFUSCATION_TOOLKIT, but in Oracle Database 10g, you can use the HASH function available in the DBMS_CRYPTO package to perform SHA-1 hashing. Here is the declaration of the function:

```
DBMS_CRYPTO.hash (
    src in raw,
    typ in pls_integer)
  return raw;
```

Because HASH accepts only the RAW datatype as input, I have to convert the input character string to RAW using the technique described earlier for encryption.

```
l_in := utl_i18n.string_to_raw (p_in_val, 'AL32UTF8');
```

This converted string can now be passed to the hash function.

In the second parameter typ (which must be declared in the PLS_INTEGER datatype) you specify the algorithm to use for hashing. You can select any of the algorithms in Table 4-7.

Table 4-7. Hashing algorithms in DBMS_CRYPTO

Constant	Description
DBMS_CRYPTO.HASH_MD5	Message Digest 5
DBMS_CRYPTO.HASH_MD4	Message Digest 4
DBMS_CRYPTO.HASH_SH1	Secure Hashing Algorithm 1

For example, to get the hash value for a RAW datatype variable, you might write a function as follows:

```
/* File on web: get_sha1_hash_val.sql */

CREATE OR REPLACE FUNCTION get_sha1_hash_val (p_in RAW)
    RETURN RAW
IS
    l_hash   RAW (4000);
BEGIN
    l_hash := DBMS_CRYPTO.HASH (src => p_in, typ => DBMS_CRYPTO.hash_sh1);
    RETURN l_hash;
END;
/
```

For MD5 hashing, you would change the value of the parameter typ from DBMS_CRYPTO.HASH_SH1 to DBMS_CRYPTO.HASH_MD5. In my function to get the hash value, I can make it generic enough to accept any algorithm.

Finally, because the return value is in RAW, I need to convert it to VARCHAR2, as follows.

```
l_enc_val := rawtohex (l_enc_val, 'AL32UTF8');
```

Putting everything together, this is what the function looks like.

```
/* File on web: get_hash_val_10g.sql */

CREATE OR REPLACE FUNCTION get_hash_val (
    p_in_val      IN    VARCHAR2,
    p_algorithm   IN    VARCHAR2 := 'SH1'
)
    RETURN VARCHAR2
IS
    l_hash_val    RAW (4000);
    l_hash_algo   PLS_INTEGER;
    l_in          RAW (4000);
    l_ret         VARCHAR2 (4000);
BEGIN
    l_hash_algo :=
        CASE p_algorithm
            WHEN 'SH1'
```

```
        THEN DBMS_CRYPTO.hash_sh1
    WHEN 'MD4'
        THEN DBMS_CRYPTO.hash_md4
    WHEN 'MD5'
        THEN DBMS_CRYPTO.hash_md5
    END;
  l_in := utl_i18n.string_to_raw (p_in_val, 'AL32UTF8');
  l_hash_val := DBMS_CRYPTO.HASH (src => l_in, typ => l_hash_algo);
  l_ret := rawtohex(l_hash_val);
  RETURN l_ret;
END;
```

Let's see how we can use it in an example:

```
SQL> SELECT get_hash_val ('Test')
  2  FROM DUAL
  3  /

GET_HASH_VAL('TEST')
----------------------------------------
640AB2BAE07BEDC4C163F679A746F7AB7FB5D1FA
```

I am using this function to hash a VARCHAR2 value, returning a VARCHAR2 field that can be stored and transmitted. By default this function uses the SHA-1 algorithm, but it can accept the other two algorithms as well.

Other Uses of Hashing

Hashing has many uses beyond cryptography—for example, in web programming and virus detection.

Web applications are stateless: they do not keep the connection open to the database server for the duration of the transaction. In other words, there is no concept of a "session," and therefore there is no locking of the type Oracle users rely upon. This means that there is no easy way to find out whether data on a web page has changed. But if a hash value is stored along with the data, a new hash value can be recalculated and compared with the stored value. If the two values do not agree, the data has changed.

Hashing is also helpful in determining whether data can be trusted. Consider the case of a virus that updates critical documents stored inside the database. This is not something that can be easily caught by a trigger. However, if the document contains a hash value, then by comparing a computed hash value with the stored value, you can determine whether the document has been tampered with and you will know whether you can trust that document.

Message Authentication Code in Oracle Database 10g

The type of hashing discussed so far in this chapter is a very helpful technique, but it has certain limitations:

- Anyone can verify the authenticity of transmitted data by using the hash function. In certain types of ultra-secure systems, where only a particular recipient is expected to verify the authenticity of the message or data, this may not be appropriate.

- Anyone can calculate the same hash value if the algorithm is known, and he can then update the values in the checksum columns, hiding the compromise in the data.

- For the reason stated in the previous problem, the hash value cannot be stored along with the data in a reliable manner. Anyone with update privileges on the table can update the hash value as well. Similarly, someone can generate the hash value and update the data in transit. For this reason, the hash value cannot accompany the data. It has to travel separately, which adds to the complexity of the system.

These limitations can be overcome by a modified implementation of hashing, one in which the exclusivity of the hashing mechanism at the receiver's end can be ascertained by a password or key. This special type of hash value is known as a *Message Authentication Code* (MAC). The sender calculates the MAC value of the data using a predetermined key that is also known to the receiver but not sent with the data. The sender then sends the MAC to the receiver along with the data, not separate from it. After receiving the data, the receiver also calculates the MAC value using the same key and matches it with the MAC value sent with the data. This mechanism is shown schematically in Figure 4-9.

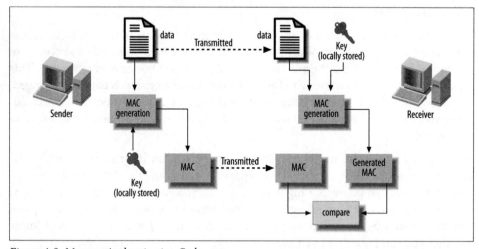

Figure 4-9. Message Authentication Code usage

Like hashing, MAC also follows the standard algorithms, MD5 and SHA-1. As with the HASH function, the parameter typ is used to specify the algorithm to be used. Select

DBMS_CRYPTO.HMAC_MD5 or DBMS_CRYPTO.HMAC_SH1, respectively. Here is how I can calculate the MAC value of an input string using the SHA-1 algorithm.

```
/* File on web: get_sha1_mac_val.sql */

CREATE OR REPLACE FUNCTION get_sha1_mac_val (p_in RAW, p_key RAW)
   RETURN RAW
IS
   l_mac   RAW (4000);
BEGIN
   l_mac :=
      DBMS_CRYPTO.mac (src     => p_in,
                       typ     => DBMS_CRYPTO.hmac_sh1,
                       key     => p_key);
   RETURN l_mac;
END;
/
```

Using my hashing function as a model, I can also create my own generic MAC calculations.

```
/* File on web: get_mac_val.sql */

CREATE OR REPLACE FUNCTION get_mac_val (
   p_in_val      IN   VARCHAR2,
   p_key         IN   VARCHAR2,
   p_algorithm   IN   VARCHAR2 := 'SH1'
)
   RETURN VARCHAR2
IS
   l_mac_val    RAW (4000);
   l_key        RAW (4000);
   l_mac_algo   PLS_INTEGER;
   l_in         RAW (4000);
   l_ret        VARCHAR2 (4000);
BEGIN
   l_mac_algo :=
      CASE p_algorithm
         WHEN 'SH1'
            THEN DBMS_CRYPTO.hmac_sh1
         WHEN 'MD5'
            THEN DBMS_CRYPTO.hash_md5
      END;
   l_in := utl_i18n.string_to_raw (p_in_val, 'AL32UTF8');
   l_key := utl_i18n.string_to_raw (p_key, 'AL32UTF8');
   l_mac_val := DBMS_CRYPTO.mac (src => l_in, typ => l_mac_algo, key=>l_key);
   l_ret := RAWTOHEX (l_mac_val);
   RETURN l_ret;
END;
```

Let's test this function to get the MAC value of the data "Test Data" and the key "Key".

```
SQL> SELECT get_mac_val ('Test Data','Key')
  2  FROM DUAL
```

```
   3  /
GET_MAC_VAL('TESTDATA','KEY')
--------------------------------------------
8C36C24C767E305CD95415C852E9692F53927761
```

Because a key is required to generate the checksum value, the MAC method provides more security than the hashing method. For example, in a banking application, the integrity of character data such as a Social Security number (SSN) in a bank account is important. Assume that the ACCOUNTS table looks like this.

```
ACCOUNT_NO      NUMBER(10)
SSN             CHAR(9)
SSN_MAC         VARCHAR2(200)
```

When an account is created, the MAC value is calculated on the SSN field using a predetermined key, such as "A Jolly Good Rancher". The column SSN_MAC is updated by the statement:

```
UPDATE accounts
    SET ssn_mac = get_mac_val (ssn, 'A Jolly Good Rancher')
  WHERE account_no = account_no;
```

Now assume that sometime afterward, an intruder updates the SSN field. If the SSN_MAC field contained the hash value of the column SSN, the intruder could calculate the hash value herself and update the column with the new value, as well. Later, when the hash value is calculated on the SSN column and compared to the stored SSN_MAC value, they would match, hiding the fact that the data was compromised! However, if the column contained the MAC value of the column, rather than the hash value, the calculation of the new value would require the key "A Jolly Good Rancher". Because the intruder does not know that, the updated value will not generate the same MAC value, thus revealing that the data was compromised.

Building a Practical Encryption System

In this section, I'll wrap up the chapter by describing a practical, real-world system that illustrates the encryption and hashing concepts we've been discussing throughout this chapter.

Sometimes your encrypted data will need to be matched with incoming data. For instance, many Customer Relationship Management (CRM) applications use different attributes of customers, such as credit card numbers, passport numbers, etc., to identify unique customers. Medical applications may need to go through the patient's diagnosis history to project a pattern and suggest treatment options. Insurance applications may need to search patient diagnoses to assess the validity of the claims, and so on. Because these data items are stored in an encrypted manner, the matching applications cannot simply match against the stored data.

There are two options for handling such situations:

Encrypt the data to be matched, and match it against the stored encrypted values

This option is possible only if the encryption key is known. If your approach is to have one key per database (or table or schema), then you know the exact key that must have been used to encrypt the values. On the other hand, if your approach is to use one key per row, then you will have an idea of what key must have been used to encrypt the value in that particular row. Hence, you can't use this approach.

The other issue with using this option is indexing. If you have an index on this encrypted column, then the index will be useful when an equality predicate is specified (e.g., "ssn = encrypt ('123-45-6789')"). The query will locate on the index the encrypted value of the string '123-45-6789' and then get the other values of the row. Because this is an equality predicate, an exact value on the index is searched and located. However, if you specified a likeness predicate (e.g., "ssn like '123-%'"), the index will be useless. Because the b-tree structure of the index provides for the values starting with similar first parts close together, this likeness operation would have been helped by the index, had it been in cleartext. For instance, index entries for '123-45-6789' and '123-67-8945' would have been close together. But when they are encrypted, the values could be something like this:

```
076A5703A745D03934B56F7500C1DCB4
178F45A983D5D03934B56F7500C1DCB4
```

Because the first characters are very different, they will be on different parts of the index. Using an index match first to determine the location in the table will be slower than doing a full table scan.

Decrypt the encrypted data in each row and match it against the cleartext value to be matched

If you use one single key per row, this is your only option. But each decryption consumes several precious CPU cycles and may affect overall database performance.

So, how can you design a system that more efficiently matches against encrypted columns? The trick is to match against a hash value, rather than the encrypted value. Creating a hash value is significantly faster than encryption, and it consumes fewer CPU cycles. Because the hashing of an input value will always produce the same value, we could store the hash value of the sensitive data, create a hash value of the match data, and match it against the stored hash value.

Here is a proposed system design. Assume that you have a table named CUSTOMERS where the credit card numbers are stored, which needs to be encrypted. Instead of storing the credit card number in the CUSTOMERS table, you would create two additional tables. Figure 4-10 shows the tables and their relationships.

CUSTOMERS table

CUST_ID (primary key)

CC (the hash value of the credit card, not the actual credit card number itself)

CC_MASTER table

    CC_HASH (primary key)

    ENC_CC# (the encrypted value of the credit card number)

CC_KEYS table

    CC_HASH (primary key)

    ENC_KEY (the encryption key used to encrypt this credit card number)

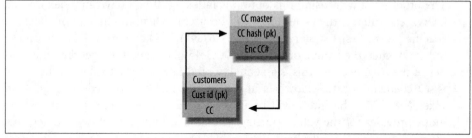

Figure 4-10. Storing encrypted credit card information

The cleartext entry of the credit card is not stored anywhere. You could write a BEFORE-row INSERT or UPDATE trigger that follows the pseudo-code shown below.

```
1   Calculate the hash value
2   Set the value of the column CC to the hash value calculated earlier
3   Search for this hash value in CC_MASTER table
4   IF found THEN
5       Do nothing
6   ELSE
7       Generate a key
8       Use this key to generate the encrypted value of the cleartext credit card number
9       Insert a record into the CC_KEYS table for this hash value and the key
10      Insert a record in the CC_MASTER table with the encrypted value and the key.
11  END IF
```

This logic ensures that the cleartext credit card is not stored in the database. Applications will continue to insert the cleartext value, but the trigger will change it to a hash value. Here is the actual code for the trigger:

```
1   CREATE OR REPLACE TRIGGER tr_aiu_customers
2       BEFORE INSERT OR UPDATE
3       ON customers
4       FOR EACH ROW
5   DECLARE
6       l_hash   VARCHAR2 (64);
7       l_enc    RAW (2000);
8       l_key    RAW (2000);
9   BEGIN
10      l_hash := get_hash_val (:NEW.cc);
11
12      BEGIN
```

```
13          SELECT cc_enc
14            INTO l_enc
15            FROM cc_master
16           WHERE cc_hash = l_hash;
17       EXCEPTION
18          WHEN NO_DATA_FOUND
19          THEN
20             BEGIN
21                l_key := get_key;
22                l_enc := get_enc_val (:NEW.cc, l_key);
23
24                INSERT INTO cc_master
25                            (cc_hash, cc_enc
26                            )
27                     VALUES (l_hash, l_enc
28                            );
29
30                INSERT INTO cc_keys
31                            (cc_hash, cc_key
32                            )
33                     VALUES (l_hash, l_key
34                            );
35             END;
36          WHEN OTHERS
37          THEN
38             RAISE;
39       END;
40
41       :NEW.cc := l_hash;
42 END;
```

The following table summarizes the logic of this code.

Lines	Description
10	First I get the hash value of the cleartext credit card number entered by the user.
13–16	I see whether this value (i.e., this credit card number) exists on the CC_MASTER table.
21	If the hash value is not found, then this is a new credit card. To encrypt it, I need to generate a key first.
22	I use this key to encrypt the cleartext credit card.
24–28	I insert this encrypted credit card number into the CC_MASTER table.
30–34	I store the key in the CC_KEYS table.
41	I replace the cleartext credit card number with its hash value and store that.

Because this trigger changes the cleartext to a hash value, the application need not be changed. Programs that match credit card numbers will need to find a match against hash values, not against cleartext or encrypted values. Using this trigger and the functions described in this chapter, you can build an effective and efficient encryption infrastructure.

Conclusion

In this chapter, we have looked at encryption, key management, hashing, and related concepts. Let's summarize the key concepts here: Encryption of data is the disguising of the data so its true meaning is not visible. It requires three basic ingredients— the input data, an encryption key, and an encryption algorithm. There are two fundamental methods of encryption: asymmetric or public key encryption, where the keys used to encrypt and decrypt are different; and symmetric key encryption, where the keys are the same. The former is typically used in data transmission and requires elaborate setup, while the latter is relatively simple to implement.

The most important and challenging aspect of building an encryption infrastructure is not using the APIs themselves, but building a reliable and secure key-management system. There are a variety of different ways to do that: you can use the database, the filesystem, or both as a key store. You can use a single key for the entire database, one key per row of the table, or something in between. You can use two different keys: one regular key stored somewhere and a master key stored at a different location. The key that is used to encrypt data is not the one stored, but is a bitwise XOR operation of the master and stored keys. If either one is compromised, the encrypted data still cannot be decrypted unless the other one is accessible as well.

Sometimes it is not necessary to hide data, but we nevertheless have to ensure that it has not changed. This is done by cryptographic hashing. A hash function will always return the same value for a given input value. Thus, if we determine that a calculated hash value differs from the value originally calculated, we know that the source data has changed. A variation of hashing, Message Authentication Code (MAC), involves hashing with a key.

Oracle Database 10g Release 2 introduced a feature called Transparent Database Encryption (TDE) that transparently encrypts and decrypts data before storing it in data files. With TDE, sensitive columns in datafiles, archived log files, and database backups are stored encrypted, so a theft of the files will not reveal the sensitive data. Note, however, that TDE is not designed to be a real encryption system so far as user control is concerned. You still need to build your own infrastructure if you want to control who will see the decrypted values and who will not.

CHAPTER 5

Row-Level Security

Row-level security (RLS) allows you to define security policies on database tables (and specific types of operations on tables) that have the effect of restricting which rows a user can see or change in the tables. Introduced in Oracle8*i* Database, RLS has become a very helpful tool for DBAs, and the facility has been enhanced in the Oracle9*i* Database and Oracle Database 10*g* releases. The RLS functionality is implemented primarily through the Oracle built-in package nDBMS_RLS.

In this chapter, I'll describe how you can use DBMS_RLS to establish and use RLS policies for your database and how the RLS features available in Oracle9*i* Database compare with those available in Oracle Database 10*g*. I'll also describe how application contexts work in conjunction with RLS and how RLS interacts with a number of other Oracle features. Because most DBAs might still be running Oracle9*i* Database, this chapter starts with a description of that version's RLS functionality, most of which works the same way in Oracle Database 10*g*. Oracle Database 10*g* enhancements to RLS are described in the section "RLS in Oracle Database 10*g*." Before getting into the details of how RLS works, let's take a step back to look at the characteristics of database access and authorization.

Introduction to RLS

Oracle has, for years, provided security at the table level and, to some extent, at the column level. Privileges may be granted to allow or restrict users to access only some tables or columns. You can grant privileges to specific users to insert only into certain tables while allowing them to select from other tables. For example, a user John can be granted SELECT access to the table EMP owned by Scott, which allows John to select any row from the table, but not to update, delete, or insert. Object-level privileges satisfy many requirements, but sometimes they are not granular enough to meet the various security requirements that are often associated with a company's data. A classic example arises from Oracle's traditional human resources demonstration tables. The employee table contains information about all the employees in the company, but a departmental manager should only be able to see information about employees in his department.

Historically, database administrators have relied on the creation of views on top of underlying tables to achieve a degree of row-level security. Unfortunately, this approach can result in a multitude of views, which are difficult to optimize and manage, especially because the rules restricting access to rows can change often over the lifetime of an application.

This is where RLS comes into play. Using RLS, you can very precisely restrict the rows in a table that a user can see, and that control can be accomplished through the creation of PL/SQL functions that encapsulate complex rules logic and that are much easier to manage than views.

At a high level, RLS consists of three main components:

Policy
> A declarative command that determines when and how to apply restrictions on a user's access during queries, insertions, deletions, updates, or combinations of these operations. For example, you may want only UPDATEs to be restricted for a user, while SELECTS remain unrestricted, or you may want to restrict access for SELECTs only if the user queries a certain column (e.g., SALARY), not others.

Policy function
> A stored function that is called whenever the conditions specified by the security policy are met.

Predicate
> A string that is generated by the policy function, and then transparently and automatically appended by Oracle to the WHERE clause of a user's SQL statements.

RLS works by automatically applying the predicate to the SQL statement issued by the user, regardless of how that statement was executed. The predicate filters out rows based on the condition defined in the policy function. If you create the condition in such a way that it excludes all rows that should not be seen by a user, you will effectively be establishing security at the row level. Oracle's automatic application of the predicate to a user's SQL statement is a key aspect of what makes RLS so secure and comprehensive.

Why Learn About RLS?

From this initial description of RLS, you might be thinking that it is a rather specialized security function, one that you are not likely to use in your daily work as a DBA. In fact, the benefits of RLS extend beyond security. I'll take a quick look here at the reasons that DBAs find RLS helpful and discuss these in greater detail throughout the chapter.

Enhance security

Certainly, RLS's primary purpose is to enhance security within your organization. For many organizations, RLS is helpful in meeting the new security and privacy initiatives and guidelines (e.g., Sarbanes-Oxley, HIPAA, Visa Cardholder Information Security Program) with which they must now comply. These days, security is no longer an afterthought, relegated to the cubicles of auditors far out in the corporate jungle. It has become an important part of the overall system design and development life cycle. Today, everyone from the most junior developers to the most senior DBAs must be knowledgeable about the security tools and technologies available to them. Oracle offers many advanced and add-on security features and options, but RLS is built into the Oracle database engine and is the first tool you should turn to when you are faced with the need to implement access policies. Whether you are a new DBA or a veteran with several years of PL/SQL development under your belt, you will quickly find that a thorough knowledge of RLS will help you to smoothly integrate security features into your database.

Simplify development and maintenance

RLS allows you to centralize your policy logic in a set of packages built around highly structured PL/SQL functions. Even if you *could* implement your row-level security requirements with views, would you even *want* to? SQL syntax can be quite convoluted when it comes to complex business requirements. And as your company puts into place new or evolved privacy policies, and as the government puts new laws into effect, you have to figure out how to translate that into SQL syntax for your views. It is far easier to make changes to PL/SQL functions in a small number of packages than to leave it to Oracle to automatically apply your rules to the specified tables—regardless of how they are accessed.

Simplify canned applications

Related to the ease of development is RLS's role in simplifying the adoption of third-party canned applications. Even if it were feasible for you to undertake changing every query in your application, you couldn't do this for canned applications, because you would not have the source code to modify. You would need the assistance of the application vendor. This problem is particularly true for legacy systems: most organizations are afraid to change anything in such systems, even something as simple as an additional predicate. RLS comes to the rescue here because it requires no code changes. You can go *beneath* the third-party application code, bypassing its logic entirely, and add your own policies to the tables with which that code works.

Control write activity

RLS offers a flexible, quick, and easy way to make tables and views read-only and read/write on the fly, and to make them so based on the credentials of the user. Oracle's native administration commands allow you to define only tablespaces as a whole to be read-only or read/write. You can use RLS to fill this gap and apply the same rules to individual tables.

A Simple Example

Let's start with a simple example of using RLS. Here is the definition of the table EMP in the schema HR, created from the example script provided with Oracle software in *$ORACLE_HOME/sqlplus/demo/demobld.sql*.

```
SQL> DESC emp
 Name                 Null?    Type
 ------------------   --------  ------------
 EMPNO                NOT NULL NUMBER(4)
 ENAME                         VARCHAR2(10)
 JOB                           VARCHAR2(9)
 MGR                           NUMBER(4)
 HIREDATE                      DATE
 SAL                           NUMBER(7,2)
 COMM                          NUMBER(7,2)
 DEPTNO                        NUMBER(2)
```

The table has 14 rows:

EMPNO	ENAME	JOB	MGR	HIREDATE	SAL	COMM	DEPTNO
7369	SMITH	CLERK	7902	17-DEC-80	800		20
7499	ALLEN	SALESMAN	7698	20-FEB-81	1,600	300	30
7521	WARD	SALESMAN	7698	22-FEB-81	1,250	500	30
7566	JONES	MANAGER	7839	02-APR-81	2,975		20
7654	MARTIN	SALESMAN	7698	28-SEP-81	1,250	1,400	30
7698	BLAKE	MANAGER	7839	01-MAY-81	2,850		30
7782	CLARK	MANAGER	7839	09-JUN-81	2,450		10
7788	SCOTT	ANALYST	7566	09-DEC-82	3,000		20
7839	KING	PRESIDENT		17-NOV-81	5,000		10
7844	TURNER	SALESMAN	7698	08-SEP-81	1,500	0	30
7876	ADAMS	CLERK	7788	12-JAN-83	1,100		20
7900	JAMES	CLERK	7698	03-DEC-81	950		30
7902	FORD	ANALYST	7566	03-DEC-81	3,000		20
7934	MILLER	CLERK	7782	23-JAN-82	1,300		10

I'll start with a very simple requirement: I want to restrict users to seeing only employees with a salary of 1,500 or less. Using these assumptions, let's suppose that a user enters the query

```
SELECT * FROM emp;
```

I would like RLS to modify this query *transparently* to:

```
SELECT * FROM emp WHERE sal <= 1500;
```

That is, whenever a user asks for data from the EMP table, Oracle (via the RLS mechanism) will automatically apply the restriction I want. For this to happen, I have to tell Oracle about my requirements.

First I need to write a function that builds and returns this predicate as a string. Given the simplicity of this requirement, I will use a standalone function; in production applications, you should define your predicate functions and related functionality in packages. Connecting as HR, I create the function authorized_emps shown here.

```
CREATE OR REPLACE FUNCTION authorized_emps (
   p_schema_name    IN    VARCHAR2,
   p_object_name    IN    VARCHAR2
)
   RETURN VARCHAR2
IS
BEGIN
   RETURN 'SAL <= 1500';
END;
```

 Notice that the two arguments (schema and object names), are not used inside the function. They are still required by the RLS architecture. Every predicate function, in other words, must pass those two arguments; this topic is explained in more detail later in the chapter.

When the function is executed, it will return my predicate: "SAL <= 1500". Let's confirm that using the following test script:

```
DECLARE
   l_return_string    VARCHAR2 (2000);
BEGIN
   l_return_string := authorized_emps ('X', 'X');
   DBMS_OUTPUT.put_line ('Return String = ' || l_return_string);
END;
```

The output is:

```
Return String = SAL <= 1500
```

Now that I have a function that returns the required predicate, I can take the next step: set up a *security policy*, also known as an *RLS policy* or, simply, a *policy*. This policy defines when and how the predicate will be applied to SQL statements. To define row-level security for the table EMP, I'll use the following code:

```
1  BEGIN
2     DBMS_RLS.add_policy (object_schema  => 'HR',
3         object_name           => 'EMP',
4         policy_name           => 'EMP_POLICY',
5         function_schema       => 'HR',
6         policy_function       => 'AUTHORIZED_EMPS',
7         statement_types       => 'INSERT, UPDATE, DELETE, SELECT'
8         );
9  END;
```

Let's look more carefully at what is going on here: I am adding a policy named EMP_POLICY (line 4) on the table EMP (line 3) owned by the schema HR (line 2). The policy will apply the filter coming out of the function AUTHORIZED_EMPS (line 6) owned by schema HR (line 5) whenever any user performs INSERT, UPDATE, DELETE, or SELECT operations (line 7).

Once I define my policy, I can immediately test it with a query against the EMP table:

```
SQL>SELECT * FROM hr.emp;

EMPNO ENAME      JOB       MGR HIREDATE     SAL    COMM DEPTNO
------ ---------- --------- ----- ---------- ------ ----------- ------
  7369 SMITH      CLERK     7902 17-DEC-80    800               20
  7521 WARD       SALESMAN  7698 22-FEB-81  1,250     500        30
  7654 MARTIN     SALESMAN  7698 28-SEP-81  1,250    1400        30
  7844 TURNER     SALESMAN  7698 08-SEP-81  1,500       0        30
  7876 ADAMS      CLERK     7788 12-JAN-83  1,100               20
  7900 JAMES      CLERK     7698 03-DEC-81    950               30
  7934 MILLER     CLERK     7782 23-JAN-82  1,300               10
```

Note how only 7 *rows* are selected, not all 14 of them. If you look closely, you'll notice that all the rows selected have a SAL value less than or equal to 1,500, which was the predicate function.

Similarly, if users try to delete from or update all the rows in the table, they will only remove those rows made visible by the RLS policy:

```
SQL> DELETE hr.emp;
7 rows deleted.

SQL> UPDATE hr.emp SET comm = 100;
7 rows updated.
```

And because Oracle applies this filtering at a very low level, users are not aware of the filtering; they don't, in effect, know what they are missing—and that is another valuable feature of RLS from the standpoint of security.

Figure 5-1 illustrates the basic flow of data and filtering as implemented by RLS.

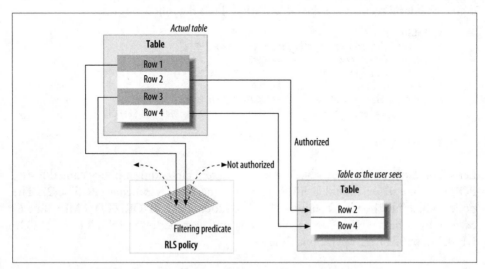

Figure 5-1. How row-level-security filters work

When a user operates on a table that is under the control of row-level security, the SQL statement is intercepted and rewritten by the database engine by adding the output of the policy function. As long as the policy function returns a valid predicate clause, it is applied to the user's original statement.

 Policies are not database schema objects: in other words, no user owns them. Any user with the EXECUTE privilege on the DBMS_RLS package can create a policy. Similarly, any user with that EXECUTE privilege can *drop* any policy. Therefore, it's important that you grant authority to run DBMS_RLS very carefully. If someone has granted the EXECUTE privilege on the package to PUBLIC, it should be revoked immediately.

You can write policy functions that are arbitrarily complex to meet virtually any application requirements. All those functions must, however, conform to these rules:

- A policy function must be a schema-level or packaged function, never a procedure.
- It must return a VARCHAR2 value, which will be applied as the predicate.
- It must have exactly two input parameters in the following order.
    a. The schema that owns the table on which the policy has been defined
    b. The object name (table or view) to which the policy is being applied

To see the policies defined on a table, you can check the data dictionary view DBA_POLICIES, which shows the name of the policy, the object on which it is defined (and its owner), the policy function name (and its owner), and much more. See Appendix A for a complete list of the columns in this view.

If you want to drop an existing RLS policy, you can do so using the DROP_POLICY program in the DBMS_RLS package. You will see examples of using this program later in this chapter.

RLS Policies in a Nutshell

- A policy is a set of instructions used to place a table under row-level security. It is not a schema object, and no user owns it.
- Oracle uses the policy to determine when and how to apply a predicate to all SQL statements that reference the table.
- The predicate is created by and returned from the policy function.

Using RLS

Now that you have seen an example of RLS fundamentals, let's look at some examples that take advantage of different aspects of RLS functionality.

Performing an Update Check

Let's consider a slight twist on our earlier example. Instead of updating the COMM column, the user now updates the SAL column. Because SAL is the column used in the predicate, it will be interesting to see the result.

```
SQL> UPDATE hr.emp SET sal = 1200;
7 rows updated.

SQL> UPDATE hr.emp SET sal = 1100;
7 rows updated.
```

Only seven rows are updated, as expected. Now, let's change the updated amount. After all, everyone deserves a better salary.

```
SQL> UPDATE hr.emp SET sal = 1600;
7 rows updated.

SQL> UPDATE hr.emp SET sal = 1100;
0 rows updated.
```

Note the last update. Why were no rows updated?

The answer lies in the first update. The first one updated the SAL column to 1,600, which is not satisfied by the filtering predicate "SAL <= 1500". Thus, after the first update, all of the rows became invisible to the user.

This is a potentially confusing situation: the user can execute a SQL statement against rows, and the statement changes the access to those rows. During application development, this seeming data instability may create bugs or at least introduce a degree of unpredictability that makes debugging a challenge. To counter this behavior, we can take advantage of another ADD_POLICY parameter, update_check. Let's take a look at the impact of setting this parameter to TRUE when we create a policy on the table.

```
BEGIN
    DBMS_RLS.add_policy (object_name   => 'EMP',
        policy_name        => 'EMP_POLICY',
        function_schema    => 'HR',
        policy_function    => 'AUTHORIZED_EMPS',
        statement_types    => 'INSERT, UPDATE, DELETE, SELECT',
        update_check       => TRUE
        );
END;
```

After this policy is placed on the table, if a user attempts to perform the same update, she gets an error.

```
SQL> UPDATE hr.emp SET sal = 1600;
update hr.emp set sal = 1600
             *
ERROR at line 1:
ORA-28115: policy with check option violation
```

The ORA-28115 error is raised because the policy now prevents any updates to the value of columns in a row that will cause a change in the visibility of those rows with the specified predicate. Users can still make changes to other columns; these changes do *not* affect the visibility of the rows:

```
SQL> UPDATE hr.emp SET sal = 1200;
7 rows updated.
```

 I recommend that you set the update_check parameter to TRUE whenever you declare a policy, to prevent unpredictable and probably undesirable behavior in the application later on.

Static RLS Policies

So far the examples have demonstrated the use of a *static* policy, which means that the value returned by the predicate function does not change even if the circumstances under which it is called change.

Given this fact, RLS need not execute the function every time a query is issued against the table. The value can be determined only once, cached, and then reused from the cache as many times as needed. To make a policy behave that way, you can define it as a *static* policy to RLS by passing TRUE for the static_policy argument:

```
 1  BEGIN
 2     DBMS_RLS.ADD_POLICY (
 3        object_name      => 'EMP',
 4        policy_name      => 'EMP_POLICY',
 5        function_schema  => 'HR',
 6        policy_function  => 'AUTHORIZED_EMPS',
 7        statement_types  => 'INSERT, UPDATE, DELETE, SELECT',
 8        update_check     => TRUE,
 9        static_policy    => TRUE
10     );
11 END;
```

The default value of the static_policy parameter is FALSE: that value makes the policy *dynamic* rather than static, and it causes the policy function to be called for each operation on the table. I'll describe dynamic policies later in the chapter in the section "Defining a Dynamic Policy." Policy types, in addition to static and dynamic, are supported in Oracle Database 10g. See the section "Other Classes of Dynamism" for more information.

There are many situations that call very precisely for a static policy. Consider a merchandise warehouse that is servicing several customers. Here, a predicate might be used to limit the entries to only the relevant records for that customer. For example, the table BUILDINGS may contain a column named CUSTOMER_ID. A predicate

"CUSTOMER_ID = *customer_id*" must be appended to the queries where *customer_id* is based on the user who is logged in. When a user logs in, his customer ID can be retrieved via a LOGON trigger, and the RLS policy can use that ID to evaluate which rows should be displayed. During a session, the value of this predicate does not change, so it makes sense to set static_policy to TRUE in such a situation.

Problems with static policies

Static policies can enhance performance, but they can also introduce bugs in applications. If the predicate derives from or depends on a changing value, such as time, IP address, client identifier, and so on, you will want to define a dynamic policy rather than a static one. Here is an example that shows why.

Let's look again at my original policy function, but let's now assume that the predicate depends on a changing value, such as the value of seconds in the current system timestamp. (This may not be a very likely real-life example, but it is close enough to explain the concept.)

```
SQL> CREATE TABLE trigger_fire
  2  (
  3      val NUMBER
  4  );

Table created.

SQL> INSERT INTO trigger_fire
  2  VALUES
  3  (1);

1 row created.

SQL> COMMIT;

Commit complete.

SQL> CREATE OR REPLACE FUNCTION authorized_emps (
  2      p_schema_name    IN    VARCHAR2,
  3      p_object_name    IN    VARCHAR2
  4  )
  5      RETURN VARCHAR2
  6  IS
  7      l_return_val    VARCHAR2 (2000);
  8      PRAGMA AUTONOMOUS_TRANSACTION;
  9  BEGIN
 10      l_return_val := 'SAL <= ' || TO_NUMBER (TO_CHAR (SYSDATE, 'ss')) * 100;
 11
 12      UPDATE trigger_fire
 13          SET val = val + 1;
 14
 15      COMMIT;
 16      RETURN l_return_val;
```

```
 17 END;
 18 /
```

```
Function created.
```

In this example, the function takes the seconds part of the current time (line 10), multiplies it by 100, and returns a predicate that shows the value of the column SAL less than or equal to this number. Because the seconds part will change with time, consecutive executions of this function will yield different results.

Now let's define a policy on the EMP table with this function as the policy function. As the policy already exists, I need to drop it first.

```
SQL> BEGIN
  2      DBMS_RLS.drop_policy (object_name => 'EMP', policy_name => 'EMP_POLICY')
;
  3  END;
  4  /
```

```
PL/SQL procedure successfully completed.
```

```
SQL> BEGIN
  2      DBMS_RLS.add_policy (object_name      => 'EMP',
  3                           policy_name      => 'EMP_POLICY',
  4                           function_schema  => 'HR',
  5                           policy_function  => 'AUTHORIZED_EMPS',
  6                           statement_types  => 'INSERT, UPDATE, DELETE, SELECT',
  7                           update_check     => TRUE,
  8                           static_policy    => FALSE
  9                           );
 10  END;
 11  /
```

```
PL/SQL procedure successfully completed.
```

It's time to test the policy. The user Lenny tries to find out the number of employees in the table.

```
SQL> SELECT COUNT(*) FROM hr.emp;
```

```
  COUNT(*)
----------
         0
```

Because the table is under row-level security, the policy function is invoked to provide the predicate string to be applied to the query. It depends on the seconds part of the current timestamp, so it is some value between 0 and 60. In this particular case, the value was such that none of the records matched the predicate; hence, no rows were satisfied.

Because the policy function updates the column VAL in the table TRIGGER_FIRE, I can check to see how many times the function was called. As the user HR, let's check the value of VAL in the table TRIGGER_FIRE.

```
SQL> SELECT * FROM trigger_fire;

       VAL
----------
         3
```

Because the policy function was called twice—once during the parse phase and once during the execution phase—the value was incremented by 2 from 1. Lenny issues the query again to know the number of employees.

```
SQL> SELECT COUNT(*) FROM hr.emp

  COUNT(*)
----------
        10
```

This time the policy function returned the predicate, which was satisfied by 10 records in the table. Again, let's check the value of VAL in the table TRIGGER_FIRE.

```
SQL> SELECT * FROM trigger_fire;

       VAL
----------
         5
```

The value is incremented by 2 from 3—proof that the policy function was executed multiple times. You can repeat the exercise as many times as you wish, to verify that the policy function is executed each time the operation occurs on the table.

Now, declare the policy as static and repeat the test. Because there is no RLS operation or API to *alter* a policy, you will need to drop it and then re-create it.

```
SQL> BEGIN
  2    DBMS_RLS.drop_policy (object_name => 'EMP', policy_name => 'EMP_POLICY');
  3  END;
  4  /

PL/SQL procedure successfully completed.
```

Now let's see the effect.

```
  1  BEGIN
  2    DBMS_RLS.add_policy (object_name      => 'EMP',
  3                         policy_name      => 'EMP_POLICY',
  4                         function_schema  => 'HR',
  5                         policy_function  => 'AUTHORIZED_EMPS',
  6                         statement_types  => 'INSERT, UPDATE, DELETE, SELECT',
  7                         update_check     => TRUE,
```

```
  8                         static_policy        => TRUE
  9                         );
 10   END;
 11   /
```

PL/SQL procedure successfully completed.

```
SQL> -- Reset the table TRIGGER_FIRE
SQL> UPDATE trigger_fire SET val = 1;
```

1 row updated.

```
SQL> COMMIT;
```

Commit complete.

As user Lenny, I select the number of rows from the table.

```
SQL> SELECT COUNT(*) FROM hr.emp;

  COUNT(*)
----------
         8
```

As user HR, I check the value of the column VAL in TRIGGER_FIRE.

```
SQL> SELECT * FROM trigger_fire;

       VAL
----------
         2
```

The value was incremented by 1, because the policy function was executed only once, not twice as it was before. I'll repeat the selection from the table EMP several times as user Lenny.

```
SQL> SELECT COUNT(*) FROM hr.emp;

  COUNT(*)
----------
         8

SQL> SELECT COUNT(*) FROM hr.emp;

  COUNT(*)
----------
         8

SQL> SELECT COUNT(*) FROM hr.emp;

  COUNT(*)
----------
         8
```

In all cases, the *same* number is returned. Why? It's because the policy function was executed only once and the predicate that was used by the policy was cached. Because the policy function was never executed after the first execution, the predicate did not change. To confirm that, I'll select from the table TRIGGER_FIRE as user HR.

```
SQL> SELECT * FROM trigger_fire;

       VAL
----------
         2
```

The value is still 2; it has not been incremented at all since the first time it was called. This output confirms that the policy function was not called during subsequent SELECTs on the table EMP.

By declaring a policy as *static*, I have effectively instructed the policy function to execute only once, and the policy to reuse the predicate originally created, even though the predicate might have changed in the course of time. This behavior might produce unexpected results in your application, so you should use static policies with great caution. The only time you're likely to want to use static policies is the case where the function positively results in a definitive predicate regardless of any of the variables, except those set at session startup and never changed—for example, the username.

Using a pragma

Another way to enforce the logic we require is to use a packaged function along with a *pragma* declaration to suppress any database operations. Here is the package specification.

```
CREATE OR REPLACE PACKAGE rls_pkg
AS
    FUNCTION authorized_emps (
        p_schema_name   IN   VARCHAR2,
        p_object_name   IN   VARCHAR2
    )
        RETURN VARCHAR2;

    PRAGMA RESTRICT_REFERENCES (authorized_emps, WNDS, RNDS, WNPS, RNPS);
END;
/
```

And here is the package body.

```
CREATE OR REPLACE PACKAGE BODY rls_pkg
AS
    FUNCTION authorized_emps (
        p_schema_name   IN   VARCHAR2,
        p_object_name   IN   VARCHAR2
```

```
    )
        RETURN VARCHAR2
    IS
        l_return_val    VARCHAR2 (2000);
    BEGIN
        l_return_val :=
            'SAL <= ' || TO_NUMBER (TO_CHAR (SYSDATE, 'ss')) * 100;
        RETURN l_return_val;
    END;
END;
/
```

In the package specification, I have defined a *pragma* to bring this function to these purity levels:

WNDS
> Write No Database State

RNDS
> Read No Database State

WNPS
> Write No Package State

RNPS
> Read No Package State

When this package body is compiled, the pragma will be violated and the compilation will fail with the following message.

```
Warning: Package Body created with compilation errors.

Errors for PACKAGE BODY RLS_PKG:

LINE/COL ERROR
-------- ----------------------------------------------------------------
2/4      PLS-00452: Subprogram 'AUTHORIZED_EMPS' violates its associated
         pragma
```

Declaring a pragma protects you from falling into potentially erroneous situations. However, it's still a good idea to use static policies as long as they are being applied only to deterministic situations, such as the warehouse example we discussed earlier.

 When you are creating a static policy, make sure that the predicate returned by the policy function will *never* have a different value within the session.

Defining a Dynamic Policy

In the previous sections, I talked about a policy that returns a predicate string that is constant—for example, SAL <= 1500. In real life, such a scenario is not very common, except in some specialized applications such as goods warehouses. In most cases, you will need to build a filter based on the user issuing the query. For instance, the HR application may require that users see only their own records, not all records in a table. This is a *dynamic* requirement, as it needs to be evaluated for each employee who logs in. The policy function can be rewritten as follows.

```
 1 CREATE OR REPLACE FUNCTION authorized_emps (
 2     p_schema_name   IN    VARCHAR2,
 3     p_object_name   IN    VARCHAR2
 4 )
 5     RETURN VARCHAR2
 6 IS
 7     l_return_val   VARCHAR2 (2000);
 8 BEGIN
 9     l_return_val := 'ENAME = USER';
10     RETURN l_return_val;
11 END;
12 /
```

In line 9, the predicate will compare the ENAME column with the USER—that is, the name of the currently logged-in user. If the user Martin (remember that Martin is the name of an employee in the table EMP) logs in and selects from the table, he sees only one row—his own.

```
SQL> CONN martin/martin
Connected.

SQL> SELECT * FROM hr.emp;

EMPNO ENAME      JOB        MGR HIREDATE     SAL   COMM DEPTNO
------ ---------- --------- ------ --------- ------ ------ ------
 7654 MARTIN     SALESMAN    7698 28-SEP-81 1,250  1,400     30
```

Now let's expand this model to let Martin show more records—not just his own, but his entire department's records. The policy function now becomes the following.

```
 1 CREATE OR REPLACE FUNCTION authorized_emps (
 2     p_schema_name   IN    VARCHAR2,
 3     p_object_name   IN    VARCHAR2
 4 )
 5     RETURN VARCHAR2
 6 IS
 7     l_deptno       NUMBER;
 8     l_return_val   VARCHAR2 (2000);
 9 BEGIN
10     SELECT deptno
11       INTO l_deptno
12       FROM emp
13      WHERE ename = USER;
14
15     l_return_val := 'DEPTNO = ' || l_deptno;
16     RETURN l_return_val;
17 END;
18 /
```

I also need to perform an additional step here. In the preceding code, the function selects from the table EMP (lines 10–13). However, the table is protected by the RLS policy whose policy function is owned by the user HR. When the function executes under the privileges of the user HR, it will not find any rows, because there is no employee with the name HR—making the predicate an incorrect one. To prevent this from happening, there are two options:

- Grant a special privilege to the user HR so that RLS policies do not apply to it, or
- Inside the policy function, indicate whether the calling user is the schema owner; if so, ignore the check

If I use the first approach, I will not need to change the policy function. As a DBA user, I must grant the special privilege to HR as follows:

```
GRANT EXEMPT ACCESS POLICY TO hr;
```

This removes the application of any RLS policies from the user HR. Because no policy—regardless of which table it is defined on—will be applied, you should use this approach with great caution. In fact, considering the breach it places in the security model, we do not recommend this approach for regular schema owners.

The other approach is to have a special schema named, say, RLSOWNER, which creates all the RLS policies and owns all the policy functions. Only this user, and no others, is granted the EXEMPT ACCESS POLICY system privilege. Because the policy function is owned by RLSOWNER, the policy-creation PL/SQL block looks like the following. This block can be run by any user that has EXECUTE privileges on the DBMS_RLS package.

```
1  BEGIN
2     DBMS_RLS.add_policy (object_name => 'EMP',
3             policy_name          => 'EMP_POLICY',
4             function_schema      => 'RLSOWNER',
5             policy_function      => 'AUTHORIZED_EMPS',
6             statement_types      => 'INSERT, UPDATE, DELETE, SELECT',
7             update_check         => TRUE
8             );
9  END;
10 /
```

Using the second approach, the policy function has to include the logic to bypass the filter for the schema owner, as shown below. Again, this block may be run by any user with EXECUTE privileges on the package DBMS_RLS.

```
1  CREATE OR REPLACE FUNCTION authorized_emps (
2     p_schema_name   IN   VARCHAR2,
3     p_object_name   IN   VARCHAR2
4  )
5     RETURN VARCHAR2
6  IS
7     l_deptno        NUMBER;
8     l_return_val    VARCHAR2 (2000);
```

```
 9  BEGIN
10     IF (p_schema_name = USER)
11     THEN
12        l_return_val := NULL;
13     ELSE
14        SELECT deptno
15          INTO l_deptno
16          FROM emp
17         WHERE ename = USER;
18
19        l_return_val := 'DEPTNO = ' || l_deptno;
20     END IF;
21
22     RETURN l_return_val;
23  END;
24  /
```

This version of the function is very similar to the previous ones; the new lines are shown in bold (line 10). Here I am checking to see if the calling user is the owner of the table; if so, I return NULL (line 12). A NULL value in the predicate returned by the function is equivalent to no policy at all—that is, no rows are filtered.

Now Martin executes the same query as before:

```
SQL> SELECT * FROM hr.emp;

EMPNO ENAME      JOB        MGR HIREDATE     SAL  COMM DEPTNO
----- ---------- --------- ---- --------- ------ ----- ------
 7499 ALLEN      SALESMAN  7698 20-FEB-81  1,600   300     30
 7521 WARD       SALESMAN  7698 22-FEB-81  1,250   500     30
 7654 MARTIN     SALESMAN  7698 28-SEP-81  1,250 1,400     30
 7698 BLAKE      MANAGER   7839 01-MAY-81  2,850             30
 7844 TURNER     SALESMAN  7698 08-SEP-81  1,500     0     30
 7900 JAMES      CLERK     7698 03-DEC-81    950             30

6 rows selected.
```

Note how all of the returned rows are from Martin's department (30).

As you can see, the policy function is crucial in building the RLS policy. The policy will be able to place filters on the rows with whatever predicate value the function can spin out, as long as it is syntactically correct. You can create quite elaborate and sophisticated predicates using policy functions.

Following the same approach, you can have the RLS filters applied to any table in the database. For instance, you could have a policy on the table DEPT as shown below.

```
1  BEGIN
2     DBMS_RLS.add_policy (object_schema  => 'HR',
3                          object_name       => 'DEPT',
4                          policy_name       => 'DEPT_POLICY',
5                          function_schema   => 'RLSOWNER',
6                          policy_function   => 'AUTHORIZED_EMPS',
7                          statement_types   => 'SELECT, INSERT, UPDATE, DELETE',
8                          update_check      => TRUE
```

```
 9                  );
10  END;
11  /
```

Here the same function—AUTHORIZED_EMPS—is used as the policy function. Because the function returns a predicate "DEPTNO = *deptno*", it can easily be used in the table DEPT as well as any other table containing a DEPTNO column.

A table that does not have a DEPTNO column probably has another column through which it has a foreign-key relationship with the EMP table. For instance, the table BONUS has a column ENAME through which it is tied to the EMP table. So I can rewrite my policy function as follows:

```
CREATE OR REPLACE FUNCTION allowed_enames (
   p_schema_name    IN   VARCHAR2,
   p_object_name    IN   VARCHAR2
)
   RETURN VARCHAR2
IS
   l_deptno         NUMBER;
   l_return_val     VARCHAR2 (2000);
   l_str            VARCHAR2 (2000);
BEGIN
   IF (p_schema_name = USER)
   THEN
      l_return_val := NULL;
   ELSE
      SELECT deptno
        INTO l_deptno
        FROM hr.emp
       WHERE ename = USER;

      l_str := '(';

      FOR emprec IN (SELECT ename
                       FROM hr.emp
                      WHERE deptno = l_deptno)
      LOOP
         l_str := '''' || emprec.ename || ''',';
      END LOOP;

      l_str := RTRIM (l_str, ',');
      l_str := ')';
      l_return_val := 'ENAME IN ' || l_str;
   END IF;

   RETURN l_return_val;
END;
/
```

If I define a policy on the BONUS table with the following policy function, this places the RLS policy on the BONUS table, as well:

```
BEGIN
   DBMS_RLS.add_policy (object_schema  => 'HR',
```

```
                object_name          => 'BONUS',
                policy_name          => 'BONUS_POLICY',
                function_schema      => 'RLSOWNER',
                policy_function      => 'ALLOWED_ENAMES',
                statement_types      => 'SELECT, INSERT, UPDATE, DELETE',
                 update_check          => TRUE
                );
    END;
    /
```

In this manner, I can define RLS polices on all related tables in the database driven
from one table. Because the facility I've described in this section essentially provides a
private view of the tables in the database based on the user or other parameters (like
the time of day or IP address), it is also known as *Virtual Private Database* (VPD).

Improving Performance

Let's assume that our requirements have changed again. (That's not surprising in a
typical organization, is it?) Now I have to set up the policy in such a way that all
employees and departments will be visible to a user who is a manager; otherwise,
only the employees of the user's department are visible. To accommodate this
requirement, my policy function might look like this.

```
CREATE OR REPLACE FUNCTION authorized_emps (
    p_schema_name    IN    VARCHAR2,
    p_object_name    IN    VARCHAR2
)
    RETURN VARCHAR2
IS
    l_deptno         NUMBER;
    l_return_val     VARCHAR2 (2000);
    l_mgr            BOOLEAN;
    l_empno          NUMBER;
    l_dummy          CHAR (1);
BEGIN
    IF (p_schema_name = USER)
    THEN
       l_return_val := NULL;
    ELSE
       SELECT DISTINCT deptno, empno
                  INTO l_deptno, l_empno
                  FROM hr.emp
                 WHERE ename = USER;

       BEGIN
         SELECT '1'
           INTO l_dummy
           FROM hr.emp
          WHERE mgr = l_empno AND ROWNUM < 2;

          l_mgr := TRUE;
       EXCEPTION
```

```
            WHEN NO_DATA_FOUND
            THEN
                l_mgr := FALSE;
            WHEN OTHERS
            THEN
                RAISE;
        END;

        IF (l_mgr)
        THEN
            l_return_val := NULL;
        ELSE
            l_return_val := 'DEPTNO = ' || l_deptno;
        END IF;
    END IF;

    RETURN l_return_val;
END;
```

Look at the complexity in selecting the data. This complexity will surely add to the response time (and, of course, in your real-world applications, the logic will be considerably more complex). Can I simplify the code and improve performance?

I certainly can. Look at the first requirement—checking to see if the employee is a manager. In the above code, we checked the EMP table for that information, but the fact that an employee is a manager does not change very often. Similarly, a manager's manager might change, but the status of a manager remains the same. So, the title of a manager is actually more like an attribute of the employee when she logs in, not something that changes during a session. Therefore, if we can somehow, during the login process, pass to the database the fact that the user is a manager, that check will not be needed later in the policy function.

How do I pass a value of this kind? Global variables come to mind. I could assign the value "Y" or "N" to designate the manager status and create a package to hold the variable.

```
CREATE OR REPLACE PACKAGE mgr_check
IS
    is_mgr CHAR (1);
END;
```

The policy function looks like this.

```
CREATE OR REPLACE FUNCTION authorized_emps (
    p_schema_name   IN   VARCHAR2,
    p_object_name   IN   VARCHAR2
)
    RETURN VARCHAR2
IS
    l_deptno        NUMBER;
    l_return_val    VARCHAR2 (2000);
BEGIN
    IF (p_schema_name = USER)
```

```
    THEN
        l_return_val := NULL;
    ELSE
        SELECT DISTINCT deptno
                    INTO l_deptno
                    FROM hr.emp
                WHERE ename = USER;

        IF (mgr_check.is_mgr = 'Y')
        THEN
            l_return_val := NULL;
        ELSE
            l_return_val := 'DEPTNO = ' || l_deptno;
        END IF;
    END IF;

    RETURN l_return_val;
END;
```

Notice how much less code is now required to check for manager status. It merely checks the status from a global packaged variable. This variable has to be set during the login process and thus is a perfect job for an *AFTER LOGON database trigger*.

```
CREATE OR REPLACE TRIGGER tr_set_mgr
    AFTER LOGON ON DATABASE
DECLARE
    l_empno    NUMBER;
    l_dummy    CHAR (1);
BEGIN
    SELECT DISTINCT empno
                INTO l_empno
                FROM hr.emp
            WHERE ename = USER;

    SELECT '1'
      INTO l_dummy
      FROM hr.emp
     WHERE mgr = l_empno AND ROWNUM < 2;

    rlsowner.mgr_check.is_mgr := 'Y';
EXCEPTION
    WHEN NO_DATA_FOUND
    THEN
        rlsowner.mgr_check.is_mgr := 'N';
    WHEN OTHERS
    THEN
        RAISE;
END;
/
```

The trigger sets the value of the packaged variable to designate the manager status of the employee, which is then picked up by the policy function. Let's do a quick test.

Connecting as King (who is a manager) and Martin (who is not), I can see that the setup works.

```
SQL> CONN martin/martin
Connected.

SQL> SELECT COUNT(*) FROM hr.emp;

  COUNT(*)
----------
    262145

SQL> CONN king/king
Connected.

SQL> SELECT COUNT(*) FROM hr.emp;

  COUNT(*)
----------
    589825
```

Martin's query retrieves fewer employees, as expected, whereas King's query retrieves all rows.

You can often use this packaged variable approach to improve performance. In the first example, where the check for manager status was done inside the policy function, the query took 199 centiseconds. Using the global variable approach, it took only 132 centiseconds, which represents a significant improvement.

Controlling the Type of Table Access

RLS has many uses beyond security and the simplification of application development models. RLS is also very helpful if you need to switch a table between read-only and read/write status, as determined by a variety of circumstances. Without RLS, DBAs could make an entire tablespace—but not the individual tables inside it—read-only or read/write. Even if a DBA wanted to take this approach, a tablespace could not be made read-only if it had any active transactions. As it may be impossible to find a period of time during which there are no transactions in a database, a tablespace may never actually be able to be made read-only. In such cases, RLS is the only viable solution.

Now, to be honest, RLS does not actually make a table read-only; it simply allows us to emulate that behavior by denying any attempts to change the contents of the table. The simplest way to do this is to apply a predicate to any UPDATE, DELETE, and INSERT that will *always* evaluate to FALSE—for example, 1=2.

Here is an example of making the EMP table read-only with this most basic of predicate functions:

```
CREATE OR REPLACE FUNCTION make_read_only (
   p_schema_name   IN   VARCHAR2,
```

```
        p_object_name    IN    VARCHAR2
    )
        RETURN VARCHAR2
    IS
    BEGIN
        -- Only the owner of the predicate policy function can change
        -- the data in the table.
        IF (p_schema_name = USER)
        THEN
            RETURN NULL;
        ELSE
            RETURN '1=2';
        END IF;
    END;
```

Using this policy function, I can create an RLS policy on the table EMP for the DML
statements that change data: INSERT, UPDATE, and DELETE.

```
    BEGIN
        DBMS_RLS.add_policy (object_name        => 'EMP',
                             policy_name        => 'EMP_READONLY_POLICY',
                             function_schema    => 'HR',
                             policy_function    => 'MAKE_READ_ONLY',
                             statement_types    => 'INSERT, UPDATE, DELETE',
                             update_check       => TRUE
                             );
    END;
```

In the line shown in bold, note that the statement_types parameter does not include
the SELECT statement, as that statement will be freely allowed.

And now it is only possible to query information on the EMP table if the current user
is not the owner of the policy's function:

```
    SQL> SHOW user
    USER is "MARTIN"

    SQL> DELETE hr.emp;
    0 rows deleted.

    SQL> SELECT COUNT(*) FROM hr.emp;

      COUNT(*)
    ----------
            14
```

When the time comes to make the table read/write again, I can simply disable the
policy.

```
    BEGIN
        DBMS_RLS.enable_policy (object_name    => 'EMP',
                                policy_name    => 'EMP_READONLY_POLICY',
                                ENABLE         => FALSE
                                );
    END;
    /
```

Now non-HR users can successfully complete DML operations on the table.

 The table is never actually set to read-only; the policy just makes sure that no rows are affected when the user issues DML statements against the table. Because no error is returned and the policy simply ignores any DML statements, you need to be careful to examine all of the application code that uses this functionality. Programmers may inadvertently mistake the no-error condition as a successful DML operation.

The power of this feature is not limited to just making tables read-only or read/write on demand; it can be created dynamically and applied automatically based on any user-defined conditions that you wish. For instance, you could write a policy function that makes the table read-only between 5:00 P.M. and 9:00 A.M. for all users, except for the batch job user, BATCHUSER, and read-only for the batch user between 9:00 A.M. and 5:00 P.M. The body of such a function might look like this:

```
BEGIN
  IF (p_schema_name = USER)
  THEN
      l_return_val := NULL;
  ELSE
      l_hr := TO_NUMBER (TO_CHAR (SYSDATE, 'HH24'));

      IF (USER = 'BATCHUSER')
      -- you can list all users here that should be
      -- read only during the daytime.
      THEN
          IF (l_hr BETWEEN 9 AND 17)
          THEN
             -- make the table read only
             l_return_val := '1=2';
          ELSE
             l_return_val := NULL;
          END IF;
      ELSE
          -- users which need to be read only during after-hours
          IF (l_hr >= 17 AND l_hr <= 9)
          THEN
             -- make the table read only
             l_return_val := '1=2';
          ELSE
             l_return_val := NULL;
          END IF;
      END IF;
  END IF;

  RETURN l_return_val;
END;
```

Based on the timestamp, you can let the table be controlled granularly on multiple fronts. The example shown here can be extended to cover other events as well (e.g., IP address, authentication type, client information, terminal, OS user, and many others). All you have to do is get the appropriate variable from the system context (SYS_CONTEXT; this feature is explored later in the chapter) of the session and check it. For example, assume that you have a requirement that the user King (the president of the company) is allowed to see every record only if he does both of the following:

- Connects from his laptop KINGLAP with a fixed IP address (192.168.1.1) and from the Windows NT domain ACMEBANK

- Connects to Windows as user King

The policy function would now look like this:

```
CREATE OR REPLACE FUNCTION emp_policy (
    p_schema_name    IN    VARCHAR2,
    p_object_name    IN    VARCHAR2
)
    RETURN VARCHAR2
IS
    l_deptno        NUMBER;
    l_return_val    VARCHAR2 (2000);
BEGIN
    IF (p_schema_name = USER)
    THEN
        l_return_val := NULL;
    ELSIF (USER = 'KING')
    THEN
        IF (
                -- check client machine name
                SYS_CONTEXT ('USERENV', 'HOST') = 'ACMEBANK\KINGLAP'
            OR
                -- check OS username
                SYS_CONTEXT ('USERENV', 'OS_USER') = 'king'
            OR
                -- check IP address
                SYS_CONTEXT ('USERENV', 'IP_ADDRESS') = '192.168.1.1'
            )
        THEN
            -- all checks satisfied for KING; allow unrestricted access.
            l_return_val := NULL;
        ELSE
            -- return the usual predicate
            l_return_val := 'SAL <= 1500';
        END IF;
    ELSE  -- All other users
        l_return_val := 'SAL <= 1500';
    END IF;

    RETURN l_return_val;
END;
```

Here I am using the built-in function SYS_CONTEXT to return the *context* attributes. I'll discuss the use of system contexts later (see the "Application Contexts" section); all you need to understand now is that the function call returns the name of the client terminal from which the user is connected. The other lines using the function call also return the appropriate values.

You can use SYS_CONTEXT to get a variety of information about the user connection. By using this information, you can easily customize your policy function to build a filter to cater to your specific needs. For a complete list of attributes available via SYS_CONTEXT, refer to Oracle's *SQL Reference Manual.*

RLS in Oracle Database 10g

This section describes the new RLS features and enhancements introduced in Oracle Database 10g.

Column-Sensitive RLS

Let's revisit the example of the HR application used in earlier sections. I designed the policy with the requirement that no user except King should have permission to see all records. Any other user can see only data about the employees in her department. But there may be cases in which that policy is too restrictive.

Suppose that I want to protect the data so people can't snoop around for salary information. Consider the following two queries.

```
SELECT empno, sal FROM emp;
```

```
SELECT empno FROM emp;
```

The first query shows salary information for employees, the very information you want to protect. In this case, I want to show only the employees in the user's own department. But the second query shows only the employee numbers. Should I filter that as well so that it shows only the numbers for the employees in the user's own department?

The answer might vary depending upon the security policy in place within my organization. There may be a good reason to let the second query show all employees, regardless of the department to which they belong.

In Oracle9i Database, RLS would not have been able to help us with this requirement, but in Oracle Database 10g, a new ADD_POLICY parameter, sec_relevant_cols, makes it easy. In the above scenario, I want the filter to be applied only when the SAL and COMM columns are selected, not any other columns. I can write the policy as follows. Note the new parameter shown in bold.

```
BEGIN
   DBMS_RLS.drop_policy (object_schema    => 'HR',
                         object_name      => 'EMP',
```

```
                    policy_name          => 'EMP_POLICY'
                 );
     --
     DBMS_RLS.add_policy (object_schema         => 'HR',
            object_name           => 'EMP',
            policy_name           => 'EMP_POLICY',
            function_schema       => 'RLSOWNER',
            policy_function       => 'AUTHORIZED_EMPS',
            statement_types       => 'INSERT, UPDATE, DELETE, SELECT',
            update_check          => TRUE,
            sec_relevant_cols     => 'SAL, COMM'
            );
   END;
```

After this policy is put in place, Martin's queries perform differently.

```
SQL> -- "harmless" query, only EMPNO is selected
SQL> SELECT empno FROM hr.emp;

... data displayed ...

14 rows selected.

SQL> -- sensitive query: SAL is present
SQL> SELECT sal FROM hr.emp;

... data displayed ...

6 rows selected.
```

Note that when the column SAL is selected, the RLS policy kicks in, preventing the display of all rows; it filters out the rows where DEPTNO is something other than 30—that is, the DEPTNO of the user (Martin) executing the query.

Column sensitivity does not apply just to being in the SELECT list, but applies whenever the column is referenced, either directly or indirectly. Consider the following query:

```
SQL> SELECT   deptno, COUNT (*)
  2     FROM hr.emp
  3    WHERE sal > 0
  4  GROUP BY deptno;

   DEPTNO   COUNT(*)
---------- ----------
       30          6
```

Here, the SAL column has been referenced in the WHERE clause, so the RLS policy applies, causing only the records from department 30 to be displayed. Consider another example, in which I try to *display* the value of SAL.

```
SQL> SELECT *
  2     FROM hr.emp
  3    WHERE deptno = 10;

no rows selected
```

Here the column SAL has not been referenced explicitly, but it is *implicitly* referenced by the "SELECT *" clause, so the RLS policy filters all but the rows from department 30. Because the query called for department 10, no rows were returned.

Let's examine a slightly different situation now. In the above case, we did protect the SAL column values from being displayed for those rows for which the user is not authorized. However, in the process, I suppressed the display of the *entire* row, not just the column. Suppose that the new requirements call for masking only the column, not the entire row, and for displaying all other non-sensitive columns. Can this be done?

It's easy with another ADD_POLICY parameter, sec_relevant_cols_opt. All I have to do is re-create the policy with the parameter set to the constant DBMS_RLS.ALL_ROWS, as follows.

```
BEGIN
    DBMS_RLS.drop_policy (object_schema      => 'HR',
                          object_name        => 'EMP',
                          policy_name        => 'EMP_POLICY'
                          );
    DBMS_RLS.add_policy (object_schema        => 'HR',
                         object_name          => 'EMP',
                         policy_name          => 'EMP_POLICY',
                         function_schema      => 'RLSOWNER',
                         policy_function      => 'AUTHORIZED_EMPS',
                         statement_types      => 'SELECT',
                         update_check         => TRUE,
                         sec_relevant_cols    => 'SAL, COMM',
                         sec_relevant_cols_opt => DBMS_RLS.all_rows
                         );
END;
```

If Martin issues the same type of query now, the results will be different (in the following output, I request that a "?" be shown for NULL values):

```
SQL> SET NULL ?
SQL> SELECT * FROM hr.emp ORDER by deptno;
```

EMPNO	ENAME	JOB	MGR	HIREDATE	SAL	COMM	DEPTNO
7782	CLARK	MANAGER	7839	09-JUN-81	?	?	10
7839	KING	PRESIDENT	?	17-NOV-81	?	?	10
7934	MILLER	CLERK	7782	23-JAN-82	?	?	10
7369	SMITH	CLERK	7902	17-DEC-80	?	?	20
7876	ADAMS	CLERK	7788	12-JAN-83	?	?	20
7902	FORD	ANALYST	7566	03-DEC-81	?	?	20
7788	SCOTT	ANALYST	7566	09-DEC-82	?	?	20
7566	JONES	MANAGER	7839	02-APR-81	?	?	20
7499	ALLEN	SALESMAN	7698	20-FEB-81	1,600	300	30
7698	BLAKE	MANAGER	7839	01-MAY-81	2,850	?	30
7654	MARTIN	SALESMAN	7698	28-SEP-81	1,250	1,400	30
7900	JAMES	CLERK	7698	03-DEC-81	950	?	30

| 7844 TURNER | SALESMAN | 7698 08-SEP-81 | 1,500 | 0 | 30 |
| 7521 WARD | SALESMAN | 7698 22-FEB-81 | 1,250 | 500 | 30 |

```
14 rows selected.
```

Notice how *all* 14 rows are shown, along with all the columns, but the values for SAL and COMM are NULL for the rows that the user is not supposed to see—that is, the employees of departments other than 30.

With these new ADD_POLICY parameters, RLS lets me meet requirements in which rows must be displayed but sensitive values must be hidden. Prior to Oracle Database 10g, I would have had to use views to accomplish the same thing, and the operations would have been a good deal more complicated.

In Oracle Database 10g Release 2, you can even apply RLS to CREATE INDEX statements. In that case, use INDEX as the value in the statement_types parameter in the ADD_POLICY procedure.

 Use this feature with extreme caution: in certain cases, it may produce unexpected results. Consider the following query issued by user Martin.

```
SQL> SELECT COUNT(1), AVG(sal) FROM hr.emp;
COUNT(SAL)   AVG(SAL)
---------- ----------
        14 1566.66667
```

The result shows 14 employees, and the average salary is 1,566, but that salary is actually the average of only the 6 employees Martin is authorized to see, not all 14 employees. This may create some confusion as to which values are correct. When the schema owner, HR, issues the same query, we see a different result.

```
SQL> CONN hr/hr
Connected.
```

```
SQL> SELECT COUNT(1), AVG(sal) FROM hr.emp;
COUNT(SAL)   AVG(SAL)
---------- ----------
        14 2073.21429
```

Because results vary by the user issuing the query, you need to be very careful to interpret the results accordingly; otherwise, this feature may introduce difficult-to-trace bugs into your application.

Other Classes of Dynamism

Perhaps the most important enhancement to RLS in Oracle Database 10g is the support of new levels of dynamism, implemented as policy types and intended to improve performance.

First, let's review the difference between static and dynamic policies. With a dynamic policy type, the policy function is executed to create a predicate string every time the policy places filters on access to the table. Although using a dynamic policy guarantees a fresh predicate every time it is called, the additional overhead resulting from multiple executions of the policy function can be quite substantial. The fact is that, in most cases, the policy function does not need to be re-executed, because the predicate will never change inside a session, as we showed earlier in the discussion of static policies.

The best approach, from a performance point of view, would be to design the policy function so that if some specific value changes, the policy function will be re-executed. Oracle Database 10g offers such a feature: if an application context on which the program depends is changed, the policy forces re-execution of the function; otherwise, the function will not be run again. We'll see how this works in the following sections.

As with Oracle9i Database, in Oracle Database 10g, you can set the static_policy parameter in the ADD_POLICY procedure to TRUE (indicating a static policy) or FALSE (indicating a dynamic policy). If this parameter is TRUE, then the value of a new Oracle Database 10g parameter, policy_type, is set to DBMS_RLS.STATIC. If static_policy is FALSE, then policy_type is set to DBMS_RLS. DYNAMIC. The default for static_policy is TRUE.

The static and dynamic policy choices behave just as they would in Oracle9i Database, but Oracle Database 10g supports some additional policy types, as well. You select these by specifying the appropriate value for the policy_type parameter in the ADD_POLICY procedure. The list below shows the new values you can specify for this parameter.

Context sensitive
> DBMS_RLS.CONTEXT_SENSITIVE

Shared context sensitive
> DBMS_RLS.SHARED_CONTEXT_SENSITIVE

Shared static
> DBMS_RLS.SHARED_STATIC

 These new policy types provide excellent performance benefits but share some of the same side effects described earlier for static policies.

Shared static policy

The shared static policy type is similar to the static type, except the same policy function is used in policies on multiple objects. In a previous example, you saw how the function authorized_emps was used as the policy function in the policies on both the DEPT and the EMP tables. Similarly, you can have the same policy defined on both tables, not merely the same function. This is known as a *shared policy*. If it can also be considered static, then the policy is known as a *shared static policy,* and the policy_type parameter is set to the constant DBMS_RLS.SHARED_STATIC. Using this policy type, here is how I can create the same policy on our two tables.

```
BEGIN
    DBMS_RLS.drop_policy (object_schema    => 'HR',
                          object_name      => 'DEPT',
                          policy_name      => 'EMP_DEPT_POLICY'
                         );
    DBMS_RLS.add_policy (object_schema => 'HR',
            object_name         => 'DEPT',
            policy_name         => 'EMP_DEPT_POLICY',
            function_schema     => 'RLSOWNER',
            policy_function     => 'AUTHORIZED_EMPS',
            statement_types     => 'SELECT, INSERT, UPDATE, DELETE',
            update_check        => TRUE,
            policy_type         => DBMS_RLS.shared_static
            );
    DBMS_RLS.add_policy (object_schema => 'HR',
            object_name         => 'EMP',
            policy_name         => 'EMP_DEPT_POLICY',
            function_schema     => 'RLSOWNER',
            policy_function     => 'AUTHORIZED_EMPS',
            statement_types     => 'SELECT, INSERT, UPDATE, DELETE',
            update_check        => TRUE,
            policy_type         => DBMS_RLS.shared_static
            );
END;
```

By declaring a single policy on both tables, I am effectively instructing the database to cache the outcome of the policy function once and then use it multiple times.

Context-sensitive policy

As you saw earlier, static policies, although quite efficient, can be dangerous: because they do not re-execute the function every time, they may produce unexpected and unwanted results. Hence, Oracle provides another type of policy—the *context-sensitive policy*, which re-executes the policy function only when the application context changes in the session. (See the "Application Contexts" section later in this chapter.) Here is a block of code that defines such a policy:

```
BEGIN
    DBMS_RLS.drop_policy (object_schema    => 'HR',
                          object_name      => 'EMP',
                          policy_name      => 'EMP_DEPT_POLICY'
                         );
    DBMS_RLS.add_policy (object_schema => 'HR',
            object_name         => 'EMP',
            policy_name         => 'EMP_DEPT_POLICY',
            function_schema     => 'RLSOWNER',
            policy_function     => 'AUTHORIZED_EMPS',
```

```
        statement_types      => 'SELECT, INSERT, UPDATE, DELETE',
        update_check         => TRUE,
        policy_type          => DBMS_RLS.context_sensitive
    );
END;
```

When you use a context-sensitive policy type (DBMS_RLS.CONTEXT_SENSI-
TIVE), performance can increase dramatically. In the following block of code, the
built-in function, DBMS_UTILITY.GET_TIME, helps calculate elapsed time down
to the hundredth of a second.

```
DECLARE
    l_start   PLS_INTEGER;
    l_count   PLS_INTEGER;
BEGIN
    l_start := DBMS_UTILITY.get_time;

    SELECT COUNT (*)
      INTO l_count
      FROM hr.emp;

    DBMS_OUTPUT.put_line (
        'Elapsed time = '
        || TO_CHAR (DBMS_UTILITY.get_time - l_start)
        );
END;
```

We then apply each of the types of policies shown in the table below and run the
block of code. As you can see from this table, the purely static policy results in the
fastest time (just a single execution of the policy function), but the context-sensitive
policy is significantly faster than the 100% dynamic version.

Policy type	Response time (cs)
Dynamic	133
Context -sensitive	84
Static	37

Shared context-sensitive policy

Shared context-sensitive policies are similar to context-sensitive policies, except that
the same policy is used for multiple objects, as we saw with shared static policies.

Troubleshooting RLS

RLS is a complex feature that interacts with a variety of elements in the Oracle architecture. You may encounter errors, either as a result of problems in your design or through
misuse by users. Fortunately, for most errors, RLS produces a detailed trace file in the
directory specified by the database initialization parameter USER_DUMP_DEST. This
section describes how you can trace RLS operations and resolve error conditions.

Interpreting Errors

The most common error you will encounter, and the easiest to deal with, is *ORA-
28110: Policy function or package has error*. The culprit here is a policy function with
one or more compilation errors. Fixing your compilation errors and recompiling the
function (or the package containing the function) solves the problem.

You may also encounter runtime errors, such as an unhandled exception, a datatype
mismatch, or a situation in which the fetched data is much larger than the variable
fetched into. In these cases, Oracle raises the *ORA-28112: failed to execute policy
function* error and produces a trace file. You can examine that file, which you will
find in the directory specified by the USER_DUMP_DEST database initialization
parameter, to find out the nature of the error. Here is an excerpt from a trace file.

```
Policy function execution error:
Logon user     : MARTIN
Table/View     : HR.EMP
Policy name    : EMP_DEPT_POLICY
Policy function: RLSOWNER.AUTHORIZED_EMPS
ORA-01422: exact fetch returns more than requested number of rows
ORA-06512: at "RLSOWNER.AUTHORIZED_EMPS", line 14
ORA-06512: at line 1
```

The trace file shows that Martin was executing the query when this error occurred.
Here the policy function simply fetched more than one row. Examining the policy
function, you notice that the policy function has a segment as follows.

```
SELECT deptno
INTO l_deptno
FROM hr.emp
WHERE ename = USER;
```

It seems there is more than one employee with the name Martin—hence, the number of rows fetched is more than one, causing this problem. The solution is to either
handle the error via an exception or just use something else as a predicate to get the
department number.

Another error, *ORA-28113: policy predicate has error*, occurs when the policy function does not construct the predicate clause correctly. Like the previous error, it produces a trace file. Here is an excerpt from the trace file.

```
Error information for ORA-28113:
Logon user     : MARTIN
Table/View     : HR.EMP
Policy name    : EMP_DEPT_POLICY
Policy function: RLSOWNER.AUTHORIZED_EMPS
RLS predicate  :
DEPTNO = 10,
ORA-00907: missing right parenthesis
```

It shows that the predicate returned by the policy function is:

```
DEPTNO = 10,
```

This string results in a syntactically incorrect SQL query, so the policy application and Martin's query failed. This can be fixed by correcting the policy function logic to return a valid string as the predicate.

Direct-Path Operations

If you are using direct-path operations—for example, SQL*Loader Direct Path Load; Direct Path Inserts using the APPEND hint (INSERT /*+ APPEND */ INTO ...); or Direct Path Export—you may run into trouble when using RLS. Because these operations bypass the SQL layer, the RLS policy on these tables is not invoked, and hence the security is bypassed. How do you deal with this problem?

In the case of exports, it's rather easy. Here is what happens when I export the table EMP, which is protected by one or more RLS policies, with the DIRECT=Y option.

```
About to export specified tables via Direct Path ...
EXP-00080: Data in table "EMP" is protected. Using conventional mode.
EXP-00079: Data in table "EMP" is protected. Conventional path may only be exporting
partial table.
```

The export is successfully done, but as you can see, the output is *conventional path*, not the direct path I wanted it to be. And in the process of performing the operation, the export still applied the RLS policies to the table—that is, the user can export only the rows he is authorized to see, not all of them.

 Because exporting a table under RLS may still successfully complete, you might get a false impression that all rows have been exported. However, be aware that only the rows the user is allowed to query are exported.

When I try to do a direct path load to the table under RLS, using SQL*Loader or Direct Path Insert, I get an error.

```
SQL> INSERT /*+ APPEND */
  2  INTO hr.EMP
```

```
  3  SELECT *
  4  FROM hr.emp
  5  WHERE rownum < 2;
FROM hr.emp
       *
ERROR at line 4:
ORA-28113: policy predicate has error
```

The error is self-explanatory; I can fix this situation either by temporarily disabling the policy on the table EMP or by exporting through a user who has the EXEMPT ACCESS POLICY system privilege.

Checking the Query Rewrite

During debugging, it may be necessary to see the exact SQL statement rewritten by Oracle when an RLS policy is applied. In this way, you will leave nothing to chance or interpretation. You can see the rewritten statement either via a data dictionary view or by setting an event.

Data dictionary view

One option is to use the V$VPD_POLICY dictionary view. VPD in the name stands for *Virtual Private Database*, another name for row-level security. This view shows all the query transformations made by the RLS policy.

```
SQL> SELECT sql_text, predicate, policy, object_name
  2  FROM v$sqlarea , v$vpd_policy
  3  WHERE hash_value = sql_hash
  4  /

SQL_TEXT                          PREDICATE
--------------------------------  --------------------------------------
POLICY                            OBJECT_NAME
--------------------------------  --------------------------------------
select count(*) from hr.emp       DEPTNO = 10
EMP_DEPT_POLICY                   EMP
```

The column SQL_TEXT shows the exact SQL statement issued by the user, while the column PREDICATE shows the predicate generated by the policy function and applied to the query. Using this view, you can identify the statements issued by the users and the predicates applied to them.

Event-based tracing

The other option is to set an event in the session and examine the trace file. When Martin issues the query, he specifies an additional command to set the event before issuing the query.

```
SQL> ALTER SESSION SET EVENTS
     '10730 trace name context forever, level 12';
```

```
Session altered.
```

```
SQL> SELECT COUNT(*) FROM hr.emp;
```

After the query finishes, you will see a trace file generated in the directory specified by the database initialization parameter USER_DUMP_DEST. Here is what the trace file shows.

```
Logon user     : MARTIN
Table/View     : HR.EMP
Policy name    : EMP_DEPT_POLICY
Policy function: RLSOWNER.AUTHORIZED_EMPS
RLS view :
SELECT "EMPNO","ENAME","JOB","MGR","HIREDATE","SAL","COMM","DEPTNO" FROM "HR"."EMP"
"EMP" WHERE (DEPTNO = 10)
```

Using either of these methods you will be able to see the exact way that the user queries are rewritten.

RLS Interactions with Other Oracle Features

RLS, like any other powerful feature, presents its share of potential concerns, issues, and complexities. This section describes the interactions between RLS and several other Oracle features.

Referential integrity constraints

If a table under RLS has a referential integrity constraint pointing to a parent table that is also under RLS, then the way Oracle deals with errors can present a security concern. Suppose that the table DEPT has an RLS policy defined on it that lets a user see only her department's information. Then an "all rows" query against DEPT reveals just a single row:

```
SQL> CONN martin/martin
Connected.
```

```
SQL> SELECT * FROM hr.dept;
```

```
    DEPTNO DNAME          LOC
---------- -------------- -------------
        10 ACCOUNTING     NEW YORK
```

The EMP table, however, is not under any RLS policy, so the user can freely select from it. A user can, therefore, be made aware that there is more than one department.

```
SQL> SELECT DISTINCT deptno FROM hr.emp;
```

```
    DEPTNO
----------
        10
        20
        30
```

Table EMP has a referential integrity constraint on the column DEPTNO that references the DEPTNO column in table DEPT.

The user can see only the details of department 10, the one to which he belongs, but he knows that there are others. Now suppose he tries to update the EMP table, and set the department number to 50.

```
SQL> UPDATE hr.emp
  2  SET deptno = 50
  3  WHERE empno = 7369;
update hr.emp
*
ERROR at line 1:
ORA-02291: integrity constraint (HR.FK_EMP_DEPT) violated - parent key not found
```

The error indicates that the integrity constraint is violated; this makes sense because the DEPT table does not have a row with DEPTNO equal to 50. The Oracle database is doing its job, but now the user knows more about the DEPT table than was intended by the security policy.

Revealing the *absence* of data can, under some circumstances, be as severe a security breach as showing the data that is *in* the table.

Replication

In multi-master replication, the receiver and propagator schemas have to be able to select data from tables in an unrestricted manner. Hence, you will need to either modify the policy function to return a NULL predicate for these users or grant the EXEMPT ACCESS POLICY system privilege to them.

Materialized views

When defining materialized views, you should be careful to make sure that the schema owner of the materialized view has unrestricted access to the underlying tables. Otherwise, only the rows satisfied by the predicate will be returned to the query defining the materialized view, and that will be incorrect. As in the case of replication, you can either modify the policy function to return a NULL predicate or grant the EXEMPT ACCESS POLICY system privilege to the schemas.

Application Contexts

In the discussion of row-level security so far, I have assumed a critical fact—that the predicate (i.e., the limiting condition that restricts the rows of the table) is constant, or fixed at the time of login. But what if I have a new requirement: users can now see employee records based not on fixed department numbers but on a list of privileges maintained for that reason. A table named EMP_ACCESS maintains the information about which users can access which employee information.

```
SQL> DESC emp_access
 Name                    Null?    Type
 ----------------------- -------- ------------
 USERNAME                         VARCHAR2(30)
 DEPTNO                           NUMBER
```

Here is some sample data.

```
USERNAME                          DEPTNO
------------------------------ ----------
MARTIN                                10
MARTIN                                20
KING                                  20
KING                                  10
KING                                  30
KING                                  40
```

I observe that Martin can see departments 10 and 20, but King can see 10, 20, 30, and 40. If an employee's name is not present in this table, he cannot see any records. The requirements also state that a user's privilege can be reassigned dynamically by updating the EMP_ACCESS table. The new privileges must take effect immediately, without requiring the user to log off and then log on again.

Given these requirements, I cannot depend on a LOGON trigger to set all the values needed for use in the policy function.

One possible option to meeting this requirement is to create a package with a variable to hold the predicate and provide the user with a PL/SQL program to assign the value to the variable. The policy function can then use the value cached in the package. Is this an acceptable approach? Consider this situation carefully: if the user can reassign another value to the package variable, what prevents him from assigning a high security level to this value, such as that for King? Martin could log in, set the variable to provide access to all departments, and then SELECT from the table to see all the records. There is no security in this case, and that is unacceptable. This scenario is precisely why we would ordinarily put the code for setting such values in the LOGON trigger, where the user will not have a chance to make such a change.

The possibility that a user may change the value of the package variable dynamically requires us to rethink our strategy. We need a way to set a global variable by some secure mechanism so that unauthorized alteration will not be possible. Fortunately, Oracle provides this capability through *application contexts*. An application context is analogous to a global package variable; once set, it can be accessed throughout the session and can also be reset.

An application context is also similar to a structure (*struct*) in the C language or a record in PL/SQL; it consists of a series of attributes, each of which is made up of a name-value pair. Unlike its counterparts in C and PL/SQL, however, the attributes are not named during the creation of the context; instead, they are named and assigned at runtime. Application contexts reside in the Process Global Area (PGA).

The mechanism by which an application context is set is what makes it more secure than a package variable. You can only change an application context value by calling a specific PL/SQL program. By restricting the way the application context is set to execution of a specific procedure, you can achieve the security needed to implement policies whose values change dynamically within a session.

A Simple Example

Let's start by using the CREATE CONTEXT command to define a new context named DEPT_CTX. Any user with the CREATE ANY CONTEXT system privilege and EXECUTE privilege on the package DBMS_SESSION can create and set a context.

```
SQL> CREATE CONTEXT dept_ctx USING set_dept_ctx;
Context created.
```

Note the clause "USING set_dept_ctx." This clause indicates that an attribute of the dept_ctx context can only be set and changed through a call to the set_dept_ctx procedure.

I have not yet specified any attributes of the context; I have simply defined the overall context (its name and the secure mechanism for changing it). So let's create the procedure. Inside this procedure, I will assign values to the context attributes using the SET_CONTEXT function from the built-in package DBMS_SESSION, as shown in the following example.

```
CREATE PROCEDURE set_dept_ctx (
    p_attr IN VARCHAR2, p_val IN VARCHAR2)
IS
BEGIN
    DBMS_SESSION.set_context ('DEPT_CTX', p_attr, p_val);
END;
```

Now, if I remain connected to the same session that owns this procedure, I can call it directly to set the attribute named DEPTNO to a value 10, as follows:

```
SQL> EXEC set_dept_ctx ('DEPTNO','10')
PL/SQL procedure successfully completed.
```

To obtain the current value of an attribute, you call the SYS_CONTEXT function, which accepts two parameters—the context name and the attribute name. Here is an example:

```
SQL> DECLARE
  2     l_ret    VARCHAR2 (20);
  3  BEGIN
  4     l_ret := SYS_CONTEXT ('DEPT_CTX', 'DEPTNO');
  5     DBMS_OUTPUT.put_line ('Value of DEPTNO = ' || l_ret);
  6  END;
/

Value of DEPTNO = 10
```

You may have noticed that I used the SYS_CONTEXT function earlier in the chapter to obtain the IP address and terminal names of the client.

The Security of Application Contexts

The set_dept_ctx procedure is nothing but an encapsulation of a call to SET_CONTEXT with appropriate parameters. Why not simply call the built-in function directly? Let's see what happens if a user calls the same code segment to set the value of the attribute DEPTNO to 10.

```
SQL> BEGIN
  2      DBMS_SESSION.set_context ('DEPT_CTX', 'DEPTNO', 10);
  3  END;
  4  /
begin
*
ERROR at line 1:
ORA-01031: insufficient privileges
ORA-06512: at "SYS.DBMS_SESSION", line 82
ORA-06512: at line 2
```

Note the error, *ORA-01031: insufficient privileges*. That's puzzling, because the user *does* have the required EXECUTE privilege on DBMS_SESSION. (It would have been impossible to compile set_dept_ctx without that privilege.)

The insufficient privilege refers not to the use of DBMS_SESSION, but to the attempt to set the context value outside of the set_dept_ctx procedure.

As you can now see, Oracle only "trusts" the set_dept_ctx procedure to set the application context values for DEPT_CTX. In fact, Oracle refers to the program referenced by the USING clause of CREATE CONTEXT as the *trusted procedure*.

The only schemas that can execute a trusted procedure are:

- The schema that owns the procedure
- Any schema to which EXECUTE authority is granted on that trusted procedure

So if you are careful about how you grant that EXECUTE authority, you can tightly control the setting of that context's values.

 You must specify the trusted procedure at the same time that you create your application context. Only the trusted procedure can set the values of that context.

Contexts as Predicates in RLS

So far you have learned that a procedure must be used to set a context value, which is akin to a global package variable. You might be tempted to ask, "How is that useful? Doesn't it increase the complexity rather unnecessarily without achieving any definite purpose?"

No. Because the trusted procedure is the *only* way to set a context attribute's value, you can use it to maintain execution control. Inside the trusted procedure, I can place all types of checks to ensure that the variable assignments are valid. I can even completely eliminate the passing of parameters and set the values from predetermined values without any input (and therefore influence) from the user. Going back to the requirement for employee access, for instance, I know that we need to set the application context value to a string of department numbers, picked from the table EMP_ACCESS, *not* passed in by the user.

To accomplish this, I will use the application context in the policy function itself. First, I need to modify the policy function.

```
 1 CREATE OR REPLACE FUNCTION authorized_emps (
 2     p_schema_name    IN    VARCHAR2,
 3     p_object_name    IN    VARCHAR2
 4 )
 5    RETURN VARCHAR2
 6 IS
 7    l_deptno        NUMBER;
 8    l_return_val    VARCHAR2 (2000);
 9 BEGIN
10    IF (p_schema_name = USER)
11    THEN
12       l_return_val := NULL;
13    ELSE
14       l_return_val := SYS_CONTEXT ('DEPT_CTX', 'DEPTNO_LIST');
15    END IF;
16
17    RETURN l_return_val;
18 END;
```

Here the policy function expects the department numbers to be passed through the attribute DEPTNO_LIST of the context DEPT_CTX (line 14). To set this value, I need to modify the trusted procedure of the context.

```
CREATE OR REPLACE PROCEDURE set_dept_ctx
IS
    l_str    VARCHAR2 (32767);
    l_ret    VARCHAR2 (32767);
BEGIN
    FOR deptrec IN (SELECT deptno
                       FROM emp_access
                      WHERE username = USER)
    LOOP
       l_str := l_str || deptrec.deptno || ',';
    END LOOP;

    IF l_str IS NULL
    THEN
       -- no access records found, no records
       -- should be displayed.
       l_ret := '1=2';
    ELSE
       l_ret := 'DEPTNO IN (' || RTRIM (l_str, ',') || ')';
       DBMS_SESSION.set_context ('DEPT_CTX', 'DEPTNO_LIST', l_ret);
    END IF;
END;
```

It's time to test the function. First, Martin logs in and counts the number of employees. Before he issues the query, he needs to set the context.

```
SQL> EXEC rlsowner.set_dept_ctx
PL/SQL procedure successfully completed.

SQL> SELECT sys_context ('DEPT_CTX','DEPTNO_LIST') FROM dual;

SYS_CONTEXT('DEPT_CTX','DEPTNO_LIST')
-------------------------------------

DEPTNO IN (20,10)

SQL> SELECT DISTINCT deptno FROM hr.emp;

    DEPTNO
----------
        10
        20
```

Here Martin sees only the employees of departments 10 and 20, as per the EMP_ ACCESS table.

Suppose now that Martin's access is changed to department 30, accomplished by the following changes to the EMP_ACCESS table:

```
SQL> DELETE emp_access WHERE username = 'MARTIN';
2 rows deleted.

SQL> INSERT INTO emp_access values ('MARTIN',30);
1 row created.

SQL> COMMIT;
Commit complete.
```

When Martin now issues the same query as before, he will see different results. First he executes the stored procedure to set the context attribute.

```
SQL> EXEC rlsowner.set_dept_ctx
PL/SQL procedure successfully completed.

SQL> SELECT sys_context ('DEPT_CTX','DEPTNO_LIST') FROM dual;

SYS_CONTEXT('DEPT_CTX','DEPTNO_LIST')
-------------------------------------------------------------

DEPTNO IN (30)

SQL> SELECT DISTINCT deptno FROM hr.emp;

    DEPTNO
----------
        30
```

This change takes effect automatically. Note that Martin did not specify which department he was allowed to see; he simply called the stored procedure set_dept_ ctx, which set the context attributes automatically. Because Martin can't set the context attributes himself, this arrangement is inherently more secure than setting a global package variable, which *can* be set directly by Martin to whatever value he chooses.

What if Martin does not execute the procedure set_dept_ctx before issuing the SELECT query? When he does execute the query, the attribute DEPTNO_LIST of the application context DEPT_CTX will be set to NULL, and hence the predicate from the policy will not list any department number. As a result, Martin will not be able to see any employees.

Analyze the above situation carefully. All I have done so far is create a policy predicate (in other words, a WHERE condition) to be applied to a user's query. I have decided to set the application context attribute first and have the policy function selected from the context attribute instead of from the table EMP_ACCESS. I could have also made the policy function select directly from the table EMP_ACCESS and construct the predicate, which could have made the policy function very easy to write. That way, the user would not have had to execute the policy function every time she logged on.

There is, however, an added advantage to having the policy function select from application contexts instead of tables directly. Let's compare the two approaches, using pseudo-code to express the fundamental logic.

First, I put logic in the policy function to select from the table EMP_ACCESS and return the predicate string:

```
1  Get the username
2  Loop
3        Select department numbers from EMP_ACCESS table
4        which are accessible to the username
5        Compile a list of department numbers
6  End loop
7  Return the list as a predicate
```

Now I do the same thing, but in the set_dept_ctx procedure:

```
1  Get the username
2  Loop
3        Select department numbers from EMP_ACCESS table
4        which are accessible to the username
5        Compile a list of department numbers
6  End loop
7  Set the attrbiute DEPTNO_LIST to the value as in the list above
```

And then the only logic needed inside the policy function is this:

```
1  Look up the context attribute DEPTNO_LIST
2  Return that as a policy predicate
```

Note the differences in the two approaches. When a user logs in, his username does not change in a session. Consequently, the set_dept_ctx function can be executed just once when the session starts to set the context attribute. The policy function built around this context attribute can then avoid querying the underlying EMP_ ACCESS table and rely solely on session memory.

If I used the version of the policy function that selects from the table, the SQL statements that trigger use of the policy function would have to do much more work. Thus, policies that access all necessary data via context attributes can increase significantly the performance of SQL statements with RLS policies.

In Oracle Database 10g, there is an added advantage to using contexts. You can define a policy as context_sensitive (see the section "RLS in Oracle Database 10g"), which indicates that the policy function is to be executed only when the context changes, not every time. In the above example, it means that the policy function is executed only once (when the user logs in and sets the context); therefore, the policy execution will be extremely fast. If the access requirements change, the user simply re-executes the set_dept_ctx procedure, which will re-execute the policy function.

Identifying Non-Database Users

Application contexts are useful well beyond the situations we've described so far. A key use of application contexts is to distinguish between different users who cannot be identified through unique sessions. This is quite common in web applications that typically use a *connection pool*—a pool of connections to the database using a single user, named, for example, CONNPOOL. Web users connect to the application server, which, in turn, uses one of the connections from the pool to get to the database. This is shown in Figure 5-2.

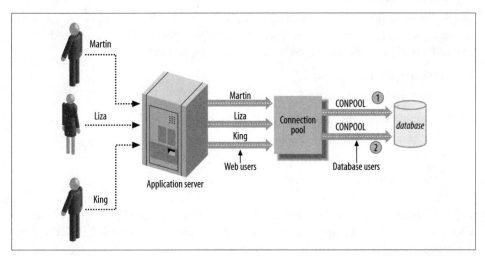

Figure 5-2. Application users and RLS

Here the users Martin and King are not database users, they are web users, and the database has no specific knowledge of them. The connection pool connects to the database using the userid CONNPOOL, which is a database user. When Martin requests something from the database, the pool might decide to use the connection labeled 1 to get it from the database. After the request is complete, the connection becomes idle. If at this point King requests something, the pool might decide to use the same connection (labeled 1). Hence, from the database perspective, a session (which is actually the connection from the pool) is from the user CONNPOOL. As a consequence, the examples we showed earlier (where the USER function identifies the actual schema name) will not work to uniquely identify the user making the calls. The USER function will always return CONNPOOL, because that is the connected user to the database.

This is where the application context comes into the picture. Assume that there is a context named WEB_CTX with attribute name WEBUSER. This value is set to the name of the actual user (e.g., Martin) by the connection pool when it gets the request from the client. The RLS policy can be based on this value instead of on the database username.

Let's see this in action. Suppose that you have a banking application in which several account managers access the client's records. You need to build an RLS system that allows an account manager to see only her clients, not others. The table has a column, ACC_MGR, that holds the username of the account manager for that account. So in this case, the policy predicate should be

```
ACC_MGR = AccountManagerUserName
```

where the value of *AccountManagerUserName* should be the Windows userid of the account manager, something the database does not know. This value needs to be passed by the connection pool to the database using contexts.

First, I will create the context:

```
CREATE CONTEXT web_ctx USING set_web_ctx;
```

Then, my main procedure to set the context looks like this:

```
CREATE OR REPLACE PROCEDURE set_web_ctx (p_webuser IN VARCHAR2)
IS
BEGIN
  DBMS_SESSION.set_context ('WEB_CTX', 'WEBUSER', p_webuser);
END;
```

This procedure takes one parameter, the actual user (WEBUSER). This is exactly what will be used by the application to set the application context WEB_CTX. After the procedure is created, I will make sure it works.

```
SQL> EXEC set_web_ctx ('LIZA')

PL/SQL procedure successfully completed.
```

```
SQL> EXEC DBMS_OUTPUT.put_line(sys_context('WEB_CTX','WEBUSER'))

LIZA

PL/SQL procedure successfully completed.
```

Note that the context setting procedure I have shown here (set_web_ctx) is rudimentary. All it does is set a context attribute. In real life, you will need to write several lines of code to perform various checks to make sure the caller of the procedure is authorized, and so on. For example, a Windows-based application server can extract the username from the client machine directly and pass it to the context using the above procedure.

Once the context is set, I can easily use it to build the policy function. My policy function looks like this:

```
CREATE OR REPLACE FUNCTION authorized_accounts (
    p_schema_name    IN    VARCHAR2,
    p_object_name    IN    VARCHAR2
)
    RETURN VARCHAR2
IS
    l_deptno        NUMBER;
    l_return_val    VARCHAR2 (2000);
BEGIN
    IF (p_schema_name = USER)
    THEN
        l_return_val := NULL;
    ELSE
        l_return_val :=
                    'acc_mgr = ''' || SYS_CONTEXT ('WEB_CTX', 'WEBUSER')
                    || '''';
    END IF;

    RETURN l_return_val;
END;
```

This policy function returns a predicate "acc_mgr = 'the username'", which is applied to the user's queries. Now the user automatically will be able to see only his records.

Conclusion

Row-level security is a very important tool for securing databases at the row level. Although RLS is very useful in security-conscious applications and databases, its utility extends beyond security. It can also be used to restrict access to certain rows of the table, eliminate the need to maintain applications for changing query conditions, and even selectively make a table effectively read-only. Using many combinations of variables inside the policy function, you can create a customized view of the data inside a table, and, in this way, both satisfy the needs of users and create more maintainable applications.

CHAPTER 6
Fine-Grained Auditing

Auditing is a mechanism for logging the activity of database users. By supplying a way to associate specific actions with specific users, auditing provides *accountability*, a cornerstone of security. Traditional Oracle auditing logs information when users make changes to the database, but not when they merely query the data. *Fine-grained auditing* (FGA), introduced in Oracle9*i* Database, extends logging to capture both changing and querying data. FGA is crucial for security, but it also provides an excellent way to analyze SQL usage and the performance of both individual statements and the overall application. It gives you a method for analyzing patterns of data access, which can be a powerful tool in improving your database performance.

This chapter describes how to use fine-grained auditing to your best advantage. By allowing you to choose which actions are to be audited and what information is to be collected, FGA lets you customize its features to suit your own database and application requirements.

FGA functionality is provided via the Oracle built-in package DBMS_FGA. In this chapter, I'll describe the DBMS_FGA programs that allow you to establish and use FGA policies for your database and how the FGA features available in Oracle9*i* Database compare with those available in Oracle Database 10g. I'll also describe how FGA interacts with another new Oracle Database 10g feature, flashback query, which allows you to see exactly what users saw when they performed actions in the database (as opposed to what you see now in the database). I'll compare FGA with database triggers, which traditionally have been used to provide some of the functionality now available through FGA.

Because many DBAs might still be running Oracle9*i* Database, this chapter starts with a description of that version's FGA functionality, most of which works the same way in Oracle Database 10g. Oracle Database 10g enhancements to FGA are described in the later section "FGA in Oracle Database 10g."

Don't confuse FGA with FGAC, which stands for fine-grained access control, a synonym for row-level security, a feature described in Chapter 5.

Introduction to FGA

To help you make the most of FGA, we will start this chapter with a review of general auditing requirements, and then move on to using FGA in a simple example.

For FGA to work correctly, your database must be in cost-based optimizer (CBO) mode; the queries must be using the cost-based optimizer (i.e., they must not be using RULE hints); and the tables (or views) in the query must have been analyzed, at least with estimates. If these conditions are not met, FGA might produce *false positives*, that is, might write an audit trail even if the necessary conditions have not been met. Note that Oracle Database 10*g* uses the cost-based optimizer by default, as described later.

What Is Auditing?

One of the basic requirements of computer security is *accountability*, that is, tracking the activities of users in such a way that you will be able to later associate specific actions with specific users. Oracle's way of achieving accountability is through its auditing feature, which tracks users' actions—in other words, who did what. Suppose that a user Scott issues this statement:

```
SELECT * FROM emp;
```

With proper auditing settings, the database will record the fact that Scott selected something from the table EMP, along with a host of other information—the time of the access, the particular terminal he used, and more. This information, known as an *audit trail*, can be used to investigate Scott's actions, if need be, in the future. Because the audit trail is owned by user SYS, ordinary users cannot alter the contents of the table, and hence cannot hide their tracks. The traditional Oracle audit trail is stored in the database table AUD$, owned by SYS, and information in it is made available through data dictionary views such as DBA_AUDIT_TRAIL. Audit trails can also be written to operating system files instead of to database tables.

By default, the statements issued by the user SYS are not audited. If you want to audit SYS objects as well, you have to set the database initialization parameter AUDIT_SYS_OPERATIONS to TRUE. However, in that case, the audit records are written to operating system files, not to database tables. As a general rule of thumb, you should never issue regular DML statements as SYS.

Regular auditing, however, has a serious limitation—it records the fact that Scott selected something from table EMP, but not *what* he selected. And in most cases, the question of *what* is as important as *who*. For example, in the case of a financial services company, the financial data of customers must be protected from prying eyes. To ensure privacy, the company might want to establish a trail of people seeing sensitive customer records. In this case, not only the identity of the person selecting the data, but the exact records she viewed must be recorded. Regular auditing, however, does not capture the exact records that users viewed, just the fact that they viewed something from the table.

One approach to capturing information about DML statements that change data is to build triggers on a table. However, most DBAs also want to capture information when someone selects from (as well as changes) a table. Because SELECT statements cannot have triggers associated with them, you cannot record such access information via DML row triggers. In Oracle versions prior to Oracle9*i* Database, there was no facility at all that could be used to capture SELECT statements.

Starting with Oracle9*i* Database, however, FGA fills this gap in functionality. Using this feature, you can track table activity without having to write or maintain triggers. Oracle records FGA auditing information in a different table from the one used by traditional auditing—that table is FGA_LOG$ in the SYS schema; the data dictionary view on the table is DBA_FGA_AUDIT_TRAIL.

You will find toward the end of this chapter a comparison of the various types of auditing now available in Oracle; this will help you determine which approach to use to meet your various application auditing requirements.

Why Learn About FGA?

There are many reasons why FGA is a very helpful tool for DBAs. We'll take a quick look at these reasons here and employ them throughout the chapter.

Enhance security
> Security is, of course, the primary purpose of FGA. The ability to record the activities of users against the database is an important security characteristic, and FGA is the best way to record information about these activities. (In certain cases, it is the only way, as traditional auditing does not capture such information as the exact query issued by a user.)

Analyze SQL execution
> FGA reveals who did what. Seeing the actual SQL statements issued by users provides a great tool for DBAs to see different types of statements issued from the applications from specific users and at certain times. Such information is helpful in deciding on indexing schemes or analyzing frequencies. It's even more useful in Decision Support Systems where queries are generally ad hoc in nature and can't be predicted in advance. Because it also shows other relevant informa-

tion, such as timestamp and originating terminal, and because all of the information is in a table, problem diagnosis and access analysis become very easy.

Optimize performance when bind variables are used

FGA audit trails also show bind-variable values, which are used widely in any well-designed application. How do you know what different values are passed during the application run? This information can help you decide more quickly and easily whether you need to define indexes on a table. The FGA audit trails will reveal the kind of information that will help you make such decisions.

Emulate SELECT triggers

Although FGA was not designed specifically for this purpose, a hidden gem is that FGA effectively allows you to define or emulate "SELECT triggers," which are otherwise not available in Oracle. FGA lets you specify execution of a PL/SQL procedure when data is selected, as well as when it is manipulated via INSERT, UPDATE, and DELETE statements. FGA can mimic a SELECT trigger by automatically executing a stored procedure when a user issues SELECT. You can further control execution by placing conditions (e.g., columns selected, value of columns referenced) upon its execution.

A Simple Example

Let's move on to show a simple example of using FGA. This example will demonstrate the basic features and functionality of FGA. Suppose that in the HR schema of the Human Resources departmental database I have defined the EMP table as follows:

```
SQL> DESC emp
 Name              Null?    Type
 ----------------- -------- ------------
 EMPID             NOT NULL NUMBER(4)
 EMPNAME                    VARCHAR2(10)
 JOB                        VARCHAR2(9)
 MGR                        NUMBER(4)
 HIREDATE                   DATE
 SALARY                     NUMBER(7,2)
 COMM                       NUMBER(7,2)
 DEPTNO                     NUMBER(2)
```

To satisfy security and privacy requirements, I need to audit any queries against this table. We can't use database triggers or traditional auditing, so I turn to FGA. My first step is to create a *policy*, which I can do using the ADD_POLICY program provided in DBMS_FGA as follows:

```
BEGIN
   DBMS_FGA.add_policy (object_schema    => 'HR',
                        object_name      => 'EMP',
                        policy_name      => 'EMP_SEL'
                        );
END;
```

You will need to have EXECUTE privileges on the DBMS_FGA package or to be connected as a SYS account to run code like that shown in the preceding example.

The FGA policy, in general, controls how the statements executed against this table will be audited. It determines the conditions under which auditing should be triggered and the actions to be taken. In the preceding example, I create a policy called EMP_SEL and apply it to the table EMP under the schema HR. The policy name must be unique in the database instance. You can define up to 256 separate policies on a single table. Support for multiple policies gives you a high degree of flexibility and eases management of the policies. I'll offer more details on policy definition and management later in the chapter.

 Although both fine-grained auditing (FGA) and row-level security (RLS) use the term *policy*, policies work quite differently for each feature, as I explain in this chapter and in Chapter 5. One similarity is that, like its namesake in RLS, a policy in FGA is not a "schema object"—that is, no user owns it. Anyone with the EXECUTE privilege on the DBMS_FGA package can create a policy and drop one created by a different user. So, it is a good practice to revoke the EXECUTE privilege from the PUBLIC role, if granted. Grant the EXECUTE privilege on this package only to people who actually need it.

Adding a policy is all that's needed to place the table under surveillance; now anyone querying this table will have his actions recorded. So, if user Scott issues the following statement:

```
SELECT salary
  FROM hr.emp
 WHERE empid = 1;
```

it will be recorded in the audit trail, SYS.FGA_LOG$.

To see the audit information, execute a query against the DBA_FGA_AUDIT_TRAIL data dictionary view. (You will, of course, need SELECT privileges on this view, either through a role or a directly granted privilege, like SELECT ANY DICTIONARY.) Here is an example:

```
SELECT db_user, sql_text
  FROM dba_fga_audit_trail
 WHERE object_schema = 'HR' AND object_name = 'EMP';
```

And the output given the previous query against EMP is:

```
DB_USER SQL_TEXT
------- -------------------------------------------------
SCOTT   select salary from hr.emp where empid = 1
```

And there it is, in broad daylight—not only the fact that Scott selected from this table, but the exact SQL statement that was executed.

If you have an FGA policy on a table, you cannot reorganize the table online using Oracle's built-in DBMS_REDEFINITION package. An attempt to redefine a table under FGA will result in the error *ORA-12090: cannot online redefine table*. So, be sure to consider a table's future reorganization needs when you put an FGA policy on it.

Auditing Differences Between Oracle Database Versions

There are a few differences between how both auditing and fine-grained auditing work in Oracle9*i* Database and Oracle Database 10*g*. The major differences are listed here. Later sections, in particular "FGA in Oracle Database 10*g*," provide more-detailed information on using these features.

- In Oracle Database 10*g*, the AUDIT statement, which is used in regular auditing to record the fact that someone selected from a particular table, has been extended to capture information about the SQL statement, something that was not available in earlier releases. (Although it may seem that this enhancement makes FGA and regular auditing in Oracle Database 10*g* nearly identical, the functionalities are quite different, as we'll explore later in this chapter.)

- In Oracle9*i* Database, only SELECT statements are audited by the FGA feature, not the DML statements INSERT, UPDATE, and DELETE. In that release, the only way to capture what has changed is to build triggers on those statements and write to a log table. In Oracle Database 10*g*, on the other hand, FGA can capture these DML statements as well. Although triggers are needed less often in Oracle Database 10*g*, it sometimes makes sense to use them in place of FGA. Both approaches have their advantages and disadvantages, as we'll explore later in this chapter.

- In Oracle9*i* Database, if *any* column of the list of columns you provide when you add a policy is referenced, FGA is invoked. In Oracle Database 10*g*, you can choose whether auditing is to be done when *any* one of the columns is referenced or only when *all* of the columns are referenced.

What Else Does FGA Capture?

In the example query from the audit trial, I selected only the user who issued the SELECT statement and the SQL statement that was actually issued by the user. FGA records more information in the audit trail, most important of which is the time of the action. The TIMESTAMP column in the DBA_FGA_AUDIT_TRAIL view records the timestamp, which you will probably want to view using this format so you can see the full timestamp:

```
TO_CHAR(TIMESTAMP,'mm/dd/yyyy hh24:mi:ss')
```

There are a number of other important columns that can be used to further establish the user's identity and provide details on the action that was audited, all of which help in accountability and analysis. Key columns in this view include:

DB_USER
: User who issued the statement.

SQL_TEXT
: SQL statement the user issued.

TIMESTAMP
: Time the user performed the action.

OS_USER
: Operating system user who connected to the database.

USERHOST
: Terminal or client machine from which the user is connected.

EXT_NAME
: Sometimes the user is externally authenticated—for example, via LDAP; in such cases, the username in the external authentication mechanism is relevant and is captured in this column.

SQL_BIND
: Values of the bind variables used in the query, if any.

Using FGA with Flashback Query

Consider the following scenario to understand why using FGA with Oracle's flashback query feature might be useful. Suppose that I (the DBA) look at the audit trail and notice that this SQL statement was issued by the user Scott:

```
SELECT salary FROM hr.emp WHERE empid = 100;
```

I happen to be represented by the employee number 100, and I realize with a shock that Scott has taken a peek at my salary! Now, Scott has always wanted my job, so it's no surprise that he checked out my salary. But then I think to myself: I just got a series of raises, changing my salary from 12,000 to 13,000, then 14,000, and finally 15,000, which gives me pause to wonder: did Scott see my new or old salary? And if he saw the old one, which one did he actually see—12,000, 13,000, or 14,000? If I now issue the same query Scott issued, I will see the current, updated value—15,000—not the old value that was present when he issued his own query.

Fortunately, Oracle9i Database offers a feature known as *flashback query* to help solve this dilemma. Using this feature you can select a value as of a specific time in the past, even though that value may have been updated and committed. Let's see how it works.

Suppose the salary was 12,000 at first.

```
SQL> SELECT salary FROM emp WHERE empid = 100;

    SALARY
----------
    12000
```

Then it was changed to 13,000 on June 10, as per a raise approved by my boss, and entered into the HR database.

```
SQL> UPDATE emp set salary = 13000 WHERE empid = 100;

1 row updated.

SQL> COMMIT;
```

I was not, however, happy with the raise. On June 11th, I renegotiated, and it was raised to 14,000.

```
SQL> UPDATE emp set salary = 14000 WHERE empid = 100;

1 row updated.

SQL> COMMIT;
```

Still, I wanted more. (What can I say? I have lots of expenses to consider.) After a long discussion with my boss, I finally convinced her that I am worth my weight in gold. On June 12th, the value was changed to 15,000.

```
SQL> UPDATE emp set salary = 15000 WHERE empid = 100;

1 row updated.

SQL> COMMIT;
```

Now, on June 13th, the salary is 15,000. If I then want to see the value as of June 9th, I will have to use the flashback query feature. So I issue a query in the following form using the AS OF syntax:

```
SQL> SELECT salary FROM emp AS OF TIMESTAMP
  2   TO_TIMESTAMP('6/9/2004 01:00:00','MM/DD/YYYY HH24:MI:SS')
  3   WHERE empid = 100;

    SALARY
----------
    12000
```

Similarly, using other appropriate timestamp values, I can then find out the values of the column at other times as well.

When you specify a timestamp in the AS OF clause after the table name, Oracle gets the value from its undo segments, not from the actual table—provided that the undo segment is big enough and that the pre-change value of the column is available in it. In this example, I assume that the undo segment is expected to hold four days worth of changes. You can set or change this number using the database initialization parameter UNDO_RETENTION, which is specified in seconds. The value I have selected—four days—is not unusual for a slowly changing database like the HR one I'm using in this example, but in the case of a rapidly changing OLTP databases, such as a reservation system, I would need to specify a larger value.

When a database change is made, Oracle records an incremental counter, the *System Change Number* (SCN), which uniquely represents a change. Because each change is tracked with an SCN number, Oracle can get the old value by first finding its SCN number and then grabbing it from the undo segment for that SCN number.

In my example, I specified a timestamp, not an SCN number. How does Oracle associate an SCN number with a timestamp, and vice versa? This is done through a table maintained by the SMON process, SMON_SCN_TIME, which records a timestamp and its associated SCN. Note, however, that the SCNs are recorded in intervals of five minutes. Here is an example of using the table.

```
SELECT time_dp, scn_bas FROM sys.smon_scn_time
```

The output is:

```
TIME_DP              SCN_BAS
-------------------- ----------
06/26/2004 15:29:26 1167826228
06/26/2004 15:34:33 1167826655
06/26/2004 15:39:41 1167827058
06/26/2004 15:44:48 1167827476
... and so on ...
```

Note the five-minute gaps in the list of timestamps. If a timestamp is specified in the AS OF clause of the flashback query, Oracle assumes that for that five-minute interval, the SCN number is the same. For instance, in the above output, the query shows the SCN number 1167826228 at 15:29:26, and 1167826655 at 15:34:33, and assumes that the SCN is always 1167826228 for the five minutes between them. That's obviously not true: the SCN has increased from 1167826228 to 1167826655, a jump of 427 for the five-minute period, which must have gradually increased as the result of a lot of changes not recorded in the table SMON_SCN_TIME. Because the flashback query does not get any more granular than the SCN number, it assumes the SCN number to be constant in that period. Therefore, it looks up the same SCN number—1167826228—at 15:29:26, at 15:30:00, and so on until 15:34:33. So if you specify any of these timestamps in the AS OF clause of the flashback query, Oracle returns the same data, because it looks it up against the same SCN number.

 Using the timestamp in a flashback query will return the results within a five-minute interval, not to a more granular time frame. To get to a specific timestamp, use the AS OF SCN clause instead.

To get these actual values, you need to specify the SCN number directly. In the previous case, you can issue the query:

```
SELECT salary
  FROM emp AS OF SCN 14122310350
 WHERE empid = 100;
```

This gets the value as of the SCN 1167826230, which will return the correct value as of that specific SCN, rather than rounding off in a five-minute interval.

The SCN number is a key component of the fine-grained audit trails. SCNs allow you to flash back tables to determine pre-changed values as of a certain time. In the view DBA_FGA_AUDIT_TRAIL, the column SCN represents the SCN during the time of audit trail generation. To find out the value of the column SALARY that the user Scott actually saw, you could use the following query to find out the SCN during the time Scott queried the record.

```
SELECT SCN
  FROM dba_fga_audit_trail
 WHERE object_schema = 'HR' AND object_name = 'EMP';
```

Suppose that this query returns 14122310350. You could then specify:

```
SELECT salary
  FROM emp AS OF SCN 14122310350
 WHERE empid = 100;
```

to see the exact value of the column SALARY that he saw.

Having a record of what the user saw at the time he issued the query is important to assign accountability, so the role of the SCN information in FGA audit trails is vital. Note, however, that the amount of undo information available to you depends on the size of the undo tablespace and the setting of the UNDO_RETENTION_PERIOD database initialization parameter. To be effective, you should issue the flashback pretty quickly. If you don't, the data may be overwritten, thus nullifying the chance of an accurate flashback.

 If it's important to be as accurate as possible in determining the value of a column as of a specific time, do not use a timestamp in the AS OF clause; use the SCN instead.

Customizing FGA

Consider the code we used in the previous section to allow a table to take advantage of FGA:

```
BEGIN
    DBMS_FGA.add_policy (object_schema    => 'HR',
                         object_name      => 'EMP',
                         policy_name      => 'EMP_SEL'
                        );
END;
```

This example illustrates the most rudimentary form of the policy. In reality, you will have to customize FGA to handle your own particular auditing needs. In the following sections, I'll show how policies can be customized.

Specifying Audit Columns

If we record information every time someone selects anything from a table, the audit trail will become very large, making it difficult to manage. You may want to limit recording of accesses to only a specific set of columns. Let's revisit the description of the table EMP.

```
SQL> DESC emp
 Name              Null?    Type
 ----------------- -------- ------------
 EMPID             NOT NULL NUMBER(4)
 EMPNAME                    VARCHAR2(10)
 JOB                        VARCHAR2(9)
 MGR                        NUMBER(4)
 HIREDATE                   DATE
 SALARY                     NUMBER(7,2)
 COMM                       NUMBER(7,2)
 DEPTNO                     NUMBER(2)
```

Examining the columns, you'll notice that some columns may be considered more important to audit than others. For example, you may want to make sure that all accesses to the column SALARY are logged, but you might not want to audit such columns as HIREDATE quite so stringently. In this example, let's assume that I want to audit accesses only to SALARY and COMM, not to all columns. I can do so by specifying a value for the ADD_POLICY procedure's audit_column parameter as follows.

```
BEGIN
   DBMS_FGA.add_policy (object_schema    => 'HR',
                        object_name      => 'EMP',
                        policy_name      => 'EMP_SEL',
                        audit_column     => 'SALARY, COMM'
                        );
END;
```

This causes the trail to be generated only if the user selects the SALARY or COMM columns. If she selects only ENAME, the trail is not recorded.

What I've described applies not only to columns named explicitly in the query, but also to columns referenced implicitly. For instance the query:

```
SELECT * FROM hr.emp;
```

selects all columns from the table EMP, including COMM and SALARY. Hence, the action is logged. Even though the columns are not explicitly mentioned, they are referenced implicitly.

In Oracle9i Database, if *any* column of the list of columns mentioned in the audit_column parameter is referenced, FGA is invoked. In Oracle Database 10g, however, there is an option to specify if auditing is to be done when *any* one of the columns is referenced or if *all* of the columns must be referenced. That option is described later in this chapter in the "FGA for Oracle Database 10g" section.

Specifying Audit Conditions

Suppose that your organization is one of those global corporations with 50,000 or more employees scattered across the world. With different labor laws and varying pay cycles, the HR database hums with activity that's more akin to that of an OLTP database. In such a case, if you try to log every access to the columns COMM and SALARY, your audit trail will quickly balloon to an unmanageable size. While thinking about solutions, you may want to limit the recording of access to high-profile cases only—for example, when someone chooses to see salaries of 150,000 or more or when someone sees *your* salary. You can set this kind of limitation in your FGA policy using a *condition*. To code the above condition, you will have to use a special parameter named audit_condition while invoking the procedure. If you already have the policy defined, you need to drop it by specifying:

```
BEGIN
    DBMS_FGA.drop_policy (object_schema    => 'ARUP',
                          object_name      => 'EMP',
                          policy_name      => 'EMP_SEL'
                         );
END;
```

Then create the policy as follows:

```
BEGIN
    DBMS_FGA.add_policy (object_schema    => 'HR',
                         object_name      => 'EMP',
                         policy_name      => 'EMP_SEL',
                         audit_column     => 'SALARY, COMM',
                         audit_condition  => 'SALARY >= 150000 OR EMPID = 100'
                        );
END;
```

Here the parameter audit_condition is used to limit the audit trail so that it is generated only when the value of the SALARY column exceeds 150,000 or when the EMPID value is 100. If a user selects a record for someone whose salary is 149,999, for example, the action is not audited. Note that *both* situations must be true for the audit record to be generated: the user must select the relevant columns *and* the audit condition must be satisfied. If the user does not specifically mention the SALARY or COMM columns in the query, the trail is not generated even if the record being accessed has a value of 150,000 or more in the SALARY column. For instance, let's say that Jake's salary is 16,000 and his EMPID is 52. A user who simply wants to find his manager's name issues this query:

```
SELECT mgr
FROM emp
WHERE empid = 52;
```

Because the user has not selected the SALARY or COMM columns, the action is not audited. However the query:

```
SELECT mgr
FROM emp
WHERE salary > 160000;
```

generates a trail. In this case, because the SALARY column is present in the WHERE clause, the user has implicitly selected it, so the relevant column condition is fulfilled. The SALARY of the records retrieved is more than 150,000, so the audit condition is fulfilled. Because both events have occurred, the audit trail is triggered.

 Both events—the audit condition evaluating to true *and* the user selecting the relevant columns—must occur for the audit trail to be generated. If only one of the events occurs, an audit entry will not be written.

The audit condition need not reference the columns of the table on which the policy is defined; it can reference other values such as pseudo-columns as well. This becomes useful if you want to audit only a certain set of users, not all. Suppose that I want to record accesses to table EMP made by Scott; I could define the policy as:

```
BEGIN
    DBMS_FGA.add_policy (object_schema    => 'HR',
                         object_name      => 'EMP',
                         policy_name      => 'EMP_SEL',
                         audit_column     => 'SALARY, COMM',
                         audit_condition  => 'USER=''SCOTT'''
                        );
END;
```

Here I have chosen to audit only the user Scott. I can easily change the condition to whatever we need; for example, specifying USER IN ("SCOTT", "FRED") enables auditing on users Scott and Fred.

I might also want to audit everything that's accessed after working hours. I would specify a policy like this one:

```
BEGIN
    DBMS_FGA.add_policy
        (object_schema    => 'HR',
         object_name      => 'EMP',
         policy_name      => 'EMP_AH',
         audit_column     => 'SALARY, COMM',
         audit_condition  =>
```

```
            'to_number(to_char(sysdate,''hh24'')) not between 09 and 17'
        );
    END;
```

Here I am auditing all accesses to the columns SALARY and COMM by all users not between 9 A.M. and 5 P.M. Because all these policies are named differently and all are defined on the table EMP, I can identify the records coming from each policy afterward from the audit trail. For instance, to identify the user who accessed EMP records after working hours, I would issue:

```
SELECT db_user, ....
FROM dba_fga_audit_trail
WHERE policy_name = 'EMP_AH';
```

You can define any number of other audit conditions to satisfy the unique auditing needs of your own database.

Recording Bind Variables

Now I have laid a nice trap for Scott, the user who has been accessing the salaries of various highly paid executives of our organization (and my salary, as well). In the future, every time Scott queries a salary, that fact will be recorded in the audit trails.

Suppose, however, that after all this careful planning, Scott smells foul and somehow realizes what I've done. Being exceptionally clever, he decides to vary his SELECT statement, using a bind variable, in hopes of avoiding the audit, like this:

```
SQL> variable EMPID number
SQL> execute :EMPID := 100
SQL> SELECT salary FROM emp WHERE empid = :EMPID;
```

His attempt will fail, because FGA captures the values of bind variables, in addition to the SQL text issued. The recorded values can be seen in the column SQL_BIND in the view DBA_FGA_AUDIT_TRAIL. In the above case, this is what will be recorded:

```
SQL> SELECT sql_text,sql_bind FROM dba_fga_audit_trail;

SQL_TEXT                                          SQL_BIND
------------------------------------------------  -----------------------
select * from hr.emp where empid = :empid         #1(3):100
```

Notice how the bind variable is captured in the format:

    #1(3):100

where:

#1

indicates the first bind variable. If the query had more than one bind variable, the others would have been shown as #2, #3, and so on.

(3)

Indicates the actual length of the value of the bind variable. In this example, Scott used 100 as the value, so the length is 3.

:100

Indicates the actual value of the bind variable, which, in this case, is 100.

The SQL_BIND column contains a string of values if more than one bind variable is used. For instance, if the query had been:

```
SQL> VARIABLE empid number
SQL> VARIABLE sal number
SQL> BEGIN
  2>     :empid := 100;
  3>     :sal := 150000;
  4> END;
  5> /

PL/SQL procedure successfully completed.

SQL> SELECT * from hr.emp WHERE empid = :empid OR salary > :sal;
```

the SQL_BIND column would look like this:

```
#1(3):100 #2(5):15000
```

The bind variables are clearly identified by their positions and their values, along with the lengths of the values.

The captured values of bind variables are very important, not just for accountability reasons, but also to analyze the pattern of data access, which is hard to examine otherwise. Suppose that you want to find out the best indexing scheme for a data warehouse system. All you have to do is to turn on the FGA audit trail for the objects for some time, and then analyze the values of the SQL_TEXT and SQL_BIND columns in the audit trail to get an idea about the types of values that users are searching for. This information can be obtained from V$SQL as well, but that view selects from the shared pool, which may age statements out as time progresses. The FGA trails, on the other hand, persist in the underlying FGA_LOG$ table, unless the DBA explicitly deletes or truncates it. Thus, the FGA trails provide a more reliable mechanism for capturing queries and values of the bind variables. You'll find such information very helpful in developing an indexing and partitioning strategy.

Turning off bind variable capture

In some cases, you may have no need for the SQL text and the values of the bind variables in the audit trails, and you may choose to turn off the logging of these values to save space. To do so (i.e., not record the bind variable values), set the audit_trail parameter in the ADD_POLICY procedure in the DBMS_FGA package to DB (which stops collecting the SQL text and bind variable information) instead of DB_EXTENDED (which collects them). The default is DB_EXTENDED. Because I want to turn off the SQL text and bind variable collection in this example, our PL/SQL block will look like this (notice that I set audit_trail to the constant DBMS_FGA.DB):

```
BEGIN
    DBMS_FGA.add_policy (object_schema       => 'HR',
```

```
                          object_name           => 'EMP',
                          policy_name           => 'EMP_SEL',
                          audit_column          => 'SALARY, COMM',
                          audit_condition       => 'SALARY >= 150000 OR EMPID = 100',
                          audit_trail           => DBMS_FGA.db
                      );
      END;
      /
```

Specifying a Handler Module

So far, you have seen how FGA can log the fact that someone SELECTed (in Oracle9i Database) from a table or performed some type of DML (in Oracle Database 10g) into an FGA audit trail table, FGA_LOG$. FGA also performs another important function: it can optionally execute a PL/SQL stored program unit such as a stored PL/SQL procedure or a Java method. If the stored procedure, in turn, encapsulates a shell or OS program, it can execute that as well. This stored program unit is known as the *handler module*. In the previous example, where I built the mechanism to audit accesses to the EMP table, you can optionally specify a stored procedure—standalone or packaged—to be executed as well. For instance, suppose that I have a stored procedure named myproc that is owned by user FGA_ADMIN; simply call the ADD_POLICY procedure with two new parameters as follows:

```
      BEGIN
          DBMS_FGA.add_policy (object_schema      => 'HR',
                               object_name        => 'EMP',
                               policy_name        => 'EMP_SEL',
                               audit_column       => 'SALARY, COMM',
                               audit_condition    => 'SALARY >= 150000 OR EMPID = 100',
                               handler_schema     => 'FGA_ADMIN',
                               handler_module     => 'MYPROC'
                          );
      END;
```

Whenever the policy's audit conditions are satisfied and the relevant columns are referenced, two things happen: the action is recorded in the audit trails, and the myproc procedure in the FGA_ADMIN schema is executed. The procedure is automatically executed as an autonomous transaction every time the audit trails are written. This means that any changes made by the handler module will be committed or rolled back without affecting the transaction in the session that fired the handler module. It will also not interfere with the auditing activity.

If the handler module fails for any reason, FGA does not report an error when you select data from the table. Instead, it simply and silently stops retrieving the rows for which the handler module fails. This is a very tricky situation because you will never know that a handler module failed. Not all rows will be returned, producing erroneous results. This makes it extremely important that you thoroughly test your handler modules.

The handler module is very useful when you want to write to your own tables, not just the regular audit trail tables. On the surface, it may seem that you would simply be replicating functionality that is already available. The following sections will, however, make clear that you can add significant value with this option.

Drawbacks with the default FGA approach

Remember that in fine-grained auditing the audit trails are written to a table called FGA_LOG$ in the SYS schema in the SYSTEM tablespace. There are three potential problems with this approach:

1. Because this table contains all types of access to all of the tables being audited by FGA, the contents are very sensitive and must be preserved. However, SYS or any other user with the DBA role can easily delete rows from this table or truncate it, thus removing the FGA trail. For very security-conscious organizations (particularly those governed by regulatory frameworks [e.g., HIPAA, Sarbanes-Oxley, Visa Cardholder Information Security Policy]), this potential for tampering is unacceptable. Securing the audit trail is critical, and the default auditing option does not provide a mechanism to do that.

2. Because the audit trails are generated not only for DML statements but also for SELECT statements, FGA may quickly generate a lot of entries. How serious a problem this is depends upon how frequently the database is accessed and how many auditing options are set. In an OLTP database, the trail (located in the SYS schema and residing in the SYSTEM tablespace) may substantially inflate the SYSTEM tablespace. Even if the table is truncated after periodic archiving, the extended datafiles may not be able to shrink back to their original size, so you can end up with a SYSTEM tablespace that contains lots of unused space.

   An alternative approach is to create a user-defined audit trail and place it in a user tablespace where it can be controlled as conveniently as any other tablespace. You can also specifically design a table of this kind to optimize performance and archival needs—for example, you can partition it to provide the most flexible management.

3. This approach only stores the audit entries; it does not send an immediate alert, notifying anyone that a problem has occurred. Oracle does not support the ability to place triggers on the audit trail table to send emails or alerts. However, in situations where you need to perform a predefined action when audit conditions are satisfied, an automatically executed stored program unit might be helpful. For example, you may want to send an alert via Oracle Advanced Queuing or through Oracle Streams to an enforcement officer when someone selects the salary of the highest-paid executives in your organization. Alternatively, you might want to send an email if a particular action occurs, or just record such instances of high-profile data access in a special table.

Creating a user-defined audit facility

I can handle these potential issues by creating a user-defined audit facility. First, I need to create a table to hold the entries. This table could be in any schema, but for security reasons, I want to put it in a schema that will not be used otherwise. So I will use the same schema—FGA_ADMIN—we used earlier. Here is an example of such a table:

```
/* File on web: cr_flagged_access.sql */

 1   CREATE TABLE flagged_access
 2   (
 3       fgasid            NUMBER(20),
 4       entryid           NUMBER(20),
 5       audit_date        DATE,
 6       fga_policy        VARCHAR2(30),
 7       db_user           VARCHAR(30),
 8       os_user           VARCHAR2(30),
 9       authent_type      VARCHAR2(30),
10       client_id         VARCHAR2(100),
11       client_info       VARCHAR2(64),
12       host_name         VARCHAR2(54),
13       instance_id       NUMBER(2),
14       ip                VARCHAR2(30),
15       term              VARCHAR2(30),
16       schema_owner      VARCHAR2(20),
17       table_name        VARCHAR2(30),
18       sql_text          VARCHAR2(64),
19       SCN               NUMBER(10)
20   )
21   TABLESPACE audit_ts
22   PARTITION BY RANGE (audit_date)
23   (
24       PARTITION y04m01 VALUES LESS THAN
25           (TO_DATE('02/01/2004','mm/dd/yyyy')),
26       PARTITION y04m02 VALUES LESS THAN
27           (TO_DATE('03/01/2004','mm/dd/yyyy')),
28       PARTITION y04m03 VALUES LESS THAN
29           (TO_DATE('04/01/2004','mm/dd/yyyy')),
30       PARTITION y04m04 VALUES LESS THAN
31           (TO_DATE('05/01/2004','mm/dd/yyyy')),
32       PARTITION y04m05 VALUES LESS THAN
33           (TO_DATE('06/01/2004','mm/dd/yyyy')),
34       PARTITION y04m06 VALUES LESS THAN
35           (TO_DATE('07/01/2004','mm/dd/yyyy')),
36       PARTITION y04m07 VALUES LESS THAN
37           (TO_DATE('08/01/2004','mm/dd/yyyy')),
38       PARTITION y04m08 VALUES LESS THAN
39           (TO_DATE('09/01/2004','mm/dd/yyyy')),
40       PARTITION def VALUES LESS THAN
41           (MAXVALUE)
42*  );
```

My purging strategy for this table is rather simple—every month, I transfer all audit data that is older than one month to a different offline storage location and delete it from the table. Accordingly, I have range-partitioned the table on the AUDIT_TABLE column with one partition per month. When the time comes to purge, I just have to convert the partition to a table using the ALTER TABLE...EXCHANGE PARTITION command and then transfer the contents to tape using Oracle's Transportable Tablespace feature. After that, I simply drop the partition. Every month I need to create new partitions for the upcoming months.

My next task is to create a procedure to populate this table. This could also be performed under the same secure schema as the table (e.g., FGA_ADMIN). This procedure calls the built-in function DBMS_FLASHBACK.GET_SYSTEM_CHANGE_NUMBER, so I need to grant the EXECUTE privilege on this package explicitly. Connected as SYS, I issue:

```
GRANT EXECUTE ON dbms_flashback TO fga_admin;
```

Now, I create the procedure.

```
/* File on web: access_flagger.sql *

 1  CREATE OR REPLACE PROCEDURE access_flagger
 2  (
 3      p_table_owner    IN VARCHAR2,
 4      p_table_name     IN VARCHAR2,
 5      p_fga_policy     IN VARCHAR2
 6  )
 7  IS
 8      l_fgasid         NUMBER(20);
 9      l_entryid        NUMBER(20);
10      l_term           VARCHAR2(2000);
11      l_db_user        VARCHAR2(30);
12      l_os_user        VARCHAR2(30);
13      l_authent_type   VARCHAR2(2000);
14      l_client_id      VARCHAR2(100);
15      l_client_info    VARCHAR2(64);
16      l_host_name      VARCHAR2(30);
17      l_instance_id    NUMBER(2);
18      l_ip             VARCHAR2(30);
19      l_sql_text       VARCHAR2(4000);
20      l_scn            NUMBER;
21  BEGIN
22      l_fgasid        := sys_context('USERENV','SESSIONID');
23      l_entryid       := sys_context('USERENV','ENTRYID');
24      l_term          := sys_context('USERENV','TERMINAL');
25      l_db_user       := sys_context('USERENV','SESSION_USER');
26      l_os_user       := sys_context('USERENV','OS_USER');
27      l_authent_type  := sys_context('USERENV','AUTHENTICATION_TYPE');
28      l_client_id     := sys_context('USERENV','CLIENT_IDENTIFIER');
29      l_client_info   := sys_context('USERENV','CLIENT_INFO');
30      l_host_name     := sys_context('USERENV','HOST');
31      l_instance_id   := sys_context('USERENV','INSTANCE');
32      l_ip            := sys_context('USERENV','IP_ADDRESS');
```

```
33     l_sql_text      := sys_context('USERENV','CURRENT_SQL');
34     l_scn           := SYS.DBMS_FLASHBACK.get_system_change_number;
35     INSERT INTOS flagged_access
36     (
37        fgasid,
38        entryid,
39        audit_date,
40        fga_policy,
41        db_user,
42        os_user,
43        authent_type,
44        client_id,
45        client_info,
46        host_name,
47        instance_id,
48        ip,
49        term,
50        schema_owner,
51        table_name,
52        sql_text,
53        scn
54     )
55     VALUES
56     (
57        l_fgasid,
58        l_entryid,
59        sysdate,
60        p_fga_policy,
61        l_db_user,
62        l_os_user,
63        l_authent_type,
64        l_client_id,
65        l_client_info,
66        l_host_name,
67        l_instance_id,
68        l_ip,
69        l_term,
70        p_table_owner,
71        p_table_name,
72        l_sql_text,
73        l_scn
74     );
75* END;
76 /
```

The following table summarizes the key points about this code.

Lines	Description
3–5	Note the input parameters used. In a handler module, you must use only the exact parameters shown here, and no others, and they must be specifically in this order—the owner of the table, the table name, and the name of the FGA policy. Of course, the names of the parameters can be anything, but their position describes their contents.
22–34	These lines show various types of information about the users' actions and sessions. They can be extended to cover as much information as the USERENV context can provide.

Lines	Description
34	The current System Change Number is obtained from the function call and will be recorded in the audit trail.
35	Here all the values collected so far are inserted into the FLAGGED_ACCESS table created earlier.

 Because of an Oracle bug, the function call SYS_CONTEXT('USERENV','SESSIONID') always returns 0 inside the FGA handler. This has been fixed in Oracle Database 10g Release 2. As of the writing of this book, there was no backported patch for versions prior to that release, so line 2 above will always have the value 0, unless a patch for this bug becomes available and is applied.

Finally, I have to add this procedure to the FGA policy so that it will be called automatically whenever the audit conditions are satisfied.

```
BEGIN
    DBMS_FGA.add_policy (object_schema       => 'HR',
                         object_name         => 'EMP',
                         policy_name         => 'EMP_SEL',
                         audit_column        => 'SALARY, COMM',
                         audit_condition     => 'SALARY >= 150000 OR EMPID = 100',
                         handler_schema      => 'FGA_ADMIN',
                         handler_module      => 'ACCESS_FLAGGER'
                        );
END;
/
```

From this point on, every time the audit conditions are satisfied, a record is written to the FGA_LOG$ table as well as to the FLAGGED_ACCESS table. In other words, the presence of a user-defined audit handler does not stop the audit records from being written to the *normal* audit logs. The reason is simple: a handler module is not just for creating a user-defined audit trail; it is also used to call a stored procedure automatically that can do a variety of things—send email, raise an alert, update some flag, and so on. So, the system audit logs must be maintained in any case.

If your stored information needs to be even *more* secure, you can create an identical table in a remote database and set up a one-way, read-only snapshot replication between them. Any records inserted into the FLAGGED_ACCESS table on the local database will create an identical row on the remote table. This process is still susceptible to abuse by a DBA who could delete the snapshot logs. However, in a relatively low-activity database, the refresh interval can be set to a low value and the values can be transmitted as soon as they materialize in the source database, which leaves very little time for the DBA to delete the records. Unfortunately, this is the only solution available to us, because distributed transactions do not work inside the handler module, making it impossible to insert directly into the remote table.

Even if the records are deleted, the values can still be obtained from the archived log files using Oracle's Log Miner. This protects the FGA trails in very secure environments.

Besides using the handler module to create a user-defined audit trail, you can also use it to perform other actions—for example, automatically sending an email to an auditor when highly sensitive data is selected after working hours.

Administering FGA

So far I have talked only about how you can set up FGA on a table. As a DBA, you will also be responsible for managing and administering the overall FGA configuration.

The DBA_AUDIT_POLICIES View

To see the FGA policies that have already been defined in the database, you can query the data dictionary view DBA_AUDIT_POLICIES, which contains the following columns:

OBJECT_SCHEMA
Name of the schema that owns the table or view on which the policy has been defined.

OBJECT_NAME
Name of the table or view on which the policy has been defined.

POLICY_NAME
Name of the policy.

POLICY_TEXT
If the policy has a condition—for example, "SALARY>=150000 OR EMPID=100"—it is shown here.

POLICY_COLUMN
If the policy has relevant columns (e.g., the audit trail is generated only if the relevant columns are referenced), they are shown here.

PF_SCHEMA
If a policy has a handler module, its owner's name is shown here.

PF_FUNCTION
If the handler module is defined and is a standalone procedure, its name is shown here. If the handler module is a packaged procedure, the name of the procedure is shown here and the name of the package is shown in the column PF_PACKAGE.

PF_PACKAGE
See the description of PF_FUNCTION above.

ENABLED
Indicates whether the policy is enabled (YES or NO).

In Oracle Database 10g, this view has several additional columns:

```
SEL
INS
UPD
DEL
AUDIT_TRAIL
POLICY_COLUMN_OPTIONS
```

These are described later in the "FGA in Oracle Database 10g" section.

Using DBMS_FGA Procedures

DBMS_FGA is a rather simple package, providing only four procedures that you use to administer fine-grained auditing in your database, ADD_POLICY, DROP_POLICY, DISABLE_POLICY, and ENABLE_POLICY.

The ADD_POLICY procedure

Remember that an FGA policy is not an *object* in the database, so the normal SQL operations do not apply to it. To administer it, you must use the ADD_POLICY procedure in the DBMS_FGA package. That procedure was described earlier in the chapter.

The DROP_POLICY procedure

To remove an FGA policy, use the DROP_POLICY procedure in the DBMS_FGA package. For example, to drop the policy we defined earlier on the EMP table, you might specify the following block of code.

```
BEGIN
   DBMS_FGA.drop_policy (object_schema    => 'HR',
                         object_name      => 'EMP',
                         policy_name      => 'EMP_SEL'
                        );
END;
/
```

If the policy does not exist, it will throw the error *ORA-28102: policy does not exist.*

The DISABLE_POLICY procedure

Sometimes you may just want to suspend the writing of the audit trail temporarily—for example, when purging the audit trail or switching it to a different table. There is no need to drop a policy in such cases; you can disable it by using the DISABLE_POLICY procedure in the DBMS_FGA package as follows:

```
BEGIN
   DBMS_FGA.disable_policy (object_schema    => 'HR',
                            object_name      => 'EMP',
```

```
                          policy_name        => 'EMP_SEL'
                      );
    END;
    /
```

The ENABLE_POLICY procedure

Once you have disabled a policy, it will remain on the object, but entries will not be written to the audit trail. After your maintenance operations are complete, you can enable the policy again by using the ENABLE_POLICY procedure in the DBMS_FGA package as follows:

```
    BEGIN
        DBMS_FGA.enable_policy (object_schema    => 'HR',
                                object_name      => 'EMP',
                                policy_name      => 'EMP_SEL'
                            );
    END;
    /
```

FGA in Oracle Database 10g

This section describes the specific features and enhancements introduced for FGA in Oracle Database 10g.

Additional DML Statements

In Oracle9i Database, FGA supports the auditing of SELECT statements only; the DML statements such as INSERT, UPDATE, and DELETE cannot be audited. In Oracle Database 10g, DML statements can also be audited. A new statement_types parameter in the ADD_POLICY procedure of the DBMS_FGA package allows you to specify the statements you want audited. To continue with our previous example, suppose that we now want to capture all types of statements—SELECT, INSERT, UPDATE, and DELETE—against the table EMP, but only when the audit conditions are satisfied as we described earlier. This can be accomplished by issuing the following:

```
    BEGIN
        DBMS_FGA.add_policy (object_schema     => 'HR',
                             object_name       => 'EMP',
                             policy_name       => 'EMP_DML',
                             audit_column      => 'SALARY, COMM',
                             audit_condition   => 'SALARY >= 150000',
                             statement_types   => 'SELECT, INSERT, DELETE, UPDATE'
                          );
    END;
    /
```

The records go to the same audit trail table, FGA_LOG$, and will be visible through the same data dictionary view, DBA_FGA_AUDIT_TRAIL. To accommodate the three additional types of access (INSERT, UPDATE, and DELETE), a new column called STATEMENT_TYPE is available in the view. If this parameter is omitted, then only SELECT statements are recorded.

DELETE statements are always audited, regardless of the audit_column parameter. This is because a DELETE removes the entire row and implicitly references or affects all of the columns in the table.

 Only simple predicates (i.e., those with just one condition) are allowed in the audit_condition when DML statements are audited by FGA. You cannot, for example, define a policy to audit DML with an audit_condition such as 'SALARY >= 150000 OR EMPID = 100'. If you create the policy, it will be successful; but the updates to the table will fail with the error ORA-28138: Error in Policy Predicate. Similarly, you cannot define a subquery in the audit_condition; it must be a simple predicate.

Additional Data Dictionary Views and Columns

In Oracle Database 10g, a number of additional items are captured in the FGA audit trail and are available in the DBA_FGA_AUDIT_TRAIL view. An additional view, FLASHBACK_TRANSACTION_QUERY, is also new in Oracle Database 10g.

The DBA_FGA_AUDIT_TRAIL view

New Oracle Database 10g columns in DBA_FGA_AUDIT_TRAIL include:

STATEMENT_TYPE
    Type of statement (e.g., SELECT, INSERT, UPDATE, or DELETE) being audited.

EXTENDED_TIMESTAMP
    In addition to the regular timestamp, an extended timestamp including microseconds, time zone information, etc., is also available in this column.

PROXY_SESSIONID
    If a user connects as a proxy when granted the proxy privileges as in the following, the proxy session ID is captured in this column:
    `ALTER USER seeta GRANT CONNECT THROUGH geeta;`

GLOBAL_UID
    If the user is an Enterprise user, such as one defined in LDAP, the user ID will differ from the regular Oracle user ID. That enterprise user or global user ID is captured in this column.

INSTANCE_NUMBER

In a Real Application Clusters (RAC) environment, each instance may have an independent session ID; thus, the combination of instance number and session ID denotes a unique user session. In previous releases, the instance number was not captured, but in Oracle Database 10g, it is. (Note that in the user-defined audit trail we built earlier, we captured this information, as well.)

OS_PROCESS

Operating system process ID of the user session. This ID might be vital in case we want to examine an associated trace file.

TRANSACTIONID

Transaction ID used in flashback queries. (To understand this column, you need to understand something about the flashback query feature, which is described earlier in this chapter.)

The FLASHBACK_TRANSACTION_QUERY view

Another new Oracle Database 10g view, FLASHBACK_TRANSACTION_QUERY, shows the transactions that have occurred in the database. It contains these columns:

XID

Each transaction is identified by a unique number. This column records it as a RAW datatype.

START_SCN

System Change Number (SCN) at the beginning of the transaction.

START_TIMESTAMP

Timestamp at the beginning of the transaction.

COMMIT_SCN

SCN at the time the commit was issued.

COMMIT_TIMESTAMP

Timestamp when the commit was issued.

LOGON_USER

Oracle user who logged in to the session.

UNDO_CHANGE#

SCN number of the undo operation.

OPERATION

Type of operation (e.g., INSERT, UPDATE, DELETE). If this is a PL/SQL block, this column shows DECLARE or BEGIN.

TABLE_NAME

Name of the table referenced in the transaction.

TABLE_OWNER

Owner of the above table.

ROW_ID
>   Rowid of the row affected or changed.

UNDO_SQL
>   SQL statement that can undo the changes made by the statement. If the original SQL is an INSERT, the UNDO_SQL is a DELETE, and so on.

Although the information in this view is mainly used for flashback query operation (another new feature in Oracle Database 10*g*), it is helpful in FGA, as well. The column XID in this view indicates the unique transaction identifier, which is also captured in the TRANSACTIONID column of the DBA_FGA_AUDIT_TRAIL view. Using this column, you can correlate the two views and thus find out everything about the transaction that caused the audit trail to be created.

Combination of Columns

In the previous example, I specified a list of columns as follows:

```
audit_column    => 'SALARY, COMM'
```

This indicates that if a user accesses either the SALARY or the COMM column, the action is logged. In some cases, however, you may have a more specific requirement that asks for logging only if *all* of the columns named in the list are referenced, not just *any* one of them. For instance, in the EMP database, you may want FGA to write a trail only if someone accesses SALARY and EMPNAME *together*. That may be because if only one column is accessed, the action is not likely to uncover sensitive information (typically, the user needs a name to match to a salary). Suppose that the user issues this query:

```
SELECT salary FROM hr.emp;
```

This displays the salaries of all of the employees, but without names next to salaries, the information is probably not very helpful. Similarly, suppose that the user issues:

```
SELECT empname FROM hr.emp;
```

This returns employee names, but without the salary column, the salary information is protected. However, if the user issues:

```
SELECT empname, salary FROM hr.emp;
```

this query *will* enable the user to see the salaries of all of the employees, the very information that is supposed to be protected. In this last case (but not in the first two), the audit trail provides meaningful information and should therefore be generated.

In Oracle9*i* Database, there was no way to specify a combination of columns as an audit condition. In Oracle Database 10*g*, this can be done through the audit_column_opts parameter in the ADD_POLICY procedure. By default, the value of that parameter is DBMS_FGA.ANY_COLUMNS, which triggers an audit trail if *any* of the columns is referenced. However, if you override that default by specifying

DBMS_FGA.ALL_COLUMNS as the value, the audit trail is generated only if *all* of the columns are referenced. In our example, if I want an FGA policy that creates an audit record only if the user selects both the SALARY and the EMPNAME columns, I can create the policy as follows:

```
BEGIN
    DBMS_FGA.add_policy (object_schema        => 'HR',
            object_name           => 'EMP',
            policy_name           => 'EMP_DML',
            audit_column          => 'SALARY, COMM',
            audit_condition       => 'SALARY >= 150000 OR EMPID = 100',
            statement_types       => 'SELECT, INSERT, DELETE, UPDATE',
            audit_column_opts     => DBMS_FGA.all_columns
            );
END;
/
```

This feature is extremely useful in focusing audit activity very tightly on the key conditions for an application (and reducing audit trail volume).

To accommodate this new feature, the DBA_AUDIT_POLICIES view in Oracle Database 10*g* has a number of additional columns, listed below:

SEL
Indicates whether the policy triggers an FGA audit trail if data is SELECTed (YES or NO).

INS
Same as above but for INSERTs.

UPD
Same as above but for UPDATEs.

DEL
Same as above but for DELETEs.

AUDIT_TRAIL
The columns SQL_TEXT and SQL_BIND are populated only if the parameter AUDIT_TRAIL is set to DB_EXTENDED (the default), as opposed to DB. This column displays the value of that parameter.

POLICY_COLUMN_OPTIONS
Indicates whether *all* the columns must be referenced in order to trigger an audit trail or *any* one of them.

FGA and Other Oracle Auditing Techniques

In this section, I describe how FGA stacks up against other types of auditing technologies provided by Oracle—in particular, triggers and traditional auditing—and why you might choose one approach over another.

FGA Compared with Triggers

Traditionally, database changes resulting from DML statements have been audited using triggers. Row-level triggers on DML statements such as INSERT, UPDATE, and DELETE are able to capture the username, the timestamp, what changed, and other information. Here is an example of how a trigger is used to capture changes on the EMP table.

```
CREATE OR REPLACE TRIGGER tr_ar_iud_emp
    AFTER INSERT OR DELETE OR UPDATE
    ON emp
    FOR EACH ROW
BEGIN
    INSERT INTO audit_trail
        VALUES (USER, SYSDATE, 'EMP', USERENV ('ip_address')
            -- ... and so on ...
            );
END;
/
```

Starting with Oracle Database 10g, FGA can also record such information for DML statements—the timestamp of the change, the IP address, and more. Does FGA thus obviate the need for triggers? Not quite. As you will see in the following sections, each approach has its advantages and disadvantages.

The case for FGA

First let's look at FGA. FGA-based auditing has some distinct benefits over triggers:

Tracking of non-DML queries
> The first benefit is one I've noted a number of times in this chapter: FGA can track and record users when they select from a table, not just when they update it. Triggers do not fire when someone issues a SELECT, so they are useless if you need to audit SELECTs.

Ease of coding
> Triggers require extensive coding and maintenance based on your specific requirements. FGA, on the other hand, requires little coding.

Differing events
> Triggers are fired only when data changes, whereas FGA audits regardless of whether data is changed or not. If data is changed first and then rolled back, triggers will not capture the change, unless you are using autonomous transactions. FGA inserts records into the audit trails using autonomous transactions, so those accesses are recorded anyway. In highly secure environments, this may be a requirement.

Number of trail entries
> After a change takes place, row triggers will insert one record into the audit trail for *each* row changed. With FGA, only one record will be inserted for one state-

ment, regardless of how many rows are affected. This approach limits the size of the trail.

Relevant columns

If you want only certain columns to be tracked and not others, you can use the WHERE clause of the triggers; for example, to track changes to the SALARY column only, you can recode the trigger as:

```
CREATE OR REPLACE TRIGGER tr_ar_iud_emp
    AFTER INSERT OR DELETE OR UPDATE
    ON emp
    FOR EACH ROW
    WHEN (:NEW.salary != :OLD.salary)
BEGIN
    INSERT INTO audit_trail
        VALUES (USER, SYSDATE, 'EMP', USERENV ('ip_address'),
                -- ... and so on ...
            );
END;
/
```

With FGA, you can simply specify the parameter:

```
audit_columns => 'SALARY'
```

Both achieve the same thing—that is, they track changes only if the SALARY column is accessed. But there is an important difference. If the SALARY column is not changed, but is simply accessed in a predicate, FGA will capture this fact but triggers will not.

Views

Now suppose that there is a view named VW_EMP on the EMP table. The view is available to end users but the table is not, so you might have defined a set of INSTEAD OF triggers to manipulate the table when users manipulate the data in the view. However, if an INSTEAD OF trigger changes a data element, the auditing triggers defined on the table will not be able to see that change and thus will not be able to track it. However, FGA will capture any change, regardless of how it is made.

The case for triggers

Is FGA always better than triggers at tracking granular changes? Not necessarily. In most cases, FGA does easily provide the fine-grained auditing mechanism necessary to satisfy your requirements, but there are some cases in which triggers work better than FGA:

Eliminate the need for a larger undo segment

When the user Scott changes a piece of data, how do you know what the value of the data was before the change? As discussed earlier, you can use Oracle's flash-back query feature to get the old value from the table using the SCN number captured in the audit trail. For example, to determine the value of SALARY before Scott changed it, you would issue:

```
SELECT salary FROM emp AS OF scn 14122310350 WHERE empid = 100;
```

This change occurred on June 6th and today is June 20th, 14 days after the change. Because the flashback query uses undo segments to reconstruct the data, the data must be available there. In this case, because you are flashing back the data 14 days into the past, you would have had to set the UNDO_RETENTION_PERIOD initialization parameter to 14 days. This, in turn, requires that the undo tablespace be large enough to hold that much undo information. In most organizations, having such a large undo tablespace may pose an operational problem. Another complication is that the undo information will be lost if the database is shut down.

If you use triggers, rather than FGA, to capture such changes, the old values can easily be stored in the audit trail itself, and you won't need such a large undo tablespace. The old values will also persist across database shutdowns. In such cases, you will probably find that using triggers makes more sense than using FGA.

Store selective data

Undo information is captured for *all* changes to the database—not just changes you are interested in. In a very active database, the undo generation could be quite significant, and it's possible that the information you need may be flushed out of undo segments before it is used in the flashback query.

As mentioned in the previous item, with triggers, the data will be immediately stored in the tables, so it will never be flushed out.

Avoid audit entries on rollback

Under some circumstances, FGA will generate a much larger and less useful audit trail than you would end up with using triggers. Consider the situation in which Scott issues the following DML statement:

```
UPDATE hr.emp SET salary = 14000 WHERE empid = 100;
```

If the EMP table has an FGA policy defined on it, this statement generates an audit trail entry. Because FGA trails are entered as autonomous transactions, the entry in the audit trail is committed regardless of what happens in Scott's transaction. Now, suppose that Scott issues a rollback instead of committing the update. In effect, he did not update the row; nevertheless, the entry in the audit trail is committed and is not rolled back. The result is that false positives are created for audit entries.

If you use a trigger instead, the insertion of the audit entry is part of the same transaction, so it will be rolled back if the main transaction rolls back, thus eliminating the possibilities of false positives. If a system does a lot of changes and then rolls back frequently, you will end up with a large audit trail under FGA—and most of it will be false. It makes sense to use triggers in such cases.

It's clear that FGA does not entirely replace a trigger-based approach to auditing; each has its place. When you are deciding where to implement FGA, consider these differences carefully and see which approach best fits your needs in each situation.

FGA Compared with Regular Auditing

Starting with Oracle Database 10g Release 1, Oracle's regular auditing (using the AUDIT command) has been enhanced so that it captures more information than it did in previous releases—for example, the text of the SQL statement issued, the bind variables, and more. In many respects it looks identical to FGA. Does it, therefore, obviate the need for FGA? Not at all. Let's look at the differences between regular and fine-grained auditing.

Types of statements

Regular auditing can track many different types of statements—DML, DDL, session control statements, privilege management statements, and so on. FGA, on the other hand, can track only one statement (SELECT) in Oracle9i Database and four (SELECT, INSERT, UPDATE, DELETE) in Oracle Database 10g.

Special parameters

FGA runs out of the box without requiring any special parameters. The FGA_LOG$ table, the repository for FGA audit entries, is already present in the SYS schema. In contrast, regular auditing must first be enabled at the database level before individual objects can be audited. You do this by setting the initialization parameter AUDIT_TRAIL. Because this parameter is not dynamic, you must also restart the database for it to take effect.

Success or failure

Regular auditing can be set up so that auditing is done regardless of the success or failure of the user's action. With FGA, tracking is done only if the action is successful.

Disable/enable

FGA can be temporarily disabled and enabled at will, but regular auditing cannot be. To pause regular auditing, you have to use the NOAUDIT command on the object. Later on, if you want to reapply the audit settings, you will have to remember what you specified in the first place because that information is lost.

Selective row auditing

FGA records access each time a user issues a statement, regardless of the number of rows changed. Regular auditing has an option that allows you to specify that an audit entry be written on either a one-row-per-access or a one-row-per-session basis. Regular auditing thus has the potential to reduce the size of the audit trail.

Database tables or OS files

Regular auditing can be set up to record its trails on either database tables (AUDIT_TRAIL=DB) or operating system files (AUDIT_TRAIL=OS). The latter is useful in situations where an auditor, rather than the DBA, will be accessing the trails. Using operating system files is also helpful because the trails will then be able to be backed up using file backup tools. In Windows, if AUDIT_TRAIL=OS, the audit trails are recorded in the Event Log and are accessed very differently. Using the OS option is a way to protect the integrity of the audit trails. Unlike the regular audit trails, the FGA audit trails can only be written to the database table FGA_LOG$. You can create handler modules in FGA to write to files, but because such modules are writable by the Oracle software owner, they are not safe from potential abuse by the DBA.

Default objects

Regular auditing can be set up for default objects, which apply to yet-to-be-created objects. For instance, you could issue "AUDIT UPDATE ON DEFAULT;", which indicates that the database should turn on auditing on updates for all tables, even for tables that have not yet been created. When a new table is created, it is automatically put under audit control for updates. In FGA, you can create policies only on tables or views that already exist.

Selective columns

Regular auditing does not have a way to discriminate between granular actions, such as whether a particular column was accessed. With FGA, you can audit only particular, relevant columns, which makes it possible to keep your trails at a manageable size.

SQL text and bind variable capture

As I've shown, FGA captures the text of SQL statements issued and the values of any bind variables. This is the default behavior, which you can change by setting the audit_trail parameter in the ADD_POLICY procedure of the DBMS_FGA package. In regular auditing, however, you must set the AUDIT_TRAIL database initialization parameter to DB_EXTENDED to capture those values, and you will have to shut down and restart the database for it to take effect.

Privileges

To issue a regular auditing command, a user needs the AUDIT SYSTEM or AUDIT ANY system privilege. To use FGA, however, a user needs only the EXECUTE privilege on the DBMS_FGA package.

As you can see, FGA differs considerably from regular auditing even though in Oracle Database 10g, the trails from both are very similar. Because they are so similar, in Oracle Database 10g, a new view, DBA_COMMON_AUDIT_TRAIL, shows entries from both regular and FGA auditing together.

The Challenge of Non-Database Users

As I've explained throughout this chapter, FGA captures not only *who* did it, but *what* was done—the row that was changed, the SCN number at the time of the action, the originating terminal, and more. The most important information is, of course, the user who performed the audited action, which is captured in the DB_USER column in the view DBA_FGA_AUDIT_TRAIL.

In some cases, however, the database username does not identify a real user. In Chapter 5, in the discussion of row-level security, you saw how in some types of architecture (e.g., three-tier web systems) a single userid is used to create a pool of connections in the database. A web user connects to the application server, which, in turn, connects to the *connection pool*, and she is assigned one connection from that pool. After the user becomes idle, that connection may be assigned to another user. In this way, a relatively small number of database sessions can service a larger number of real users.

This scenario, however, creates a problem: how can the database identify actual users? From the database perspective, the username is the shared id used by the connection pool, not the real user behind the connection pool. Hence, the DB_USER column in the FGA trail records the shared userid, which cannot be used to assign true accountability. For accurate recording of the user performing this action, I must identify the actual, distinct user from within the pool. How can I capture that information?

There are several approaches. Most of them work by conveying additional information about the real user in the ancillary data elements associated with the session. These elements are populated by the client and are read by the database while capturing the changes. Two key elements are the *client identifier* and the *application context*. I described those at some length in Chapter 5, so here we'll jump right into how they can be used in the FGA environment.

Client Identifier

Starting with Oracle9*i* Database, a variable-length character string can be assigned as an attribute of a user's session. It can then be retrieved later from another program through a query against the V$SESSION view, effectively providing distinguishing information about the real user. Suppose that the user connects to the database as a user named DBUSER and then issues a statement:

```
BEGIN
   DBMS_SESSION.set_identifier ('REAL_USER');
END;
/
```

This populates the CLIENT_IDENTIFIER column of the V$SESSION view with the value REAL_USER. So, from another session you will be able to see the value of this column.

```
SELECT client_identifier
  FROM v$session
 WHERE SID = sid;
```

This returns REAL_USER.

This information is not limited to V$SESSION; it also shows up in the FGA trails—for example:

```
SELECT client_id
  FROM dba_fga_audit_trail;
```

This also returns REAL_USER.

If this value is populated with the name of the real user, you will be able to accurately assign accountability to that user.

There are several ways that the client identifier can be set securely and reliably, as discussed in Chapter 5.

Application Contexts

Application contexts are sets of name-value pairs that can be defined in a session by executing a specially defined stored procedure. They are most commonly used to control access to database resources according to rules that vary depending on the current user and discussed in detail for row-level security in Chapter 5. As with the client identifier discussed in the previous section, they can be used to convey the identity of the real user. Either approach (or a combination of the two) gives you a way to identify non-database users.

See Chapter 5 for explanations and examples of using application contexts.

Troubleshooting FGA

Like any other complex and low-level feature in Oracle, FGA might at times produce unexpected results. In this section, I'll go over some of the common FGA-related errors and how to handle them. Please note that I am not going to talk about FGA bugs—published or unpublished—that might affect its behavior. Bugs are often platform-specific and transient. I will instead focus on errors that can occur with typical use of FGA.

Any time there is a problem with FGA, a trace file is produced in the directory specified by the database initialization parameter USER_DUMP_DEST. This trace file shows important information about the exact error condition and offers clues for diagnosing it further. Here is an except from one such trace file:

```
/opt/app/oracle/admin/gridr/udump/gridr_ora_14424.trc
Oracle Database 10g Enterprise Edition Release 10.1.0.3.0 - 64bit Production
With the Partitioning, Oracle Label Security, OLAP and Data Mining options
ORACLE_HOME = /opt/app/oracle/product/10g_gridr
System name:     SunOS
Node name:       smiley2.proligence.com
Release:         5.9
Version:         Generic_117171-12
Machine:         sun4u
Instance name: gridr
Redo thread mounted by this instance: 1
Oracle process number: 54
Unix process pid: 14424, image: oraclegridr@smiley2.proligence.com

*** 2005-07-12 19:01:44.337
*** ACTION NAME:( ) 2005-07-12 19:01:44.288
*** MODULE NAME:(SQL*Plus) 2005-07-12 19:01:44.288
*** SERVICE NAME:(SYS$USERS) 2005-07-12 19:01:44.288
*** SESSION ID:(165.51503) 2005-07-12 19:01:44.288
FGA supports simple predicates only - error 28138
FGA Policy EMP_DML
```

Note the last two (highlighted) lines, which show two important facts:

- The policy name—in this case, EMP_DML
- The error—in this case, FGA supports simple predicates only

This error was caused when a user updated the table. You can view the audit condition of the policy by specifying:

```
SQL> SELECT policy_text
  2    FROM dba_audit_policies
  3    WHERE policy_name = 'EMP_DML';

POLICY_TEXT
-----------------------------------------------
SALARY >= 1500 or EMPID=304
```

Note that this policy's audit condition, "SALARY >= 1500 or EMPID=304", has more than one condition and thus is not a simple predicate. The error message simply confirms that observation. The solution is straightforward: you need to re-create the policy with a simple predicate such as "SALARY >= 1500" or "EMPID=304", not both at the same time. Policies with non-simple predicates work for SELECT statements—just not for DML statements.

In some cases, FGA will raise errors that occur *silently*—in other words, the user is not made aware of the error. One good example is when the handler module (if defined) fails for some rows: in this case, no error is reported to the user. In addition, the rows for which the handler module failed are not returned in the user's query, so the user doesn't have the slightest idea that some rows were *not* returned by the query. In such a case, an entry in the trace file is the only evidence that an error has occurred. An excerpt from a trace file is shown below.

```
*** 2005-07-12 17:52:07.590
*** ACTION NAME:( ) 2005-07-12 17:52:07.536
*** MODULE NAME:(SQL*Plus) 2005-07-12 17:52:07.536
*** SERVICE NAME:(SYS$USERS) 2005-07-12 17:52:07.536
*** SESSION ID:(165.50693) 2005-07-12 17:52:07.536
-------------------------------------
Error during execution of handler in Fine Grained Auditing
Audit handler   : begin ARUP.ACCESS_FLAGGER(:sn, :on, :pl); end;
Error Number 1  : 604
Logon user      : SYSMAN
Object Schema: ARUP, Object Name: EMP, Policy Name: EMP_SEL
*** 2005-07-12 17:52:32.891
Error Number 2: 1438-----------------------------------
Error during execution of handler in Fine Grained Auditing
Audit handler   : begin ARUP.ACCESS_FLAGGER(:sn, :on, :pl); end;
Error Number 1  : 604
Logon user      : SYSMAN
Object Schema: ARUP, Object Name: EMP, Policy Name: EMP_SEL
```

There are two different sections here. The first starts from the top, ending at the second date line, "*** 2005-07-12 17:52:32.891", indicating the first time this error occurred. The set of lines in the next section shows the true error; note the line shown in bold: "Error Number 2: 1438". This error is the true reason why the operation failed. You can look up the error code using the *oerr* utility as follows.

```
Smiley2:/opt/app/oracle/admin/gridr/udump>oerr ora 1438
01438, 00000, "value larger than specified precision allows for this column"
// *Cause:
// *Action:
```

The cause of the error is clear now: the handler module was trying to insert a value larger than the column allowed. Fixing that value will fix this error.

The last error drives home a very important point: if you enable FGA on any of the tables in your database, always check for trace files in the USER_DUMP_DEST directory so that you will catch these silent errors. You may be already checking for trace files anyway, but this is another reason to continue doing so.

Conclusion

Fine-grained auditing provides an excellent tool for logging user accesses to your database by storing information that you can use to track user activities and enforce accountability. You can customize FGA logging to record accesses on specified tables by specified users and under certain conditions (e.g., whether particular columns are referenced or whether the access occurs at a particular time of the day). Although many DBAs think of FGA simply as a security-related tool for ensuring accountabil-

---

FGA in a Nutshell

- FGA can record SELECT accesses to a table (in Oracle9*i* Database) or all types of DML access (in Oracle Database 10*g*) into an audit table named FGA_LOG$ in the SYS schema.

- For FGA to work correctly, you must be using the cost-based optimizer (CBO); otherwise, many "false positives" will likely be written to the audit table.

- With FGA, the recording of the trail is done via an autonomous transaction; even if the DML operation fails and issues a rollback, the trail will still exist. This can also lead to false positives.

- The audit trails show the exact SQL statement used by the user, the value of any bind variables, the System Change Number at the time of the query, and various attributes of the session such as the database username, the operating system username, the timestamp, and much more.

---

ity, you can also use FGA to analyze data access patterns, examine SQL statement usage, and otherwise improve performance. It provides a way to eliminate, or at least reduce dependence on, the complex trigger-based mechanisms that many DBAs use for tracking and responding to database access.

CHAPTER 7
Generating Random Values

Databases are supposed to be about predictable facts; we meticulously collect data that defines our business or activity and then go to any lengths to protect and enforce its integrity. Why would you want to generate something that is just the contrary—an unpredictable, random value? Let's look at some common situations in which DBAs might need a randomizer:

- You are creating temporary passwords or generating web site user IDs for registered users.

- You are involved in the development of an application that needs thorough testing from all angles (performance, scalability, accuracy, and more), and as part of that development, you must create a test bed with some representative data. *Representative* here means that the data has to relate in some way to the actual entity it represents; for example, a column containing an account number must reflect the format of an actual account number, a name should be alphabetic, and so on.

- You want to test the effect of some important database structural components such as indexes. Answers to questions such as how many indexes, on what columns, how many histograms you should collect while analyzing, whether it will be beneficial to enable block sampling, and so on, all require a lot of data representing real-life scenarios. It might be impractical to get this set of data from another source, so you might need to generate it. The focus here is on creating a data set that is random enough but that closely follows a real-life pattern.

- You are building an encryption infrastructure and need to generate a key. Oracle9i Database and later releases provide ways to generate true random keys; in prior versions, however, you will need to generate your own keys.

This chapter explains how to use PL/SQL to generate random values (numbers and strings) representing real-world values. It also explores the use of seeding techniques to randomize generated values. The chapter contains extensive examples and code samples, built around the need to generate test data (account names and balances) for a banking application, which you can easily use in your own development work.

Most of the examples shown in this chapter take advantage of Oracle's built-in package, DBMS_RANDOM. Two key functions provided in this package return random values as follows:

For numbers
> The VALUE function returns a positive floating-point number greater or equal to zero and less than 1 with 38 digits of precision—for example, 0.034869472.

For characters
> The STRING function returns a random string of characters of a user-specified length and distribution of characters.

I'll show examples of using these functions, and the other functions provided in DBMS_RANDOM, throughout this chapter.

Generating Random Numbers

One of the most common applications of random value generators is to generate random numbers. Numbers may be of many types—positive or negative, whole numbers or decimal values, and so on. Let's start with the simplest type: positive numbers.

Generating Positive Numbers

I need to generate a variety of account balances for our test data, all of which are numbers. My representative balance could be a whole number or a floating-point number with two places after the decimal, such as 12,345.98. For simplicity's sake, let's assume the bank does not allow overdrafts—that is, the balance cannot be negative. The DBMS_RANDOM package's VALUE function returns a positive number greater or equal to zero and less than 1 with 38 spaces after the decimal point. Here is how I can use that function to get a number.

```
CREATE OR REPLACE FUNCTION get_num
    RETURN NUMBER
IS
    l_ret    NUMBER;
BEGIN
    l_ret := DBMS_RANDOM.VALUE;
    RETURN l_ret;
END;
```

When this function is called, it returns a number such as the following.

```
SQL> COLUMN get_num FORMAT 0.999999999999999999999999999999999999

SQL> SELECT get_num FROM dual;

                             GET_NUM
-------------------------------------
.461751213136117718759559812185463755
```

Because the function has a purity level of WNDS (write no database state), we can also call this function directly in a SELECT statement or use it inside an INSERT.

For the moment, let's take a detour into a different kind of application. Assume that I am building a scientific application where temperature readings from a thermometer have to be captured for later analysis. I can generate a list of numbers via the following code:

```
BEGIN
    FOR ctr IN 1 .. 10
    LOOP
        DBMS_OUTPUT.put_line ('Temperature = ' || get_num || ' Celsius');
    END LOOP;
END;
```

The output is:

```
Temperature = .724576305545640729229926652249281988851 Celsius
Temperature = .451538982479795965269933874403385861333 Celsius
Temperature = .595537532390531350522195022991038210943 Celsius
Temperature = .045799374332632779724746861736688343983 Celsius
Temperature = .167376547635414030450225123995535308709 Celsius
Temperature = .414184373944667510171500965808344866541 Celsius
Temperature = .669388307838355080076573164263047730733 Celsius
Temperature = .544391586663112986741260677896884537473 Celsius
Temperature = .017014710246600241582833438780085188688 Celsius
Temperature = .784265307132044634900116542166003383283 Celsius
```

Note how the temperatures generated are clearly random. Now let's assume that we need to store these values for future analysis. I'll use the following code to store them in a table called TEMPERATURES, which looks like this:

```
SQL> DESC temperatures
 Name                    Null?    Type
 --------------------    -------- -------

 READING_ID                       NUMBER
 TEMPERATURE                      NUMBER
```

The program to insert random values in this table is:

```
BEGIN
    FOR ctr IN 1 .. 10
    LOOP
        INSERT INTO temperatures
            VALUES (ctr, get_num);
    END LOOP;
END;
```

Selecting from the table later, I can see the values.

```
SQL> COLUMN temperature FORMAT 0.99999999999999999999999999999999999999
SQL> SELECT *
  2> FROM temperatures;
```

```
READING_ID                        TEMPERATURE
---------- ----------------------------------------
         1 .66733860224728195452640954263069321 56
         2 .35450999225882783787205590007510881 59
         3 .08924257081517234678511286780155604 74
         4 .15999791864667727452301250894734830 32
         5 .42912397921866978084502657397654556 86
         6 .01239183199089496432172490631238397 75
         7 .19263860983177949906369436544412476 79
         8 .96313834520200160615433405863247828 69
         9 .76786019851712011806264458824732587 94
        10 .09449342480565941126832144763342112 63
```

This example can be modified to cover a much larger number of readings; extended to multiple sources of readings, such as different thermometers; and so on.

Controlling the precision

In the preceding example, the number generated was a positive floating-point number with 38 spaces after the decimal. A number like this may not be hugely beneficial in applications involving bank account numbers that must be whole numbers and generally of a specific number of digits. No problem! I can increase the function's usefulness by adding some modifiers. For instance, I can modify the function as follows to return a random number between 1 and 100.

```
CREATE OR REPLACE FUNCTION get_num
    RETURN PLS_INTEGER
IS
    l_ret    PLS_INTEGER;
BEGIN
    l_ret := ROUND (100 * DBMS_RANDOM.VALUE);
    RETURN l_ret;
END;
```

Using larger multipliers inside the function, I can also generate random numbers of higher precision.

The same principle can be extended to the generation of floating-point numbers. In the United States, account balances are generally stored in units of dollars and cents. The latter is one hundredth of a dollar, and therefore occupies two digits after the decimal point. The currency systems of many countries follow this pattern. To create an appropriate random balance in this case, you have to generate a number with two places after the decimal point. The simplest approach is to modify the function to supply a scale to the ROUND function. However, let's create a more generic utility by modifying the function to accept parameters:

```
CREATE OR REPLACE FUNCTION get_num (
    p_precision   IN   PLS_INTEGER,
    p_scale       IN   PLS_INTEGER := 0
)
    RETURN NUMBER
IS
    l_ret    NUMBER;
```

```
BEGIN
    l_ret := ROUND (10 * p_precision * DBMS_RANDOM.VALUE, p_scale);
    RETURN l_ret;
END;
```

With these arguments, I can easily obtain random numbers that fit my specific requirements.

Controlling the range

Suppose that I need to generate account balances that fall within a particular range. For example, the bank may have a minimum balance requirement, so the random-ized balance would have to be above that range and likely below a certain perceived maximum number. To handle this requirement, the VALUE function is overloaded in the DBMS_RANDOM package to accept two parameters, low and high, and return a number between those values. Here is an example of using this overloading to obtain random numbers between 1,000 and 9,999:

```
l_ret := DBMS_RANDOM.VALUE(1000,9999)
```

The large number of digits after the decimal point in the random number generated may be rather intimidating, but I can get rid of them using the ROUND function. I can now modify our account-balance-generation function to generate within a range as shown here.

```
/* File on web: get_num_1.sql */
CREATE OR REPLACE FUNCTION get_num (
    p_highval    NUMBER,
    p_lowval     NUMBER := 0,
    p_scale      PLS_INTEGER := 0
)
    RETURN NUMBER
IS
    l_ret    NUMBER;
BEGIN
    l_ret := ROUND (DBMS_RANDOM.VALUE (p_lowval, p_highval), p_scale);
    RETURN l_ret;
END;
```

Notice that this function is generic enough to handle a wide variety of random-number-generation requirements, including:

- Generate bank account numbers, which are 10-digit whole numbers. These numbers are strictly 10-digit—that is, they can't have leading zeros.
  ```
  SQL> EXEC DBMS_OUTPUT.put_line(get_num(1000000000,9999999999))

  2374929832
  ```
- Use the same function for account balances, which carry two places after the decimal and are between 1,000 (the bank's minimum-balance requirement) and

1,000,000 (the perceived maximum of an account balance). Because I need to generate two places after the decimal, I must specify a p_scale parameter of 2.

```
SQL> EXEC DBMS_OUTPUT.put_line(get_num(1000,1000000,2))
```

```
178861.81
```

• Use the function for scientific data, such as readings from a highly sensitive thermometer used in nuclear facilities, where numbers have three places before and 10 places after the decimal point; that is, a number may be between 100.0000000000 and 999.9999999999:

```
BEGIN
    DBMS_OUTPUT.put_line (
        get_num(100,999.9999999999,10));
END;
/
607.1872599141
```

Generating Negative Numbers

So far I have generated only positive numbers, not negative ones. But suppose that my banking application allows overdrafts—that is, borrowing money from the accounts temporarily. In this case, the account balance can be negative—a condition known as "being overdrawn." In the test data, I may want to throw in some of those accounts, too. The DBMS_RANDOM.RANDOM function allows you to do this from within PL/SQL.

The RANDOM function

The DBMS_RANDOM package provides a function that can be used to generate random whole numbers, called RANDOM, which accepts no parameters and returns a binary integer in the range -2^{31} through 2^{31}—that is, a whole number up to 10 digits long. The usage is straightforward:

```
DECLARE
    l_ret    NUMBER;
BEGIN
    l_ret := DBMS_RANDOM.random;
    DBMS_OUTPUT.put_line ('The number generated = ' || l_ret);
    l_ret := DBMS_RANDOM.random;
    DBMS_OUTPUT.put_line ('The number generated = ' || l_ret);
    l_ret := DBMS_RANDOM.random;
    DBMS_OUTPUT.put_line ('The number generated = ' || l_ret);
END;
/
```

The output is:

```
The number generated = 865225855
The number generated = 1019041205
The number generated = -1410740185
```

Note how the numbers *in this particular execution* contain a mixture of negative and positive integers up to 10 digits long. There is no guarantee when calling this program that you *will* get a negative random number. If you need to be sure that your possibly negative random number conforms to specific formats, you will want to use a combination of both the RANDOM and the VALUE functions, as shown below.

I can modify the function get_num to accept a parameter to allow for the generation of negative numbers as follows.

```
/* File on web: get_num_2.sql */
CREATE OR REPLACE FUNCTION get_num (
   p_highval            NUMBER,
   p_lowval             NUMBER := 0,
   p_negatives_allowed  BOOLEAN := FALSE,
   p_scale              PLS_INTEGER := 0
)
   RETURN NUMBER
IS
   l_ret   NUMBER;
   l_sign  NUMBER := 1;
BEGIN
   IF (p_negatives_allowed)
   THEN
      l_sign := SIGN (DBMS_RANDOM.random);
   END IF;

   l_ret := l_sign *
            ROUND (DBMS_RANDOM.VALUE (p_lowval, p_highval)
                  , p_scale);
   RETURN l_ret;
END;
```

Here I have preserved the functionality provided by my original get_num function (which accepts high and low values and the scale of the number), but have extended it to allow for the possibility of generating negative as well as positive random numbers.

Seeding Random Number Generation

What makes random numbers truly random? To visualize the mechanism, here is an exercise: quickly think of a number, *any* number. What number came to mind? That number is very likely significant to you in some way: your age, a part of your telephone number, your street address number—something that you are either familiar with or just happened to see at that time. That number, in other words, was not randomly selected and is, therefore, likely to be repeated or predicted.

Fine, you might say. You want a random number? I will close my eyes and punch at keys randomly on my calculator. Surely *that* will result in a random number.

Probably not. If you examine the number closely, you will notice that some digits are repeated next to each other. That is natural: if you hit a key—say, 9—it's likely that you will hit 9 again next because your finger was hovering in the general vicinity of the 9 key.

I hope you can see, after these simple thought-exercises, that it is quite difficult for a human being to come up with a truly random number. Similarly, a machine can't just pull a number from thin air. There are several methods to achieve true randomness based on complex mathematical formulas that are beyond the scope of this book. The most common component of any random number generator is some randomizer found elsewhere, such as system time, which is guaranteed to be different between two points in time. This randomizer component, which is conceptually similar to the general area where your finger was hovering over the calculator keypad to produce a random number, is called a *seed*. If the seed chosen is sufficiently random, the generated number will be truly random. If the seed is constant, the random number generated may not be truly random. The pattern might be repeated and might be easy to guess. Therefore, a seed is very important in random number generation.

The DBMS_RANDOM package contains an INITIALIZE procedure that provides an initial seed that will then be used by its randomizer function. Here is an example of a call to this program.

```
BEGIN
    DBMS_RANDOM.initialize (10956782);
END;
```

This procedure accepts a BINARY_INTEGER argument and sets that value as the seed. The larger the number of digits in this seed, the higher the degree of randomness for the generated number. You would generally want to use a number greater than five digits to achieve an acceptable degree of randomness.

 Explicitly calling the INITIALIZE procedure is purely optional and is not required when you are using the DBMS_RANDOM package. By default, Oracle will automatically initialize with the date, user ID, and process ID if no explicit initialization is performed.

For true randomness, though, the number should not be a constant. A good variable for this seed is the system time, which is guaranteed to be different every time it is used within a 24-hour period; for example:

```
BEGIN
    DBMS_RANDOM.initialize (
        TO_NUMBER (TO_CHAR (SYSDATE, 'MMDDHHMISS')));
END;
```

Here I have fed the month, day, hour, minute, and second as the seed. This seed is used initially; however, if the same seed is used throughout the session, the randomness might be compromised. Hence, you will need to supply a new seed at regular intervals. This can be accomplished via the SEED procedure, which, like INITIALIZE, accepts a BINARY_INTEGER as a parameter.

```
BEGIN
    DBMS_RANDOM.seed (TO_CHAR (SYSDATE, 'mmddhhmiss'));
END;
```

When the session does not need any further generation of new seeds, you can issue the TERMINATE procedure as follows, to stop generating new random numbers (and stop wasting CPU cycles).

```
BEGIN
    DBMS_RANDOM.terminate;
END;
```

Generating Characters

The previous sections introduced randomizers, random functions, and seeding, but all of the examples included in those sections were oriented to random number generation. In this section, we'll look at the generation of random character strings using the DBMS_RANDOM package's STRING function. STRING accepts two parameters, opt and len.

The first parameter, opt, specifies the type of string to be generated. The following table lists possible values.

opt value	Effect
u	Generates uppercase alphabets only (e.g., DFTHNDSW)
l	Generates lowercase alphabets only (e.g., pikdcdsd)
a	Generates mixed-case alphabets (e.g., DeCWCass)
x	Generates a mixture of uppercase alphabets and numbers (e.g., A1W56RTY)
p	Generates any printable characters (e.g., $\$2sw&*)

The second parameter, len, specifies the length of the character string to be generated. This is necessary if your application requires a random string of a particular length. Using this function, I can build my first random string generator function as follows:

```
CREATE OR REPLACE FUNCTION get_random_string (
    p_len    IN    NUMBER,
    p_type   IN    VARCHAR2 := 'a'
)
    RETURN VARCHAR2
AS
    l_retval    VARCHAR2 (200);
BEGIN
    l_retval := DBMS_RANDOM.STRING (p_type, p_len);
    RETURN l_retval;
END;
/
```

To produce a 40-character string of mixed-case letters using this newly created function, I can specify:

```
SQL> EXEC DBMS_OUTPUT.put_line(get_random_string(40))
XaCbNwzpkGEsgqzCCdEykCycEtLlvoMOxrPnwanj

PL/SQL procedure successfully completed.

SQL> EXEC DBMS_OUTPUT.put_line(get_random_string(40))
hUctRtmsTWsedxqcTNNIlMDhyTgcQmmkyhrCwkUY

PL/SQL procedure successfully completed.
```

As shown in the table, I can use different values of the p_opt parameter to generate different types of random strings, such as only uppercase letters, only lowercase letters, a mixture of letters and numbers, and any printable characters.

As with numbers, I can specify a seed value for the generation of random strings, using the same SEED procedure, which is overloaded to accept a VARCHAR2 value. I can use the same technique of using the system time as the seed, but in this case I make it a character.

```
BEGIN
    DBMS_RANDOM.seed (TO_CHAR (SYSDATE, 'mmddhhmiss'));
END;
```

Let's revisit the original goal stated at the outset of this chapter: we wanted to develop test data with bank account names and balances, using good randomization techniques so that the account names and balances will be generated as truly random characters and numbers. We have already seen the technique for generating the account balance, but what about the name?

I could use my get_random_string function, but it currently always returns a string of the specified length. In real life, names are of varying lengths. To generate a sufficiently varied set of names, let's enhance our function to specify the minimum and maximum lengths and to randomize the string length within that range. Here is version two of our string randomizer:

```
CREATE OR REPLACE FUNCTION get_random_string (
    p_minlen    IN    NUMBER,
    p_maxlen    IN    NUMBER,
    p_type      IN    VARCHAR2 := 'a'
)
    RETURN VARCHAR2
AS
    l_retval    VARCHAR2 (200);
BEGIN
    l_retval :=
        DBMS_RANDOM.STRING (p_type
                        , DBMS_RANDOM.VALUE (p_minlen, p_maxlen));
    RETURN l_retval;
END;
```

In the DBMS_RANDOM.STRING call, I passed the length of the string parameter a random number between the parameter values passed. Let's test this function:

```
SQL> EXEC DBMS_OUTPUT.put_line(get_random_string(10,20))
DPZmDqQFcwhnqRL

PL/SQL procedure successfully completed.

SQL> EXEC DBMS_OUTPUT.put_line(get_random_string(10,20))
goJVifYdSeQ

PL/SQL procedure successfully completed.
```

Note how the lengths of the strings generated in these two cases are different. Using this approach, I can generate random strings for a wide variety of applications, including account names, web site user IDs, and temporary passwords. The most valuable use in the context of this chapter, however, is the generation of seeds and keys for encryption, as we will see later on.

Let's build a program to populate account records with random data. The ACCOUNTS table looks like this:

```
SQL> DESC accounts
 Name                  Null?    Type
 -------------------- -------- -------

 ACCOUNT_NO                    NUMBER
 BALANCE                       NUMBER(9,4)
 ACCOUNT_NAME                  VARCHAR2(20)
```

The program to insert random values into the accounts table is:

```
DECLARE
    i   NUMBER;
BEGIN
    FOR i IN 1 .. 10
    LOOP
        DBMS_RANDOM.seed (TO_NUMBER (TO_CHAR (SYSDATE, 'hhmiss')));

        INSERT INTO accounts (account_no, balance, account_name)
            VALUES (i
                 , DBMS_RANDOM.VALUE (10000, 99999)
                 , DBMS_RANDOM.STRING ('x', DBMS_RANDOM.VALUE (10, 20)));
    END LOOP;
END;
/
```

After the PL/SQL block has been run, I can see the records inserted.

```
SQL> SELECT * FROM accounts;

ACCOUNT_NO    BALANCE ACCOUNT_NAME
---------- ---------- --------------------
         1 91772.2043 FZIGIONR8OU
         2 91772.2043 FZIGIONR8OU
         3 91772.2043 FZIGIONR8OU
         4 91772.2043 FZIGIONR8OU
         5 91772.2043 FZIGIONR8OU
         6 91772.2043 FZIGIONR8OU
```

```
 7 91772.2043 FZIGIONR8OU
 8 91772.2043 FZIGIONR8OU
 9 86258.8032 65YJYV9NMMBGMRP5CMP7
10 86258.8032 65YJYV9NMMBGMRP5CMP7
```

Do you see that something is seriously wrong here? Pretty much all the balances are the same, and the names are the same, too. This does not look like a true randomized data set. What's the problem?

The problem is with the seeding value. Note that in line 6 of the code segment, I set the seed value to a combination of hours, minutes, and seconds. However, this program runs for less than a second, and the seed value is reset to the *same* value every time; hence, the random numbers generated are the same. In the above example, in iterations 1 through 8, the seed value was the same; hence, all the "random" values are simply the same. The seed *changed* at the ninth iteration, and that caused the "random" values to change.

To resolve this problem, I can just remove the seeding line from the above PL/SQL code. Here is the modified code with the line commented.

```
DECLARE
   i   NUMBER;
BEGIN
   FOR i IN 1 .. 10
   LOOP
      -- DBMS_RANDOM.seed (TO_NUMBER (TO_CHAR (SYSDATE, 'hhmiss')));

      INSERT INTO accounts
            VALUES (i, DBMS_RANDOM.VALUE (10000, 99999),
                    DBMS_RANDOM.STRING ('x', DBMS_RANDOM.VALUE (10, 20)));
   END LOOP;
END;
/
```

Now if I check the values generated, I will see a truly randomized data set.

```
SQL> SELECT * FROM accounts;

ACCOUNT_NO    BALANCE ACCOUNT_NAME
---------- ---------- --------------------
         1 18344.0416 ELR8PWCSIAPKF1POH
         2  94702.904 XQGBFVQGQI8QPAV6NIN
         3 64261.8317 POF99DU2DAHOXE5AC7
         4 95369.3182 42IT6V7XOAF7
         5 65451.8237 6ZU5H91XEGMVO
         6 68695.4939 4VNP4KWJN6Y
         7 71474.0692 9OLNOSJNKE5CO
         8 78402.0396 IG9Z3KEFZ35YCXIER9N
         9 63726.3395 86JK18HJEON
        10 12416.5512 JRQC39C5KOLA
```

Carefully review the lesson learned here. Resetting the seed to the *same* value results in a predictable value in the randomizer. Leaving the seed unchanged results in the generation of true random numbers. In the above code sample, the program ran too fast for seed changes, however. If we are not sure about the speed of the program and want to use the seed, how can we achieve randomness?

The solution is to throw another element into the seed, an element that will *definitely* change. In the code sample, the element could be the iteration variable i, which definitely changes inside the loop. So the code could be written as:

```
 1  DECLARE
 2     i   NUMBER;
 3  BEGIN
 4     FOR i IN 1 .. 10
 5     LOOP
 6        DBMS_RANDOM.seed (i || TO_NUMBER (TO_CHAR (SYSDATE, 'hhmiss')));
 7
 8        INSERT INTO accounts
 9            VALUES (i, DBMS_RANDOM.VALUE (10000, 99999),
10                     DBMS_RANDOM.STRING ('x', DBMS_RANDOM.VALUE (10, 20)));
11     END LOOP;
12* END;
```

Note that in line 6, the seed value now has the value of i as a component, too. This guarantees a different seed value each time, even if the program runs too fast. Using this technique, we can code for all possible scenarios involving random numbers.

 Never reset the seed to the same value it was before you called a randomizer function. If you use as a seed some variable whose value could potentially be the same—such as the current time—use another variable that is guaranteed to change, such as a loop counter variable.

Checking for Randomness

After generating the random numbers as discussed in the previous sections, you may want to make sure that they really *are* random. To do this, check the distribution of the data inside the table of random data from a statistical point of view.

```
SQL> SELECT MIN (balance), MAX (balance)
  1        , AVG (balance), STDDEV (balance)
  2    FROM accounts;

MIN(BALANCE) MAX(BALANCE) AVG(BALANCE) STDDEV(BALANCE)
------------ ------------ ------------ ---------------
    10008.03     99889.97   54948.4654      25989.9271
```

As shown, the average (often referred to in statistics as the *mean*) balance is 54,948.4654 and the standard deviation is 25,989.9271. As per statistical analysis, here is the distribution of values inside a table:

Assume that A = average and S = standard deviation; thus:

- About 68% of values lie within A - S and A + S

- About 95% of values lie within A - 2 × S and A + 2 × S
- About 99.7% of values lie between A - 3 × S and A + 3 × S

If the pattern of distribution is such, it is said to be in *normal distribution*. In my case, however, I want an even spread of data, *not* normally distributed. Here I have:

A = 54,948.4654, and S = 25,989.9271

Therefore, 68% of the data lies between 28,958.5383 and 80,938.3925 as shown in the following expression:

54948.4654 - 25989.9271 = 28958.5383

and

54948.4654 + 25989.9271 = 80938.3925

These numbers indicate that the list is well varied, not too crowded around the average value. It therefore satisfies our definition of a truly random sample. In creating a test bed to validate assumptions, you will have to build several random samples of data, and the type of analysis performed here will be very helpful in making sure the sample is truly random. I'll explore this topic more in the following section.

Following Statistical Patterns

Suppose that you are building a table of customers and populating it with names that will be used later in searches. How would you generate the values? For example, should the values be random collections of characters like the following?

```
-32nr -32nr3121ne -e21e
323-=11r- r
0-vmdw-dwv0-[o- rr0-32r2 0
r4i32r -rm32r3p=x ewifef-432fr32o3-==
```

I got these values by merely pecking randomly at the keyboard. But it's unlikely that these values would serve well as sample customer names. After all, names have some acceptable variation (such as Jim or Jane), and when you develop a table of test data, it's important that those values reflect possible data as much as possible. Your values should be from a set of known values, but should occur randomly within that set, without following a predictable pattern.

Another aspect to consider is the variance. Very few names are unique. For instance, in the United States, you will find frequent occurrences of the male names John, James, or Scott (but few cases of names like Arup). So when you generate test data, you usually want to make sure that the distribution is random but also that it follows a real-world statistical model. For instance, let's say that in our population the distribution of first names should look like the following:

10%	Alan
10%	Barbara

5%	Charles
5%	David
15%	Ellen
20%	Frank
10%	George
5%	Hillary
10%	Iris
10%	Josh

When populating the column FIRST_NAME in the table ACCOUNTS according to this pattern, therefore, 10% of the records should have the FIRST_NAME Alan, 10% Barbara, and so on. Let's further assume that we want to populate the rest of the columns as well to represent real-world scenarios. First let's see the columns of the modified ACCOUNTS table.

```
SQL> DESC accounts
 Name              Null?    Type
 ----------------- -------- ------------
 ACC_NO            NOT NULL NUMBER
 FIRST_NAME        NOT NULL VARCHAR2(30)
 LAST_NAME         NOT NULL VARCHAR2(30)
 ACC_TYPE          NOT NULL VARCHAR2(1)
 FOLIO_ID                   NUMBER
 SUB_ACC_TYPE               VARCHAR2(30)
 ACC_OPEN_DT       NOT NULL DATE
 ACC_MOD_DT                 DATE
 ACC_MGR_ID                 NUMBER
```

Suppose that to make the data distribution realistic, I have to create the data to follow the column pattern shown in the following table.

Column name	Purpose	Data pattern
ACC_NO	Account number	Any number with fewer than 10 digits
FIRST_NAME	First name	10% -Alan
		10% -Barbara
		5% -Charles
		5% - David
		15% - Ellen
		20% - Frank
		10% - George
		5% - Hillary
		10% -Iris
		10% - Josh
LAST_NAME	Last name	Any alphabetic character between 4 and 30, but 25% should be "Smith"

Column name	Purpose	Data pattern
ACC_TYPE	Type of account: savings, checking, etc.	20% each of S, C, M, D, and X
FOLIO_ID	Folio ID from the other systems	One-half NULL and the other half a number related to the account number
SUB_ACC_TYPE	If the customer is incorporated, then sub-account types, if any	75% null. From the values populated: 5% - S 20% - C
ACC_OPEN_DT	Date account was opened	A date between now and 500 days ago
ACC_MGR_ID	ID of the account manager servicing the account	There are 5 account managers, with the percent of accounts as follows: 1 – 40% 2 – 10% 3 – 10% 4 – 10% 5 – 30%

As you can see, these are moderately complex requirements; they accurately reflect how the data will be distributed in a real database. In real life, there will be customers with the first names "Josh" and "Ellen," not "XepqjEuF," so the names must be chosen from the set of possible names. In the United States, there are many different last names. Here, I want a semi-random distribution with 25% of a very popular last name, "Smith." The rest of the last names can be scattered.

So how can I generate data that conforms to this complex set of rules? I will borrow a page or two from probability theory and follow the path of statisticians, who often use the *Monte Carlo simulation*. With this approach, I generate a random number, between 1 and 100 (inclusive). Over a long period of time, the probability that a specific number, such as 6, will be generated is exactly one out of 100, or 1%. In fact, all the numbers have 1/100 probability of being generated. Using the same approach, the probability of either of two numbers, such as 1 and 2, will be 2%; and that of any of three numbers—1, 2, or 3—will be 3%. And, of course, the probability that any one of the numbers between 1 and 10 will turn up is 10%. I will use these rules to configure the probability of the random value generated.

Generating Strings

Take, for instance, the value of the column ACC_TYPE, which calls for equal probability of S, C, M, D, and X, or 20% probability each. If we generate a whole number between 1 and 5 (inclusive), the probability of each generated number will be 20%. Then I can use a SQL DECODE function to get the ACC_TYPE value based on the number generated.

```
1  SELECT DECODE (FLOOR (DBMS_RANDOM.VALUE (1, 6)),
2                    1, 'S',
3                    2, 'C',
4                    3, 'M',
5                    4, 'D',
6                       'X'
7                    )
8* FROM DUAL;
```

Let's see what's going on here. First, I am generating a number between 1 and 5 (line 1). Because the number generated is less than the highest value passed as a parameter, I have specified 6. Because I want a whole number, I use the FLOOR function in line 1. It truncates all decimal values from the generated number. Depending on the number obtained, I use DECODE to get one of the values—S, C, M, D, or X. Because the numbers 1, 2, 3, 4, and 5 all have an equal probability of getting generated, so will the letters—at 20% each.

This technique is very useful in generating random but predetermined values of the type shown in the example. The same approach can be used to generate almost all types of predetermined random values.

Generating Random Values with NULLs

Remember from the discussion earlier that the requirement for the column FOLIO_ID is a little different. It needs only 50% of the values populated; the rest should be NULL. How can I achieve that result?

I will use the same probability approach with a twist; I will simply use a determination of "yes" or "no." Generating a random number between 1 and 100 will ensure 1% probability of each number. Hence, a number below 51 will have exactly 50% probability. I can use this in a CASE statement to get the value:

```
SQL> SELECT CASE
2            WHEN DBMS_RANDOM.VALUE (1, 100) < 51
3              THEN NULL
4            ELSE FLOOR (DBMS_RANDOM.VALUE (1, 100))
5          END
6* FROM DUAL;
```

On line 2, I check if the number generated is less than 51. If so, I return NULL. Because the probability of a number under 51 is 50%, I have NULLs occurring 50% of the time, as well. In the other 50%, I have generated a random number between 1 and 100 to be used as a FOLIO_ID.

Generating Random Strings of Random Length

In DMBS_RANDOM.STRING, the string generated is random but of *fixed* length. In reality, however, people have last names of *varying* lengths. In this next example, the requirement is to have a length between 4 and 30 characters. To accommodate this

---

requirement, I can pass the length as a random number as well to the STRING function in line 6 below.

```
 1  BEGIN
 2     FOR i IN 1 .. 10
 3     LOOP
 4        DBMS_OUTPUT.put_line (   'Random String='
 5                    || DBMS_RANDOM.STRING ('A'
 6                                  , DBMS_RANDOM.VALUE (4, 30)
 7                                  )
 8                    );
 9     END LOOP;
10* END;
```

The output is:

```
Random String=RniQZGquFVJYFpGLOvtNd
Random String=GhcphpcsaCXlhigRQY
Random String=JtakoelUf
Random String=BgCOu
Random String=QFBzQxcHqGlHWkZFmnN
Random String=lSxVjqJvpwBB
Random String=jfhNARzALrLOKZRpOwnhrzz
Random String=KuFtdJcqQpjkrFmzFbzcXnYFGjWo
Random String=BhuZ
Random String=GebcqcgvzBfEpTYnJPmYAQdb
```

Note how the generated strings are not only random but also of randomly different lengths.

I also need 25% of the last names to be "Smith" and the rest to have random values. I can accomplish that by combining the random strings and the Monte Carlo simulation as follows:

```
DECODE (
     FLOOR(DBMS_RANDOM.value(1,5)),
         1,'Smith',
         DBMS_RANDOM.string ('A',DBMS_RANDOM.value(4,30))
     )
```

This expression will return "Smith" 25% of the time and a random alphabetic string between 4 and 30 characters the rest of the time.

Putting It All Together

Now that you understand the building blocks of the randomization approach, you can put them together to build the account-record-generation PL/SQL code segment shown below. In this example, I load 100,000 records into the table ACCOUNTS. Here is the complete loading program.

```
/* File on web: ins_acc.sql */
BEGIN
   FOR l_acc_no IN 1 .. 100000
   LOOP
```

```
INSERT INTO accounts
    VALUES (l_acc_no,

        -- First Name
        DECODE (FLOOR (DBMS_RANDOM.VALUE (1, 21)),
                1, 'Alan',
                2, 'Alan',
                3, 'Barbara',
                4, 'Barbara',
                5, 'Charles',
                6, 'David',
                7, 'Ellen',
                8, 'Ellen',
                9, 'Ellen',
                10, 'Frank',
                11, 'Frank',
                12, 'Frank',
                13, 'George',
                14, 'George',
                15, 'George',
                16, 'Hillary',
                17, 'Iris',
                18, 'Iris',
                19, 'Josh',
                20, 'Josh',
                'XXX'
                ),

        -- Last Name
        DECODE (FLOOR (DBMS_RANDOM.VALUE (1, 5)),
                1, 'Smith',
                DBMS_RANDOM.STRING ('A'
                                    , DBMS_RANDOM.VALUE (4, 30))
                ),

        -- Account Type
        DECODE (FLOOR (DBMS_RANDOM.VALUE (1, 5)),
                1, 'S',
                2, 'C',
                3, 'M',
                4, 'D',
                'X'
                ),

        -- Folio ID
        CASE
           WHEN DBMS_RANDOM.VALUE (1, 100) < 51
              THEN NULL
           ELSE l_acc_no + FLOOR (DBMS_RANDOM.VALUE (1, 100))
        END,

        -- Sub Acc Type
        CASE
           WHEN DBMS_RANDOM.VALUE (1, 100) < 76
```

```
                   THEN NULL
                   ELSE DECODE (FLOOR (DBMS_RANDOM.VALUE (1, 6)),
                                1, 'S',
                                2, 'C',
                                3, 'C',
                                4, 'C',
                                5, 'C',
                                NULL
                                )
              END,

              -- Acc Opening Date
              SYSDATE - DBMS_RANDOM.VALUE (1, 500),
              -- Acc Mod Date
              SYSDATE,

              -- Account Manager ID
              DECODE (FLOOR (DBMS_RANDOM.VALUE (1, 11)),
                         1, 1,
                         2, 1,
                         3, 1,
                         4, 1,
                         5, 2,
                         6, 3,
                         7, 4,
                         8, 5,
                         9, 5,
                         10, 5,
                         0
                         ));
   END LOOP;

   COMMIT;
END;
```

How do I know that all these exercises yield the required result? The proof is in the pudding. After this table has been loaded, let's examine the actual distribution:

```
SQL> SELECT   first_name, COUNT (*)
  2      FROM accounts
  3  GROUP BY first_name
  4  ORDER BY first_name
  5  /

FIRST_NAME                     COUNT(*)
------------------------------ ----------
Alan                                9766
Barbara                            10190
Charles                             5066
David                               5000
Ellen                              15023
Frank                              15109
George                             14913
Hillary                             5019
```

```
Iris                             9932
Josh                             9982
```

```
10 rows selected.
```

Each first name is exactly as per the desired distribution. For example, remember that I wanted to have 10% of the rows contain the first name "Alan," and I got 9,766 out of 100,000, which equates to approximately 10%? I wanted 15% containing "Ellen" and I got 15.023%, pretty close to that number and statistically significant. You can continue to check through all of the other columns, verifying that they are actually distributed as per the required pattern.

Conclusion

Being able to generate random values is important in a variety of applications. Randomization is an integral part of encryption, but it plays a role in many other areas, as well. In this chapter, I showed how to generate all types of random numbers and strings of different precisions and lengths, how to control randomness using the proper seeding techniques, and how to avoid the risk of generating non-random values by resetting the seed to the same value. To make the generation better approximate real-world values, I also discussed how to create random values that follow certain statistical patterns and, finally, how to verify the randomness of the data generated.

CHAPTER 8
Scheduling

Administering a database requires running lots of tasks, sometimes on the spur of the moment, but often at regularly and predictably scheduled times. Examples include collecting statistics on database objects, gathering information on free space inside the database, analyzing and reporting problems with an instance directly to the DBA on call, and so on. Such tasks may be database-related or may be related to the operating system—for example, checking space in filesystems, making sure that other servers are reachable, and so on. As a DBA, you can probably think of hundreds of situations where a specific task, usually referred to as a *job*, needs to be scheduled to run at some point in the future rather than executed immediately.

This chapter describes PL/SQL's facilities for scheduling jobs in the database, as well as outside the database (in the same server). This functionality is provided via two built-in packages: DBMS_JOB and DBMS_SCHEDULER. DBMS_JOB, first introduced in the Oracle8i Database, is quite limited in functionality. With Oracle Database 10g Release 1, Oracle effectively replaced DBMS_JOB with DBMS_SCHEDULER. The newer package is a much more robust utility and should be used in place of DBMS_JOB. This chapter focuses solely on showing you how to use DBMS_SCHEDULER. Oracle Enterprise Manager in Oracle Database 10g provides a graphical user interface that may be used to manage job scheduling, but that discussion is outside the scope of this chapter.

Oracle scheduling encompasses four basic components, shown conceptually in Figure 8-1:

- A *job*, an object that specifies which program runs at what time
- A *schedule*, a named object that stores a calendar of specific execution times
- A *program*, a named object that specifies the executable that is to run
- A *window*, which specifies a particular duration and resource allocation scheme for a job

A job has the following associated with it:

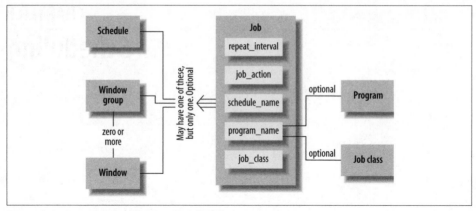

Figure 8-1. Components of the Oracle Scheduler

- A job_action, which may be a stored procedure, a PL/SQL anonymous block, or an operating system executable.

- A repeat_interval, which shows how often and when the job should be executed.

A job may optionally be assigned a named schedule, which specifies calendar strings inside it. The schedule_name parameter may specify a schedule, a window, or a window group. Instead of a job_action, a job may execute a named program, which references the types of actions the job_action parameter can reference; these may be stored procedures, anonymous PL/SQL blocks, or operating system executables.

A job may belong to a *job class*, which groups similar jobs and defines some common properties for them—for example, a logging level.

A window represents a particular start and end time and a resource manager plan. When a window is assigned to a job, the job starts and ends at the time specified by the window, and it is governed by the same resource manager plan. A window may belong to a *window class*. If a window class is assigned to a job, then the windows of the window class take effect for the job.

I'll explain all of these components in detail, with examples of usage, as the chapter progresses.

Why Schedule Jobs from Within Oracle?

Oracle DBAs who need to schedule a job for execution—either at a specific, future time or at regularly scheduled intervals—generally have two options from which to choose:

Use the operating system scheduler

Execute the program or code segment from an operating system-specific utility such as *cron* in Unix or *AT* in Microsoft Windows. These tools let you execute an operating system-specific command as needed. You can even run an Oracle job from the frontend, usually by constructing it as a SQL script and then running it through SQL*Plus as a command-line execution.

Use the database scheduler from within Oracle

Schedule the operation as a job in the database to be run either one time or repeatedly using DBMS_SCHEDULER. This database job runs within the context of the database, not the operating system.

Given that you have the ability to schedule jobs in the operating system using standard operating system utilities, why would you even consider scheduling them inside the database? There are several compelling reasons:

Database dependence

An operating system job runs regardless of whether the database is available. So what happens if the job to collect optimizer statistics starts at its scheduled time but the database is down for some reason? The job fails, which may then lead to a variety of unpleasant consequences. Collecting statistics is a rather benign example; in other cases, this scenario could present more serious issues. Suppose, for example, that you have an operating system job that goes through a series of database and operating system tasks, and pages the on-call DBA when it fails. If the database is down, the page is still generated, albeit incorrectly. Of course, you could write the first few lines of your code in such a way that it checks for database availability before starting, but you will then have to add that code to every one of your utilities, which becomes a maintainability issue. On the other hand, a database job will run only when the database is up, never when it is down. This results in better and more accurate control over the execution process.

Protection

Jobs are part of the database and therefore come with the same protection as the other objects in that database. You can grant or revoke access on specific jobs to or from individual users. When the database is backed up, so are the jobs, along with the metadata information on them (e.g., comments, schedules, etc.).

Operating system independence

Consider the syntax of the *cron* command on Unix and the Windows Task Scheduler or the *AT* command on Windows. They are entirely different. What if you want to port your database from one platform to the other? You will have to change each execution to accommodate the target platform, which will be a rather painstaking process. On the other hand, if you perform scheduling from within the database, the database will carry its job definitions along with it; there will be no need to change any aspect of your job definitions.

Location independence

Suppose you store all your utilities in the */u01/app/dbatools* directory, but later you decide to move them to a different directory, */u02/app/dbatools*. If you are using *cron* or *AT* for scheduling, this simple change will require you to make several changes in every one of your schedule definitions. On the other hand, if you use database scheduling, it's a snap; no location information needs to be provided.

Security

When you call a PL/SQL code segment or even a simple SQL script from the operating system, you have to pass the username and password in the scheduled job. Let's look at the simplest case. Suppose that you have a shell script that calls a SQL script called *myjob.sql* as follows:

```
$ORACLE_HOME/bin/sqlplus -s scott/tiger @/u01/app/dbatools/myjob.sql
```

The username (scott) and password (tiger) are passed in cleartext in the command. Anyone who looks for this process using a *ps -aef* command will easily see this crucial information, which of course opens up a security hole.

You could try to minimize the risk of exposing Scott's password by creating the script a little differently—placing the username/password inside the SQL script file *myjob.sql* as a connection as follows:

```
CONNECT scott/tiger
blah ... blah ... blah ...
```

Now your calling script would look like this:

```
$ORACLE_HOME/bin/sqlplus -s /nolog @/u01/app/dbatools/myjob.sql
```

The switch /nolog instructs SQL*Plus not to expect any login information in the command line (as there is no login). This approach is a little better: the username and password are not visible from the process lookup; however, if a user checks the script file, this information will be revealed—and you certainly don't want your users to see each other's passwords.

The last alternative would be to use what is called an OPS$ login, which allows the OS to perform the authentication. You could have a Unix user called scott and an Oracle user called OPS$SCOTT which is identified externally. The *cron* job would look like this:

```
$ORACLE_HOME/bin/sqlplus -s / @/u01/app/dbatools/myjob.sql
```

There is a key disadvantage of this approach, however. Not only does it depend on your Oracle login being the same as your OS login, it also means that if someone gains access to your OS password, she can also connect to your database schema without further authentication.

If, on the other hand, you use the database to schedule jobs, you will not need scripts of this kind, so the user's password will never be revealed. Many security-conscious organizations have strict rules against revealing passwords under any circumstances. Database scheduling is the only option in such environments.

Flexibility

If you are using operating system scheduling and need to change a user's password, you will have to go through all of the necessary shell scripts to change that password. Some organizations may try to minimize this effort by creating a central password file and reading from it for every shell script. That may save some effort, but if a user wants to change his password, this password file will have to be updated as well. If operating system access to your database server is restricted to only DBAs (as it should be), a regular user won't be able to change the password file and will have to ask the DBA for help in making the change. Involving another person in the password management process is never a desirable situation.

On the other hand, if you are using database scheduling, the password need not be stored anywhere.

All in all, if you need to execute Oracle-related functionality, it is easier, more secure, and more efficient to do so through DBMS_SCHEDULER.

 Throughout this chapter, I will refer to Oracle's scheduling subsystem as either DBMS_SCHEDULER or the Scheduler.

Managing Jobs

The job is the fundamental unit of work in scheduling. This section describes how you can create and manage jobs in the database using the CREATE_JOB procedure in the DBMS_SCHEDULER package. I'll start with a simple example that illustrates job scheduling concepts.

A Simple Example

Suppose that I am working with a banking application and want to schedule the execution of a job that applies interest daily to the account balances. A stored procedure called apply_interest is used to apply the interest. I can use DBMS_SCHEDULER's CREATE_JOB program to create a scheduler job named "apply_daily_interest" as follows:

```
1  BEGIN
2     DBMS_SCHEDULER.create_job (job_name       => 'apply_daily_interest',
3                       job_type              => 'STORED_PROCEDURE',
4                       job_action            => 'apply_interest',
5                       repeat_interval       => 'FREQ=DAILY; INTERVAL=1',
6                       enabled               => TRUE,
7                       comments              => 'Apply Daily Interest'
8                    );
9* END;
```

Let's examine the lines in detail in the following table.

Line	Description
2	I define the name of the job. The name must be a valid Oracle identifier, which means that it must start with a letter; contain some combination of letters, numbers, #, _, or $; and cannot be longer than 30 characters. The name also must be unique in the Oracle namespace; it cannot, for example, have the same name as a table.

Line	Description
3	Here I specify what type of program is to be run. This is a wonderful enhancement of DBMS_SCHEDULER over the functionality available in DBMS_JOB. In this case, the program to be executed (apply_interest) is a stored procedure, indicated by the value ("STORED_PROCEDURE") of the job_type parameter. Other valid values for this argument are "PLSQL_BLOCK" and "EXECUTABLE".
4	The job_action parameter indicates what this job does—in this case, it executes the stored procedure apply_interest.
5	The repeat_interval parameter indicates how often this job should be run, in this case every day. (I'll explore the use of intervals in more detail later in this chapter.)
6	The value (TRUE) of the enabled parameter is the default, which means that the job is immediately enabled and run.
7	Here I can specify optional comments for the job, which may later help explain what a job does.

Once you have created a job, you will be able to find information about it in the data dictionary view DBA_SCHEDULER_JOBS. Let's take a quick look now at that view to confirm the results of the call to CREATE_JOB above; I'll explore it in more detail below.

```
SELECT owner, job_name, job_type
    , job_action, repeat_interval, comments
  FROM dba_scheduler_jobs
```

The following shows the output in a vertical format for easy viewing, the column names on the left and their contents on the right.

```
OWNER             : ARUP
JOB_NAME          : APPLY_DAILY_INTEREST
JOB_TYPE          : STORED_PROCEDURE
JOB_ACTION        : apply_interest
REPEAT_INTERVAL   : FREQ=DAILY; INTERVAL=1
COMMENTS          : Apply Daily Interest
```

I have now created a job that calls a stored procedure. Although there are some syntactical differences, the core functionality will at first glance appear quite similar to that offered by DBMS_JOB. After reading the following sections, however, you will understand more clearly how much more DBMS_SCHEDULING does for us.

Running OS executables and anonymous blocks

Suppose that the job you want to schedule involves a Unix script, not a PL/SQL program. A common example is an RMAN incremental backup. The full path for the RMAN script is *u01/app/oracle/admin/tools/kick_rman_inc.sh*. As a Unix executable, the script is not entirely within the purview of the Oracle database. Do you have to resort to a *cron* job to schedule it? As discussed earlier, a drawback of operating system scheduling is that it will run even when the database is down, and in this case you want the job to run only when the database is up. A compelling advantage of DBMS_SCHEDULER over DBMS_JOB is its ability to directly specify and execute non-database programs from within the database context.

The following example uses the CREATE_JOB procedure in the DBMS_SCHED-ULER package to schedule the RMAN incremental backup.

```
 1  BEGIN
 2     DBMS_SCHEDULER.create_job
 3        (job_name          => 'RMAN_INC',
 4         repeat_interval   => 'FREQ=DAILY; BYHOUR=2',
 5         job_type          => 'EXECUTABLE',
 6         job_action        => '/u01/app/oracle/admin/tools/kick_rman_inc.sh',
 7         enabled           => TRUE,
 8         comments          => 'Take RMAN Inc Backup'
 9        );
10* END;
```

This job will call the Unix executable *kick_rman_inc.sh*. Note that in line 5 the job_type parameter is set to EXECUTABLE.[*]

You can use the CREATE_JOB procedure to create jobs that call anonymous PL/SQL code segments—for example:

```
BEGIN
   DBMS_SCHEDULER.create_job
           (job_name          => 'RMAN_INC',
            repeat_interval   => 'FREQ=DAILY; BYHOUR=2',
            job_type          => 'PLSQL_BLOCK',
            job_action        => 'DECLARE i number; BEGIN code; END;',
            enabled           => TRUE,
            comments          => 'Take RMAN Inc Backup'
            );
END;
```

Here the parameter job_action specifies the whole PL/SQL code segment: a DECLARE-BEGIN-END block terminated by a semicolon. You can include any valid anonymous PL/SQL block in the placeholder marked **code** in the above example.

DBA_SCHEDULER_JOBS view

After you have created a job, you can check it in the data dictionary view DBA_SCHEDULER_JOBS. Here are some key columns of the view. Appendix A shows the complete set of columns.

OWNER
　　Owner of the job.

JOB_NAME
　　Name of the job.

---

[*] By contrast, in the first example, it was set to STORED_PROCEDURE.

CLIENT_ID
If the user specified the client identifier for the session while creating a job, it is recorded here. You can set the client identifier by calling DBMS_SESSION.SET_IDENTIFIER.

GLOBAL_UID
If the user is a global (or enterprise) user, the global user id is recorded here.

JOB_TYPE
The type of job; valid values are EXECUTABLE, PLSQL_BLOCK, and STORED_PROCEDURE.

JOB_ACTION
What the job does. If it is a PL/SQL code segment, then the entire segment is shown here. If it is an executable or a stored procedure, its name is recorded here.

START_DATE
Start time of the job in the TIMESTAMP datatype.

REPEAT_INTERVAL
Calendar string that specifies the schedule of the job (e.g., FREQ=DAILY; BYHOUR=2). (See also the later section "Calendar Strings.")

ENABLED
Whether the job is enabled (TRUE or FALSE).

STATE
Current state this job is in (e.g., SCHEDULED, RUNNING, SUCCEEDED, FAILED).

RUN_COUNT
Number of times this job has been run.

FAILURE_COUNT
Number of times this job has failed.

RETRY_COUNT
If the job failed, it is retried; this column shows how many times it has been retried.

LAST_START_DATE
Timestamp of the last time the job started.

LAST_RUN_DURATION
Duration of the last time the job ran.

NEXT_RUN_DATE
Next time the job is scheduled to run.

SYSTEM
Whether a job is a system job (TRUE or FALSE).

COMMENTS
Comments entered by you earlier.

I'll discuss additional columns as we describe other aspects of DBMS_SCHEDULER functionality.

Simple Job Management

Now that you understand basically how to create a job, let's see how to manage the job we just created. Unless otherwise stated, all tasks are performed by various programs in the DBMS_SCHEDULER package.

Enabling and disabling jobs

You can temporarily disable or enable a job using the DISABLE and ENABLE procedures, respectively. For example, to disable the job RMAN_INC, specify:

```
BEGIN
    DBMS_SCHEDULER.disable (NAME => 'RMAN_INC');
END;
```

If this job is currently running, the above command will return an error. You can include the FORCE parameter to override the default behavior:

```
BEGIN
    DBMS_SCHEDULER.disable (NAME => 'RMAN_INC', FORCE=> TRUE);
END;
```

Specifying FORCE will disable the job, but will allow the currently running process to complete.

You can enable a currently disabled job by calling the procedure ENABLE as follows.

```
BEGIN
    DBMS_SCHEDULER.enable (NAME => 'RMAN_INC');
END;
```

 When you create a job and do not set the enabled parameter, the job is created but is disabled. You must explicitly enable it.

Stopping running jobs

When a job is running and you want to stop it, you can run the STOP_JOB procedure as follows.

```
BEGIN
    DBMS_SCHEDULER.stop_job (JOB_NAME => 'RMAN_INC');
END;
```

STOP_JOB will attempt to gracefully stop a job. There are times, unfortunately, when a graceful shutdown is not possible, in which case the above statement returns an error. You can force a job to shut down by using the FORCE parameter. For example, to stop the job APPLY_INTEREST (which executes a stored procedure), created earlier in this chapter, I can run the following block to immediately shut down the job, even if it is currently running.

```
BEGIN
    DBMS_SCHEDULER.stop_job (job_name    => 'APPLY_INTEREST',
                            FORCE        => TRUE);
END;
```

The owner of a job can shut that job down normally without requiring the FORCE=>TRUE parameter. Any other user with ALTER privileges on that job can also stop it normally. For example, the owner of the job (ACC_MASTER) can grant the privilege to the user ARUP as follows:

```
GRANT ALTER ON apply_daily_interest TO arup;
```

Now ARUP will be able to stop the job.

To use the FORCE parameter in your call to DBMS_SCHEDULER.STOP_JOB, you must have the MANAGE SCHEDULER system privilege.

 Only jobs that run PL/SQL code segments and stored procedures can be stopped by setting the FORCE parameter. Jobs that run operating system executables cannot be stopped with the FORCE parameter. You will need to wait until they have completed.

Running a job

The Scheduler allows you to explicitly request the running of a job. There are a number of circumstances requiring manual execution of a job:

- You stopped a job to take care of an issue, and now you want to run that job to completion.
- The job is not yet scheduled to run, but you decide that you need to run it immediately anyway.
- The job is scheduled to run now, but it is failing, and you want to see the reason. (In other words, you run the job to debug the job.)

You can run a job using the RUN_JOB procedure. For example, to run the job CALCULATE_DAILY_INTEREST, you would specify:

```
BEGIN
    DBMS_SCHEDULER.run_job (job_name => 'CALCULATE_DAILY_INTEREST');
END;
```

This will cause the job to be run in the session to which you are currently connected. To do this, you must

- Be connected as the owner of the job or
- Have the system privilege ALTER ANY JOB

RUN_JOB is a very helpful program. If the job fails for some reason, you will find out immediately; you won't have to wait to examine the job log at a later time. (The job log is described later in the "Managing Logging" section.) Even if the job is currently running as scheduled or if someone else is also running it, RUN_JOB *still* lets you run it immediately in your session. Running a job this way will help you to determine any problems with the job's execution or scheduling because if it fails, information about it will display right away in your execution environment.

When you call DBMS_SCHEDULER.RUN_JOB, the columns RUN_COUNT, LAST_START_DATE, LAST_RUN_DURATION, and FAILURE_COUNT in the data dictionary view DBA_SCHEDULER_JOBS are *not* updated. There will, in other words, be no record of that job's execution in the metadata for the job.

Suppose that you want to start a job, but it will take five or six hours to complete. You are likely, then, to want to run the job in the background, outside of the current session. You can do this by setting the use_current_session parameter in the RUN_JOB procedure to FALSE. In the example below, I schedule CALCULATE_DAILY_INTEREST to run as a task in the background, and control is immediately returned to my session.

```
BEGIN
   DBMS_SCHEDULER.run_job (
      job_name             => 'CALCULATE_DAILY_INTEREST',
      use_current_session  => FALSE
      );
END;
```

If the program runs successfully, it will also update the columns RUN_COUNT, LAST_START_DATE, LAST_RUN_DURATION, and FAILURE_COUNT in the data dictionary view DBA_SCHEDULER_JOBS. However, if the job fails for some reason, the failure will not show immediately on the screen, but instead will show up in the job logs, described later in the "Managing Logging" section.

Dropping a job

When you no longer need a job, you can drop it altogether using the procedure DROP_JOB. For example, to drop the job APPLY_DAILY_INTEREST, you would specify:

```
BEGIN
   DBMS_SCHEDULER.drop_job (job_name => 'APPLY_DAILY_INTEREST');
END;
```

If the job is running at the time, then this code will return an error. If you include the FORCE parameter, the Scheduler will first attempt to stop the job and will then remove it:

```
BEGIN
   DBMS_SCHEDULER.drop_job (job_name        => 'APPLY_DAILY_INTEREST',
```

```
              FORCE        => TRUE);
   END;
```

Managing the Calendar and Schedule

In the previous section, I focused on the first basic component of scheduling: the job. In this section, I'll explore the second key component (and the most visible one), the *schedule*, which is the definition of times when a job is supposed to run. You can specify the schedule when you create a job with the CREATE_JOB procedure either by entering a calendar string as the value of the repeat_interval parameter or by referencing a named schedule that you have already created.

Calendar Strings

The syntax of the calendar string you can specify in CREATE_JOB's repeat_interval parameter is quite simple and English-like. For example, if you want to schedule a job that runs Monday through Friday at exactly 7 A.M. and 3 P.M., you would specify the following calendar string as the value for repeat_interval:

```
FREQ=DAILY; BYDAY=MON,TUE,WED,THU,FRI; BYHOUR=7,15
```

The calendar string has two distinct types of clauses, FREQ and BY..., separated by semicolons. You specify only one FREQ clause, but you may specify several different types of BY clauses, depending on your calendar. Each clause consists of a keyword and a value, separated by an equal sign. Together, the clauses specify how often a job is expected to run, as follows:

Unit of frequency (FREQ)
> The FREQ clause specifies the repetition unit. In the example, I want the job to be repeated every day, so I specify FREQ = DAILY. Valid keywords are YEARLY, MONTHLY, WEEKLY, DAILY, HOURLY, MINUTELY, and SECONDLY.

Limits (BY...)
> The BY clause limits exactly when the job will execute. In the example, I start by specifying the unit of frequency as every day (FREQ=DAILY). I then limit execution to only specific days (Monday, Tuesday, Wednesday, Thursday, and Friday), by specifying BYDAY=MON,TUE,WED,THU,FRI. I then further limit execution by requesting that the job be run at 7 A.M. and 3 P.M., by specifying BYHOUR=7,15. Valid keywords are BYMONTH, BYMONTHDAY, BYYEARDAY, BYHOUR, BYMINUTE, and BYSECOND. These are described in Table 8-1.

Suppose that my job needs to be run every day, regardless of the day of the week, at 10 A.M., 2 P.M., and 8 P.M.; I could specify the repeat_interval parameter as:

```
FREQ=DAILY; BYHOUR=10,14,20
```

What if I want to run the job every *other* day, not every day? A new keyword, INTERVAL, takes care of that:

```
FREQ=DAILY; INTERVAL=2, BYHOUR=10,14,20
```

Here, the INTERVAL=2 clause changes the frequency to 2 units of what is defined in the FREQ clause. Because the FREQ keyword is set to DAILY, the job executes every two days.

A negative number indicates counting from the end of the period. For example, the following indicates the second hour counting from the end of the day.

```
FREQ=DAILY; BYHOUR=-2
```

Table 8-1 shows some key interval commands for the repeat_interval parameter.

Table 8-1. BY keywords for calendar strings in the repeat_interval parameter

Keyword	Description

BYMONTH	Schedules the job to run in certain months. For example, to schedule an interest calculation job to run in June and December only, specify:
	
	`BYMONTH=JUN,DEC`
	
	Alternatively, you can specify numeric month numbers:
	
	`BYMONTH=6,12`
	
	The exact date of the month when the job will execute is the date when it started. For example, if the job started on the 4th of July, then it will execute every June and December on the 4th. If you want to schedule it on a different date, use the BYMONTHDAY keyword instead.

BYMONTHDAY	Specifies exactly which day of the month the job should execute. For example, to execute the job on the 1st day of every month, at 3:00 P.M., specify: `FREQ=MONTHLY; BYMONTHDAY=1; BYHOUR=15` If you omit the BYHOUR clause, the job defaults to midnight of the day.
BYYEARDAY	Specifies the day of the year when the job should run. For example, to execute a job on the 15th day of every year, specify: `FREQ=YEARLY; BYYEARDAY=15`

BYHOUR	Schedules the job to run at certain hours. For example, to execute a job every day at 3 A.M., 6 A.M., and 9 A.M., specify:
	
	`FREQ=DAILY; BYHOUR=3,6,9`
	
	A schedule based on the above calendar string will be:
	
	`07/06/2005 03:00:00`
	`07/06/2005 06:00:00`
	`07/06/2005 09:00:00`
	`07/07/2005 03:00:00`
	`07/07/2005 06:00:00`
	`07/07/2005 09:00:00`
	`... and so on.`
	
	A variation on the previous example is the following calendar string:
	
	`FREQ=MINUTELY; BYHOUR=3,6,9`
	
	An interval of MINUTELY means that the job will execute every minute. A schedule based on the above is:
	
	`07/06/2005 03:00:00`
	`07/06/2005 03:01:00`
	`07/06/2005 03:02:00`
	`07/06/2005 03:03:00`
	`07/06/2005 03:04:00`
	`07/06/2005 03:05:00`
	`... and so on till 03:59:00. The series repeats at 6:00:00 A.M. and goes on till 06:59:00 A.M.`

Table 8-1. BY keywords for calendar strings in the repeat_interval parameter (continued)

Keyword	Description

BYMINUTE	Schedules a job at a certain minute of the day. To execute a job every 30th minute, specify the calendar string:
	
	`FREQ=MINUTELY; BYMINUTE=30`
	
	A schedule based on this calendar string is:
	
	`07/06/2005 00:30:00`
	`07/06/2005 01:30:00`
	`07/06/2005 02:30:00`
	… and so on.
	
	If you specify FREQ=HOURLY instead of MINUTELY above, the effect will be the same, because the hour is still omitted in this case. However, if the above interval is specified as:
	
	`FREQ=DAILY; BYMINUTE=30`
	
	then rounding will be done at the day level. A schedule based on this calendar is:
	
	`07/06/2005 00:30:00`
	`07/07/2005 00:30:00`
	`07/08/2005 00:30:00`
	`07/09/2005 00:30:00`
	… and so on.
	
	Here, the job executes at 00:30 hours of every day, because the FREQ clause shows DAILY.

BYSECOND	Similar to BYMINUTE and BYHOUR, BYSECOND executes schedules on the specified seconds.

If you specify a negative number as a value for any of these keywords, counting will start from the end instead of from the beginning. For example, the calendar string:

```
FREQ=YEARLY; BYYEARDAY=-1
```

indicates the first day of the year from the end of the year. So the above calendar string will execute the job on December 31st of each year.

Examples of calendar strings

Let's look at some additional examples of calendar strings. Suppose that all of these are first specified on jobs starting on July 5th, 2005. I will show you how to specify this calendar string starting with larger intervals and then specifying more granular ones.

FREQ=YEARLY

> Because the frequency is specified as yearly, the schedule is once a year. I have not specified any dates, so the schedule defaults to July 5th every year starting with 2006. This job will execute every year on July 5th at midnight.

FREQ=YEARLY; INTERVAL=2

> Because the INTERVAL clause is specified, the schedule will be set for every other year. This job will execute on July 5th in 2007, 2009, 2011, and so on.

FREQ=YEARLY; BYMONTH=JAN

> Because I specified a BYMONTH clause, the yearly execution will not default to this month (July), but because I have not specified any dates, it will default to

today's date (the 5th). This job will execute every year on January 5th—again, at midnight.

```
FREQ=YEARLY; BYMONTH=JAN; BYMONTHDAY=2
```

Note the additional clause BYMONTHDAY. This indicates that the schedule will be operational on the 2nd day of the month, not the default. This job will execute on January 2nd 2006, January 2nd 2007, and so on.

```
FREQ=YEARLY; BYMONTH=JAN; BYDAY=SUN
```

Here, instead of specifying a date, I have specified a day of the week in that month. This job will execute on every Sunday in January of every year. Some example schedules, in mm/dd/yyyy format, are:

01/01/2006
01/08/2006
01/15/2006
01/22/2006
01/29/2006
01/07/2007

All these are Sundays.

```
FREQ=YEARLY; BYMONTH=JAN; BYMONTHDAY=2; BYDAY=SUN
```

This is a slight twist on the previous two schedules. The clause BYMONTH-DAY specifies a specific day of the month (2nd), but the BYDAY clause specifies a specific day of the week (Sunday). Hence, this job will execute every Sunday in January when the date is the 2nd. The schedule is:

01/02/2011
01/02/2022
01/02/2028
01/02/2033

Note that the first occurrence is on January 2nd, 2011, because that happens to be a Sunday.

```
FREQ=YEARLY; BYYEARDAY=60
```

Here I specify every 60th day of the year. The schedule is:

03/01/2006
03/01/2007
02/29/2008
03/01/2009

Note how the Scheduler takes care of the leap year, 2008, where the 60th day falls on February 29th. On all other years the 60th day of the year is March 1st.

```
FREQ=YEARLY; BYYEARDAY=60; BYMONTHDAY=1
```

By combining conditions, I can get the specific results I need. In this case I specify the 60th day of the year but on the 1st of the month. The schedule is:

03/01/2006
03/01/2007
03/01/2009
03/01/2010

Note that the year 2008 is not included. On that year, the 60th day falls on February 29th, not on the first of any month, so it is not included in the schedule.

FREQ=YEARLY; BYWEEKNO=2

Here I indicate that the schedule should be repeated every day for the second week of the year. The schedule is:

```
01/09/2006
01/10/2006
01/11/2006
01/12/2006
01/13/2006
01/14/2006
01/15/2006
01/08/2007
```

Note how all seven days of the second week of all of the years show up in the schedule.

FREQ=DAILY; BYHOUR=3,6,9

This job executes every day at 3 A.M., 6 A.M., and 9 A.M., exactly on the hour.

```
07/06/2005 03:00:00
07/06/2005 06:00:00
07/06/2005 09:00:00
07/07/2005 03:00:00
...and so on.
```

FREQ=DAILY; INTERVAL=2; BYHOUR=3,6,9

This specification is the same as the previous one, except that the INTERVAL is set to 2. This means that the actual interval between two executions should be two times the interval specified in the FREQ clause—that is, two days.

```
07/06/2005 03:00:00
07/06/2005 06:00:00
07/06/2005 09:00:00
07/08/2005 03:00:00
... and so on.
```

Note how it executes on July 6th and then on July 8th.

FREQ=DAILY; BYHOUR=3,6,9; BYMINUTE=00,15,30,45

This job executes every day at 3 A.M., 6 A.M., and 9 A.M. as above, but because the BYMINUTE clause is specified, the execution occurs at those minute markers. So the schedule is:

```
07/06/2005 03:00:00
07/06/2005 03:15:00
07/06/2005 03:30:00
... and so on.
```

Determining future calendar strings

Because calendar strings are English-like, they are easy to write. However, it's possible to get confused and end up with a schedule that isn't quite what you meant it to be. The EVALUATE_CALENDAR_STRING procedure available in DBMS_SCHEDULER

ISO-8601 Week Numbering

When BYWEEKNO is specified, the Scheduler uses week numbering as specified by the ISO-8601 standard, which introduces its own idiosyncrasies. Here is what you need to know about ISO-8601 week numbering:

- The first day of the week is considered to be Monday, not Sunday, because this is common practice in many businesses and programs.
- Week numbers may be from 1 to 53.
- The first week starts from the first Monday of the year; hence, there may be some days before the first week of the year. For example, in 2005 if your scheduling calendar specifies "FREQ=YEARLY; BYWEEKNO=1", the first day this schedule will start is January 2nd, 2005, because that is the first Monday of the year 2005. This means that the date January 1st will never appear in any of the schedules. This may not present a problem for you, but you should be aware of it.
- Similarly, the last week of the year may not cover all of the year. Part of the year may be left out, and will be included in the first week of the next year.
- The last week of the year may contain some parts from the next year. Consider the calendar string "FREQ=YEARLY; BYWEEKNO=52". When specified in 2005, it shows the following schedule:

```
12/26/2005
12/27/2005
12/28/2005
12/29/2005
12/30/2005
12/31/2005
01/01/2006
12/25/2006
... and so on
```

- Note that the last week of the year includes January 1st, 2006, which is in 2006, not 2005. Even though it shows up as the 52nd week of the year 2005, the schedule actually goes into 2006. If you aren't aware of this important fact when you build your schedule, the outcome may be very different from what you anticipate.

will examine your calendar string and produce a sample schedule that you can scrutinize to make sure that your job will execute as you expect it to.

The procedure accepts four parameters:

calendar_string
    Calendar string to be evaluated

start_date
    Date (specified as a TIMESTAMP datatype) where you want to start

return_date_after

> If you need to specify dates and times that fall after a certain date, use this parameter to start the sequence of scheduled dates after that date.

next_run_date

> This is an OUT parameter. The procedure places the date and time when the Scheduler will execute this calendar string here.

Let's look at an example of using this procedure to get the execution schedules for the calendar string "FREQ=MONTHLY;INTERVAL=2".

```
    /* File on web: cal_eval.sql */
 1  DECLARE
 2     l_start_date     TIMESTAMP;
 3     l_next_date      TIMESTAMP;
 4     l_return_date    TIMESTAMP;
 5  BEGIN
 6     l_start_date := TRUNC (SYSTIMESTAMP);
 7     l_return_date := l_start_date;
 8
 9     FOR ctr IN 1 .. 10
10     LOOP
11        dbms_scheduler.evaluate_calendar_string ('FREQ=MONTHLY;INTERVAL=2',
12                                                  l_start_date,
13                                                  l_return_date,
14                                                  l_next_date
15                                                  );
16        DBMS_OUTPUT.put_line (    'Next Run on: '
17                   || TO_CHAR (l_next_date, 'mm/dd/yyyy hh24:mi:ss')
18                   );
19        l_return_date := l_next_date;
20     END LOOP;
21  END;
```

The output is:

```
Next Run on: 09/06/2005 00:00:00
Next Run on: 11/06/2005 00:00:00
Next Run on: 01/06/2006 00:00:00
Next Run on: 03/06/2006 00:00:00
Next Run on: 05/06/2006 00:00:00
Next Run on: 07/06/2006 00:00:00
Next Run on: 09/06/2006 00:00:00
Next Run on: 11/06/2006 00:00:00
Next Run on: 01/06/2007 00:00:00
Next Run on: 03/06/2007 00:00:00
```

You can check over the exact dates and times of future executions to make sure they are what you expect them to be.

Named Schedules

Calendar strings provide a very helpful tool for specifying the schedule for executing your jobs. But suppose you have several jobs that run at the same time—for example, you might be collecting optimizer statistics for several tables. Here is an excerpt from the data dictionary view showing the schedule for these jobs:

```
SQL> SELECT job_name, repeat_interval
  2  FROM dba_scheduler_jobs;

JOB_NAME                          REPEAT_INTERVAL
--------------------------------  ------------------------------
TABSTAT_ACCOUNTS                  FREQ=DAILY; BYHOUR=3
TABSTAT_SAVINGS                   FREQ=DAILY; BYHOUR=3
TABSTAT_CHECKING                  FREQ=DAILY; BYHOUR=3
... and so on ...
```

Notice that the jobs have all the same calendar string, "FREQ=DAILY; BYHOUR=3", which indicates execution at 3:00 A.M. every day. Now, suppose you want to change the timing to 4:00 A.M. instead of 3:00; what will you have to do?

You will have to go through each job painstakingly and change the calendar string. The more jobs you have, the more work you have to do—it will be a very tedious experience, and it will also be very prone to error. These are the drawbacks to any hardcoding inside an application.

The Scheduler gives you another option that helps you avoid this hardcoding. It allows you to create a *named* schedule, which all of your jobs can reference. If you use a named schedule, you won't need to explicitly state the calendar string; maintenance of your schedules will be much simpler. Let's see how this works.

Using the CREATE_SCHEDULE procedure, I can create a schedule called opt_stat_coll_sched, which specifies the calendar string I defined above.

```
1  BEGIN
2     DBMS_SCHEDULER.create_schedule
3        (schedule_name       => 'opt_stat_coll_sched',
4         start_date          => SYSTIMESTAMP,
5         repeat_interval     => 'FREQ=DAILY; BYHOUR=3',
6         comments            => 'Run daily at 3 AM'
7        );
8  END;
```

Let's examine the lines in detail in the following table.

Line	Description
3	Name of the schedule.
4	Time the named schedule should start. In this example, I define it to start now. The time is in the TIMESTAMP datatype, so I specify SYSTIMESTAMP instead of SYSDATE.

Line	Description
5	Calendar string that defines the schedule.
6	Comments that describe the schedule.

Once I have created the schedule, my job creation script can simply reference it by name. To illustrate, I'll drop the jobs I have created and start over.

```
BEGIN
    DBMS_SCHEDULER.drop_job (job_name => 'tabstat_savings');
END;
```

Similarly, I'll drop all of my jobs and then re-create them using the named schedule. Here is one example for a job named TABSTAT_SAVINGS.

```
1  BEGIN
2      DBMS_SCHEDULER.create_job (job_name  => 'tabstat_savings',
3              job_type         => 'stored_procedure',
4              job_action       => 'collect_stats_checking',
5              schedule_name    => 'opt_stat_coll_sched',
6              enabled          => TRUE,
7              comments         => 'Collect Optimizer Stats'
8                      );
9* END;
```

This code is almost identical to the previous job creation code except for line 5, which shows a new parameter—schedule_name, where I can reference the named schedule I just created.

To check a schedule for a job, I can query the DBA_SCHEDULER_JOBS view as before. Assume that I have just re-created the job TABSTAT_SAVINGS to use a named schedule. The other two jobs are still on a calendar.

```
SQL> SELECT job_name, repeat_interval, schedule_name, schedule_owner, schedule_type
  2  FROM dba_scheduler_jobs;

JOB_NAME              REPEAT_INTERVAL       SCHEDULE_NAME          SCHEDU SCHEDULE_
-------------------   -------------------   --------------------   ------ ---------
TABSTAT_ACCOUNTS     FREQ=DAILY; BYHOUR=3                                 CALENDAR
TABSTAT_SAVINGS                            OPT_STAT_COLL_SCHED    ARUP   NAMED
TABSTAT_CHECKING     FREQ=DAILY; BYHOUR=3                                 CALENDAR
```

Note the SCHEDULE_TYPE column, which shows NAMED for the job I just turned over to a named schedule. That column shows CALENDAR for the jobs still using the calendar string as schedules. The column SCHEDULE_NAME shows the name of the schedule you just assigned to the job. Also, when I provide a named schedule for a job, the column REPEAT_INTERVAL becomes NULL for that job.

Owner of the Schedule

Another important column in the output from the DBA_SCHEDULER_JOBS view is SCHEDULE_OWNER. In this case, it shows ARUP, the user that created the schedule. The implication of this column is significant: a schedule need not be created by the user who actually runs a job; it could be defined by another user. Note, however, that the user who creates a schedule must have the CREATE JOB system privilege. Because the schedule is created using the DBMS_SCHEDULER package, that user must also have the EXECUTE privilege on the package.

Suppose that I am creating a single user named SCHED_MANAGER, to manage all of the schedules for your database. Doing so will make it easier to manage schedules and will establish a single point of control for these schedules. As I noted above, that user must be given the following privileges:

```
CREATE JOB
EXECUTE ON DBMS_SCHEDULER
```

My job creation code now looks like this.

```
 1  BEGIN
 2     DMS_SCHEDULER.create_job
 3         (job_name        => 'tabstat_savings',
 4          job_type        => 'stored_procedure',
 5          job_action      => 'collect_stats_checking',
 6          schedule_name   => 'SCHED_MANAGER.opt_stat_coll_sched',
 7          enabled         => TRUE,
 8          comments        => 'Collect SAVINGS Stats'
 9         );
10* END;
```

Note that line 6 has changed. Now the schedule_name parameter shows SCHED_MANAGER.opt_stat_coll_sched, which indicates the owner of the schedule. In my earlier examples, I did not include a prefix for the schedule name; if you omit the prefix, the default is that the schedule belongs to the user who is creating the job.

 Once a schedule has been created by one user, it can be used by *any* other user. There is no fine-grained access control that may be used to control access to a specific schedule. Keep this mind when you are creating your schedules.

Managing Named Programs

I've explained two basic scheduling concepts: the job and the schedule. A third important concept is the *program*: the actual code that will be executed as scheduled. Now that you've learned how to call different types of programs, you might be tempted (quite justifiably) to place all scheduled processes—whether in stored procedures, PL/SQL anonymous blocks, or operating system executables—under Scheduler control. There is, however, one complication that you will need to be aware of.

According to the syntax you've seen so far, you need to pass the full path of your executable (or your PL/SQL block or stored procedure) to the parameter job_action in the CREATE_JOB procedure. If the path is long (as it may often be), it may be inconvenient to specify the entire path. And if you supply it more than once, you are again introducing opportunities for errors to enter your scheduling process.

Fortunately, DBMS_SCHEDULER allows you to define *named* programs, which make it extremely easy to reference the program to be executed. Named programs are essentially synonyms for the actual code being executed. Instead of calling the actual code segment, you simply reference the name you have given the program. Then, if you ever need to change your job to run a different program, you will not need to change the job definition. All you have to do is swap the new executable into the program, and your job will call the right one.

Creating a Program

In this next example, I'll use DBMS_SCHEDULER's CREATE_PROGRAM procedure to give a frequently called executable program the name KICK_RMAN_INC.

```
BEGIN
    DBMS_SCHEDULER.create_program
            (program_name    => 'KICK_RMAN_INC',
             program_type    => 'EXECUTABLE',
             program_action  => '/u01/app/oracle/admin/tools/kick_rman_inc.sh',
             enabled         => TRUE,
             comments        => 'Take RMAN Inc Backup'
            );
END;
```

After the program is created, my original RMAN incremental backup job will not need to specify the full path of the program or what type of job it is. The new definition looks like this:

```
BEGIN
    DBMS_SCHEDULER.create_job (job_name       => 'RMAN_INC',
                               program_name   => 'KICK_RMAN_INC',
                               schedule_name  => 'EVERY_DAY',
                               comments       => 'RMAN Inc Backup',
                               enabled        => TRUE
                              );
END;
```

Note that I've specified only the schedule name and the program name. Because the program (with its whole path) has already been defined as an executable, there is no need to specify what type of program it is (PL/SQL block, stored procedure or executable), so the program_type parameter is no longer needed in the job description. Furthermore, now that this program has been defined, you can also use it in another job without specifying any details. You can even change the job entirely—for example, make it a PL/SQL block or a stored procedure instead of an OS executable—and you will not have to change any of the code that creates the job.

Running Other Users' Programs

As I described when covering schedules, programs can be owned by users other than their creators. By default, a program defined in the CREATE_JOB procedure is assumed to be owned by the user creating the job. However, if you want, you can use a program owned by another user. For example, suppose that a user known as INTEREST_ADMIN owns the program to apply interest as follows:

```
SQL> CREATE USER interest_admin IDENTIFIED BY interest_admin;
User created.

SQL> GRANT CREATE SESSION, CREATE JOB, CREATE PROCEDURE to interest_admin;
Grant succeeded.

SQL> CONN interest_admin/interest_admin
Connected.

SQL> CREATE PROCEDURE calc_int
  2  AS
  3  BEGIN
  4      NULL;
  5  END;
  6  /

Procedure created.
```

I can now use this procedure in a named program called CAL_INTEREST as the user INTEREST_ADMIN:

```
BEGIN
    DBMS_SCHEDULER.create_program (program_name      => 'CALC_INTEREST',
                                   program_type      => 'STORED_PROCEDURE',
                                   program_action    => 'calc_int',
                                   enabled           => TRUE,
                                   comments          => 'Calculate Interest'
                                  );
END;
```

Once the program has been created, I can create a schedule owned by the user SCHED_MANAGER. The schedule is named EVERY_DAY.

```
SQL> CONN sched_manager/sched_manager
Connected.
SQL> BEGIN
  2      DBMS_SCHEDULER.create_schedule (schedule_name   => 'every_day',
  3                                      start_date      => SYSTIMESTAMP,
  4                                      repeat_interval => 'FREQ=DAILY; BYHOUR=3',
  5                                      comments        => 'Schedule Run for Int Calc'
  6                                     );
  7  END;
  8  /

PL/SQL procedure successfully completed.
```

Before user ACC_MANAGER can use this program, she must be granted the EXECUTE privilege on the program or she must have the EXECUTE ANY PROGRAM system privilege.

```
SQL> CONN interest_admin/interest_admin
Connected.

SQL> GRANT EXECUTE ON calc_interest TO acc_manager;
Grant succeeded.
```

Now as user ACC_MANAGER, I can create the job.

```
BEGIN
    DBMS_SCHEDULER.create_job (job_name          => 'Calculate_Daily_Interest',
                              program_name      => 'INTEREST_ADMIN.CALC_INTEREST',
                              schedule_name     => 'SCHED_MANAGER.EVERY_DAY',
                              comments          => 'Daily Interest Calculation',
                              enabled           => TRUE
                             );
END;
```

This will create a job called Calculate_Daily_Interest, which executes the program referenced by the named program CALC_INTEREST owned by the user INTEREST_ADMIN as per the schedule defined in the named schedule EVERY_ DAY owned by the user SCHED_ADMIN. Whew!

> The ability to execute named programs can be controlled by the EXECUTE privilege, but no privileges exist to reference any named schedule owned by a different user.

Using named programs can significantly reduce administrative overhead. When you make a change in the executable, the path, or the name of the stored procedure, you will not have to change your job definitions.

Managing Priorities

Oracle allows you to assign priorities to jobs, and that is critical functionality for any robust scheduling mechanism.

Suppose that you have created several jobs in the database with a variety of schedules. There is always a possibility that some jobs will overlap with others. After all, there are only 24 hours in a day. When two jobs run at the same time, they might consume resources such as CPU and memory at a pace not usually seen during the normal operation of the database. The resource consumption—more accurately, the resource contention—may cause *both* jobs to slow down (as well as other applications running on the system). In such a case, what should be done? You may want to give Job A all the resources it needs, and let Job B suffer a little until Job A completes. Or you may want to give Job B more resources.

Using the Resource Manager

Oracle job scheduling priorities are managed through a database feature called the Resource Manager, which in turn is made available through the built-in package, DBMS_RESOURCE_MANAGER. It's beyond the scope of this book to discuss the Resource Manager, so I will assume you are aware of and familiar with it.

Let's look at an example. First, I define a resource manager group known as OLTP_GROUP to handle the database load during regular OLTP activities.

```
BEGIN
   DBMS_RESOURCE_MANAGER.clear_pending_area ();
   DBMS_RESOURCE_MANAGER.create_pending_area ();
   DBMS_RESOURCE_MANAGER.create_consumer_group
         (consumer_group       => 'oltp_group',
          COMMENT              => 'OLTP Activity Group'
         );
   DBMS_RESOURCE_MANAGER.submit_pending_area ();
END;
```

Next, I need to define plan directives that show how resources are allocated among various groups in the plan. Oracle comes with a predefined group known as OTHER_GROUP. In this example, I define a second group known as OLTP_GROUP, which serves as the group for all OLTP activities. I am going to assign 80% of the CPU to OLTP activities and the rest to the OTHER_GROUP.

```
BEGIN
   DBMS_RESOURCE_MANAGER.clear_pending_area ();
   DBMS_RESOURCE_MANAGER.create_pending_area ();
   DBMS_RESOURCE_MANAGER.create_plan ('OLTP_PLAN',
                              'OLTP Database Activity Plan'
                             );
   DBMS_RESOURCE_MANAGER.create_plan_directive
                        (PLAN                    => 'OLTP_PLAN',
                         group_or_subplan         => 'OLTP_GROUP',
                         COMMENT                  => 'This is the OLTP Plan',
                         cpu_p1                   => 80,
                         parallel_degree_limit_p1 => 4,
                         switch_group             => 'OTHER_GROUPS',
                         switch_time              => 10,
                         switch_estimate          => TRUE,
                         max_est_exec_time        => 10,
                         undo_pool                => 500


                        );
   DBMS_RESOURCE_MANAGER.create_plan_directive
                        (PLAN                    => 'OLTP_PLAN',
                         group_or_subplan         => 'OTHER_GROUPS',
                         COMMENT                  => NULL,
                         cpu_p1                   => 20,
                         parallel_degree_limit_p1 => 0,
```

```
                                  active_sess_pool_p1            => 0,
                                  queueing_p1                    => 0,
                                  switch_estimate                => FALSE,
                                  max_est_exec_time              => 0,
                                  undo_pool                      => 10
                                  );
        DBMS_RESOURCE_MANAGER.submit_pending_area ();
    END;
```

After the resource plans have been established, I can use them when scheduling jobs.

There are two different ways to use resource plans: in a job class and in a window. The next section describes the use of a job class. The later section "Managing Windows" describes how to use windows with DBMS_SCHEDULER, including their use with resource plans.

Job Class

A job class is a collection of properties. I can create a job class with DBMS_SCHEDULER's CREATE_JOB_CLASS procedure. When I create a job, I can specify the name of an already created job class using the job_class parameter in CREATE_JOB. Here is how to create a scheduler job class that follows the resource allocation group OLTP_GROUP.

```
1  BEGIN
2      DBMS_SCHEDULER.create_job_class
3              (job_class_name              => 'OLTP_JOBS',
4              logging_level                => dbms_scheduler.logging_full,
5              log_history                  => 45,
6              resource_consumer_group      => 'OLTP_GROUP',
7              comments                     => 'OLTP Related Jobs'
8              );
9  END;
```

Let's examine the lines in detail in the following table.

Line	Description
3	Name of the job class.
4	When a job executes, it creates a log of its activities in a SYS-owned table named SCHEDULER$_EVENT_LOG. You can expose this table to others via the DBA_SCHEDULER_JOB_LOG view. The log entries can be full or partial. (See the "Managing Logging" section for an explanation.)
5	If the execution of the job is logged, then the log entries must be purged periodically; otherwise, the log will become unmanageably large. The log_history parameter determines how many days of logs must be kept. The default is 30 days. In this example, I increase the number of days to 45.
6	This job class is assigned the resource group OLTP_GROUP, which governs the resource allocation and utilization of the jobs defined in this job class.
7	Comments for this job class.

After the job class is created, I can check its attributes or those of any previously defined job classes in the DBA_SCHEDULER_JOB_CLASSES data dictionary view. Here is a record from the view, shown in vertical format for easy readability.

```
JOB_CLASS_NAME                    : OLTP_JOBS
RESOURCE_CONSUMER_GROUP           : OLTP_GROUP
SERVICE                           :
LOGGING_LEVEL                     : FULL
LOG_HISTORY                       : 45
COMMENTS                          : OLTP Related Jobs
```

When you define a job class, you can also define a service name under which the jobs in the job class will run. The service name must have been defined in the database. For example, if I use a service name called INTCALC_SRVC, I must have enabled it as follows:

```
ALTER SYSTEM SET SERVICE_NAME = 'INTCALC_SRVC';
```

After that, I can define the job class under that service name by specifying the service parameter in the CREATE_JOB_CLASS procedure (see the highlighted line below).

```
BEGIN
    DBMS_SCHEDULER.create_job_class
                    (job_class_name           => 'INT_JOBS',
                     logging_level            => dbms_scheduler.logging_full,
                     log_history              => 45,
                     service                  => 'INTCALC_SRVC',
                     comments                 => 'Interest Calculation Related Jobs'
                     );
END;
```

Service names are useful when you want to control a session connected to a service, instead of to an instance. An Oracle instance can have many services defined in it, and when sessions connect, they can specify a SERVICE_NAME parameter in the *TNSNAMES.ORA* file instead of using the SID in the connect string. When a session connects that way, the SERVICE_NAME column in V$SESSION shows it for that session. When the service is not enabled in the instance, the sessions can't connect, even if the instance is up.

Services are helpful in other ways as well. For example, if you are running a multi-instance RAC database, you might want to define a service in only one instance of that database, thus restricting the job to only that one instance. When the instance fails, the sessions will be transferred over to the other surviving instances. Defining a service allows you to specify to which node the sessions get transferred when the instance fails. A service may also be used to control resource manager plans allocated to the sessions assigned the service.

 Because a service also controls resource allocation, you cannot specify both the resource_consumer_plan and the service parameters; you must choose between these two approaches.

As a last step, create a job that has the definition of that job class. In this case, I have created a job to collect optimizer statistics.

```
BEGIN
    DBMS_SCHEDULER.create_job (job_name          => 'COLLECT_STATS',
                               job_type          => 'STORED_PROCEDURE',
                               job_action        => 'collect_opt_stats',
                               job_class         => 'OLTP_JOBS',
                               repeat_interval   => 'FREQ=WEEKLY; INTERVAL=1',
                               enabled           => TRUE,
                               comments          => 'Collect Optimizer Stats'
                               );
END;
```

Note the highlighted line—that is the only difference from the other examples we've seen. The job_class parameter here is set to OLTP_JOBS, which is the job class I created. The job COLLECT_STATS inherits all the properties of the job class OLTP_JOBS. Because the job class has been assigned the resource consumer group OLTP_GROUP, all of the resource control parameters defined for the resource consumer group will be applicable to the job COLLECT_STATS.

Managing Windows

Windows are defined durations within which a specified job runs. Using windows, you can control how resources (e.g., CPU, parallel query servers, undo pool size) are allocated and governed. When a job runs, the resource allocation method specified by the window active at that time is in effect, and it controls the resource allocation for that job.

A window has three distinct components:

- A *schedule*, which defines the starting time of the window
- A *time duration* of the window, indicating how long it is open
- A *resource allocation plan* that is applied to a job attached to the window

The first component may be specified using either a calendar string or a named schedule, as I described earlier for jobs. The third component may be specified via a resource manager plan, as described for programs in the previous section. In the following sections, I'll explain the second component, the time duration of windows.

Creating a Window

You can create a window using the CREATE_WINDOW procedure in the DBMS_SCHEDULER package. Suppose that I want to create a window called LOW_LOAD, which has the following characteristics:

- It starts each day at 3:00 A.M.

- It is 14 hours long.
- It uses the resource plan OLTP_PLAN.

I can create this window as follows.

```
 1  BEGIN
 2      DBMS_SCHEDULER.create_window (window_name         => 'low_load',
 3              resource_plan       => 'OLTP_PLAN',
 4              schedule_name       => 'SCHED_MANAGER.EVERY_DAY',
 5              DURATION            => NUMTODSINTERVAL
 6                                      (840,
 7                                      'minute'
 8                                      ),
 9              comments            => 'This is a low load window'
10          );
11  END;
```

Let's examine the lines in detail in the following table.

Line	Description
2	Name of the window.
3	Name of the resource manager plan, OLTP_PLAN, which was previously created.
4	Name of the schedule, which was previously created. It starts at 3:00 A.M. every day.
5–8	Duration of this window. The duration parameter is specified in the datatype INTERVAL DAY TO SECOND. I must specify the 14-hour period in the manner shown.
9	Comment for the window.

Once this window has been created, I can create a job that uses this window. When I run the CREATE_JOB procedure, I can specify the window name in the schedule_ name parameter, as shown below. Earlier, I described how to set this parameter to define a schedule. Here, the same parameter I used to specify a window named LOW_LOAD.

```
BEGIN
    DBMS_SCHEDULER.create_job (job_name        => 'Calculate_Daily_Interest',
                            program_name    => 'INTEREST_ADMIN.CALC_INTEREST',
                            schedule_name   => 'SYS.LOW_LOAD',
                            comments        => 'Daily Interest Calculation',
                            enabled         => TRUE
                            );
END;
```

Because windows are always owned by SYS, I qualify the window name with "SYS". Because the job was assigned this window, its resource allocation method is governed by the resource allocation scheme for the window.

When a window is supposed to become active, it is said to be *opened*; subsequently, when it becomes inactive, it is said to be *closed*. So a window opens when the time comes for it to be opened based on the calendar defined or the schedule associated with the window.

When a window closes, what happens to the jobs that are running at that time? There are two possibilities: you could let them run as usual or just stop them. Sometimes it is important to stop a job when the window closes. For example, you may have a job that collects optimizer statistics for tables. This job usually runs during the night—perhaps until 6:00 A.M. Suppose that on one particular day it does not finish at 6:00 A.M. and instead continues on until 8:00 A.M. By that time it might be affecting regular database processing. This is a case where you may want to stop the job before completion when its associated window closes. This property of the window is controlled by the CREATE_JOB parameter stop_on_window_close. If it is set to TRUE, the specified job is stopped when the window closes.

 Windows can be created by any user with the MANAGE SCHEDULER system privilege. However, windows are not owned by that user. Technically, the window objects are owned by SYS.

Prioritizing Windows

Because windows are defined according to a time scale, only one window is active at any point in time. Suppose that you have defined two windows as follows:

- Window W1 starts at 7 A.M. and ends at 9 P.M.
- Window W2 starts at 7 P.M. and ends at 7 A.M.

These two windows overlap between 7 P.M. and 9 P.M. During that time, which window will be active?

The Scheduler resolves this situation according to the priority you have assigned to each window. You specify the priority in the window_priority parameter of the CREATE_WINDOW procedure. The only two possible values are "low" (the default) and "high." For example:

```
window_priority => 'high'
```

When windows overlap, the one with the "high" priority will be activated. If two windows with the same priority overlap, then the window that is going to end sooner is given precedence, and the other window waits.

Specifying an End Date for Windows

DBMS_SCHEDULER allows you to specify a date when a window will end. What does that mean?

Suppose that your accounting database receives data from an outside source. You discover that the outside source has been compromised and that the data coming from there is not accurate. You decide to code a stored procedure that will fix the data in the database, and use a schedule to execute this procedure every day. However, the source for this fix is available to you only until August 2nd, and today is

July 5th. After August 2nd, you want this job to end. You defined a window in the first place so that this job will not consume all your resources. Because the issue will be resolved by August 2nd, you want the window to have a definite lifespan. To effectively end this window on that day, and thus conserve resources, you could specify an end date when you create the window. You do this with the end_date parameter of the CREATE_WINDOW procedure.

Getting Information About Windows

You can obtain information about windows in the database from the view DBA_ SCHEDULER_WINDOWS. Here are the important columns of the view.

Column name	Description
WINDOW_NAME	Name of the window.
RESOURCE_PLAN	Name of the Resource Manager plan associated with the window.
SCHEDULE_OWNER	If the window has a named schedule, this is the name of the owner of the schedule.
SCHEDULE_NAME	Name of the schedule, if any.
START_DATE	Timestamp when the window will open. This is effective only when the window's calendar properties are provided inline, not via a schedule. Shows the date in the TIMESTAMP(6) WITH TIME ZONE datatype.
REPEAT_INTERVAL	If the window has an inline schedule (calendar string, as opposed to a named schedule), this is the calendar string.
END_DATE	When a window has an inline schedule (calendar string, as opposed to a named schedule), this specifies the timestamp when the window will close permanently. Similar to start_date, this column shows the date in the TIMESTAMP(6) WITH TIME ZONE datatype.
DURATION	How long the window is open. Shown in the DURATION datatype.
WINDOW_PRIORITY	When two windows overlap, the one with the higher priority will be opened, and the other one will be closed. The priorities are shown as HIGH and LOW.
NEXT_START_DATE	Next timestamp the window is scheduled to open. Shows the date in the datatype TIMESTAMP(6) WITH TIME ZONE.
LAST_START_DATE	Timestamp of the last time the window was opened. Shows the date in the datatype TIMESTAMP(6) WITH TIME ZONE.
ENABLED	Indicates whether a window is enabled; may be TRUE or FALSE.
ACTIVE	Indicates whether a window is open now; may be TRUE or FALSE.
COMMENTS	Comments about the window.

Dropping Windows

When you no longer need a window, you can drop it with the DROP_WINDOW procedure. If you attempt to drop a window and any jobs are currently using this window as their schedules, you will not be able to drop the window normally. Instead, you will have to use the FORCE option as follows.

```
BEGIN
    DBMS_SCHEDULER.drop_window (window_name => 'window1', FORCE => TRUE);
END;
```

If FORCE is specified for a window, that window will be dropped regardless of its association with any job. In this example, if there are any jobs using the window named window1 as their schedule, they will be disabled, and the window will be dropped.

Disabling and Enabling Windows

Instead of dropping a window, you may want to disable it so that it will never open automatically. To disable a window, use the procedure DISABLE, as shown here.

```
BEGIN
    DBMS_SCHEDULER.disable (NAME => 'window1');
END;
```

If the window named window1 is currently open, this operation will fail. To forcibly disable a window, you must use the FORCE parameter as follows:

```
BEGIN
    DBMS_SCHEDULER.disable (NAME => 'window1', FORCE=>TRUE);
END;
```

This will *not* close the currently open window, but it will force the window not to open in the future.

Similarly, to enable a disabled window, use the ENABLE procedure:

```
BEGIN
    DBMS_SCHEDULER.enable (NAME => 'window1');
END;
```

Note that the ENABLE and DISABLE procedures shown here are the same ENABLE/ DISABLE procedures used for other Scheduler objects, such as jobs, schedules, and programs.

Forcing Windows Open and Closed

Let's suppose that you have defined a window for regular OLTP activities named OLTP_WINDOW, starting at 9:00 A.M. Today, uncharacteristically, the processing started early—perhaps at 7:00 A.M. You have defined the resource manager group associated with the window, and you want this job to be under the resource plan, if possible. But the window is not scheduled to be open until two hours from now. What can you do?

In a case like this, you can force a window to open, using the procedure OPEN_ WINDOW, as shown here:

```
BEGIN
    DBMS_SCHEDULER.open_window (
        window_name => 'OLTP_WINDOW', DURATION => NULL);
END;
```

This immediately opens the specified window, and any jobs using this window can immediately use the resource plan.

In this example, the duration parameter is specified as NULL, which means that the normal duration of the window will be followed. Suppose the normal duration, specified when the window was created, is eight hours, ending at 5:00 P.M. Because the window was manually opened at 7:00 A.M., it will automatically close eight hours after that, at 3:00 P.M. That may not be acceptable to you: you may want to keep the window open until 5:00 P.M. anyway. In that case, you can open the window with a specified duration, as shown below; the duration must be in the INTERVAL datatype.

```
BEGIN
    dbms_scheduler.open_window (
        window_name     => 'OLTP_WINDOW',
        DURATION        => NUMTODSINTERVAL (600, 'minute')
        );
END;
```

Window Groups

Let's suppose that I have defined three different windows:

MORNING
1:00 A.M. through 9:00 A.M. Most of the management jobs, such as statistics collection, etc., run during this window.

WORKDAY
9:00 A.M. through 5:00 P.M. The entire regular database OLTP processing occurs during this window. No management or batch jobs are allowed to run.

EVENING
5:00 P.M. through 1:00 A.M. Most of the batch jobs and ETL processing occur during this window.

However, some jobs have to run at all times, regardless of whatever window is active at that time—for example, jobs that monitor performance. I can't define another window because at any point in time, only one window is active. So what can I do?

I can define a window group, which is a collection of windows. When I create a job, I can specify this window group as a schedule, and it will inherit the properties of the windows. I create a window group using the CREATE_WINDOW_GROUP procedure. For example, to create a window group named ALL_DAY as a collection of the three windows listed above, I issue the following code segment:

```
BEGIN
    DBMS_SCHEDULER.create_window_group (
        group_name      => 'all_day',
        window_list     => 'MORNING, WORKDAY, EVENING',
        comments        => 'All day window group'
        );
END;
```

I can specify the names of all of the windows in the window group as a comma-separated list in the window_list parameter. I can also create a window group with no windows assigned to it yet. The parameter will be NULL in that case. This is useful when a window group has just been created and you have not decided which windows should be applied.

When I create a job, I can specify the name of the window group in the CREATE_JOB schedule_name parameter as shown here:

```
BEGIN
    DBMS_SCHEDULER.create_job (job_name          => 'DB_Monitor',
                               program_name      => 'INTEREST_ADMIN.CALC_INTEREST',
                               schedule_name     => 'SYS.ALL_DAY',
                               comments          => 'DB Monitor',
                               enabled           => TRUE
                              );
END;
```

After I define a window group, I can add windows to it and remove windows from it. To remove the window MORNING from the window group ALL_DAY, I'll use the REMOVE_WINDOW_GROUP_MEMBER procedure as follows:

```
BEGIN
    DBMS_SCHEDULER.remove_window_group_member
                          (group_name    => 'all_day',
                           window_list   => 'MORNING'
                          );
END;
```

To add it later, I will use the ADD_WINDOW_GROUP_MEMBER procedure:

```
BEGIN
    DBMS_SCHEDULER.add_window_group_member
                          (group_name    => 'all_day',
                           window_list   => 'MORNING'
                          );
END;
```

When I want to remove a window group, I can use the DROP_WINDOW_GROUP procedure as shown here:

```
BEGIN
    DBMS_SCHEDULER.drop_window_group (group_name => 'all_day');
END;
```

If the window group has windows defined under it, then it cannot be dropped normally. In this example, the window group ALL_DAY has three windows: MORNING, WORKDAY, and EVENING. To drop the window group, use the FORCE parameter:

```
BEGIN
    DBMS_SCHEDULER.drop_window_group (group_name => 'all_day', FORCE => TRUE);
END;
```

Note, however, that this merely drops the window group, not the windows defined under it; they remain intact.

If there are any jobs running that use this window group, the jobs are disabled. They can, however, be manually restarted.

Managing Logging

Like most scheduling systems, the Oracle Scheduler executes programs in the background, where no direct feedback to users or administrators can take place. Given this situation, how can you diagnose issues related to jobs after those jobs have stopped running? The Scheduler allows you to do so with the extensive logging information generated by your job operations and window operations. I'll describe logging for both in the following sections.

Job Logs

There are two data dictionary views that show information about job logs: DBA_SCHEDULER_JOB_LOG and DBA_SCHEDULER_JOB_RUN_DETAILS.

DBA_SCHEDULER_JOB_LOG

When jobs are created, altered, dropped, and run, the results are loaded into a summary table that is visible through the DBA_SCHEDULER_JOB_LOG view. Its columns are listed in the following table.

Column name	Description
LOG_ID	Unique identifier for each record.
LOG_DATE	Timestamp of the log entry.
OWNER	Owner of the job.
JOB_NAME	Name of the job.
JOB_CLASS	Job class, if any.
OPERATION	What happened during the job entry (e.g., CREATE, RUN, BROKEN).
STATUS	What happened after the operation was performed by the job (e.g., SUCCEEDED, FAILED).
USER_NAME	Name of the user who invoked the job.
CLIENT_ID	Client identifier, if set using DBMS_SESSION.SET_IDENTIFIER.
GLOBAL_UID	If the user is a global user, the global UID is shown here.
ADDITIONAL_INFO	Any additional information about the job execution is stored as a CLOB in this column. For example, if the job was dropped automatically after it was successfully executed (provided that the auto_drop parameter was set to TRUE), then the OPERATION column shows DROP. However, you will not know from that column whether the job was dropped automatically or explicitly by a user. This column shows the specific reason for the drop. In this case, the column shows:
	`REASON="Auto drop job dropped".`
	Similarly, any other relevant information about the job execution is also stored here.

DBA_SCHEDULER_JOB_RUN_DETAILS

The DBA_SCHEDULER_JOB_LOG view described in the previous section shows the summary log for your jobs, not the details. For detailed information about job execution, see the view DBA_SCHEDULER_JOB_RUN_DETAILS. Its columns are listed in the following table.

Column name	Description
LOG_ID	Unique number representing the specific log entry.
LOG_DATE	Timestamp of the log entry, shown in the TIMESTAMP with TIMEZONE datatype.
OWNER	Owner of the job.
JOB_NAME	Name of the job.
STATUS	Status of the job after the operation (e.g., FAILED, SUCCEEDED).
ERROR#	Oracle error number, if there was an error.
REQ_START_DATE	Scheduled or requested time of the job run, which may not be the actual time the job started.
ACTUAL_START_DATE	The job may not start at the scheduled or requested time—perhaps because the window was not opened before the job was scheduled, a higher priority job was running, or the like. In this case, the actual timestamp of the start of the job is recorded here.
RUN_DURATION	Duration of the job run, shown in the TIMESTAMP datatype.
INSTANCE_ID	If this is a RAC database, then the job must have run on a specific instance of the database; the instance number is recorded here.
SESSION_ID	SID of the session that kicked off the job process.
SLAVE_PID	Process ID of the job slave process.
CPU_USED	Amount of CPU used in execution of the job.

ADDITIONAL_INFO	Additional information about the specific detail of the job execution is stored as a CLOB in this column. This information may be very helpful in diagnosing job execution issues. For example, suppose that a job fails and you find the following information in this column:
	
	`ORA-01014: ORACLE shutdown in progress`
	
	Or suppose that a statistics collection job failed and you find the following information in this column:
	
	`ORA-28031: maximum of 148 enabled roles exceeded`
	
	In both cases, you will be able to find out specifically why the job failed. Similarly, any other relevant information related to this line in the DETAILS view is also shown here.

Pruning the job log

Job logging provides very helpful information, but unless the logs are pruned from time to time, they will grow to an unmanageable size and overwhelm your database space. By default, the table where this information is stored (SYS. SCHEDULER$_JOB_RUN_DETAILS) is located in the SYSAUX tablespace. Oracle addresses this issue by automatically pruning the log entries after a certain period of time. This operation is accomplished by a Scheduler job, named PURGE_LOG, which is owned by the SYS user. This job is automatically installed when the Oracle database is created as a part of the job class DEFAULT_JOB_CLASS. It calls a named program called PURGE_LOG_PROG, which points to the stored procedure AUTO_PURGE in the DBMS_SCHEDULER package itself.

The job is scheduled on a named schedule called DAILY_PURGE_SCHEDULE, which runs at 3:00 A.M. every day. Although this is an automatic job, it is still a scheduling job. As with any other kind of job, you can change its properties—for example, when it runs, what program it calls, and whether it is assigned a window.

PURGE_LOG prunes only the log entries that are marked for deletion because their retention periods have expired. To control this retention period, see the later section "Setting the retention period."

Log levels

One way that you can control the size of your log is to limit the amount of logging information that is recorded for a job. For example, you may want to record when the jobs are run but not when they are created. In some cases, you may not want any logging at all.

You can control the level of logging by assigning a value for the CREATE_JOB_CLASS parameter logging_level when you create a job class. Later, when the job class is referenced in a job creation, the properties of the job will be inherited from the job class.

DBMS_SCHEDULER supports three levels of logging:

DBMS_SCHEDULER.LOGGING_OFF
    Logging is completely disabled.

DBMS_SCHEDULER.LOGGING_RUNS
    Logs are written only when the job runs. This is the default.

DBMS_SCHEDULER.LOGGING_FULL
    Logs are written when the job runs; in addition, all actions on the job (e.g., creation, drop, alteration) are also logged.

I can specify the logging_level parameter in the CREATE_JOB_CLASS procedure as follows:

```
BEGIN
   DBMS_SCHEDULER.create_job_class
             (job_class_name      => 'MONITOR',
              logging_level       => dbms_scheduler.logging_full
              );
END;
```

I can also change the level by setting the logging_level attribute of the job class as follows. (See the discussion of attributes in the later section "Managing Attributes.")

```
BEGIN
   DBMS_SCHEDULER.set_attribute (NAME       => 'sys.default_job_class',
                                 ATTRIBUTE  => 'logging_level',
```

```
                    VALUE           => dbms_scheduler.logging_full
                    );
    END;
```

Setting the retention period

Another way to limit the size of your logs is to set the retention period of the log entries in the log tables. When the automatic PURGE_LOG job runs, it purges from the logs only those entries that are older than the associated retention period. The default retention period is 30 days. After 30 days, the 31st oldest day's log is automatically deleted.

If you wish, you can specify a different retention period for each job class. You do this by setting the log_history parameter in the CREATE_JOB_CLASS procedure. (The default value is 30 days.) You can also modify the retention period for an existing job class by setting the log_history attribute at a later time.

In the following example, I specify a log retention period of 120 days when the job class is created:

```
    BEGIN
        DBMS_SCHEDULER.create_job_class (job_class_name    => 'MONITOR',
                                         log_history       => 120
                                         );
    END;
```

The next example sets the retention period for an existing job class called DEFAULT_JOB_CLASS:

```
    BEGIN
        DBMS_SCHEDULER.set_attribute (NAME          => 'sys.default_job_class',
                                      ATTRIBUTE     => 'log_history',
                                      VALUE         => 120
                                      );
    END;
```

I can check the current settings for log retention in the data dictionary view DBA_SCHEDULER_JOB_CLASSES, as shown here:

```
    SQL> SELECT job_class_name, logging_level, log_history
      2    FROM dba_scheduler_job_classes;

    JOB_CLASS_NAME                       LOGG LOG_HISTORY
    ------------------------------------ ---- -----------
    DEFAULT_JOB_CLASS                    RUNS         120
    AUTO_TASKS_JOB_CLASS                 RUNS
    MONITOR                              RUNS         120
```

The default logging level and retention period are adequate in most cases. However, in certain cases, you may want to override these defaults. Logs usually provide the only way that you can diagnose problems after jobs have completed. For particularly important jobs, you may want to enable full logging. For jobs where you may need to look further into the past than is customary, you may want to specify a higher retention period than the default.

Window Logs

Like jobs, windows produce logging entries, which you can examine via the two data dictionary views described in the following sections.

 You do not have the same ability to fine-tune the level and the retention period of the logs for window operations as you do for job operations.

DBA_SCHEDULER_WINDOW_LOG

When windows are created, altered, and dropped, the results are loaded into a summary table that is visible through the DBA_SCHEDULER_WINDOW_LOG view. Its columns are listed in the following table.

Column name	Description
LOG_ID	Unique identifier for the record.
LOG_DATE	Timestamp of the log entry.
WINDOW_NAME	Name of the window.
OPERATION	What happened to the window during the log entry (e.g., CLOSE, DISABLE, ENABLE, OPEN, UPDATE).
STATUS	What happened after the operation was performed by the job (e.g., SUCCEEDED, FAILED).
USER_NAME	Name of the user who invoked the job.
CLIENT_ID	The client identifier, if set using DBMS_SESSION.SET_IDENTIFIER, is recorded here. If this command was issued from Oracle's Enterprise Manager or Grid Control, this column is populated as follows: `SYSMAN@192.168.1.1@Mozilla/4.0 (compatible; MSIE 6.0; Windows N` This example shows that the Grid Control user was SYSMAN, logged in from the IP address 192.168.1.1, and so on.
GLOBAL_UID	If the user is a global user, the global UID is recorded here.
ADDITIONAL_INFO	Any additional information is stored as a CLOB in this column. For example, if the program is disabled forcibly, the OPERATION column shows DISABLE, but not specifically how the program was disabled. The ADDITIONAL_INFO column shows detailed information. For example, if the window was manually disabled, this column will show: `FORCE="TRUE", REASON="manually disabled"`

DBA_SCHEDULER_WINDOW_DETAILS

The DBA_SCHEDULER_WINDOW_LOG view described in the previous section shows the summary log for your windows, not the details. For detailed information about window use, see the view DBA_SCHEDULER_WINDOW_DETAILS. Its columns are listed in the following table.

Column name	Description
LOG_ID	Unique number representing the specific log entry.
LOG_DATE	Timestamp of the log entry, shown in the TIMESTAMP with TIMEZONE datatype.
WINDOW_NAME	Name of the window.
REQ_START_DATE	Scheduled or requested time of the window operation, which may not be the actual time the operation started.
ACTUAL_START_DATE	The window may not open or close at the scheduled or requested time. There are a variety of reasons why this might occur—for example, the window was not enabled; a higher priority window was open; and so on. In this case, the actual timestamp of the start of the window operation is recorded here.
WINDOW_DURATION	Specified duration of the window, shown in the INTERVAL datatype. This might be different from the actual duration of the window.
ACTUAL_DURATION	Actual duration of the window, shown in the INTERVAL datatype. This might be different from the specified duration of the window.
INSTANCE_ID	If this is a RAC database, the instance number is recorded here.
ADDITIONAL_INFO	Any additional information is stored as a CLOB in this column. This information may help in diagnosing window problems.

Managing Attributes

Throughout this chapter I have illustrated how you can assign properties for various scheduling components at the time you create them—for example, with the CREATE_JOB or CREATE_WINDOW commands. Sometimes, however, you may have to change the properties of a scheduling component after it has been created. For example, you may want to change the repeat interval of a job that has already been created in the database. One approach to changing properties is to drop and then re-create the object, but this is not always an option.

Properties such as repeat intervals, schedule names, logging level, and so on are known as the *attributes* of a job, program, or schedule object. The DBMS_SCHED-ULER package provides the SET_ATTRIBUTE procedure, which allows you to change the attributes of an existing job, job class, program, schedule, window, or window group.

For example, suppose that I want to change the comments for the job PURGE_LOG to "This job purges the log entries of jobs and windows". I could issue the following:

```
BEGIN
    DBMS_SCHEDULER.set_attribute
                    ('PURGE_LOG',
                     'comments',
                     'This job purges the log entries of jobs and windows'
                     );
END;
```

This procedure accepts three parameters:

component_name
> Name of the component whose property is to be changed. Because jobs, windows, programs, job classes, window groups, and schedules all have unique names, there is no need to specify the type of component here.

attribute
> Property to be changed as a VARCHAR2 datatype. Valid values will be different for each type of component—for example, "max_failures" is a valid attribute for jobs but not for programs.

value
> Value of the attribute. The datatype of this parameter depends on the particular attribute. For example, for windows, the attribute window_priority accepts a VARCHAR2 value ("LOW" or "HIGH"), but the attribute duration expects an INTERVAL datatype.

With this structure in mind, let's explore the valid values for the different types of attributes. Because they are different for each component, I'll examine one component at a time. Because attributes are set explicitly, one at a time, attributes have no default values. (Earlier, I described the default values of parameters when objects are created.)

Jobs

Attribute	Datatype	Description
auto_drop	BOOLEAN	Whether the job should be dropped after having completed. Valid values are TRUE and FALSE.
comments	VARCHAR2	Comments.
end_date	TIMESTAMP	Date after which the job will no longer run. The job will be dropped if auto_drop is set or disabled, and the state is changed to COMPLETED if it is. If this attribute is set, schedule_name must be NULL.
instance_stickiness	BOOLEAN	If this is a RAC database, then the job starts on any one of the instances. The next run may be on a different instance, where the load is light. If this attribute is set to TRUE, the same instance is used, even if that is not the one with the lightest load. Valid values are TRUE and FALSE.
job_action	VARCHAR2	Nature of the program: • For a PL/SQL block, specify the anonymous block to execute. • For a stored procedure, specify the name of the stored procedure. You can also qualify it with a schema and package name. • For an executable, specify the full path name for the operating system executable or shell script.
job_class	VARCHAR2	Job class with which this job is associated.

Attribute	Datatype	Description
job_priority	PLS_INTEGER	Priority of this job relative to other jobs in the same job class. If multiple jobs within a class are scheduled to be executed at the same time, the job priority determines the order in which jobs from that class are picked up for execution by the job coordinator. Valid values are between 1 (highest priority) and 5 (lowest priority). Default is 3.
job_type	VARCHAR2	Type of this job. Valid values are: • PLSQL_BLOCK • STORED_PROCEDURE • EXECUTABLE If this is set, program_name must be NULL.
job_weight	PLS_INTEGER	Degree of parallelism for the job. Valid values are between 1 and 100. Default is 1.
logging_level	PLS_INTEGER	How much information is logged for the job. Overrides the job class properties. Valid values are: • DBMS_SCHEDULER.LOGGING_OFF • DBMS_SCHEDULER.LOGGING_RUNS (default) • DBMS_SCHEDULER.LOGGING_FULL
max_failures	PLS_INTEGER	How many failures of the job are allowed before the status is set to BROKEN. Must be between 1 and 1,000,000. Default is NULL, which indicates that new instances of the job will be started regardless of how many previous instances have failed. This is also a departure from the old DBMS_JOB package, which only allowed a maximum of 16 failures before marking the job as BROKEN (that number was not configurable).
max_runs	NUMBER	Maximum number of consecutive scheduled runs of the job. Once max_runs is reached, the job is disabled and its state is changed to COMPLETED. Must be between 1 and 1,000,000. Default is NULL, which means that the job will repeat forever or until end_date or max_failures is reached.
number_of_arguments	PLS_INTEGER	Number of arguments if the program is included inline. If this attribute is set, program_name must be NULL.
program_name	VARCHAR2	Name of a program object to use with this job. If this attribute is set, job_action, job_type, and number_of_arguments must be NULL.
repeat_interval	INTERVAL	Character expression using the calendar string syntax (see the earlier description). For example: "FREQ=YEARLY; BYMONTH=12"
restartable	BOOLEAN	Specifies whether the job should be retried after failing; valid values are TRUE and FALSE. Default is TRUE.
schedule_limit	PLS_INTEGER	In heavily loaded systems, jobs are not always started at their scheduled time. This attribute tells the Scheduler not to start a job at all if the delay in starting the job is longer than the interval specified. Valid values are between 1 minute and 99 days. For example, if a job was supposed to start at noon and the schedule limit is set to 60 minutes, the job will not be run if it has not started to run by 1:00 P.M. If schedule_limit is not specified, the job is executed at some later date as soon as there are resources available to run it. By default, this attribute is set to NULL, which indicates that the job can be run at any time after its scheduled time. A scheduled job run that is skipped because of this attribute does not count against the number of runs and failures of the job. An entry in the job log will be made to reflect the skipped run.

Attribute	Datatype	Description
schedule_name	VARCHAR2	Name of a schedule, window, or window group to use as the schedule for this job. If this attribute is set, end_date, start_date, and repeat_interval must all be NULL.
start_date	VARCHAR2	Original timestamp at which this job started or will be scheduled to start. If this attribute is set, schedule_name must be NULL.
stop_on_window_close	BOOLEAN	Window close choice. When a job is assigned a window and the window closes while the job is running, what should happen? If this attribute is set to TRUE, the job will stop as well. If FALSE, the job runs to completion even if the window closes.

Job Classes

Attribute name	Datatype	Description
comments	VARCHAR2	Comments.
log_history	PLS_INTEGER	Amount of history (in days) to keep in the logs for this job class. The range of valid values is 1 through 999.
logging_level	PLS_INTEGER	Specifies how much information is logged; valid values are: • DBMS_SCHEDULER.LOGGING_OFF • DBMS_SCHEDULER.LOGGING_RUNS (default) • DBMS_SCHEDULER.LOGGING_FULL
resource_consumer_group	VARCHAR2	Resource consumer group with which this job class should be associated. If this attribute is set, service must be NULL.
service	VARCHAR2	Service name defined in the database to which the job class belongs. Default is NULL, which implies the default service. If this attribute is set, resource_consumer_group must be NULL.

Schedules

Attribute name	Datatype	Description
comments	VARCHAR2	Comments.
end_date	TIMESTAMP	Cutoff timestamp after which the schedule will not specify any dates.
repeat_interval	VARCHAR2	Character expression using the calendar string syntax (see the earlier description). For example: "FREQ=YEARLY; BYMONTH=12"
start_date	TIMESTAMP	Starting timestamp used by the calendar syntax.

Programs

Attribute name	Datatype	Description
comments	VARCHAR2	Comments.
number_of_arguments	PLS_INTEGER	Number of arguments of the program.

Attribute name	Datatype	Description
program_action	VARCHAR2	Nature of the program: • For a PL/SQL block, specify the anonymous block to execute. • For a stored procedure, specify the name of the stored procedure. You can also qualify it with a schema and package name. • For an executable, specify the full path name for the operating system executable or shell script.
program_type	VARCHAR2	Type of program; valid values are: • PLSQL_BLOCK • STORED_PROCEDURE • EXECUTABLE

Windows

Attribute name	Datatype	Description
comments	TIMESTAMP	Comments.
duration	INTERVAL	Duration of the window.
end_date	TIMESTAMP	Timestamp after which the window will no longer open. If this attribute is set, schedule_name must be NULL.
repeat_interval	VARCHAR2	Character string using the calendar string syntax (see the earlier description). If this attribute is set, schedule_name must be NULL.
resource_plan	VARCHAR2	Resource plan to be associated with a window.
schedule_name	TIMESTAMP	Name of a schedule to use with this window. If this attribute is set, start_date, end_date, and repeat_interval must all be NULL.
start_date	TIMESTAMP	Next timestamp on which this window is scheduled to open. If this attribute is set, schedule_name must be NULL.
window_priority	VARCHAR2	Priority of the window. Must be either LOW or HIGH.

Window Groups

Attribute name	Datatype	Description
comments	TIMESTAMP	Comments for the Window group. This is the only attribute allowed for a window group.

Conclusion

The Oracle Scheduler is a new job management utility introduced in Oracle Database 10g. It is far superior to its predecessor, DBMS_JOB. Using the Scheduler you can schedule both PL/SQL code units (stored procedures and anonymous blocks) and operating system executables for execution. It allows you to use an almost English-like notation to specify a calendar showing the desired times of execution. All Scheduler-related activities are available as APIs in the DBMS_SCHEDULER built-in package. In addition, Enterprise Manager in Oracle Database 10g provides a graphical user interface that may be used to manage job scheduling, making scheduling extremely easy even for those using the utility for the first time. The Scheduler allows you to define a named schedule that can be called independently to execute an action, which may be a complete executable name or a named program that references the executable. Jobs may also be subject to Oracle's resource management framework, which may be used to control the amount of resources (e.g., CPU, parallel query servers) available to individual jobs. In summary, the Scheduler is the only job management system you will need for any jobs except those that definitely need to be de-linked from the database—for example, for starting the database itself.

Quick Reference

This appendix contains summaries of the parameters and datatypes for all of the built-in packages described in this book, as well as lists of the columns in the data dictionary views related to these packages.

DBMS_OBFUSCATION_TOOLKIT

This package is available in Oracle9*i* Database and above, although it is deprecated in Oracle Database 10*g*. It provides support for encryption, decryption, key generation, and hashing.

DES3GETKEY

This program generates an encryption key that is cryptographically secure. The key can be used with the Triple Data Encryption Standard (DES3) encryption algorithm, both the two-pass and three-pass variants. It is overloaded as a function and a procedure, and is further overloaded for different datatypes.

Procedure—Version 1

Accepts two input parameters and returns the key in the OUT parameter.

Parameter name	Datatype	Description
which	BINARY_INTEGER	Number of passes for Triple DES algorithm: 1 for two-pass, 2 for three-pass. The default is 1 (two-pass).
seed_string	VARCHAR2	Seed string to be used in generating the key.
key	VARCHAR2	The only OUT parameter; the generated key is placed here.

Procedure—Version 2

Identical to the first version in that it also accepts two input parameters and returns the key in the OUT parameter. The difference is that the parameters are RAW.

Parameter name	Datatype	Description
which	BINARY_INTEGER	Number of passes for Triple DES algorithm: 1 for two-pass, 2 for three-pass. The default is 1 (two-pass).
seed	RAW	Seed string to be used in generating the key.
key	RAW	The only OUT parameter; the generated key is placed here.

Function—Version 1

Accepts two input parameters and returns the generated key. Returns the key as a VARCHAR2.

Parameter name	Datatype	Description
which	BINARY_INTEGER	Number of passes for Triple DES algorithm: 1 for two-pass, 2 for three-pass. The default is 1 (two-pass).
seed_string	VARCHAR2	Seed string to be used in generating the key.

Function—Version 2

Identical to the first version, except that it deals with RAW datatypes. Returns the key as a RAW value.

Parameter name	Datatype	Description
which	BINARY_INTEGER	Number of passes for Triple DES algorithm: 1 for two-pass, 2 for three-pass. The default is 1 (two-pass).
seed_string	RAW	Seed to be used in generating the key.

DESGETKEY

This program generates the keys for the Data Encryption Standard (DES) algorithm. Like DES3GETKEY, it is overloaded with two procedures and two functions. The parameters are the same, except that there is no *which* parameter. (The DES algorithm uses only a single pass, so there is no need to have a parameter specify two-pass or three-pass schemes as for DES3.)

DES3ENCRYPT

This program is used to encrypt input data using the DES3 algorithm. It is overloaded as a function and a procedure, and is further overloaded for different datatypes.

Procedure—Version 1

Accepts four input parameters and returns the encrypted value in the OUT parameter.

Parameter name	Datatype	Description
input_string	VARCHAR2	Input string to be encrypted. Its length must be a multiple of eight.
key_string	VARCHAR2	Encryption key. Its length must be a multiple of eight.

Parameter name	Datatype	Description
encrypted_string	VARCHAR2	The only OUT parameter; the encrypted value is placed here.
which	BINARY_INTEGER	Number of passes for Triple DES algorithm: 1 for two-pass, 2 for three-pass. The default is 1 (two-pass).
iv_string	VARCHAR2	Initialization vector. This value is added to the input value to reduce the repetition of encrypted values. It is optional. If used, then the combined length of the input string and the IV must be a multiple of eight.

Procedure—Version 2

Identical to the first version, except that it accepts inputs in RAW.

Parameter Name	Datatype	Description
input	RAW	Input string to be encrypted.
key	RAW	Encryption key.
encrypted	RAW	The only OUT parameter; the encrypted value is placed here.
which	BINARY_INTEGER	Number of passes for Triple DES algorithm: 1 for two-pass, 2 for three-pass. The default is 1 (two-pass).
iv	RAW	Initialization vector. This value is added to the input value to reduce the repetition of encrypted values. It is optional.

Function—Version 1

Identical to the procedure version. It accepts four parameters and returns the encrypted value as a VARCHAR2.

Parameter name	Datatype	Description
input_string	VARCHAR2	Input string to be encrypted. Its length must be a multiple of eight.
key_string	VARCHAR2	Encryption key. Its length must be a multiple of eight.
which	BINARY_INTEGER	Number of passes for Triple DES algorithm: 1 for two-pass, 2 for three-pass. The default is 1 (two-pass).
iv_string	VARCHAR2	Initialization vector. This value is added to the input value to reduce the repetition of encrypted values. It is optional. If used, then the combined length of the input string and the IV must be a multiple of eight.

Function—Version 2

Identical to the first version, except that it accepts parameters in RAW and returns the encrypted value as a RAW.

Parameter name	Datatype	Description
input	RAW	Input string to be encrypted.
key	RAW	Encryption key.
which	BINARY_INTEGER	Number of passes for Triple DES algorithm: 1 for two-pass, 2 for three-pass. The default is 1 (two-pass).

Parameter name	Datatype	Description
iv	RAW	Initialization vector. This value is added to the input value to reduce the repetition of encrypted values. It is optional.

DESENCRYPT

This program performs encryption for the DES algorithm. It is overloaded and its programs (two procedures and two functions) are identical to DES3ENCRYPT except that there is no *which* parameter. Because the DES algorithm uses only one pass, there is no need to specify a two- or three-pass scheme as there is with the DES3 algorithm.

DES3DECRYPT

This program decrypts an encrypted data using the DES3 algorithm. As with its encryption sister program DES3ENCRYPT, it is overloaded as a function and a procedure, and is further overloaded for different datatypes.

Procedure—Version 1

Accepts four input parameters and returns the decrypted value in the OUT parameter.

Parameter name	Datatype	Description
input_string	VARCHAR2	Encrypted string to be decrypted.
key_string	VARCHAR2	Encryption key; this must be the same one used during encryption.
decrypted_string	VARCHAR2	The only OUT parameter; the decrypted value is placed here.
which	BINARY_INTEGER	Number of passes for Triple DES algorithm: 1 for two-pass, 2 for three-pass. The default is 1 (two-pass).
iv_string	VARCHAR2	Initialization vector. This value is added to the input value to reduce the repetition of encrypted values. It is optional, but if an IV was used during encryption, it must be specified for decryption as well.

Procedure—Version 2

Identical to the first version, except that it accepts inputs in RAW.

Parameter name	Datatype	Description
input	RAW	Encrypted value to be decrypted.
key	RAW	Encryption key that was used during encryption.
decrypted_data	RAW	The only OUT parameter; the decrypted value is placed here.
which	BINARY_INTEGER	Number of passes for Triple DES algorithm: 1 for two-pass, 2 for three-pass. The default is 1 (two-pass).
iv	RAW	Initialization vector. This value is added to the input value to reduce repetition of encrypted values. It is optional, but if an IV was used during encryption, it must be specified for decryption as well.

Function—Version 1

Identical to the procedure version. It accepts four parameters and returns the decrypted value in VARCHAR2.

Parameter name	Datatype	Description
input_string	VARCHAR2	Input string to be decrypted.
key_string	VARCHAR2	Encryption key; must be the same one used during encryption.
which	BINARY_INTEGER	Number of passes for Triple DES algorithm: 1 for two-pass, 2 for three-pass. The default is 1 (two-pass).
iv_string	VARCHAR2	Initialization vector. This value is added to the input value to reduce the repetition of encrypted values. This parameter must be specified if it was used during encryption, and it must be the same value used for encryption.

Function—Version 2

Identical to the first version, except that it accepts parameters in RAW and returns the decrypted value in RAW.

Parameter name	Datatype	Description
input_string	RAW	Input string to be decrypted.
key_string	RAW	Encryption key; must be the same one used during encryption.
which	BINARY_INTEGER	Number of passes for Triple DES algorithm: 1 for two-pass, 2 for three-pass. The default is 1 (two-pass).
iv_string	RAW	Initialization vector. This value is added to the input value to reduce the repetition of encrypted values. This parameter must be specified if it was used during encryption, and it must be the same value used for encryption.

DESDECRYPT

This program performs encryption for the DES algorithm. Like DES3DECRYPT, it is overloaded and its programs (two procedures and two functions) are identical to DES3ENCRYPT except that there is no *which* parameter. Because the DES algorithm uses only one pass, there is no need to specify a two- or three-pass scheme as there is with the DES3 algorithm.

MD5

This program is used to produce a Message Digest 5 (MD5) hash value of an input value. It is overloaded as a function and a procedure, and is further overloaded for different datatypes.

Procedure—Version 1

Accepts one input parameter and returns the hash value in the OUT parameter.

Parameter name	Datatype	Description
input_string	VARCHAR2	String whose hash value is to be calculated
checksum_string	VARCHAR2	OUT parameter where the hash value is returned

Procedure—Version 2

Identical to the first version, except that the datatypes are RAW.

Parameter name	Datatype	Description
input	RAW	Value whose hash value is to be calculated
checksum	RAW	OUT parameter where the hash value is returned

Function—Version 1

Accepts one input parameter. Returns the hash value as a 16-byte VARCHAR2 value.

Parameter name	Datatype	Description
input_string	VARCHAR2	String whose hash value is to be calculated

Function—Version 2

Accepts one input parameter. Returns the hash value as a 16-byte RAW value.

Parameter Name	Datatype	Description
input	RAW	Value whose hash value is to be calculated

DBMS_CRYPTO

This package is available only in Oracle Database 10*g*. Like the DBMS_OBFUSCATION_ TOOLKIT used in Oracle9*i* Database, it provides encryption, decryption, key generation, and hashing programs. It also provides message authentication code (MAC) programs.

GETRANDOMBYTES

This function generates a cryptographically secure key for encryption. It accepts one input parameter and returns the key as a RAW datatype.

Parameter name	Datatype	Description
number_bytes	BINARY_INTEGER	Length of the random value to be generated

ENCRYPT

This program produces encrypted values from input values. The program is overloaded as a function and two procedures, and is further overloaded for different datatypes.

Function Version

Accepts four input parameters and returns the encrypted value as a RAW datatype.

Parameter name	Datatype	Description
src	RAW	Value to be encrypted. This value may be of any length.
typ	BINARY_INTEGER	Combines the encryption algorithm, padding method, and chaining method.
key	RAW	Encryption key.
iv	RAW	Initialization vector. This value is added to the input value to reduce the repetition of encrypted values. This parameter must be specified if it was used during encryption, and it must be the same value used for encryption.

Procedure—Version 1

Encrypts LOBs. To encrypt non-LOB values, use the function version of ENCRYPT. This version accepts four input parameters and returns the encrypted value as a RAW datatype.

Parameter name	Datatype	Description
dst	BLOB	OUT parameter; the encrypted value is passed back to the user in this parameter.
src	BLOB	BLOB value or resource locator to be encrypted.
typ	BINARY_INTEGER	Combines the encryption algorithm, padding method, and chaining method.
key	RAW	Encryption key.
iv	RAW	Initialization vector. This value is added to the input value to reduce the repetition of encrypted values. It is optional.

Procedure—Version 2

Identical to the first procedure version, except that it is used to encrypt CLOB data.

Parameter name	Datatype	Description
dst	BLOB	OUT parameter; the encrypted value passed back to the user in this parameter.
src	CLOB	CLOB value or resource locator to be encrypted.
typ	BINARY_INTEGER	Combines the encryption algorithm, padding method, and chaining method.
key	RAW	Encryption key.
iv	RAW	Initialization vector. This value is added to the input value to reduce the repetition of encrypted values. It is optional.

DECRYPT

This program decrypts encrypted values. Like ENCRYPT, the program is overloaded as a function and two procedures, and is further overloaded for different datatypes.

Function Version

Accepts four input parameters and returns the decrypted value as a RAW datatype.

Parameter name	Datatype	Description
src	RAW	Encrypted value to be decrypted.
typ	BINARY_INTEGER	Combines the encryption algorithm, padding method and chaining method. It must be the same one used during encryption.
key	RAW	Encryption key; must be the same one used during encryption.
iv	RAW	Initialization vector. This value is added to the input value to reduce the repetition of encrypted values. This parameter must be specified if it was used during encryption, and it must be the same value used for encryption.

Procedure—Version 1

Decrypts encrypted LOBs. To decrypt encrypted non-LOB values, use the function variant of DECRYPT instead. This version accepts four input parameters and returns the decrypted value in the BLOB datatype.

Parameter name	Datatype	Description
dst	BLOB	Decrypted value is placed here.
src	BLOB	Encrypted BLOB value or resource locator to be decrypted.
typ	BINARY_INTEGER	Combines the encryption algorithm, padding method, and chaining method. It must be the same one used during encryption.
key	RAW	Encryption key; must be the same one used during encryption.
iv	RAW	Initialization vector. This value is added to the input value to reduce the repetition of encrypted values. This parameter must be specified if it was used during encryption, and it must be the same value used for encryption.

Procedure—Version 2

Identical to the first procedure version, except that it is used to decrypt encrypted CLOB data.

Parameter name	Datatype	Description
dst	CLOB	Decrypted value is placed here.
src	BLOB	Encrypted BLOB value or resource locator to be decrypted.

Parameter name	Datatype	Description
typ	BINARY_INTEGER	Combines the encryption algorithm, padding method, and chaining method. This value must be the same as the one used during encryption.
key	RAW	Encryption key; must be the same as the one used during encryption.
iv	RAW	Initialization vector. This value is added to the input value to reduce the repetition of encrypted values. This parameter must be specified if it was used during encryption, and it must be the same value used for encryption.

HASH

This program generates cryptographic hash values from the input values. You can generate Message Digest (MD) or Secure Hash Algorithm 1 (SHA-1) hash values by specifying the appropriate typ parameter. This program is overloaded with three functions

Function—Version 1

Generates hash values of non-LOB datatypes. This version accepts two parameters and returns the hash value as a RAW datatype.

Parameter name	Datatype	Description
src	RAW	Input value whose hash value is to be generated
typ	BINARY_INTEGER	Hash algorithm to be used: DBMS_CRYPTO.HASH_MD5 for MD5 or DBMS_CRYPTO.HASH_SH1 for SHA-1

Function—Version 2

Generates hash values of BLOB datatypes. This version accepts two parameters and returns the hash value as a RAW datatype.

Parameter name	Datatype	Description
src	BLOB	Input BLOB value or resource locator whose hash value is to be generated
typ	BINARY_INTEGER	Hash algorithm to be used: DBMS_CRYPTO.HASH_MD5 for MD5 or DBMS_CRYPTO.HASH_SH1 for SHA-1

Function—Version 3

Generates hash values of CLOB datatypes. This version accepts two parameters and returns the hash value as a RAW datatype.

Parameter name	Datatype	Description
src	CLOB	Input CLOB value or resource locator whose hash value is to be generated

Parameter name	Datatype	Description
typ	BINARY_INTEGER	Hash algorithm to be used: DBMS_CRYPTO.HASH_MD4 for MD4, DBMS_CRYPTO.HASH_MD5 for MD5, or DBMS_CRYPTO. HASH_SH1 for SHA-1

MAC

This program generates Message Authentication Code (MAC) values from the input values. MAC values are similar to hash values, but they have an added key. You can generate either Message Digest (MD) or Secure Hash Algorithm 1 (SHA-1) MAC values by specifying the appropriate typ parameter. Like HASH, this program is overloaded with three functions.

Function—Version 1

Generates MAC values of non-LOB datatypes. This version accepts three parameters and returns the MAC value as a RAW datatype.

Parameter name	Datatype	Description
src	RAW	Input value whose MAC value is to be generated
typ	BINARY_INTEGER	MAC algorithm to be used: DBMS_CRYPTO.HMAC_MD5 for MD5 or DBMS_CRYPTO.HMAC_SH1 for SHA-1
key	RAW	Key used to build the MAC value

Function—Version 2

Generates hash values of BLOB datatypes. This version accepts two parameters and returns the hash value as a RAW datatype.

Parameter name	Datatype	Description
src	BLOB	Input value whose MAC value is to be generated
typ	BINARY_INTEGER	MAC algorithm to be used: DBMS_CRYPTO.HMAC_MD5 for MD5 or DBMS_CRYPTO.HMAC_SH1 for SHA-1
key	RAW	Key used to build the MAC value

Function—Version 3

Generates hash values of CLOB datatypes. This version accepts two parameters and returns the hash value as a RAW datatype.

Parameter name	Datatype	Description
src	CLOB	Input value whose MAC value is to be generated
typ	BINARY_INTEGER	MAC algorithm to be used: DBMS_CRYPTO.HMAC_MD5 for MD5 or DBMS_CRYPTO.HMAC_SH1 for SHA-1
key	RAW	Key used to build the MAC value

DBMS_RLS

This package contains all of the programs used to implement row-level security by adding, dropping, enabling, disabling, and refreshing policies. Because some program parameters are new or different in Oracle Database 10*g*, the tables below indicate the differences between the Oracle9*i* Database and Oracle Database 10*g* releases.

ADD_POLICY

This procedure adds an RLS policy on a table.

Parameter name	Datatype	Description	Oracle Database version 9*i*	10*g*
object_schema	VARCHAR2	Owner of the table on which the RLS policy is placed. Default is the current user.	Yes	Yes
object_name	VARCHAR2	Name of the table on which the RLS policy is placed.	Yes	Yes
policy_name	VARCHAR2	Name of the RLS policy being created.	Yes	Yes
function_schema	VARCHAR2	Owner of the policy function. This function produces the predicate that is applied to the query to restrict rows. Default is the current user.	Yes	Yes
policy_function	VARCHAR2	Name of the policy function.	Yes	Yes
statement_types	VARCHAR2	Types of statements to which this policy is applied—SELECT, INSERT, UPDATE, and/or DELETE. Default is all. In Oracle Database 10*g* Release 2, a new type, INDEX, is also available.	Yes	Yes
update_check	BOOLEAN	Possible values—TRUE or FALSE. If set to TRUE, the policy makes sure that the user sees the rows even after the change. Default is FALSE.	Yes	Yes
enable	BOOLEAN	Possible values—TRUE or FALSE. Indicates whether the policy is enabled.	Yes	Yes
static_policy	BOOLEAN	Included if the policy is static.	Yes	Yes
policy_type	BINARY_INTEGER	Dynamism of the policy; STATIC, SHARED_STATIC, CONTEXT_SENSITIVE, SHARED_ CONTEXT_SENSI-TIVE, or DYNAMIC. Prefix with DBMS_RLS, as in POLICY_TYPE=> DBMS_RLS. STATIC. Default is DYNAMIC.	No	Yes
long_predicate	BOOLEAN	If the length of the predicate returned by the policy function is more than 4,000 bytes, you must set this parameter to TRUE; that allows the policy function to return predicates up to 32,000 bytes long. Default is FALSE.	No	Yes
sec_relevant_cols	VARCHAR2	Specifies the list of columns whose selection causes the RLS policy to be applied; otherwise, the RLS policy is not applied to the query.	No	Yes

Parameter name	Datatype	Description	Oracle Database version 9*i*	10*g*
sec_relevant_cols_opt	VARCHAR2	If there are specific columns whose selection triggers use of the RLS policy, then there is a choice: when the user selects the sensitive columns, should the row be displayed with the values of the columns shown as NULL, or should the row not be displayed at all? Setting this parameter to ALL_ROWS chooses the former behavior. Prefix with DBMS_RLS, as in SEC_RELEVANT_COLS_OPT => DBMS_RLS.ALL_ROWS. Default is NULL, which indicates that the rows containing these values should not be displayed.	No	Yes

DROP_POLICY

This procedure drops an existing RLS policy on a table.

Parameter name	Datatype	Description	Oracle Database version 9*i*	10*g*
object_schema	VARCHAR2	Owner of the table on which the RLS policy is placed. Default is the current user.	Yes	Yes
object_name	VARCHAR2	Name of the table on which the RLS policy is placed.	Yes	Yes
policy_name	VARCHAR2	Name of the RLS policy to be dropped.	Yes	Yes

ENABLE_POLICY

This procedure enables or disables an RLS policy on a table.

Parameter name	Datatype	Description	Oracle Database version 9*i*	10*g*
object_schema	VARCHAR2	Owner of the table on which the RLS policy is placed. Default is the current user.	Yes	Yes
object_name	VARCHAR2	Name of the table on which the RLS policy is placed.	Yes	Yes
policy_name	VARCHAR2	Name of the RLS policy to be enabled or disabled.	Yes	Yes
enable	BOOLEAN	TRUE means enable this policy; FALSE means disable this policy.	Yes	Yes

REFRESH_POLICY

This procedure refreshes the predicate on an RLS policy. When a policy is defined as being anything other than DYNAMIC, the policy predicate may not execute. The predicate cached in memory will be used until the expiring condition specified for that predicate occurs. When you want to refresh the policy, simply call the REFRESH_POLICY procedure. It re-executes the policy function and refreshes the cached predicate.

Parameter name	Datatype	Description	Oracle Database version 9i	10g
object_schema	VARCHAR2	Owner of the table on which the RLS policy is placed. Default is the current user.	Yes	Yes
object_name	VARCHAR2	Name of the table on which the RLS policy is placed.	Yes	Yes
policy_name	VARCHAR2	Name of the RLS policy to be refreshed.	Yes	Yes

RLS Data Dictionary Views

This section summarizes the columns in the data dictionary views that are relevant to row-level security.

DBA_POLICIES

This view shows all the RLS policies on the database, whether they are enabled or not.

Column name	Description	Oracle Database version 9i	10g
OBJECT_OWNER	Owner of the table on which the policy is defined.	Yes	Yes
OBJECT_NAME	Name of the table on which the policy is defined.	Yes	Yes
POLICY_GROUP	If this is part of a group, the name of the policy group.	Yes	Yes
POLICY_NAME	Name of the policy.	Yes	Yes
PF_OWNER	Owner of the policy function, which creates and returns the predicate.	Yes	Yes
PACKAGE	If the policy function is a packaged one, this is the name of the package.	Yes	Yes
FUNCTION	Name of the policy function.	Yes	Yes
SEL	Indicates that this is a policy for SELECT statements on this table.	Yes	Yes
INS	Indicates that this is a policy for INSERT statements on this table.	Yes	Yes
UPD	Indicates that this is a policy for UPDATE statements on this table.	Yes	Yes
DEL	Indicates that this is a policy for DELETE statements on this table.	Yes	Yes
IDX	Indicates that this is a policy for CREATE INDEX statements on this table (only for Oracle Database 10g Release 2).	No	Yes
CHK_OPTION	Indicates whether the update check option was enabled when the policy was created.	Yes	Yes
ENABLE	Indicates whether the policy is enabled.	Yes	Yes
STATIC_POLICY	Indicates whether this is a static policy.	Yes	Yes
POLICY_TYPE	Dynamism of the policy (e.g., STATIC). See ADD_POLICY for a complete list.	No	Yes
LONG_PREDICATE	Indicates whether this policy function returns a predicate longer than 4,000 bytes.	No	Yes

DBMS_FGA

This package is used to add, drop, enable, and disable fine-grained auditing policies. Because some program parameters are new or different in Oracle Database 10*g*, the tables below indicate the differences between the Oracle9*i* Database and Oracle Database 10*g* releases.

ADD_POLICY

This procedure adds an FGA policy on a table.

Parameter name	Datatype	Description	Oracle Database version 9*i*	10*g*
object_schema	VARCHAR2	Schema name whose tables are to be under FGA.	Yes	Yes
object_name	VARCHAR2	Name of the table on which FGA is enabled.	Yes	Yes
policy_name	VARCHAR2	Name of the policy.	Yes	Yes
audit_condition	VARCHAR2	Condition under which the audit trail will be generated (e.g., USER='SCOTT').	Yes	Yes
audit_column	VARCHAR2	Auditing will be triggered only if columns from this list are selected.	Yes	Yes
handler_schema	VARCHAR2	If the policy has a handler module, the owner of that module. Handler modules are either procedures or packages that execute automatically when the audit condition is satisfied.	Yes	Yes
handler_module	VARCHAR2	Name of the handler procedure or package.	Yes	Yes
enable	BOOLEAN	Indicates whether the policy is created as enabled. Default is enabled.	Yes	Yes
statement_types	VARCHAR2	Which types of statements are audited. Valid values are SELECT, INSERT, DELETE, and UPDATE.	No	Yes
audit_trail	BINARY_INTEGER	If you need to capture bind variables as well as SQL text, set this parameter to DB_EXTENDED (which is the default). Otherwise, set it to DB. In Oracle Database 10*g* Release 2, you can define another type—XML—that writes audit trails in XML format in the filesystem.	No	Yes
audit_column_opts	BINARY_INTEGER	When the parameter audit_column is set, auditing is triggered only if those columns are selected. If this parameter is set to ALL_COLUMNS, auditing is triggered only if all of the columns mentioned in the parameter audit_column are selected. If this parameter is set to ANY_COLUMNS, then auditing kicks in if any of the columns are selected.	No	Yes

DROP_POLICY

This procedure drops an FGA policy that was previously created on a table.

Parameter name	Datatype	Description	Oracle Database version 9i	10g
object_schema	VARCHAR2	Owner of the table under FGA	Yes	Yes
object_name	VARCHAR2	Name of the table on which FGA is enabled	Yes	Yes
policy_name	VARCHAR2	Name of the policy to be dropped	Yes	Yes

DISABLE_POLICY

This procedure disables an FGA policy that was previously created on a table. The policy is not dropped, but its effect is disabled.

Parameter name	Datatype	Description	Oracle Database version 9i	10g
object_schema	VARCHAR2	Owner of the table under FGA	Yes	Yes
object_name	VARCHAR2	Name of the table on which FGA is enabled	Yes	Yes
policy_name	VARCHAR2	Name of the policy to be disabled	Yes	Yes

ENABLE_POLICY

This procedure enables an FGA policy that was previously created on a table. The specified policy must have already been created.

Parameter name	Datatype	Description	Oracle Database version 9i	10g
object_schema	VARCHAR2	Owner of the table under FGA	Yes	Yes
object_name	VARCHAR2	Name of the table on which FGA is established	Yes	Yes
policy_name	VARCHAR2	Name of the policy to be enabled	Yes	Yes

FGA Data Dictionary Views

This section summarizes the columns in the data dictionary views that are relevant to fine-grained auditing.

DBA_AUDIT_POLICIES

This view shows the FGA policies created on the database.

Column name	Description	Oracle Database version 9i	Oracle Database version 10g
OBJECT_SCHEMA	Owner of the table on which the policy is defined.	Yes	Yes
OBJECT_NAME	Name of the table on which the policy is defined.	Yes	Yes
POLICY_NAME	Name of the defined policy.	Yes	Yes
POLICY_TEXT	Condition under which the auditing should be triggered (e.g., "SALARY>1500") is recorded here.	Yes	Yes
POLICY_COLUMN	Columns whose selection triggers the audit.	Yes	Yes
PF_SCHEMA	If the policy has a handler module, its owner is recorded here. The handler module executes automatically when the audit condition is satisfied.	Yes	Yes
PF_PACKAGE	If the handler module is a packaged procedure, the name of package is recorded here.	Yes	Yes
PF_FUNCTION	Name of the handler. If the handler module is a packaged procedure, this column shows the name of the procedure.	Yes	Yes
ENABLED	Indicates whether the policy is currently enabled.	Yes	Yes
SEL	Indicates whether the policy applies to SELECT statements.	No	Yes
INS	Indicates whether the policy applies to INSERT statements	No	Yes
UPD	Indicates whether the policy applies to UPDATE statements.	No	Yes
DEL	Indicates whether the policy applies to DELETE statements.	No	Yes
AUDIT_TRAIL	Type of auditing. If the value is DB_EXTENDED, it records bind variables in the trail. If the value is DB, bind variables are not recorded. In Oracle Database 10g Release 2, this column might also show XML, which indicates that the audit trail is in XML format in the operating system.	No	Yes
POLICY_COLUMN_OPTIONS	Indicates whether auditing is triggered when *all* of the columns are selected or just *any* one of them, from the list shown in the column POLICY_COLUMN.	No	Yes

DBA_FGA_AUDIT_TRAIL

This view shows the FGA audit trail.

Column name	Description	Oracle Database version 9i	Oracle Database version 10g
SESSION_ID	AUDIT SESSION identifier. This is a unique session ID number; it is not the same as the SID column from the V$SESSION view.	Yes	Yes
TIMESTAMP	Time of the trail entry.	Yes	Yes
DB_USER	Database user that issued this query recorded in the trail.	Yes	Yes
OS_USER	Operating system user.	Yes	Yes
USERHOST	Hostname of the user.	Yes	Yes

Column name	Description	Oracle Database version 9i	10g
CLIENT_ID	Client identifier of the session, if defined.	Yes	Yes
ECONTEXT_ID	Only in Oracle Database 10g Release 2. If a context is defined, the context ID is shown here.	No	Yes (R2)
EXT_NAME	If the user is externally authenticated, the external name is shown here.	Yes	Yes
OBJECT_SCHEMA	Owner of the table referenced by the statement.	Yes	Yes
OBJECT_NAME	Name of the table.	Yes	Yes
POLICY_NAME	Name of the policy that triggered this entry.	Yes	Yes
SCN	System Control Number of the database when this audit trail entry was generated. Used for flashback queries.	Yes	Yes
SQL_TEXT	Text of the SQL statement issued by the user.	Yes	Yes
SQL_BIND	Bind variables and their values in the SQL statement.	Yes	Yes
COMMENT$TEXT	Additional information about the audit trails is recorded here, if available.	Yes	Yes
STATEMENT_TYPE	Indicates the type of statement (e.g., SELECT).	No	Yes
EXTENDED_TIMESTAMP	Extended timestamp of the audit entry. This is recorded in the TIMESTAMP datatype, which offers a precision up to one-thousandth of a second.	No	Yes
PROXY_SESSIONID	If the user has logged in as a proxy user, this indicates the SID of the proxy session.	No	Yes
GLOBAL_UID	If the user is an enterprise user, authenticated by LDAP or some other mechanism, then the global UID is listed here.	No	Yes
INSTANCE_NUMBER	Instance ID, relevant only if the database is a Real Application Cluster (RAC).	No	Yes
OS_PROCESS	Operating system Process ID.	No	Yes
TRANSACTIONID	If the statement is a transaction, then the transaction ID is recorded here.	No	Yes
STATEMENTID	A single session may have several statements (e.g., a user selected from one table, then from another, etc.). Each statement has a unique statement ID.	No	Yes
ENTRYID	A single statement may, in turn, invoke several recursive statements, which are identified by a unique entry ID.	No	Yes

FLASHBACK_TRANSACTION_QUERY

This view shows the transactions in the system available in the undo segments. You can use this information to find out details on transactions. Available only in Oracle Database 10g.

Column name	Description
XID	Transaction identifier.
START_SCN	SCN number at the start of the transaction.

Column name	Description
START_TIMESTAMP	Start time of the transaction, in TIMESTAMP format.
COMMIT_SCN	SCN when the transaction was committed.
COMMIT_TIMESTAMP	Time when the transaction was committed, in TIMESTAMP format.
LOGON_USER	User who performed the transaction.
UNDO_CHANGE#	SCN number of the undo operation.
OPERATION	Operation performed by the transaction (e.g., SELECT). PL/SQL blocks will show up as either DECLARE or BEGIN.
TABLE_NAME	Name of the table on which the operation was performed.
TABLE_OWNER	Owner of the table.
ROW_ID	Rowid of the row that was modified by this transaction.
UNDO_SQL	SQL that can be used to undo the transaction.

DBMS_RANDOM

This package contains programs that generate random values (numbers or strings) and perform other randomization operations.

SEED

This program initializes the DBMS_RANDOM package with a user-specified "seed" that will be used to generate random values. Having a different seed value for different programs ensures the generation of sufficiently random values. SEED is overloaded: both versions are functions, each accepting a parameter of a different datatype.

Function—Version 1

Accepts a single parameter, val, which will be used as the seed value. The parameter is a VARCHAR2 value, which may be up to 2,000 bytes.

Function—Version 2

Accepts a single parameter, val, which will be used as the seed value. The parameter is a BINARY_INTEGER value.

VALUE

This program returns a random number: a positive, floating-point number less than one. VALUE is overloaded: both versions are functions, one with parameters and one without.

Function—Version 1 (no parameters)

Returns a random number in the NUMBER datatype. There are no parameters.

Function—Version 2 (parameters)

Returns a random number in the NUMBER datatype. This version accepts two input parameters: low and high. The returned value will be between the low and high values.

Parameter name	Datatype	Description
low	NUMBER	Lower-bound for the returned random number
high	NUMBER	Upper-bound for the returned random number

STRING

This function returns a random string. This string is of a user-specified length and distribution of characters. It accepts two input parameters.

Parameter name	Datatype	Description
opt	VARCHAR2	Option specifying the random string to be generated (see the following table for options)
len	NUMBER	Length of random string to be generated

The opt parameter may have any of the values shown in the following table.

opt value	Effect
u	Generates uppercase alphabets only (e.g., DFTHNDSW)
l	Generates lowercase alphabets only (e.g., pikdcdsd)
a	Generates mixed-case alphabets (e.g., DeCWCass)
x	Generates a mixture of uppercase alphabets and numbers (e.g., A1W56RTY)
p	Generates any printable characters (e.g., $\$2sw&*)

NORMAL

This function, like the VALUE function, returns a random number. However, the pattern of random number generation for NORMAL follows a normal distribution. That means that if you execute this function several times in succession, the generated numbers will follow a random number distribution. The NORMAL function has no input parameters.

DBMS_SCHEDULER

This package is used to schedule jobs in the database to be executed at some given point in time and with some specified periodicity. It contains all the programs necessary to create and maintain jobs, job classes, schedules, programs, windows, and window groups.

CREATE_JOB

This program creates a job to be executed either immediately or later. It is overloaded as four versions, all procedures.

Procedure—Version 1 (no named objects)

This version is the quickest way to create a job. It accepts all of the components needed to creat a job (e.g., calendar, job action) defined in a granular manner without explicit names.

Parameter name	Datatype	Description
job_name	VARCHAR2	Name of the job.
job_type	VARCHAR2	Type of the job. Valid values are PLSQL_BLOCK, STORED_PROCEDURE, and EXECUTABLE.
job_action	VARCHAR2	What the job actually does. It depends on the previous parameter. If job_type is PLSQL_BLOCK, this is the entire PL/SQL block. STORED_PROCEDURE requires the name of the stored procedure. EXECUTABLE requires the name of the OS executable with the full path.
number_of_arguments	PLS_INTEGER	If the job's action, as shown in the previous parameter, accepts some input parameter, then the number of parameters is shown here. Default is 0.
start_date	TIMESTAMP WITH TIMEZONE	Date and time the job is to start. If this is NULL (the default), then the job starts immediately.
repeat_interval	VARCHAR2	Calendar string, which determines when the job should repeat—for example, "FREQ=DAILY BYHOUR=3". For a complete list of values in the calendar string, see Chapter 8. Default is NULL, which indicates that the job will never be repeated; it will be executed only once at the start_date.
end_date	TIMESTAMP WITH TIMEZONE	If set, this indicates when the job should stop executing. Default is NULL, which means never stop.
job_class	VARCHAR2	Job classes determine the resource consumption profile of the job as well as the logging level, etc. Oracle comes with a predefined job class, "DEFAULT_JOB_CLASS". If this parameter is not specified, then this job belongs to the default job class.
enabled	BOOLEAN	Specified if this job is enabled to be run. Default is FALSE, which indicates that the job is created disabled by default. You must set this parameter to TRUE to enable it at creation.
auto_drop	BOOLEAN	If set to TRUE, the job is dropped after execution. Set it to FALSE to avoid having it be dropped. Default is TRUE.
comments	VARCHAR2	Comments on the job.

Procedure—Version 2 (named schedule but inline action)

Identical to Version 1, except that the schedule is specified as a named schedule, not in calendar string format.

Parameter name	Datatype	Description
job_name	VARCHAR2	Name of the job.
schedule_name	VARCHAR2	Name of the schedule created earlier. If this schedule is owned by a different user, then the owner's name is prefixed, (e.g., SCHED_ADMIN.EVERY_DAY). Because the schedule defines when the job starts, ends, and how often it runs, the corresponding parameters (start_date, end_date, and repeat_interval) are absent.
job_type	VARCHAR2	Type of job. Valid values are PLSQL_BLOCK, STORED_PROCEDURE, and EXECUTABLE.
job_action	VARCHAR2	What the job actually does. It depends on the previous parameter. If job_type is PLSQL_BLOCK, this is the entire PL/SQL block. STORED_PROCEDURE requires the name of the stored procedure. EXECUTABLE requires the name of the OS executable with the full path.
number_of_arguments	PLS_INTEGER	If the job's action (shown in the previous parameter) accepts some input parameter, the number of parameters is shown here. Default is 0.
job_class	VARCHAR2	Job classes determine the resource consumption profile of the job as well as the logging level, etc. Oracle comes with a predefined job class, "DEFAULT_JOB_CLASS". If this parameter is not specified, then this job belongs to the default job class.
enabled	BOOLEAN	Specified if this job is enabled to be run. Default is FALSE, which indicates that the job is created disabled by default. You must set this parameter to TRUE to enable it at creation.
auto_drop	BOOLEAN	If set to TRUE, the job is dropped after execution. Set it to FALSE to avoid having it be dropped. Default is TRUE.
comments	VARCHAR2	Comments on the job.

Procedure—Version 3 (named program as action but inline schedule)

Identical to Version 2 except that it accepts the calendar as a string and a named program. With this version, you use a named program instead of declaring the job action on the fly.

Parameter name	Datatype	Description
job_name	VARCHAR2	Name of the job.
program_name	VARCHAR2	Name of the named program, which you must have defined earlier. If the program is owned by a different owner, then the program name must be qualified with the owner's name (e.g., JOB_ADMIN.CALC_INT). Because the program defines all of the characteristics of the action, the corresponding parameters (e.g., job_action) are not present.

Parameter name	Datatype	Description
start_date	TIMESTAMP WITH TIMEZONE	Date and time the job is to start. If this is NULL (the default), then the job starts immediately.
repeat_interval	VARCHAR2	Calendar string, which determines when the job should repeat—for example, "FREQ=DAILY BYHOUR=3". For a complete list of values in the calendar string, see Chapter 8. Default is NULL, which indicates that the job will never be repeated; it will be executed only once at the start_date.
end_date	TIMESTAMP WITH TIMEZONE	If set, this indicates when the job should stop executing. Default is NULL, which means never stop.
job_class	VARCHAR2	Job classes determine the resource consumption profile of the job as well as the logging level, etc. Oracle comes with a predefined job class, "DEFAULT_JOB_CLASS". If this parameter is not specified, then this job belongs to the default job class.
enabled	BOOLEAN	Specified if this job is enabled to be run. Default is FALSE, which indicates that the job is created disabled by default. You must set this parameter to TRUE to enable it at creation.
auto_drop	BOOLEAN	If set to TRUE, the job is dropped after execution. Set it to FALSE to avoid having it be dropped. Default is TRUE.
comments	VARCHAR2	Comments on the job.

Procedure—Version 4 (named program and named schedule)

The simplest of all job creation procedures. If you create a job using this version, you have to specify only the program name and the schedule name, both of which must have been defined earlier.

Parameter name	Datatype	Description
job_name	VARCHAR2	Name of the job.
program_name	VARCHAR2	Name of the named program, which you must have defined earlier. If the program is owned by a different owner, then the program name must be qualified with the owner's name (e.g., JOB_ADMIN.CALC_INT). Because the program defines all of the characteristics of the action, the corresponding parameters (e.g., job_action) are not present.
schedule_name	VARCHAR2	Name of the schedule created earlier. If this schedule is owned by a different user, then the owner's name is prefixed, e.g., SCHED_ADMIN.EVERY_DAY. Because the schedule defines when the job starts, ends, and how often it runs, the corresponding parameters (start_date, end_date, and repeat_interval) are absent.

Parameter name	Datatype	Description
job_class	VARCHAR2	Job classes determine the resource consumption profile of the job as well as the logging level, etc. Oracle comes with a predefined job class, "DEFAULT_JOB_CLASS". If this parameter is not specified, then this job belongs to the default job class.
enabled	BOOLEAN	Specified if this job is enabled to be run. Default is FALSE, which indicates that the job is created disabled by default. You must set this parameter to TRUE to enable it at creation.
auto_drop	BOOLEAN	If set to TRUE, the job is dropped after execution. Set it to FALSE to avoid having it be dropped. Default is TRUE.
comments	VARCHAR2	Comments on the job.

CREATE_JOB_CLASS

This procedure creates a job class that can be subsequently associated with jobs. A job class need not contain any job. When jobs are defined as a part of a class, the attributes of the job class, such as logging level, resource consumer group, and so on, are also applied to the jobs in that class.

Parameter name	Datatype	Description
job_class_name	VARCHAR2	Name of the job class. Must be unique in the database.
resource_consumer_group	VARCHAR2	Name of the resource consumer group defined in the database earlier. There is no default. If not specified, NULL is assumed. In that case, the job class is not associated with any resource plans in the database and is not subject to any restrictions on resources.
service	VARCHAR2	Service name (if the database has service names defined on it) to which the job class must belong.
logging_level	PLS_INTEGER	Amount of log information written on the jobs under this job class. Three possible values are: DBMS_SCHEDULER.LOGGING_OFF indicates that no log information is written. DBMS_SCHEDULER.LOGGING_RUNS indicates that logs are written only when jobs are run. DBMS_SCHEDULER.LOGGING_FULL indicates that logs are written on every operation on the job (e.g., ALTER, DROP) in addition to the usual runs.
log_history	PLS_INTEGER	How many days worth of logs are kept. After this many days, the log entries are deleted.
comments	VARCHAR2	Comments on the job class.

STOP_JOB

This procedure stops a running job.

Parameter name	Datatype	Description
job_name	VARCHAR2	Name of the job to be stopped. You can also specify a series of jobs separated by commas (e.g., "JOB1,JOB2", etc.).
		Alternately, you may specify the name of a job class. If a job class is specified, then all the jobs under the job class are stopped.
force	BOOLEAN	If the job is currently running, this procedure attempts to stop the job using an interrupt. However, the job may not be stopped immediately, and the stop job command will have to wait. If this parameter is set to TRUE, then the procedure kills the job slaves. Default is FALSE.

RUN_JOB

This procedure runs a job now, even if it is not scheduled to execute right now.

Parameter name	Datatype	Description
job_name	VARCHAR2	Name of the job.
use_current_session	BOOLEAN	If set to TRUE, the job runs in the current session and the messages appear on the user's screen immediately. This is very useful in helping to debug a job. If set to FALSE, then the job runs in the background as another session, just as it normally would. Default is TRUE.

COPY_JOB

This procedure creates a new job from an old job's definition. It is very useful to be able to quickly create a job "like" an existing one, but with a new name.

Parameter name	Datatype	Description
old_job	VARCHAR2	Name of the job whose attributes are to be copied.
new_job	VARCHAR2	Name of the new job that is created as the old one. The new job is created disabled; you must explicitly enable it.

DISABLE

This procedure is used to disable components of the job system. It is very useful in cases where a temporary halt in scheduling is necessary. For example, suppose that you have a job to calculate and apply interest to accounts, but the program has a bug that is currently being investigated. Until that is fixed, you want to make sure the apply_interest job does not run. Instead of dropping it, you can disable it. Disabling a job preserves all the information about the job, but does not execute it. Later on, you can enable it.

This procedure is used to disable all types of Scheduler components—jobs, job classes, schedules, programs, windows, and window groups. Based on the object specified, the behavior differs.

Parameter name	Datatype	Description
name	VARCHAR2	Name of the object (prefixed by owner, if this is an application) that needs to be disabled. You can also include a comma-delimited list to specify many objects.
force	BOOLEAN	Based on the input name, this parameter shows different properties. Basically, if set to TRUE, it forces the dependent objects to be altered as well, Default is FALSE, which does not alter the dependent objects.

ENABLE

This procedure is the corollary to the DISABLE procedure. It is used to enable disabled objects. Like its cousin, it is used to enable all types of Scheduler components—jobs, job classes, schedules, programs, windows, and window groups.

Parameter name	Datatype	Description
name	VARCHAR2	Name of the object (prefixed by owner, if it is an application) that needs to be enabled. You can also include a comma-delimited list to specify many objects.

DROP_JOB

This procedure drops a job when it is no longer needed.

Parameter name	Datatype	Description
job_name	VARCHAR2	Name of the job to be dropped. You can also specify a series of jobs separated by commas (e.g., "JOB1,JOB2", etc.).
		Alternatively, you may specify the name of a job class. If a job class is specified, then all the jobs under the job class are dropped.
		Note that you cannot drop a job class by specifying it here. You have to use DROP_JOB_CLASS procedure.
force	BOOLEAN	If the job is currently running, then it can't be dropped. Setting this parameter to TRUE makes the procedure attempt to stop the job first before dropping it. The default is FALSE, which results in an error when DROP_JOB is issued.

DROP_JOB_CLASS

This procedure drops a job class when it is no longer needed.

Parameter name	Datatype	Description
job_class_name	VARCHAR2	Name of the job class to be dropped. You can also specify a series of jobs separated by commas (e.g., "JOB_CLASS1,JOB_CLASS2", etc.).

Parameter name	Datatype	Description
force	BOOLEAN	If you have jobs defined under this class, you cannot drop the job class. Setting this parameter to TRUE marks the jobs disabled and allows dropping of the job class. Default is FALSE. If a job belonging to the job_class is running now, it is not affected.

CREATE_SCHEDULE

This procedure creates a named schedule that can be used while creating a job. This allows you to use a named schedule instead of a string of calendar values.

Parameter name	Datatype	Description
schedule_name	VARCHAR2	Name of the schedule. It must be unique in the database.
start_date	TIMESTAMP WITH TIMEZONE	Date when the schedule starts to take effect. Default is NULL, which means immediately.
repeat_interval	VARCHAR2	Calendar string that determines how often the schedule should be repeated, (e.g., "FREQ=DAILY; BYHOUR=3"). For a complete list, see Chapter 8.
end_date	TIMESTAMP WITH TIMEZONE	Date when the schedule will end. Default is NULL, which means it never ends.
comments	VARCHAR2	Comments on the schedule.

DROP_SCHEDULE

This procedure drops a named schedule.

Parameter name	Datatype	Description
schedule_name	VARCHAR2	Name of the schedule to be dropped.
force	BOOLEAN	If the schedule is referenced by a job or a window, then you cannot drop it. If this parameter is set to TRUE, it will disable the job or the window and then drop the schedule. Default is FALSE.

CREATE_WINDOW

This program creates a named window, which can be used as a schedule for a job. The program is overloaded into two versions, both procedures.

Procedure—Version 1 (named schedule)

Creates a named window. The schedule of the window (i.e., the information on how often the window is to be repeated) is specified as a named schedule, which must have been defined earlier.

Parameter name	Datatype	Description
window_name	VARCHAR2	Name of the window. Must be unique in the database.
resource_plan	VARCHAR2	Resource Manager plan under which this window will be placed. You must specify this parameter, and you must supply a valid Resource Manager plan.
schedule_name	VARCHAR2	Named schedule this window will follow.
duration	INTERVAL DAY TO SECOND	How long this window will stay open.
window_priority	VARCHAR2	Priority of the window. Valid values are LOW and HIGH; default is LOW. This parameter is only relevant if two windows overlap. The priority determines which window will close to make room for the other.
comments	VARCHAR2	Comments on the window.

Procedure—Version 2 (inline schedule)

Identical to Version 1, but the schedule is specified as an inline calendar string.

Parameter name	Datatype	Description
window_name	VARCHAR2	Name of the window. Must be unique in the database.
resource_plan	VARCHAR2	Resource Manager plan under which this window will be placed. You must specify this parameter, and you must supply a valid Resource Manager plan.
start_date	TIMESTAMP WITH TIMEZONE	Date and time the job is to start. If this is NULL (the default), then the job starts immediately.
repeat_interval	VARCHAR2	Calendar string that determines when the job should repeat (e.g., "FREQ=DAILY BYHOUR=3"). For a complete list of calendar string values, see Chapter 8. The default is NULL, which indicates that the job will never be repeated; it will be executed only once at the start_date.
end_date	TIMESTAMP WITH TIMEZONE	If set, this indicates when the job should stop executing. Default is NULL, which means that it will never stop.
duration	INTERVAL DAY TO SECOND	How long this window will stay open.
window_priority	VARCHAR2	Priority of the window. Valid values are LOW and HIGH; default is LOW. This parameter is only relevant if two windows overlap. The priority determines which window will close to make room for the other.
comments	VARCHAR2	Comments on the window.

CREATE_WINDOW_GROUP

This procedure creates a named window group, that is, a collection of windows. A window group can be used as a schedule for a job.

Parameter name	Datatype	Description
group_name	VARCHAR2	Name of the window group. Must be unique in the database.
window_list	VARCHAR2	Comma-separated list of windows in the window group (e.g., WIN1,WIN2). You can have a window group with no members yet in it. Specifying NULL creates such a window group.
comments	VARCHAR2	Comments on the window group.

ADD_WINDOW_GROUP_MEMBER

While you create a window group, you can define it as having no windows in it. You can add windows to it later on using this procedure. You can also add windows to a window group that already has windows in it.

Parameter name	Datatype	Description
group_name	VARCHAR2	Name of the window group, which must have been already created.
window_list	VARCHAR2	Comma-separated list of windows to be added to the window group (e.g., WIN1,WIN2).

DROP_WINDOW

This procedure drops a window.

Parameter name	Datatype	Description
window_name	VARCHAR2	Name of the window to be dropped.
force	BOOLEAN	If a schedule is referenced by a job or a window, then you cannot drop it. When this parameter is set to TRUE, it will disable the job or the window and then drop the schedule. Default is FALSE.

OPEN_WINDOW

This procedure manually opens a window. A window that has not yet reached its scheduled time is considered closed. You can manually open a closed window using this procedure. Doing so will make sure the jobs associated with the window are run.

Parameter name	Datatype	Description
window_name	VARCHAR2	Name of the window to be opened.
duration	INTERVAL DAY TO SECOND	How long the window will stay open.
force	BOOLEAN	If the window is already open, you cannot reopen it; this procedure will return an error. When this parameter is set to TRUE, the window opening will not cause an error but instead will reset the duration of the window to the duration specified in the previous parameter, starting from that instant.

CLOSE_WINDOW

This procedure allows you to manually force the closing of a window before its scheduled closing time.

Parameter name	Datatype	Description
window_name	VARCHAR2	Name of the window to be closed. The window must currently be open or an error will be generated.

Scheduler Data Dictionary Views

This section summarizes the columns in the data dictionary views that are relevant to scheduling.

DBA_SCHEDULER_JOBS

This view shows the jobs defined in the database.

Column name	Description
OWNER	Owner of the job.
JOB_NAME	Name of the job.
CLIENT_ID	If the user specified the client identifier for the session while creating a job, it is recorded here. You can set the client identifier by calling DBMS_SESSION.SET_IDENTIFIER.
GLOBAL_UID	If the user is a global (or enterprise) user, the global user id is recorded here.
JOB_TYPE	The type of job; valid values are EXECUTABLE, PLSQL_BLOCK, and STORED_PROCEDURE.
JOB_ACTION	What the job does. If it is a PL/SQL code segment, then the entire segment is shown here. If it is an executable or a stored procedure, its name is recorded here.
START_DATE	Start time of the job in the TIMESTAMP datatype.
REPEAT_INTERVAL	Calendar string that specifies the schedule of the job (e.g., "FREQ=DAILY; BYHOUR=2"). (See the section "Calendar Strings" in Chapter 8.)
ENABLED	Whether the job is enabled (TRUE or FALSE).
STATE	Current state this job is in (e.g., SCHEDULED, RUNNING, SUCCEEDED, FAILED).
RUN_COUNT	Number of times this job has been run.
FAILURE_COUNT	Number of times this job has failed.
RETRY_COUNT	If the job failed, it is retried; this column shows how many times it has been retried.
LAST_START_DATE	Timestamp of the last time the job started.
LAST_RUN_DURATION	Duration of the last time the job ran.
NEXT_RUN_DATE	Next time the job is scheduled to run.
SYSTEM	Indicates whether a job is a system job (TRUE or FALSE).
COMMENTS	Comments entered by you earlier.

In Oracle Database 10*g* Release 2, a new feature, event-based jobs (not described in this book), enable some jobs to be run based not on time but on the occurrence of certain events. To support this feature, Oracle Database 10*g* Release 2 adds the following new columns to the DBA_SCHEDULER_JOBS view.

JOB_SUBNAME	Name of the secondary job.
SCHEDULE_TYPE	Type of the schedule; valid values are ONCE, CALENDAR, or EVENT.
EVENT_QUEUE_OWNER	Name of the owner of the event queue.
EVENT_QUEUE_NAME	Name of the event queue.
EVENT_QUEUE_AGENT	Agent name of the event queue.
EVENT_CONDITION	Condition that will trigger the occurrence of the event.
EVENT_RULE	Rule that governs the firing of the event and subsequent execution of the job.
RAISE_EVENTS	When a job is completed, another event (or other events) may trigger a different job. Those events are recorded here.

DBA_SCHEDULER_WINDOWS

This view shows the windows defined in the database.

Column name	Description
WINDOW_NAME	Name of the window.
RESOURCE_PLAN	Name of the Resource Manager plan associated with the window.
SCHEDULE_OWNER	If the window has a named schedule, this column shows the name of the owner of the schedule.
SCHEDULE_NAME	Name of the schedule, if any.
START_DATE	Timestamp when the window will open. This is effective only when the window's calendar properties are provided inline, not via a schedule. Shown in the TIMESTAMP(6) WITH TIMEZONE datatype.
REPEAT_INTERVAL	If the window has an inline calendar string, not a named schedule, the calendar string is shown here. (See the section "Calendar Strings" in Chapter 8.)
END_DATE	When a window has an inline schedule (calendar string, not a named schedule), this specifies the timestamp when the window will close permanently. Shown in the TIMESTAMP(6) WITH TIMEZONE datatype.
DURATION	How long the window is open. Shown in the DURATION datatype.
WINDOW_PRIORITY	When two windows overlap, the one with the higher priority will be opened, and the other one will be closed. The priorities are shown as HIGH and LOW.
NEXT_START_DATE	Next timestamp the window is scheduled to open. Shown in the TIMESTAMP(6) WITH TIMEZONE datatype.
LAST_START_DATE	Timestamp of the last time the window was opened. Shown in the TIMESTAMP(6) WITH TIMEZONE datatype.
ENABLED	Specifies whether a window is enabled (TRUE/FALSE).
ACTIVE	Specifies whether a window is open now (TRUE/FALSE).
COMMENTS	Comments about the window.

Oracle Database 10g Release 2 adds several new columns to the DBA_SCHEDULER_ WINDOW view. These are very useful in cases in which the window was manually opened.

SCHEDULE_TYPE	Type of the schedule; may be ONCE, CALENDAR, or EVENT.
MANUAL_OPEN_TIME	If the window was manually opened, the time is recorded here in the TIMESTAMP datatype.
MANUAL_DURATION	If the window is manually opened, the duration is recorded here in the INTERVAL datatype.

DBA_SCHEDULER_SCHEDULES

This view shows the named schedules defined in the database.

Column name	Description
OWNER	Owner of the schedule.
SCHEDULE_NAME	Name of the schedule.
START_DATE	Date and time when the schedule is supposed to start.
REPEAT_INTERVAL	Repeat interval (calendar string) that determines how often the schedule is repeated. Shown in the calendar string syntax (e.g., "FREQ=DAILY; BYMONTH=2"). See the section "Calendar Strings" in Chapter 8.
END_DATE	Date when the schedule ends.
COMMENTS	Comments on the schedule.

Oracle Database 10g Release 2 adds several new columns to the DBA_SCHEDULER_ SCHEDULES view to support the event-based job triggering mechanism.

SCHEDULE_TYPE	Type of the schedule; may be ONCE, CALENDAR, or EVENT.
EVENT_QUEUE_OWNER	Name of the owner of the event queue.
EVENT_QUEUE_NAME	Name of the event queue.
EVENT_QUEUE_AGENT	Agent name of the event queue.
EVENT_CONDITION	Condition that will trigger the occurrence of the event.

DBA_SCHEDULER_PROGRAMS

This view shows the named programs in the database.

Column name	Description
OWNER	Owner of the program.
PROGRAM_NAME	Name of the program.
PROGRAM_TYPE	Type of program; may be PLSQL_BLOCK, STORED_PROCEDURE, or EXECUTABLE.
PROGRAM_ACTION	What the program does. For instance, if the program is a stored procedure, then the name of the stored procedure is shown here. If the program is an executable, then the full path is here.
NUMBER_OF_ARGUMENTS	Number of arguments of the program, if any. If no arguments, then this shows 0.
ENABLED	Whether this is enabled (TRUE/FALSE).
COMMENTS	Comments on the program.

DBA_SCHEDULER_JOB_CLASSES

This view shows the job classes in the database.

Column name	Description
JOB_CLASS_NAME	Name of the job class.
RESOURCE_CONSUMER_GROUP	Name of the resource consumer group that controls the resource allocation for this job class.
SERVICE	Service name this job class should use.
LOGGING_LEVEL	Amount of logging; possible values are: • OFF –no logging is performed here. • RUNS—logs are written only when the jobs are run. • FULL—logs are written during any job activity (e.g., ALTER, DROP).
LOG_HISTORY	Number of days to keep the logs.
COMMENTS	Comments on this job class.

DBA_SCHEDULER_WINDOW_GROUPS

This view shows the window groups defined in the databases.

Column name	Description
WINDOW_GROUP_NAME	Name of the window group.
ENABLED	Whether the window group is enabled; valid values are TRUE and FALSE.
NUMBER_OF_WINDOWS	Number of windows assigned to this group. For the exact window names, refer to the DBA_SCHEDULER_WINGROUP_MEMBERS view.
COMMENTS	Comments on this window group.

DBA_SCHEDULER_WINGROUP_MEMBERS

This view shows the window groups and their associated windows.

Column name	Description
WINDOW_GROUP_NAME	Name of the window group.
WINDOW_NAME	Name of the window.

DBA_SCHEDULER_JOB_LOG

See the detailed description of this view in the section "Managing Logging" in Chapter 8.

DBA_SCHEDULER_JOB_RUN_DETAILS

See the detailed description of this view in the section "Managing Logging" in Chapter 8.

DBA_SCHEDULER_RUNNING_JOBS

This view shows all jobs currently running in the database.

Column name	Description
OWNER	Owner of the job.
JOB_NAME	Name of the job.
SESSION_ID	Session ID, as shown in V$SESSION, of this job process.
SLAVE_PROCESS_ID	Process ID of the slave process.
RUNNING_INSTANCE	Instance number of the database in which this job is running. This parameter is only relevant if this is a clustered database.
RESOURCE_CONSUMER_GROUP	Name of the resource consumer group this job is associated with. This governs how much resource—such as CPU, parallel query server, etc.—is assigned to the job.
ELAPSED_TIME	Elapsed time since this job run started. Shown in the INTERVAL datatype.
CPU_USED	Amount of CPU cycles (in time) consumed by this job. Shown in the INTERVAL datatype.

Oracle Database 10g Release 2 adds several new columns to the DBA_SCHEDULER_ RUNNING_JOBS view.

JOB_SUBNAME	Sub-name of this current job
SLAVE_OS_PROCESS_ID	Operating system process ID of the slave process

Index

We'd like to hear your suggestions for improving our indexes. Send email to *index@oreilly.com*.

B

BEGIN statement, 4, 79
BFILE datatype, 12
BINARY_DOUBLE datatype, 11
BINARY_DOUBLE_INFINITY constant, 7
BINARY_DOUBLE_MAX_NORMAL
    constant, 7
BINARY_DOUBLE_MAX_SUBNORMAL
    constant, 7
BINARY_DOUBLE_MIN_NORMAL
    constant, 7
BINARY_DOUBLE_MIN_SUBNORMAL
    constant, 7
BINARY_DOUBLE_NAN constant, 7
BINARY_FLOAT datatype, 11
BINARY_FLOAT_INFINITY constant, 7
BINARY_FLOAT_MAX_NORMAL
    constant, 7
BINARY_FLOAT_MAX_SUBNORMAL
    constant, 7
BINARY_FLOAT_MIN_NORMAL
    constant, 7
BINARY_FLOAT_MIN_SUBNORMAL
    constant, 7
BINARY_FLOAT_NAN constant, 7
BINARY_INTEGER parameter, 313
bind variables
    cursors, 111
    FGA and, 274, 300
    literals and, 93
    matching algorithms, 91
    NDS and, 102
    performance and, 271
    queries and, 46
    recording, 281–282
BIT_XOR function, 198, 199
bitwise XOR operation, 198, 199
BLOB datatype
    defined, 12
    ENCRYPT procedure, 186
    encryption and, 172
    TDE and, 208
block chaining, 188
block ciphering, 168, 183
blocks
    anonymous, 332, 333, 347
    comment delimiters, 5, 9
    overview, 2–4
    procedures and, 33
Boolean datatype, 12, 76
Boolean literals, 8
BULK COLLECT clause, 52–53, 60, 78

BULK COLLECT INTO clause, 48, 63,
    104–106
bulk fetching
    cursors and, 104–106
    table functions, 117, 136, 137
%BULK_EXCEPTIONS attribute, 47
%BULK_ROWCOUNT attribute, 47, 97
BY clause, 338
BYDAY keyword, 341
BYHOUR keyword, 338, 339–340, 342
BYMINUTE keyword, 338, 340, 342
BYMONTH keyword, 338, 339, 340
BYMONTHDAY keyword, 338, 339, 341
BYSECOND keyword, 338, 340
BYWEEKNO keyword, 342, 343
BYYEARDAY keyword, 338, 339, 341

C

calendar_string parameter (EVALUATE_
    CALENDAR_STRING), 343
calendars
    managing, 338–347
    named schedules and, 328
    schedules and, 327
    windows and, 354, 355, 357
CASE expressions, 16, 17
case sensitivity
    PL/SQL and, 5
    string literals, 7
    wallet passwords, 205
CASE statement, 17, 18
CAST_TO_RAW function, 190
CBC (Cipher Block Chaining), 165, 187, 189
CBO (cost-based optimizer), 82, 93, 269
CFB (Cipher Feedback), 165, 187, 188
CHAIN_CBC constant, 187, 188
CHAIN_CFB constant, 187, 188
CHAIN_ECB constant, 187
CHAIN_OFB constant, 187
chaining
    defined, 165
    ENCRYPT function, 192
    encryption and, 187
    typ parameter, 188
CHAR datatype, 10
character set, 4–6
characters
    datatypes, 10
    generating, 314–318
    returning random values, 307
    statistical patterns, 319–326
checksum parameter (MD5), 378

checksum_string parameter (MD5), 378
CHK_OPTION column, 385
Cipher Block Chaining (CBC), 165, 187, 189
Cipher Feedback (CFB), 165, 187, 188
cleartext
    defined, 161
    encrypting, 169, 207
    hash values and, 218
    security and, 330
client identifiers, 301–302, 361, 365
CLIENT_ID column, 334, 361, 365, 389,
        401
CLIENT_IDENTIFIER column, 302
client-side PL/SQL, 2
CLOB datatype
    defined, 11
    ENCRYPT procedure, 186
    job logs, 361, 362
    TDE and, 208
    window logs, 365, 366
CLOSE statement, 99
CLOSE_WINDOW procedure, 401
closing cursors
    explicit, 50, 101
    implicit, 49
    queries, 47
    soft, 98, 99
CLUSTER clause, 127, 131, 132
cluster streaming, 131, 132
collection methods, 32–33
collections
    BULK COLLECT clause, 52
    defined, 27
    NDS support, 76
    overview, 27–33
    as parameters, 153
    referencing elements, 62
    result sets as, 118, 122
    standardizing names, 152
colon (:), 5, 71, 76
columns
    auditing and, 273, 278, 280, 292–295
    cluster streaming, 131
    combining, 69
    cursors and, 81
    encrypted, 167, 204, 206
    FGA and, 297, 300
    hash values based on, 130
    ORA-28115 error, 229
    records and, 24, 25, 127
    REF cursor and, 106
    RLS and, 221, 247–250

in tables, 25, 30, 44
    updating, 56, 57, 58
    VARRAYs as, 30
    (see also specific columns)
comment block delimiters, 5, 9
comment indicator (--), 5, 9
COMMENT keyword, 65
COMMENT$TEXT column, 389
comments, 5, 8, 9
comments attribute, 367, 369, 370
COMMENTS column
    job classes, 404
    managing jobs, 334
    programs, 403
    scheduling, 401, 402, 403
    window groups, 404
    windows, 357
comments parameter
    CREATE_JOB procedure, 392, 393, 394,
        395
    CREATE_JOB_CLASS procedure, 395
    CREATE_SCHEDULE procedure, 398
    CREATE_WINDOW procedure, 399
    CREATE_WINDOW_GROUP
        procedure, 400
COMMIT statement
    autonomous transactions and, 67
    DML triggers and, 68
    functionality, 64
    overview, 64
COMMIT_SCN column, 293, 390
COMMIT_TIMESTAMP column, 293, 390
commits
    autonomous transactions and, 60
    DDL statements and, 75
    SCN and, 293
    timestamps, 293
compilation, 82, 254
concatenation operator, 5
conditional control statements, 16
conditional expressions, 37
connection pool, 265–267, 301
constants
    declaring, 14, 15
    naming, 10
    package specifications and, 41
constrained declaration, 38
context switch, 60, 104
context-sensitive policy, 251–254, 265
control statements, 16–18
COPY_JOB procedure, 396
cost-based optimizer (CBO), 82, 93, 269

COUNT function, 32
COUNT method, 52
CPU_USED column, 362, 405
CREATE ANY CONTEXT system
    privilege, 260
CREATE CONTEXT statement, 260, 261
CREATE INDEX statement, 250
CREATE JOB system privilege, 347
CREATE TABLE statement, 72, 75
CREATE TYPE statement, 30, 31
CREATE_JOB procedure
    creating windows, 355
    job classes, 352
    managing attributes, 366
    managing jobs, 331–333
    named programs, 348
    parameters, 392–395
    program ownership, 349
    schedules and, 338
    stopping jobs, 356
    window groups, 360
CREATE_JOB_CLASS procedure, 352, 353,
    363, 395
CREATE_PROGRAM procedure, 348
CREATE_SCHEDULE procedure, 345, 346,
    398
CREATE_WINDOW procedure
    creating windows, 354
    end dates for windows, 357
    managing attributes, 366
    parameters, 398–399
    prioritizing windows, 356
CREATE_WINDOW_GROUP
    procedure, 359, 399
CRM (Customer Relationship Management)
    applications, 216
cron command, 328, 329
cryptoanalysis, 169
cryptographic hashing, 208–216
cursor attributes
    DML statements, 58
    explicit, 51, 52
    implicit, 49, 50
    overview, 47, 96, 97
    REF cursors, 108
    referencing, 47
cursor expressions, 46, 103, 110–113
cursor variables
    defined, 54
    functionality, 46
    querying data, 55–56
    referencing cursor attributes, 47

CURSOR_SHARING parameter, 84, 91, 93
cursors
    additional uses, 103–113
    anchoring records to, 16
    closing, 47
    declaration section and, 3
    nested, 103, 110–113, 146–149
    opening, 46
    overview, 81
    packages and, 41, 45
    records and, 25
    reusing, 82–95
    SELECT statements and, 120
    soft-closing, 98–103, 112
    table functions and, 120–122
    (see also explicit cursors; implicit cursors)
Customer Relationship Management (CRM)
    applications, 216

D

daisy-chaining, 124, 143
data
    binary, 12
    changing, 56–63
    cryptographic hashing, 208–216
    decrypting, 169–171, 192, 194, 217
    dynamic access, 108
    encrypting, 165–168, 186–192
    representative, 306
    (see also querying data)
Data Definition Language statements (see
    DDL statements)
data dictionary views
    auditing and, 269, 270, 272, 292–295
    RLS and, 385
    VPD and, 256
    (see also specific views)
data encryption (see encryption)
Data Encryption Standard (see DES)
Data Manipulation Language statements (see
    DML statements)
data warehouses, 115, 120
databases
    administering, 327
    auditing version differences, 273
    key management, 194–202
    nested tables and, 28
    PL/SQL programs and, 2
    program data and, 9
    randomizers, 306
    scheduling jobs within, 329–331
    security, x

NORMAL function, 391
RANDOM function, 311, 312
SEED function, 390
STRING function, 314, 315, 322, 391
VALUE function, 307, 310, 390
(see also random numbers)
DBMS_REDEFINITION package, 272
DBMS_RESOURCE_MANAGER
package, 351
DBMS_RLS package
ALL_ROWS constant, 249
components, 383–385
dropping policies, 227
EXECUTE privilege, 227, 237
new policy types, 251
update checks, 228
(see also RLS)
DBMS_SCHEDULER package
calendar strings, 342
components, 391–405
creating programs, 348
creating windows, 354
end dates for windows, 356
EXECUTE privilege, 347
job classes, 352
log levels supported, 363
managing attributes, 366
managing jobs, 331–337
overview, 327, 329, 331
pruning job logs, 363
windows and, 352
(see also scheduling)
DBMS_SESSION package, 260, 261, 334
DBMS_SQL package, 74, 77
DBMS_TRACE package, 144
DBMS_UTILITY package, 23, 253
DBMS_XMLGEN package, 13
DDL (Data Definition Language) statements
commits and, 75
DDL triggers and, 67, 72–73
debugging, 253–257
(see also exception handling;
troubleshooting)
Decision Support Systems, 270
declaration section
autonomous transactions and, 67
defined, 3
example, 4
explicit cursors, 46, 48, 51
package body and, 43
purpose, 14

declarations
cursor variables, 55
explicit cursors, 51
functions and, 36
package body and, 42
procedures and, 34
program data and, 14–16
records, 25, 26
REF CURSOR types, 54, 150
DECLARE keyword, 79
DECRYPT program, 380, 381
decrypted_data parameter
(DES3DECRYPT), 376
decrypted_string parameter
(DES3DECRYPT), 376
decryption
building tool, 175–176
of data, 169–171, 192, 194, 217
packages and, 373–382
(see also DBMS_CRYPTO package;
DBMS_OBFUSCATION_
TOOLKIT package)
DEFAULT keyword, 15
DEFAULT_JOB_CLASS job class, 363, 364
definer rights model, 34, 36
DEL column, 290, 295, 385, 388
DELETE procedure, 32
DELETE statement
auditing and, 273, 291, 292
controlling table access, 243, 244
DML triggers, 68
EXECUTE IMMEDIATE statement, 75
explicit cursors, 50
FORALL statement and, 61
functionality, 56
implicit cursors, 48
pseudo-records and, 71
RETURNING clause, 63
savepoints and, 66
syntax, 58
triggers and, 271, 296
DELETING function, 72
delimiters
comment block, 5, 9
label, 5
as lexical units, 5
semicolons, 8
DES (Data Encryption Standard)
DBMS_CRYPTO and, 187, 189
ENCRYPT function, 190
Oracle9i Database, 177
overview, 164

EXTENDED_TIMESTAMP column, 292, 389
Extensible Markup Language (XML), 13
Extraction, Transformation, Loading (see ETL processes)

F

FAILURE_COUNT column, 334, 337, 401
false positives, 269
FALSE value, 8, 12
FETCH INTO clause, 52
FETCH statement
    cursor variables, 54, 55
    functionality, 47
    LIMIT clause, 53
fetching
    bulk, 104–106, 117, 136, 137
    cursor variables, 54, 55
    cursors and, 47, 81
    explicit cursors, 50
    implicit cursors, 49
    records, 104–106
Feuerstein, Steven, xviii
FGA (fine-grained auditing)
    administering, 289–291
    application contexts, 301, 302
    auditing techniques, 295–300
    client identifiers, 301–302
    customizing, 277–288
    functionality, 268
    non-database users, 301–302
    Oracle Database 10g, 291–295
    overview, 269–277
    troubleshooting, 302–304
    (see also DBMS_FGA package)
FGA_LOG$ table
    audit trails, 270, 272, 282–284, 288, 292, 300
    SYS schema and, 299
FGAC (fine-grained access control), 269
filtering
    policies and, 226, 238, 247, 248
    predicate and, 222
    tables, 238
fine-grained access control (FGAC), 269
fine-grained auditing (see FGA)
fingerprint match, 162
FIPS Publication 197, 164
FIRST function, 32
FIRST method, 29
FLAGGED_ACCESS table, 288

flashback query, 274–277, 294, 298
FLASHBACK_TRANSACTION_QUERY view, 292–293, 389–390
floating-point type, 7
FOR loops, 11, 14, 19
FORALL statement, 47, 52, 60–63
force parameter (DBMS_SCHEDULER)
    disabling windows, 358, 397
    dropping job classes, 398
    dropping jobs, 337, 397
    dropping schedules, 398
    dropping windows, 358, 400
    job management, 335, 336
    opening windows, 400
    stopping jobs, 396
    window groups, 360
FORCE setting, 93
FORMAT_ERROR_BACKTRACE function, 23
FORMAT_ERROR_STACK function, 23
%FOUND attribute, 47, 51, 97
FREQ clause, 338, 339, 340–342
FROM clause, 115
FUNCTION column, 385
function_schema parameter (ADD_POLICY), 383
functions
    autonomous transactions and, 67
    defined, 33
    error, 23
    exception handling, 24
    named blocks and, 2
    as operational directives, 71
    overview, 35–37
    package specifications and, 41
    parameters and, 37
    predicate, 225
    result sets and, 118
    (see also policy functions; table functions)

G

GET_SYSTEM_CHANGE_NUMBER function, 286
GET_TIME function, 253
GETRANDOMBYTES function, 177
global UID, 361, 365
global variables
    application context and, 259, 264
    policy functions and, 241, 242, 243
GLOBAL_UID column
    audit trails, 292, 389
    job logs, 361

len parameter (STRING), 314, 391
LIMIT clause, 53, 105
LIMIT function, 32
literals
    cursor reuse and, 88–90
    overview, 6–8
    reformatting, 85, 86
LOB datatype
    defined, 11
    encryption and, 157, 172, 184
    NDS support, 76
LOCK TABLE statement, 64
Log Miner feature, 288
LOG_DATE column, 361, 362, 365, 366
log_history attribute, 369
LOG_HISTORY column, 404
log_history parameter (CREATE_JOB_
        CLASS), 395
LOG_ID column, 361, 362, 365, 366
logging, managing, 361–366
logging_level attribute, 363, 368, 369
LOGGING_LEVEL column, 404
logging_level parameter (CREATE_JOB_
        CLASS), 363
LOGOFF trigger, 73, 74
LOGON trigger, 73, 74, 259
LOGON_USER column, 293, 390
LONG datatype, 11
LONG RAW datatype, 12
LONG_PREDICATE column, 385
long_predicate parameter (ADD_
        POLICY), 383
loops
    associative arrays, 29
    index variables, 14
    overview, 18
    PLS_INTEGER datatype and, 11
    table functions, 136
low parameter, 310, 391

M

MAC (Message Authentication Code)
    functionality, 183
    hash values and, 382
    overview, 213–216
    support for, 157
MAC function, 382
main transaction, 66
MANAGE SCHEDULER system
        privilege, 336, 356
MANUAL_DURATION column, 403
MANUAL_OPEN_TIME column, 403

master key, 197, 199–205
max_failures attribute, 368
max_runs attribute, 368
MD (Message Digest), 209, 212
MD4 algorithm, 382
MD5 algorithm, 209–211, 214, 382
Message Authentication Code (see MAC)
Message Digest (MD), 209, 212
methods, 32–33, 67
Monte Carlo simulation, 321, 323
multiline comments, 9
MULTISET EXCEPT set operator, 29, 30

N

name parameter
    DISABLE procedure, 397
    ENABLE procedure, 397
named blocks, 2, 3
named notation, 39, 40
named programs, 328, 347–350
named schedules, 328, 345–346, 354
naming conventions, 10, 152
National Bureau of Standards, 164
National Institute of Standards and
        Technology (NIST), 164
National Language Support (NLS), 93, 172
native dynamic SQL (see NDS)
NCHAR datatype, 10
NCLOB datatype, 11
NDS (native dynamic SQL)
    datatype support, 76
    defined, 74
    dynamic PL/SQL and, 78
    OPEN FOR statement, 77
    soft-closing cursors, 102–103
negative numbers, 311, 339, 340
nesting
    cursors, 103, 110–113, 146–149
    REF CURSOR datatype, 151
    table functions, 120, 124–125, 143
    tables, 28–30
NEW pseudo-record, 71
new_job parameter (COPY_JOB), 396
NEXT function, 32
NEXT_RUN_DATE column, 334, 401
next_run_date parameter (EVALUATE_
        CALENDAR_STRING), 344
NEXT_START_DATE column, 357, 402
NIST (National Institute of Standards and
        Technology), 164
NLS (National Language Support), 93, 172

NO_DATA_FOUND exception, 30, 49–50, 52, 152
NOAUDIT command, 299
normal distribution, 319
NORMAL function, 391
not equal relational operator, 5
NOT NULL clause, 14
%NOTFOUND attribute, 47, 51, 53, 97
NULL statement, 16
NULL value
  Boolean datatype, 12
  Boolean expressions, 8
  column-sensitive RLS and, 249, 250
  generating random values with, 322
  implicit cursor attributes, 50
  NOT NULL clause and, 14
  overview, 6
  passing, 76
  predicates and, 238
NUMBER datatype, 7, 11, 172
number_bytes parameter
    (GETRANDOMBYTES), 378
number_of_arguments attribute, 368, 369
NUMBER_OF_ARGUMENTS column, 403
number_of_arguments parameter (CREATE_
    JOB), 392, 393
NUMBER_OF_WINDOWS column, 404
numbers
  BULK COLLECT clause, 52
  negative, 311, 339, 340
  passing, 76
  positive, 307–311
  predefined datatypes, 11
numeric literals, 7
NVARCHAR2 datatype, 10

O

OBJECT_NAME column, 289, 385, 388, 389
object_name parameter
  ADD_POLICY procedure, 383, 386
  DISABLE_POLICY procedure, 387
  DROP_POLICY procedure, 384, 387
  ENABLE_POLICY procedure, 384, 387
  REFRESH_POLICY procedure, 385
OBJECT_OWNER column, 385
OBJECT_SCHEMA column, 289, 388, 389
object_schema parameter
  ADD_POLICY procedure, 383, 386
  DISABLE_POLICY procedure, 387
  DROP_POLICY procedure, 384, 387

  ENABLE_POLICY procedure, 384, 387
  REFRESH_POLICY procedure, 385
objects
  auditing and, 300
  cursors and, 81
  instances and, 33
  package ownership, 44
  passing, 153
  result sets and, 118
  standardizing names, 152
oerr utility, 304
OFB (Output Feedback), 165, 187
OLD pseudo-record, 71
old_job parameter (COPY_JOB), 396
OPEN FOR statement, 77, 78
OPEN_CURSORS parameter, 99
OPEN_WINDOW procedure, 358, 400
opening
  cursor variables, 55
  cursors, 46
  explicit cursors, 50, 99–101
  implicit cursors, 49, 99–101
OPERATION column, 293, 361, 365, 390
operational directives, 71
operators, 5
OPS$ login, 330
opt parameter (STRING), 314, 315, 391
OPTIMIZER_MISMATCH column, 95
ORA-01000 error, 99
ORA-01007 error, 150
ORA-01031 error, 261
ORA-01555 error, 105
ORA-04081 error, 69, 72
ORA-04085 error, 71
ORA-06550 error, 108
ORA-12090 error, 272
ORA-28102 error, 290
ORA-28110 error, 254
ORA-28112 error, 254
ORA-28113 error, 255
ORA-28115 error, 229
ORA-28138 error, 292
ORA-28233 error, 176, 199
Oracle Advanced Queuing (AQ), 284
Oracle Advanced Security Option
    (ASO), 156, 163, 201
Oracle Database 10g
  auditing version differences, 273
  CBO and, 269
  customizing FGA, 278
  DBA_AUDIT_POLICIES view, 290

comments, 8, 9
identifiers, 6
literals, 6–8
semicolon delimiter, 8
SYS user, 269, 284, 355
SYS_CONTEXT function, 246–247, 260
SYS_REFCURSOR datatype
    examples, 13, 54, 106–109
    table functions and, 149–151
SYSAUX tablespace, 362
System Change Number (SCN), 276–277,
        288, 293
SYSTEM column, 334, 401
System Global Area (SGA), 107, 111, 112
SYSTEM tablespace, 284

T

table functions
    applying criteria, 151
    bulk fetching criteria, 136, 137
    calling, 117
    CURSOR expression, 46
    cursors and, 120–122
    defined, 115
    defining result set structure, 119
    examples, 116, 117, 133, 134, 144–149
    headers for, 135, 136
    nesting, 120, 124–125, 143
    parallelizing, 125–133
    pipelining, 117, 120, 122–124, 142
    repeating records, 137–140
    result set structure, 118, 119
    running, 141–142
    tips for, 149–154
    totals, 142–144
TABLE_NAME column, 293, 390
TABLE_OWNER column, 293, 390
tables
    AUDIT statement, 273
    columns in, 25, 30, 44
    controlling access, 243–247
    controlling activity, 223
    customizing FGA, 277–288
    DDL statements and, 72
    filtering, 238
    foreign-key relationship, 239
    index-by, 27
    index-organized, 12
    key management, 194–202
    materialized views and, 258
    nested, 28–30
    object name parameter and, 227

ORA-12090 error, 272
performance, 105
records and, 25
referential integrity constraints, 257
RLS and, 221
standardizing names, 152
storing keys, 182
TDE and, 203, 204, 206
triggers on, 270
V$SYSSTAT, 82, 83
views and, 222
TDE (Transparent Data
        Encryption), 203–208
TERMINATE procedure, 314
3DES168 encryption algorithm, 206
TIMESTAMP column, 273, 274, 388
TIMESTAMP datatype
    calendar strings, 343
    introduction of, 11
    job logs, 362
    named schedules, 345
    scheduling jobs, 334
    window logs, 366
    windows and, 357
timestamps
    commits and, 293
    controlling table access, 246
    data dictionary view, 273
    datatypes, 11
    extended, 292
    FGA and, 271, 296
    flashback query, 275, 276, 293
    job start, 334
    log entries, 361
    triggers and, 296
    window logs, 365
    windows and, 357
TO clause, 65
TOO_ MANY_ROWS exception, 49
trace file, 256, 302–304
TRANSACTIONID column, 293, 294, 389
transactions, 64, 66, 68
    (see also autonomous transactions)
Transparent Data Encryption
        (TDE), 203–208
Transportable Tablespace feature, 286
triggers
    audit trail, 280, 295, 298
    auditing version differences, 273
    autonomous transactions and, 67
    database event, 67, 73–74
    defined, 33

global, 241, 242, 243, 259, 264
  as identifiers, 6
  index, 14
  initializing, 14
  naming, 10
  package specifications and, 41
  packages and, 45
  randomness and, 313
  (see also bind variables)
variance, 319
VARRAYs (variable-sized arrays), 28, 30, 31
versions, PL/SQL, xiv–xvi
views
  controlling activity, 223
  data dictionary, 256, 269, 270, 272
  FGA and, 297
  materialized, 258
  object name parameter and, 227
  security and, 222
  (see also specific views)
virtual local area network (VLAN), 201
Virtual Private Database (VPD), 240, 256
virus detection, 213
VLAN (virtual local area network), 201
VPD (Virtual Private Database), 240, 256

W

wallets, 203–206
weak types
  cursor variables, 55
  defined, 54
  REF cursors, 107–108
  SYS_REFCURSOR, 54
WHEN clause
  DDL triggers, 73
  DML triggers, 70
  exceptions and, 21, 22
WHEN OTHERS clause, 23
WHERE clause
  audit conditions and, 280
  column sensitivity and, 248
  cursor expressions and, 111
  DELETE statement, 58
  EXECUTE IMMEDIATE statement, 76

predicate and, 222
  triggers and, 297
  UPDATE statement, 57
which parameter
  DES3DECRYPT program, 376, 377
  DES3ENCRYPT program, 172, 375
  DES3GETKEY program, 178, 373, 374
  encryption and, 174
WHILE loops, 20, 29
whitespace, 5, 6
window classes, 328, 391–405
window groups, 328, 359–361, 370
WINDOW_DURATION column, 366
WINDOW_GROUP_NAME column, 404
window_list parameter
  ADD_WINDOW_GROUP_MEMBER
    procedure, 400
  CREATE_WINDOW_GROUP
    procedure, 400
WINDOW_NAME column, 357, 365–366,
    402, 404
window_name parameter
  CLOSE_WINDOW procedure, 401
  CREATE_WINDOW procedure, 399
  OPEN_WINDOW procedure, 400
window_priority attribute, 367, 370
WINDOW_PRIORITY column, 357, 402
window_priority parameter (CREATE_
    WINDOW), 356, 399
windows
  DBMS_SCHEDULER package, 352
  defined, 327
  logging entries, 365–366
  managing, 354–361
  managing attributes, 370
  overview, 328
  schedule_name parameter and, 328
Windows environment, 328, 329
WORK keyword, 65

X

XID column, 293, 294, 389
XML (Extensible Markup Language), 13
XMLType datatype, 13

About the Author

Arup Nanda became a production-support Oracle DBA in the spring of 1993 on Oracle Version 6, where Transaction Processing was an option (i.e., if you didn't purchase it, the entire table would be locked). Ever since, he has swum through the rough waters of many ORA-600s, corrupted disks, and lots of OOPS! while still maintaining his sanity. Arup specializes in such Oracle database areas as Disaster Recovery, High Availability, Real Application Clusters, Grid Control, and Security.

Arup is an active member of the user community (Independent Oracle Users Group and New York Oracle Users Group, for example); writes for several publications (including *Oracle Magazine*, *DBAZine*, and *SELECT Journal*); and speaks at many technical events (including Oracle Open World, IOUG Live!, and local events sponsored by NYOUG). Acknowledging his professional accomplishments and contributions to the user community, Oracle honored him with the title of "DBA of the Year" in 2003. He lives in Danbury, Connecticut with his wife Anindita and son Anish.

Steven Feuerstein is the author or coauthor of *Oracle PL/SQL Programming*, *Oracle PL/SQL Best Practices*, *Oracle PL/SQL for DBAs*, *Oracle PL/SQL Programming: A Developer's Workbook*, *Oracle Built-in Packages*, and several pocket reference books (all from O'Reilly Media). Steven has been developing software since 1980, spent five years with Oracle (1987–1992), and serves as a Senior Technology Advisor to Quest Software. His products include utPLSQL (an open source unit-testing framework for PL/SQL) and Qnxo (an Oracle development toolkit that helps generate, reuse, and unit-test code *http://www.qnxo.com*). He has won numerous awards for his writing and trainings, offers a PL/SQL portal at *http://www.oracleplsqlprogramming.com*, and can be reached via email at *steven@stevenfeuerstein.com*. He lives in Chicago with his wife, Veva, and three cats. Two sons, Eli and Chris, orbit nearby.

Colophon

Our look is the result of reader comments, our own experimentation, and feedback from distribution channels. Distinctive covers complement our distinctive approach to technical topics, breathing personality and life into potentially dry subjects.

The animals on the cover of *Oracle PL/SQL for DBAs* are butterflies. Moths and butterflies comprise a very large group called *Lepidoptera*, or "scaly-winged" insects. An estimated 150,000 different species are included in this group—more than any other type of insect except beetles. Although most species of butterflies are found in tropical areas such as rainforests, they inhabit almost all types of environments throughout the world. The butterfly's only climate demand is adequate heat since it must maintain a body temperature of 86 degrees in order to fly. To solve this problem, some butterflies are not butterflies in the winter, but pupa. Other species hibernate in tree trunks or migrate south. The monarch, for example, has been known to migrate as far as 2,000 miles in the fall, flying from Canada to central Mexico.

The butterflies appearing on this cover are members of the family *Pieridae*, of which there are about 60 species in North America and more than 1,000 species world-wide. Butterflies of this family are characterized by their medium size, forked claws, and full-sized forelegs. Many also exhibit sexual dimorphism and have wings that reflect and absorb ultraviolet light in specific patterns, helping them to identify potential mates of the same species.

The lifespan of the butterfly ranges from one week to nine months, with most species living an average of one month. As a butterfly ages, its colors fade and its wings become ragged. Yet it is rare to find geriatric butterflies in the wild, as predators, disease, and automobiles generally get the better of them before too long. Butterfly defense mechanisms include camouflage, flight of up to 30 miles per hour, and, as a last resort, being a terrible dinner. Some butterflies are poisonous to eat and cause their predators to vomit, protecting their species—and other species that look like them—from a similar fate.

Darren Kelly was the production editor, and Asa Tomash was the copyeditor for *Oracle PL/SQL for DBAs*. Cindy Gierhart proofread the book. Adam Witwer and Colleen Gorman provided quality control. Lucie Haskins wrote the index.

Karen Montgomery designed the cover of this book, based on a series design by Edie Freedman. The cover image is a 19th-century engraving from Cassell's *Natural History*. Karen Montgomery produced the cover layout with Adobe InDesign CS using Adobe's ITC Garamond font.

David Futato designed the interior layout. This book was converted by Andrew Savikas to FrameMaker 5.5.6 with a format conversion tool created by Erik Ray, Jason McIntosh, Neil Walls, and Mike Sierra that uses Perl and XML technologies. The text font is Linotype Birka; the heading font is Adobe Myriad Condensed; and the code font is LucasFont's TheSans Mono Condensed. The illustrations that appear in the book were produced by Robert Romano, Jessamyn Read, and Lesley Borash using Macromedia FreeHand MX and Adobe Photoshop CS. The tip and warning icons were drawn by Christopher Bing. This colophon was written by Lydia Onofrei.

Better than e-books

Buy *Oracle PL/SQL for DBAs* and access the digital edition FREE on Safari for 45 days.

Go to www.oreilly.com/go/safarienabled
and type in coupon code J2MG-XNML-PUFX-HTLM-L4H9

Search
thousands of
top tech books

Download
whole chapters

Cut and Paste
code examples

Find
answers fast

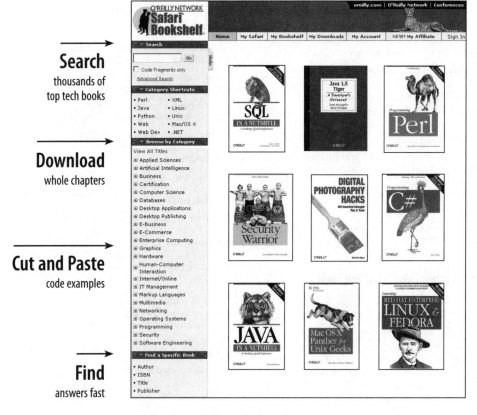

Search Safari! The premier electronic reference
library for programmers and IT professionals.

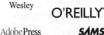

Keep in touch with O'Reilly

Download examples from our books

To find example files from a book, go to: *www.oreilly.com/catalog* select the book, and follow the "Examples" link.

Register your O'Reilly books

Register your book at *register.oreilly.com* Why register your books? Once you've registered your O'Reilly books you can:

- Win O'Reilly books, T-shirts or discount coupons in our monthly drawing.
- Get special offers available only to registered O'Reilly customers.
- Get catalogs announcing new books (US and UK only).
- Get email notification of new editions of the O'Reilly books you own.

Join our email lists

Sign up to get topic-specific email announcements of new books and conferences, special offers, and O'Reilly Network technology newsletters at:

elists.oreilly.com

It's easy to customize your free elists subscription so you'll get exactly the O'Reilly news you want.

Get the latest news, tips, and tools

www.oreilly.com

- "Top 100 Sites on the Web"—PC Magazine
- CIO Magazine's Web Business 50 Awards

Our web site contains a library of comprehensive product information (including book excerpts and tables of contents), downloadable software, background articles, interviews with technology leaders, links to relevant sites, book cover art, and more.

Work for O'Reilly

Check out our web site for current employment opportunities:

jobs.oreilly.com

Contact us

O'Reilly Media, Inc.
1005 Gravenstein Hwy North
Sebastopol, CA 95472 USA
Tel: 707-827-7000 or 800-998-9938
    (6am to 5pm PST)
Fax: 707-829-0104

Contact us by email

For answers to problems regarding your order or our products:
order@oreilly.com

To request a copy of our latest catalog:
catalog@oreilly.com

For book content technical questions or corrections: **booktech@oreilly.com**

For educational, library, government, and corporate sales: **corporate@oreilly.com**

To submit new book proposals to our editors and product managers:
proposals@oreilly.com

For information about our international distributors or translation queries:
international@oreilly.com

For information about academic use of O'Reilly books:
adoption@oreilly.com
or visit:
academic.oreilly.com

For a list of our distributors outside of North America check out:
international.oreilly.com/distributors.html

Order a book online

www.oreilly.com/order_new